SELECTED EDUCATIONAL HERESIES

SELECTED EDUCATIONAL HERESIES

Some Unorthodox Views Concerning the Nature and Purposes of Contemporary Education

WILLIAM F. O'NEILL
University of Southern California

SCOTT, FORESMAN AND COMPANY

PREFACE

Someone once said that, since we have all been children, we are all implicitly convinced that we are experts in child psychology. The same sort of thing might very well be said of public education. Since we have all been through it, we all feel fully qualified to comment on it.

In a sense, however, this is one of the refreshing things about the study of education. It is a controversial issue—a "live question"—and, since neither the questions nor the answers are the exclusive province of any self-elected group who have passed through the required mysteries and been invested with sacred knowledge, anyone with the necessary ability and a willingness to become informed "can play."

One of the special features of educational theory—and, indeed, of virtually all of the supportive disciplines in the area of professional education—is that it is fundamentally an "open" and interdisciplinary kind of undertaking. The educational process is infinitely complex, and it draws upon the widest range of supportive insights from a vast variety of different fields. As a result, educational theories do not, on the whole, have "sharp boundaries" which identify them with one or more of the traditional areas of academic inquiry and not with others. In the province of educational theory, ideas are typically expected to work when applied to practical classroom situations. Under these conditions, ideas from different areas tend to interpenetrate and, in so doing, frequently undergo a strange sort of change. They often tend to become blurred in terms of the usual academic disciplines, and their somewhat hybrid nature frequently nettles the more stalwart champions of the orthodox classifications of knowledge.

What this costs in terms of traditional curricular clarity is often effectively counterbalanced by an increase in intellectual vitality. Ideas that derive from a practical context and which have been cross-fertilized by scholars representing different academic denominations frequently have a peculiar sort of force and fascination about them.

For better or worse, educational theorists have never been able to decide whether they are primarily speculative scholars or practical educators. The problems of education are vast and complicated problems, and the demands of education have always compelled the educational theorist to become conversant with many ideas and points of view that might otherwise remain separate and unrelated. In one sense, this has been extraordinarily fortunate, because they have necessarily been forced to function as wide-ranging intellectuals with broad humanistic interests and a genuine concern for whatever knowledge appears to be most appropriate to the questions at hand. As a result of this cross-disciplinary involvement, educational philosophy—if that term may be used to encompass the general area sometimes referred to as the social and philosophical foundations of education—has never become a stagnant pond. It has always, and virtually by necessity, been a point of confluence where many rivers meet.

The catholicity of interest which is characteristic of the broader reaches of educational theory is well represented by the selections included in this book. Speculation about the nature and goals of education is not limited to a narrow range of ideas which comprise the closed content of "philosophy," "educational philosophy," or even "education." The fundamental task of "educational philosophy" has always been to select, integrate, and relate all of the more significant intellectual insights which pertain to the basic problems confronting education.

The selections included in this book not only represent the leading edge of intellectual speculation which is currently influencing the course of American education. In a basic sense, they also represent "what's happening" on the American intellectual scene. In the current slang of American adolescence, this is "where the action is," and these are the men and women who are intellectually "with it" when it comes to the various difficulties which currently afflict our schools.

This is not to say, of course, that the selections presented in this book are in any sense either final or definitive. Any collection of this sort is necessarily both partial and selective. Many fascinating topics and ideas have necessarily been omitted. It is with the greatest regret that I have been forced, by practical considerations, to avoid including some of the controversial ideas of such exciting and disparate individuals as Jacob Bronowski, Bertrand Russell, Daisetz Suzuki, Dorothy Lee, Pitirim Sorokin, C. Wright Mills, Alan Watts, Ayn Rand, Norman O. Brown, Susanne Langer, O. H. Mowrer, Harold Rugg, V. Krishnamurti, Viktor Frankl, and many, many others who have had provocative things to say about teaching and learning.

Most of the selections included in this collection have not been previously anthologized for use in courses dealing with education. Many have not, to the best of my knowledge, been included in any sort of academic collection at all. It goes without saying that the final list of selections is necessarily somewhat idiosyncratic. "All serious fiction," Thomas Wolfe once said, "is autobiographical." Even obscure academic anthologies, he might have added, are merely intellectual itineraries which retrace someone else's travels in some particular realm of speculation. I can only say that I have traveled this way myself and that the students who have accompanied me have generally been enthusiastic about the trip.

One criticism that can very well be leveled at many of these selections is that they are essentially "negative" — predominantly critical of existing policies and practices within our schools. This is quite true, and the criticism is scarcely unfounded. I can only say that whatever risk is entailed by such a lack of balance seems to be warranted. It has been my observation that it frequently pays, in purely pedagogical terms, to play the devil's advocate rather than the booster. It is no indictment of American education to say that there *is* much which is wrong with our schools. It should be added, quite quickly, however, that much of that which is *wrong* cannot be facilely dismissed as the result of sloth, ignorance, or incompetence on the part of the educators themselves. American education is, after all, essentially a *public* and not a *professional* enterprise, and the responsibility for education is not properly restricted to those who are directly involved with teaching our children.

Many of the individuals represented in this collection feel very strongly that what we are doing in our schools is grievously flawed in either design or execution. Many take extreme—frequently even untenable—positions. They speak, however, with the force of real concern and often with the eloquence of indignation. Anyone, William Pitt once said, can speak sense. It takes an extraordinary man to talk nonsense. Undoubtedly, some nonsense is included in these selections. Hopefully, however, it is the kind of nonsense which promotes thought and, indirectly, creates sense.

It takes a certain amount of courage to risk significant error. The truly wise man, Robert Louis Stevenson once remarked, is wise enough not to be afraid of making a fool out of himself. He is wise enough to risk small errors in the search for significant truth.

Bold and innovative ideas are seldom presented by innocuous men in measured prose. "The peril of excluding too much of life," notes literary critic Henri Peyre, "is greater than that of accepting it too liberally and running the risk of presenting violence, vulgarity and sadism as the whole of life." "If a thing is worth doing," the elegant Mr. Chesterton once noted, "it is worth doing badly."

This book is intended for use at either the undergraduate or graduate levels in introductory courses in education wherever there is a desire or requirement in the teacher training curriculum to treat the philosophy and the philosophical foundations of education. It also contains many selections that are of great value to the student concerned with the social foundations of education.

The selections in this book are not safe, dull, and respectable. They are intended to excite, arouse, provoke, and even irritate. They are, above all, designed to cause thinking to take place — to stimulate the kind of interest which will make the usual sort of classroom approaches increasingly relevant and worthwhile. These selections are not designed to provide a systematic sort of textbook coverage of a particular content area or to serve as a loosely knit supplementary text which adheres systematically to the usual pattern of academic inquiry. Clearly, they are not recommended for those who prefer a bland and balanced presentation of accepted or acceptable ideas. They are purposefully controversial. They are designed to make people think, to arouse interest, and to create the sort of intellectual climate which is necessary for real learning to occur.

A secondary advantage of this kind of book stems from the fact that much of the more promising materials which are available in the broader and more humanistic reaches of educational theory—and in contrast to many other areas—is not to be found in scholarly journals but must be excerpted from books. A major virtue of a collection of this sort is that it makes certain materials — as, for example, Skinner's remarks on education from *Walden II* or Marshall McLuhan's comments on the educational implications of the communications revolution from his book *Understanding Media* —readily available to students without the necessity of time-consuming library assignments or the purchase of intimidating numbers of costly volumes which are often only partially relevant to the larger objectives of the course.

An incidental advantage of this sort of anthology is that it fosters precisely the kind of creativity which education so frequently purports to seek. It is a sad indictment of contemporary education that many students will stay up all night reading about the Revolutionary War and yet fail to keep up with contemporary revolutions because no one has told them that they are "history." In a similar sense, philosophy seldom comes packaged as "philosophy," neatly contained within the confines of the usual sort of appropriately labeled textbooks. One of the hallmarks of the truly educated man is his capacity to discover the sort of knowledge which is relevant to the solution of his problems in a variety of different places and frequently in the most unlikely spots. As McLuhan indicates so well in one of the selections included in this book, fragmented, academic specialism has largely seen its day. For better or worse, the new questions are no longer appropriately classified with reference to the old labels appended to the traditional catalogues of prior answers. The student who is discomfited to find "educational philosophy" in the writings of a mathematician (like Norbert Wiener) or an anthropologist (like Margaret Mead) or a lawyer (like David Riesman) has simply not come to terms with the realities of a radically changing world and yearns to return to the Linus blanket of outmoded academic formulas.

W.F.O.

CONTENTS

Part 3

"THINKING ABOUT THINKING": CYBERNETICS, COMMUNICATIONS, AND EDUCATION

Part 4

PROGNOSIS AND PRESCRIPTION

Part 1

VALUES, CULTURE,
AND EDUCATION

Introduction

This is, Max Scheler once said, the first age in which man seems to have succeeded in becoming problematic to himself. " 'The end of the world,' " comments social critic Lewis Mumford, "is no longer an apocalyptic hyperbole . . . . We have reached a point in history where man has become his own most dangerous enemy."[1] Even "progress," which is perhaps the last absolute — the residue left over after God and immortality have disappeared — has become a source of grave doubt, and life has become "scandalously provisional."[2]

"We are," Swedish philosopher Gunther Anders has remarked, "the first men with the power to unleash a world cataclysm, we are also the first to live continually under its threat . . . . Accordingly," he continues, "all history can be divided into three chapters, with the following captions: (1) All men are mortal, (2) All men are exterminable, and (3) Mankind as a whole is exterminable."[3]

It may be, of course, that we all suffer from "the facile social pessimism of our time"[4] — that our present generation, like that of Thoreau's time, "inclines a little to congratulating itself on being the last of an illustrious line."[5] It may even be, as the old saying has it, that the world gets better every day and then worse again in the morning.

On the other hand, it is becoming increasingly evident that time may really be running out — that "mankind has not aeons and eternities to spare for trying out discredited systems."[6] There is, after all, a significant difference between a perceived crisis (every age has *experienced itself* as in crisis) and a *perceived crisis* which can be *objectively substantiated* (such as that posed by the present threat of nuclear cataclysm).

The entire world today is smaller, in a practical sense, than the world of classical Greece. Generations, which were previously measured in life spans, have now shrunk to decades and even less. "Parents," comments

---

1. Lewis Mumford, *The Conduct of Life* (New York: Harcourt, Brace and Company, 1951), pp. 8 and 11.
2. José Ortega y Gasset, *The Revolt of the Masses* (New York: New American Library, Inc., 1952), p. 135.
3. Gunther Anders, "Reflections on the H Bomb," in *Man Alone: Alienation in Modern Society*, ed. Eric and Mary Josephson (New York: Dell Publishing Co., Inc., 1962), pp. 290–291.
4. C. P. Snow, *The Two Cultures and a Second Look* (New York: New American Library, Inc., 1959), p. 71.
5. Henry David Thoreau, *Walden* (New York: New American Library, Inc., 1960), p. 220.
6. Morrison I. Swift, "Human Submission," quoted in William James, *Pragmatism* (New York: The World Publishing Company, 1961), p. 33.

social critic Kenneth Keniston, "can no longer hope to be literal models for their children; institutions cannot hope to persist without change in rite, practice and custom."[7]

For better or worse, we find ourselves faced with a crisis of belief. "No one," counsels anthropologist Margaret Mead, "will live all his life in the world into which he was born, and no one will die in the world in which he worked in his maturity."[8] In many cases, the traditional ways are insufficient precisely because they perpetuate outmoded patterns of response. "Tradition," remarks communications theorist Marshall McLuhan, " . . . is the sense of the total past as *now*."[9] The problem, as G. K. Chesterton observed so many years ago, is that "in dealing with any historical answer, the point is not whether it was given in our time, but whether it was given in answer to our question."[10]

It has been remarked that there are no "natural" ways of doing 95 per cent of the things we do. Virtually all of our behavior is socially determined. Human activity is determined primarily through the superorganic instrumentality of culture. "Essentially," states Lewis Mumford in his book *The Conduct of Life,*

> *a culture is an extra-organic means of changing man's nature and his environment, without leaving indelible marks on his organism or curtailing his essential flexibility and plasticity. A heated house for winter living is the equivalent of the horse's trick of acquiring a shaggy winter coat of hair: an X-ray tube is the equivalent of acquiring a more penetrating form of vision—and so on.*[11]

Cultures, like individuals, however, are also motivated by certain internal dynamics. Every culture has its implicit world view or hidden "axiom-set." "The culturally prevalent, implicit, dominant ontology," states philosopher James K. Feibleman, "is the greatest force in the life of every individual."[12] "Culture is not," remarks anthropologist Dorothy Lee in a similar vein, " . . . 'a response to the total needs of a society'; but rather a system which stems from and expresses . . . the basic values of society."[13]

---

7. Kenneth Keniston, "Social Change and Youth in America," in *The Challenge of Youth*, ed. Erik H. Erikson (Garden City, N.Y.: Doubleday & Company, Inc., Anchor Books, 1963), p. 220.
8. Margaret Mead, "Thinking Ahead," *Harvard Business Review*, XXXVI (November–December 1958), 34.
9. Marshall McLuhan, *Understanding Media: The Extensions of Man* (New York: McGraw-Hill Book Company, 1964), p. 301.
10. G. K. Chesterton, *Orthodoxy* (Garden City, N.Y.: Doubleday & Company, Inc., Image Books, 1959), p. 75.
11. Mumford, *op. cit.*, p. 38.
12. James K. Feibleman, "An Ontological Philosophy of Education," in *Modern Philosophies and Education*, ed. Nelson B. Henry, Fifty-Fourth Yearbook of the National Society for the Study of Education, Part I (Chicago: University of Chicago Press, 1955), p. 347.
13. Dorothy Lee, *Freedom and Culture* (Englewood Cliffs, N. J.: Prentice-Hall, Inc., 1959), p. 76.

In large part, of course, "the crisis of our age" is a value crisis. A "value," comments anthropologist Clyde Kluckhohn, is "a conception, explicit or implicit, distinctive of an individual or characteristic of a group, of the desirable which influences the selection from available modes, means, and ends of action."[14] The reason we place such emphasis upon cultural value orientations is because they serve as the strategically crucial *point of articulation* between a culture and the various personalities and social systems within that culture.

An attempt to define values is always implicitly an attempt to define personal and social identity. To ask what a culture's values *should be* is always, indirectly, to ask what a culture *is* and how it should *change*. As philosopher Eliseo Vivas has said,

> *values are not all, like water lilies, on the surface and since even those which are have groping roots entangled with other roots sunk in the slime of the subconscious, the search for them is, in fact, a search for one's personality. But the search is a creative search, since one's formulation of what one truly is influences in a creative way what one becomes: the act of expression leads to a clarification of what one is, what one stands for, the values essentially constitutive of one's self. A clarification, then, is not merely an ordering of what is there, a mere verbalizing of what hitherto has remained unexpressed, but an ordering which sets one in motion toward completion of what one is. In achieving a clearer notion of ourselves, we thus create ourselves, and the process has the stamp of spontaneity.*[15]

What Vivas says of the search for personal values is also applicable in large degree to the question of social values, for, as linguistic scholar Edward Sapir once noted, "the more fully one tries to understand a culture, the more it takes on the characteristics of a personality organization."[16] The selections in Part One are all concerned with the relationship between values and culture and, less directly, with the relationship between cultural values and the educational process.

In the first selection Cora Du Bois focuses on the question of what contemporary American values — and, more specifically, the dominant values of middle-class Americans — actually *are*. "For the American middle class," she notes, "it is postulated that: (1) the universe is mechanistically conceived, (2) man is its master, (3) men are equal, and (4) men are perfectible." These four premises imply three basic focal values: "material well-

---

14. Clyde Kluckhohn, "Values and Value-Orientations in the Theory of Action: An Exploration in Definition and Classification," in *Toward a General Theory of Action,* ed. Talcott Parsons and Edward A. Shils (New York: Harper and Brothers, 1951), p. 395.

15. Eliseo Vivas, *The Moral Life and the Ethical Life* (Chicago: Henry Regnery Co., 1963), p. 162. Reprinted by permission.

16. Edward Sapir, quoted in Dorothy Eggan, "Instruction and Affect in Hopi Cultural Continuity," in *Education and Culture: Anthropological Approaches,* ed. George D. Spindler (New York: Holt, Rinehart and Winston, Inc., 1963), p. 32.

being that derives from the premise that man is master of a mechanistic universe; conformity that derives from the premise of man's equality; effort-optimism that derives from the premise of man's perfectibility."[17]

Social scientists David Riesman, Nathan Glazer, and Reuel Denney, who are celebrated for their monumental study of changing American values, *The Lonely Crowd,* are represented by two selections. In the first, "Tradition-Direction, Inner-Direction, and Other-Direction," they elaborate upon their basic thesis that there are three basic types of culturally determined character structure. They define these types, and they compare and contrast the different ways in which each one operates. In their second selection, "Changing Values and the Changing Teacher," they discuss the way in which evolving social values have affected the role of the teacher.

Social critic William H. Whyte, Jr., who is best known as the author of *The Organization Man,* an analysis of the changing American character structure, is also represented by two selections. In the first, "Groupthink," he presents his basic thesis that Americans have become increasingly dominated by an implicit philosophy of *"rationalized* conformity — an open, articulate philosophy which holds that group values are not only expedient but right and good as well." As Whyte sees it, this commitment has given rise to three mutually supporting ideas: "(1) that moral values and ethics are relative; (2) that what is important is the kind of behavior and attitudes that makes for the harmonious functioning of the group; (3) that the best way to achieve this is through the application of 'scientific' techniques."[18] Most of the credit for this vision of man as a unit of the group, a view which conveniently offers freedom from moral choice, states Whyte,

> goes to John Dewey, who, with William Kilpatrick, gave "progressive" education its impetus. But there were many others — Veblen in economics, for example, and Roscoe Pound in the law ("The law is social engineering"). Like a fresh breeze, through almost every field of American thought, the new concepts swept, as converts enthusiastically fell to whacking away at the restrictions of the old absolutes. Social man was coming of age.

> When the cultural anthropologists got to work on him, his final link to the old moral absolutes was severed.[19]

In his second selection, "Education and the Organization Man," Whyte contrasts the traditional American value-orientation, what he terms "the Protestant Ethic," emphasizing hard work, thrift, and competitive struggle, with the emerging "Social Ethic," which he defines as "that contemporary body of thought which makes morally legitimate the pressures of society

---

17. Cora Du Bois, "The Dominant Value Profile of American Culture," *American Anthropologist,* LVII (December 1955), pp. 1233–1234.
18. William H. Whyte, Jr., "Groupthink," *Fortune,* March 1952, p. 114.
19. *Ibid.,* p. 116.

against the individual."[20] He describes how these are expressed in two contrasting industrial training programs.

Psychologist B. F. Skinner, in a selection taken from his novel *Walden II*, explores the possibilities of using existing psychological techniques for conditioning behavior to create a new and more positive type of society—a society which would be structured along purely scientific lines and which would be directed to the fullest realization of the common good. He proposes a government based on a purely experimental ethic which would be regulated by the science of human behavior itself. As he states,

> *an efficient state culture must be discovered by experimentation . . . .*
> *I'm not arguing for no government at all, but only for none of the*
> *existing forms. We want a government based upon a science of human*
> *behavior. Nothing short of that will produce a permanent social*
> *structure. For the first time in history we're ready for it, because*
> *we can now deal with human behavior in accordance with simple*
> *scientific principles. The trouble with a program of anarchy was that*
> *it placed too much faith in human nature. It was an offshoot of the*
> *philosophy of perfectionism . . . . We have no truck with phi-*
> *losophies of innate goodness—or evil . . . . We can* make *men*
> *adequate for group living—to the satisfaction of everybody.*[21]

Skinner would delegate authority for all really significant decisions to experts. Democracy, he states, is based on an invalid concept of man; man is determined by the state and not vice versa. Popular skill in government declines with the complexity of culture, government has become a special skill which requires experts. The general public is in no position to evaluate the experts, and, where choice is reliant on expertise, democracy no longer works. In such cases, democracy in practice operates as a despotism of neglect, ignorance, and accident. It guarantees only that a *majority* will not be despotically ruled.

> *The government of Walden II . . . will have the virtues of democ-*
> *racy, but none of the defects. It's much closer to the theory or intent*
> *of democracy than the actual practice in America today. The will of*
> *the people is carefully ascertained. We have no election campaigns*
> *to falsify issues or obscure them with emotional appeals, but a careful*
> *study of the satisfaction of the membership is made. Every mem-*
> *ber has a direct channel through which he may protest to the Man-*
> *agers or even the Planners. And these protests are taken as seriously*
> *as the pilot of an airplane takes a sputtering engine. We don't need*
> *laws and a police force to compel a pilot to pay attention to a defec-*
> *tive engine. Nor do we need laws to compel our Dairy Manager to*

20. William H. Whyte, Jr., *The Organization Man* (Garden City, N.Y.: Doubleday & Company, Inc., Anchor Books, 1957), p. 7.
21. B. F. Skinner, *Walden II* (New York: The Macmillan Company, 1948), pp. 195–196. Reprinted by permission.

> *pay attention to an epidemic among his cows. Similarly, our Behavioral and Cultural Managers need not be compelled to consider grievances. The grievance is a wheel to be oiled, or a broken pipeline to be repaired.*[22]

In Skinner's version of utopia, then, good government stands above politics. It is a science and not an art. It is *for the people* but not *of the people;* and it is based on the principle that the *end* of democracy — self-actualization — is better attained without democratic *means.*[23] In Walden II there would be absolute control of human behavior, but the population would continue to *feel* free, because they would be trained *to want to do what they need to do.* Indeed, the question of "freedom" never arises at all, for such a question occurs only in cases of restraint; and the inhabitants of Walden II have been conditioned to desire only those things which are socially constructive. Choice continues to exist but only within a context of possibilities delimited by prior social conditioning. The type of education which Skinner proposes in the selection "Education in Walden II" is, accordingly, an education which emphasizes the transmission of effective habits in ways of thinking and the elimination of destructive inclinations directed against the common good.

George Orwell's alarming fictional prognosis "Thinking and Learning in 1984" envisions a world which has finally been divided into warring totalitarian megastates. These are capable of exerting total control, not only over individual actions, but over individual thought and desire as well. Aldous Huxley's anti-utopia is projected somewhat further into the future than 1984. It goes even further than Orwell's by envisioning a world in which not only education per se, but even sexual behavior, physical development, and subjective emotional states are subject to external manipulation and overall control by the state.

Not everyone, however, agrees with the new sociological moralists or concurs with the fictional forecasts of Orwell or Huxley. Part One closes on a note of dissent. Social critic Harold Rosenberg, in his essay "The Orgamerican Phantasy," rejects the positions presented by Riesman and Whyte. "What is new in America," he counters, "is not the socially reflexive person but the presence of a self-conscious intellectual caste whose disillusionment has induced its members to volunteer for the part."[24] "What the Orgman-critics [i.e., the critics of an other-directed 'organization' society] expose is not a flaw in society but the injurious realities of its normal everyday life . . . . Loosed from action, for which it can see no aim, [such] post-radical criticism often exaggerates its complaints, producing a worse impression of conditions than is warranted by the facts, at the same time that it seeks remedies in the wrong direction."[25]

---

22. *Ibid.,* p. 269.
23. *Ibid.,* p. 3.
24. Harold Rosenberg, "The Orgamerican Phantasy," *The Tradition of the New* (New York: Horizon Press, Inc., 1959), p. 283.
25. *Ibid.,* pp. 274 and 279.

Extremist but neither radical nor conservative, the Organization criticism is inspired not by a passion for social correction but by nostalgia. A sigh over the lost person mars the phantasy of American unanimity which has supplanted the ideological Passion Plays of Marxian condemnation and conflict. Whyte's memoir on his training in the Vick's Vaporub rugged individualist sales force of "the old days" (the late 'thirties) is the most eloquent and touching passage in his entire literature. The Age of the Giants—alas, gone forever. With Vicks' Richardson extinct, every human degradation may be logically anticipated. Today, the Orgman, the "dominant member of society," still lives among the relics of older types. Tomorrow he will tread the stage alone, in conflict only with himself.[26]

---

26. *Ibid.*, pp. 278–279.

CORA DU BOIS

Cora Du Bois is currently a professor of anthropology at Harvard University and Radcliffe College. She is particularly noted for her studies in the relationship between culture and personality and for her social and ethnological studies of Southeast Asia, People of Alor *(1960) and* Social Forces in Southeast Asia *(1959). She is also the author of* Foreign Students of Higher Education in the United States *(1956), an extensive study of foreign students in American colleges and universities.*

The Dominant Value Profile
of American Culture

This paper is an attempt to synthesize and systematize the relevant insights on American values advanced by a diverse group of writers from De Tocqueville through Myrdal to the authors of the polemic or conversational pieces that have been so numerous in the last decade. It will be addressed to the dominant value system of middle-class Americans. This system is rooted in the Protestant ethic and eighteenth-century rationalism. Many of its specific values are shared with other societies, but its configuration has come to be considered peculiarly American.

Since the allotted space is limited, what is said here must be condensed, schematic, and highly selective. There is no attempt to give a new definition of value or to adhere rigidly to existing ones. Distinctions between value and related concepts like themes, configurations, etc., will not be argued. Furthermore, the comments made here do not stem from scientific investigations. Readers interested in the attempt of anthropologists to grapple with such subtle and difficult questions are referred to more competent and exhaustive materials. Dr. Ethel Albert's still unpublished material furnishes whatever logical coherence this paper may have, but for the content and interpretations the writer must assume full responsibility.

"The Dominant Value Profile of American Culture" by Cora Du Bois is reproduced by permission of the American Anthropological Association and the author from *American Anthropologist*, LVII, (December 1955), 1232–1239.

THE OPPOSITIONAL MODE

Oppositional propositions are a consistent aspect of Western European culture. They represent recurrent dilemmas in logic and ethics. They are reflected in, and fostered by, the structure of Indo-European languages. They have permeated sociological and psychological conceptualization. A wide range of oppositional propositions can be offered as illustrations: thesis-antithesis; good-evil; subject-predicate; folk-urban; aggression-submission; superordinate-subordinate; mind-body. Of these oppositional propositions some may be genuine in the sense that they are, logically speaking, contraries. But it seems probable that most oppositional propositions current in Western culture are preponderantly spurious in the sense that they are poorly conceived contradictories.

The assumption is made here that no system of values can encompass genuine contraries and therefore that the oppositional propositions in any value system are spurious. The further assumption is made that in any value system where such spurious oppositions exist there will be a strain for consistency.

The implication of these assumptions for the processes of value change are clear. Analytically, any attempt to present a value system should avoid the formulation of new and spurious oppositions. The avoidance of analytic oppositions may help to reveal those already extant in the existing value system, and the associated strains for consistency may emerge more clearly.

The strain for consistency in the American value system may be one of the forces accounting for changes in its configuration over the last three hundred years. Whether that strain is more intense in the American value system than in others it is impossible to estimate here. However, that the strain exists has been manifest in two major directions: (1) the prizing of change itself, usually expressed as effort, struggle, and progress, which will be discussed again in connection with the focal value called "effort-optimism"; and (2) compromise, which is not exclusively American but has received characteristic expression in the phrase "splitting the difference." This phrase reveals particularly an appreciation of the spurious quality of the oppositions, since it implies that neither oppositional term represents "truth" and that by retreating from false dichotomies a valid equilibrium may be achieved.

FOUR BASIC PREMISES

For our purposes the value premises of any culture can be considered to rest upon the assumptions made concerning man's cognitive view of the universe, man's relation to it, and man's relation to other men. For the American middle class it is postulated that: (1) the universe is mechanistically conceived, (2) man is its master, (3) men are equal, and (4) men are perfectible. From these four basic premises alone many of the focal and specific values, as well as the directives, of the American value system can be derived. In the context of the last three hundred years of American history these assumptions have proved valid both experientially and integratively (i.e., in a self-reinforcing sense) for the United States as a whole and, more specifically, for the American middle class. Despite changed situations and therefore the potential loss of experiential and integrative validation, we may nevertheless expect these assumptions to persist for a considerable period of time. There may be lags in a value system as there are in other aspects of culture.

FOCAL VALUES AND THEIR DIRECTIVES

Albert uses the term "focal" to designate a value about which numerous specific values cluster. Directives are used to designate the do's and dont's inherent in specific as well as in focal values.[1]

The four premises given above yield at least three major focal values: material well-being that derives from the premise that man is master of a mechanistic universe; conformity that derives from the premise of man's equality; effort-optimism that derives from the premise of man's perfectibility. (The fortunate term "effort-optimism" was coined by the Kluckhohns.[2])

The nexus of specific values and directives clustering around each of these focal values can now be considered. Simultaneously the mutual reinforcement that occurs between the basic premises and their focal values, as well as the constant effort to resolve spurious oppositions through change, can be underlined. The inner consistency of the value system here presented accounts for much of the traditional vigor of "the American way of life" in the past. However, such vigor could not have existed without the reinforcement provided by the geographic setting of the American nation and the historic forces operative in the broader setting of Western European commercial, industrial, technical, and scientific growth in which the American nation shared.

1. Effort-Optimism

Work is a specific value in American society. It is not so much a necessary condition of existence as a positive good. It is a specific instrumental value through which man strives to reach not only the goal of his own perfectibility but also the goal of mastering a mechanistically conceived universe. But in values Vaihinger's "law of the preponderance of the means over the ends" is frequently operative. Thus work becomes a goal in itself and in the process may acquire the quality of activity for its own sake. Thus recreation, although theoretically the antithesis of work, nevertheless in its activism shows many of the aspects of work. "Fun" is something that most

1. Ethel M. Albert, "Theory Construction for the Comparative Study of Values in Five Cultures: A Report on the Value Study," Harvard University, Laboratory of Social Relations: Value Study. (Dittoed.)
2. Clyde Kluckhohn and Florence Kluckhohn, "American Culture: Generalized Orientations and Class Patterns," in *Conflicts of Power in Modern Culture: Seventh Symposium*, ed. Lyman Bryson (New York: Conference on Science, Philosophy and Religion in Their Relation to the Democratic Way of Life, Inc.), pp. 106–128. (Distributed by Harper and Brothers.)

Americans work hard for and at, so that they must be warned at forty to give up tennis for golf, or hunting trips for painting. Touring, whether at home or abroad, acquires the quality of a marathon. And this in turn is closely associated with another specific value linked with the effort-optimism syndrome, the importance placed on education. However, as we shall see later, the educational effort acquires a particularly American cast when taken in conjunction with the other two focal values, material well-being and conformity. In sum, as many foreigners have observed, American life gives the impression of activism. The directives, as well as the virtues and vices, associated with this optimistic activism are numerous: "If at first you don't succeed, try, try again"; or, in the more contemporary idiom, "Let's get this show on the road." The optimistic quality that pervades the American mood is clearly conveyed by the "bigger ergo better" mentality; the "never say die"; the "up and at 'em."

Vigor, at least as motility, connotes biologic youth. The cult of youthfulness in this society is again a specific value frequently commented upon by foreign observers. This observation is borne out by the popularity of the heroes manufactured in Hollywood and in the world of sports, by the advertisements of styles and cosmetics. As the average age of the population increases, this value is already showing signs of being given new interpretations in terms of geriatrics, etc. This will be alluded to again in following paragraphs.

2. Material Well-Being

If indeed effort is optimistically viewed in a material universe that man can master, then material well-being is a consistent concomitant value. Not only is it consistent within the value system, but it has been amply demonstrated in our national experience. It has been manifest in the American standard of living. The nation's geographic frontier and its natural resources, combined with an era of invention, have convinced most Americans of the validity of such a proposition. In the American scene progress and prosperity have come to have almost identical meaning. So deeply convinced are most Americans of what is generally called "prosperity" that material well-being is close to being considered a "right" due to those who have conscientiously practiced the specific value of work. The congruence of this view with the new science of geriatrics, social insurance, and the growth of investment trusts is obvious. It represents a consistent adjustment of specific values to a changing situation. However, as the situational context changes it may weaken the present linkage between effort and optimism with the resulting devaluation of both and thereby set up a new strain for consistency that may alter the present configuration of the American value system.

One of the most common stereotypes about the United States is its materialism. Viewed in the context of the value system presented here, materialism is less a value *per se* than an optimistic assertion of two value premises (mastery over material nature and the perfectibility of man) that have operated in a favorable environment. What foreign observers may call materialism, with derogatory or envious innuendos, is to the American a success that carries the moral connotation of "rightness"—of a system that proves itself or, as Americans would say with complete consistency, that "works." Within the frame of American value premises, success phrased as material well-being resolves the material-spiritual opposition and becomes a proof of right-mindedness. "Hard work pays off." The old and widely known proverb that, "Virtue is its own reward" has a particularly American slant, meaning not that virtue is in itself a reward but rather that virtue is rewarded.

If hard work is a "good thing" in a material universe and since it has been rewarded by material well-being, consistency requires that manual labor should be accorded dignity or, at least, should not be considered undignified. Furthermore, manual labor is an unambiguous manifestation of that activism alluded to earlier.

The salience of material well-being as a focal value in American life leads into many by-ways, some of which confuse and confound members of societies founded on a different value configuration. In military terms, for example, Americans are so profoundly convinced of the correctness of the material well-being formula that logistics forms our basic strategy. Personal heroism, though it may amply exist, is not assumed to be the fundamental requisite for victory, as it is in France. In American terms, victory is won by the sheet of matériel laid down in front of advancing infantry and by the lines of supply that must be built up to provide such a barrier between hand-to-hand combat.

In the same vein, there is little room in the American middle-class value system for the realities of physical pain, brutality, and death. Since they are nonetheless natural and undeniable, they are given a highly stylized treatment in detective fiction, newspapers, and movies that provide an acceptable discharge of tension created by the discrepancy between values and reality. Many Americans are alienated and morally repelled when they encounter the poverty and misery prevalent in certain lands. They manage to go through life untouched experientially even by those in our own population who have not succeeded—those who exist hopelessly in rural or urban slums or those who are victims of physical or psychic disasters. We have provided for the latter so effectively that they are whisked away into institutions that our national surpluses permit us to provide comparatively lavishly. Death itself has been surrounded with appurtenances of asepsis. Evelyn Waugh's *The Loved Ones* could never have been written with India as a setting. The compelling quality of this value emerges when we consider world statistics on human welfare facilities. In this respect, the United States is consistently in the lead. Yet, if we compare these statistics with the outbursts of compassion that a newspaper account of a "blue baby" will elicit, we become aware not only of the power of this focal value but also the resultant constellation that might be summarized as compulsive compassionate activism.

3. Conformity

Viewed historically it seems probable that conformity is a more recent focal value in American culture than effort-optimism and material well-being. It may represent one of the valuational changes induced by the strain for consistency assumed earlier in the paper to be one of the forces that alter value systems. Over a century ago De Tocqueville saw with singular clarity the potential threat to national solidarity inherent in the values of individual liberty, on the one hand, and of the sovereignty of enfranchised masses, on the other hand. In the contemporary American value system, conformity represents an attempt to resolve this dilemma. The France of today, with a comparable dilemma, has still to find a resolution.

If the premises of perfectibility and equality are linked with the focal value labeled effort-optimism, then each middle-class American may legitimately aspire to maximal self-realization. But, if man is to master through his efforts a mechanistic universe, he must co-operate with his fellow-men, since no single man can master the universal machine. In other words, people are individuated and prized, but if they are to co-operate with their fellow-men for mastery of the universe or, in more modest terms, of the immediate physical and sociopolitical environment, too great a degree of individualization would be an impediment. Also since the American value premises—in contradistinction to much of the rest of the world—include equality, the realization of the self in such a context would not necessarily imply the development of highly personalized and idiosyncratic but rather of egalitarian traits. Self-cultivation in America has as its goal less the achievement of uniqueness and more the achievement of similarity. This is a proposition many Frenchmen, for example, find difficult to grasp. The Japanese, with their stress upon self-cultivation in order more perfectly to discharge the obligations they owe their family and society, might come closer to understanding this American formulation. (For a formulation of Japanese values, see William Caudill, "Japanese-American Personality and Acculturation," Genetic Psychology Monographs, No. 45 (1952), pp. 3–102. On p. 93, the author points out the compatibility of Japanese and American middle-class values.)

The assimilation of diverse immigrant groups to middle-class American values has been one of the remarkable sociopolitical achievements of the nation and testifies to the compelling vigor of its value system. As resources and space were more fully manned, the very lack of tolerance for differences that facilitated assimilation was finally to curtail the admission to this country of those who presented such differences.

Earlier in our history self-reliance and initiative were specific values attached to the focal value of liberty. Today these specific values have a new focus. Individual self-reliance and initiative are attached to the promotion of the commonweal and to the progress of society. Conformity has replaced liberty as a focal value to which these specific traits are attached. Co-operation has been added as a specific value that has facilitated the shift-over. The present American value system manifests a highly effective integration of the individual to society.

The ramification of this nexus into the sphere of education has been alluded to already. Education is envisaged as a means by which all men through effort can realize themselves. But since co-operativeness is a specific value also inserted into this equation, education comes to be envisaged as a means to make more men more effective workers and better citizens.

The land-grant colleges, the vast network of public schools, and the system of free and compulsory education with its stress on education for citizenship and on technical skills have set the American educational system apart from that of many other countries. In the American context the linkage between conformity, effort-optimism, and material well-being leads inevitably to mass education with the emphasis on the common man rather than the uncommon man, to its technical and practical cast, to what seems to many observers its low standards. Simultaneously, to many Americans schooling has acquired the weight of a goal rather than a means. A college degree is a "good thing" in itself, whether or not the education entailed is prized. This concatenation does not lead one to expect perfection as a directive for performance in American life.

In a society where co-operation and good citizenship are valued and where the commonweal is served by having each man develop himself through his own efforts, a generous friendliness, openness, and relaxation of interpersonal relations are not only possible but desirable so long as the associated expanding economy furnishes the situational possibilities. Rigid class structures and protective privacies are inconsistent with the values here enumerated. Doors need not be closed to rooms; fences need not be built around properties. The tall hedges of England and the enclosing walls of France are not appropriate to the American scene, where life faces outward rather than inward. If every individual is as "good as" the next and all are good citizens—what is there to hide? The open front yards, the porches, or more recently the picture windows that leave the home open to everyone's view, the figurative and literal klieg lights under which our public figures live are all evidence of the value placed in American life on likeness and the pressure exerted for conformity. This is very different from saying that American middle-class individuals are in fact all alike. It means merely that likeness is valued.

The American hostility to figures in authority has been frequently noted, and in this connection the almost placatory informality and familiarity of American manners that serve to play down status differences have been pointed out. The apparent contradiction between the striving for upward mobility and the distrust of those who achieve pre-eminent positions can now be seen in more balanced terms. If the argument advanced here is correct, upward mobility is valued as successful activity, but when it reaches a point where it outstrips the premise of equality and the focal value of conformity it borders on *hubris*.

In this connection then the relaxed, friendly manner of American life so frequently commented upon by foreign observers can be gauged in the broader context of an adjustment to incompatible values. The search for popularity, the desire to be like, the wish to be considered a "good fellow," are searches for reassurance that, in striving to achieve all the ends implied by the focal value of effort-optimism, one has not exceeded the bounds set by the other focal value of conformity. That this process can operate at any level of actual achievement, from the presidency of the United States to chairmanship of an Elks Club committee, need not be stressed. It is the boss, the politician, the teacher, the "big shots" who are disvalued figures to the extent that their superordinate position implies authority. It is the movie star and the baseball hero who are valued figures since their pre-eminence connotes no authority but at the same time dramatizes the me-teoric rise to fame and popularity through hard work and youthful striving.

Another aspect of American social life is thrown into relief in the effort to balance effort-optimism, material well-being, and conformity and their linked specific values. In the business and financial world, despite conser-vative tendencies, there has been a steady trend toward consolidation and standardization. Although the familiar and now perhaps inappropriate hue and cry is still raised about monopoly and big business, the latter, at least, serves the greater material well-being of the American mass consumer, whose values are geared to conformity. "Big business" is consonant with the American value system here portrayed so long as the owners of such enterprises are pictured as the American middle class, so long as savings are invested in the stocks and bonds of these enterprises so that the middle class shares "equally" in its successes, and so long as the authorities in such enterprises are presented as servants of the people. In these terms the American value system is served. The dangers of a too extreme individual-istic power-centered authority are thus allayed, and competitive rivalry is brought under control.

SUMMARY AND CONCLUSIONS

Two basic assumptions were made: (1) that no viable value system *qua* sys-tem can entertain logical contraries, and (2) that there is a strain for consis-tency among the spurious contradictions that may be inherent in any value system. Four major premises were assumed to underlie the Ameri-can middle-class value system: (1) a mechanistically conceived universe, (2) man's mastery over that universe, (3) the equality of men, (4) man's per-fectibility. From these four premises three focal values were suggested: (1) effort-optimism, (2) material well-being, and (3) conformity. Each of these focal values is envisaged as being more or less directly derived from each of the premises. Each in turn constitutes a series (here not fully ex-plored) of specific values and directives. Each of the three focal and their constituent specific values are more or less consistently interlocked. But the viability of a value system does not rest exclusively on its internal coherence. It must also manifest a considerable degree of congruence with the situa-tional context within which it exists. Changes in value systems will result, therefore, from a strain for consistency not only within the value system but also between values and situational factors.

DAVID RIESMAN
NATHAN GLAZER
REUEL DENNEY

David Riesman has had a varied career. A lawyer, he at one time served as law clerk to Supreme Court Justice Brandeis. Best known for his provocative and controversial study of changing American character, The Lonely Crowd, *he has also authored or co-authored such books as* Individualism Reconsidered *(1954) and, of particular interest to educators,* Constraint and Variety in American Education *(1956). He is currently writing a book with Christopher Jencks on American universities and is a professor in the Department of Social Relations at Harvard University.*

Nathan Glazer is a well-known sociologist who has worked with David Riesman on both The Lonely Crowd *and* Faces in the Crowd *(1952). Among his other books are* American Judaism *(1957) and* Beyond the Melting Pot *(1963). He is currently pursuing research on urban problems and race relations.*

Reuel Denney is the author of a number of books and articles on a wide range of subjects. He is perhaps best known for his contribution to The Lonely Crowd *and for his book* The Astonished Muse *(1957). Denney is currently a professor of American studies in English at the University of Hawaii.*

Tradition-Direction, Inner-Direction, and Other-Direction

In their book The Lonely Crowd, *the authors formulate the provocative thesis that there is a relationship between social character and population growth. Western society since the Middle Ages, they state, can be shown to demonstrate an S-shaped curve of population growth.*

The bottom horizontal line of the S represents a situation where the total population does not increase or does so very slowly, for the number of births equals roughly the number of deaths, and both are very high. In societies of this type, a high proportion of the population is young, life expectancy is low, and the turnover of generations is extremely rapid. Such societies are said to be in the phase of "high growth potential"; for should something happen to decrease the very high death rate (greater production of food, new sanitary measures, new knowledge of the causes of disease, and so on), a "population explosion" would result, and the population would increase very rapidly. This in effect is what happened in the West, starting with the seventeenth century. This spurt in population was most marked in Europe, and the countries settled by Europeans, in the nineteenth century. It is represented by the vertical bar of the S. Demographers call this the stage of "transitional growth," because the birth rate soon begins to follow the death rate in its decline. The rate of growth then slows down, and demographers begin to detect in the growing proportion of middle-aged and aged in the population the signs of a third stage, "incipient population decline." Societies in this stage are represented by the top horizontal bar of the S, again indicating, as in the first stage, that the total population growth is small — but this time because births and deaths are low.

The authors' thesis is, in essence, then

that each of these three different phases on the population curve appears to be occupied by a society that enforces conformity and molds social character in a definably different way.

The society of high growth potential develops in its typical members a social character whose conformity is insured by their tendency to follow tradition: these I shall term *tradition-directed* people and the society in which they live *a society dependent on tradition-direction.*

The society of transitional population growth develops in its typical members a social character whose conformity is insured by their tendency to acquire early in life an internalized set of goals. These I shall term *inner-directed* people and the society in which they live *a society dependent on inner-direction.*

Finally, the society of incipient population decline develops in its typical members a social character whose conformity is insured by their tendency to be sensitized to the expectations and preferences of others. These I shall term *other-directed* people and the society in which they live one *dependent on other-direction.*

Let me point out, however, before embarking on a description of these three "ideal types" of character and society, that I am not concerned here with making the detailed analysis that would be necessary before one could prove that a link exists between population phase and character type. Rather, the theory of the curve of population provides me with a kind of shorthand for referring to the myriad institutional elements that are also—though usually more heatedly—symbolized by such words as "industrialism," "folk society," "monopoly capitalism," "urbanization," "rationalization," and so on. Hence when I speak here of transitional growth or incipient decline of population in conjunction with shifts in character and conformity, these phrases should not be taken as magical and comprehensive explanations.

My reference is as much to the complex of technological and institutional factors related—as cause or effect—to the development of population as to the demographic facts themselves. It would be almost as satisfactory, for my purposes, to divide societies according to the stage of economic development they have reached. Thus, Colin Clark's distinction between the "primary," "secondary," and "tertiary" spheres of the economy (the first refers to agriculture, hunting and fishing, and mining; the second to manufacturing; the third to trade, communications, and services) corresponds very closely to the division of societies on the basis of demographic characteristics. In those societies which are in the phase of "high growth potential," the "primary" sphere is dominant (for example, India); in those that are in the phase of "transitional" growth, the "secondary" sphere is dominant (as for example, Russia); in those that are in the phase of "incipient decline," the "tertiary" sphere is dominant (for example, the United States). And of course, no nation is all of a piece, even in its population characteristics or its economy—different groups and different regions reflect different stages of development, and social character reflects these differences.

A DEFINITION OF TRADITION-DIRECTION

Since the [traditional] type of social order . . . is relatively unchanging, the conformity of the individual tends to reflect his membership in a particular age-grade, clan, or caste; he learns to understand and appreciate patterns which have endured for centuries, and are modified but slightly as the generations succeed each other. The important relationships of life may be controlled by careful and rigid etiquette, learned by the young during the years of intensive socialization that end with initiation into full adult membership. Moreover, the culture, in addition to its economic tasks, or as part of them, provides ritual, routine, and religion to occupy and to orient everyone. Little energy is directed toward finding new solutions of the age-old problems, let us say, of agricultural technique or medicine, the problems to which people are acculturated.

It is not to be thought, however, that in these societies, where the activity of the individual member is determined by characterologically grounded obedience to traditions, the individual may not be highly prized and, in many instances, encouraged to develop his capabilities, his initiative, and even, within very narrow time limits, his aspirations. Indeed, the individual in some primitive societies is far more appreciated and respected than in some sectors of modern society. For the individual in a society dependent on tradition-direction has a well-defined functional relationship to other members of the group. If he is not killed off, he "belongs" — he is not "surplus," as the modern unemployed are surplus, nor is he expendable as the unskilled are expendable in modern society. But by very virtue of his "belonging," life goals that are *his* in terms of conscious choice appear to shape his destiny only to a very limited extent, just as only to a limited extent is there any concept of progress for the group.

In societies in which tradition-direction is the dominant mode of insuring conformity, relative stability is preserved in part by the infrequent but highly important process of fitting into institutionalized roles such deviants as there are. In such societies a person who might have become at a later historical stage an innovator or rebel, whose belonging, as such, is marginal and problematic, is drawn instead into roles like those of the shaman or sorcerer. That is, he is drawn into roles that make a socially acceptable contribution, while at the same time they provide the individual with a more or less approved niche. The medieval monastic orders may have served in a similar way to absorb many characterological "mutations."

In some of these societies certain individuals are encouraged toward a degree of individuality from childhood, especially if they belong to families of high status. But, since the range of choice, even for high-status people, is minimal, the apparent social need for an individuated type of character is also minimal. It is probably accurate to say that character structure in these societies is very largely "adjusted," in the sense that for most people it appears to be in tune with social institutions. Even the few misfits "fit" to a degree; and only very rarely is one driven out of his social world.

This does not mean, of course, that the people are happy; the society to whose traditions they are adjusted may be a miserable one, ridden with anxiety, sadism, and disease. The point is rather that change, while never completely absent in human affairs, is slowed down as the movement of molecules is slowed down at low temperature; and the social character comes as close as it ever does to looking like the matrix of the social forms themselves.

In western history the Middle Ages can be considered a period in which the majority were tradition-directed. But the term tradition-directed refers to a common element, not only among the people of precapitalist Europe but also among such enormously different types of people as Hindus and Hopi Indians, Zulus and Chinese, North African Arabs and Balinese. There is comfort in relying on the many writers who have found a similar unity amid diversity, a unity they express in such terms as "folk society" (as against "civilization"), "status society" (as against "contract society"), "*Gemeinschaft*" (as against "*Gesellschaft*"), and so on. Different as the societies envisaged by these terms are, the folk, status, and *Gemeinschaft* societies resemble each other in their relative slowness of change, their dependence on family and kin organization, and — in comparison with later epochs — their tight web of values. And, as is now well recognized by students, the high birth rate of these societies in the stage of high growth potential is not merely the result of a lack of contraceptive knowledge or techniques. A whole way of life—an outlook on chance, on children, on the place of women, on sexuality, on the very meaning of existence—is the basis of distinction between the societies in which human fertility is allowed to take its course and toll and those which prefer to pay other kinds of toll to cut down on fertility by calculation, and, conceivably, as Freud and other observers have suggested, by a decline in sexual energy itself . . . .

A DEFINITION OF INNER-DIRECTION

In western history the society that emerged with the Renaissance and Reformation and that is only now vanishing serves to illustrate the type of society in which inner-direction is the principal mode of securing conformity. Such a society is characterized by increased personal mobility, by a rapid accumulation of capital (teamed with devastating technological shifts), and by an almost constant *expansion:* intensive expansion in the production of goods and people, and extensive expansion in exploration, colonization, and imperialism. The greater choices this society gives—and the greater initiatives it demands in order to cope with its novel problems—are handled by character types who can manage to live socially without strict and self-evident tradition-direction. These are the inner-directed types.

The concept of inner-direction is intended to cover a very wide range of types. Thus, while it is essential for the study of certain problems to differentiate between Protestant and Catholic countries and their character types, between the effects of the Reformation and the effects of the Renaissance, between the puritan ethic of the European north and west and the somewhat more hedonistic ethic of the European east and south, while all these are valid and, for certain purposes, important distinctions, the concentration of this study on the development of modes of conformity permits their neglect. It allows the grouping together of these otherwise distinct developments because they have one thing in common: *the source of direction for the individual is "inner" in the sense that it is implanted early in life by the elders and directed toward generalized but nonetheless inescapably destined goals.*

We can see what this means when we realize that, in societies in which tradition-direction is the dominant mode of insuring conformity, attention is focused on securing strict conformity in generally observable words and actions, that is to say, behavior. While behavior is minutely prescribed, individuality of character need not be highly developed to meet prescriptions that are objectified in ritual and etiquette—though to be sure, a social character *capable* of such behavioral attention and obedience is requisite. By contrast, societies in which inner-direction becomes important, though they also are concerned with behavioral conformity, cannot be satisfied with behavioral conformity alone. Too many novel situations are presented, situations which a code cannot encompass in advance. Consequently the problem of personal choice, solved in the earlier period of high growth potential by channeling choice through rigid social organization, in the period of transitional growth is solved by channeling choice through a rigid though highly individualized character.

This rigidity is a complex matter. While any society dependent on inner-direction seems to present people with a wide choice of aims—such as money, possessions, power, knowledge, fame, goodness—these aims are ideologically interrelated, and the selection made by any one individual remains relatively unalterable throughout his life. Moreover, the means to those ends, though not fitted into as tight a frame of social reference as in the society dependent on tradition-direction, are nevertheless limited by the new voluntary associations—for instance, the Quakers, the Masons, the Mechanics' Associations—to which people tie themselves. Indeed, the term "tradition-direction" could be misleading if the reader were to conclude that the force of tradition has no weight for the inner-directed character. On the contrary, he is very considerably bound by traditions: they limit his ends and inhibit his choice of means. The point is rather that a splintering of tradition takes place, connected in part with the increasing division of labor and stratification of society. Even if the individual's choice of tradition is largely determined for him by his family, as it is in most cases, he cannot help becoming aware of the existence of competing traditions—hence of tradition as such. As a result he possesses a somewhat greater degree of flexibility in adapting himself to ever changing requirements and in return requires more from his environment.

As the control of the primary group is loosened—the group that both socializes the young and controls the adult in the earlier era—a new psychological mechanism appropriate to the more open society is "invented": it is what I like to describe as a psychological gyroscope.[1] This instrument, once it is set by the parents and other authorities, keeps the inner-directed person, as we shall see, "on course" even when tradition, as responded to by his character, no longer dictates his moves. The inner-directed person becomes capable of maintaining a delicate balance between the demands upon him of his life goal and the buffetings of his external environment.

This metaphor of the gyroscope, like any other, must not be taken literally. It would be a mistake to see the inner-directed man as incapable of learning from experience or as insensitive to public opinion in matters of external conformity. He can receive and utilize certain signals from outside, provided that they can be reconciled with the limited maneuverability that his gyroscope permits him. His pilot is not quite automatic.

Huizinga's *The Waning of the Middle Ages* gives a picture of the anguish and turmoil, the conflict of values, out of which the new forms slowly emerged. Already by the late Middle Ages people were forced to live under new conditions of awareness. As their self-consciousness and their individuality developed, they had to make themselves at home in the world in novel ways. They still have to . . . .

A DEFINITION OF OTHER-DIRECTION

The type of character I shall describe as other-directed seems to be emerging in very recent years in the upper middle class of our larger cities: more prominently in New York than in Boston, in Los Angeles than in Spokane,

---

1. Since writing the above I have discovered Gardner Murphy's use of the same metaphor in his volume *Personality* (New York: Harper and Brothers, 1947).

in Cincinnati than in Chillicothe. Yet in some respects this type is strikingly similar to the American, whom Tocqueville and other curious and astonished visitors from Europe, even before the Revolution, thought to be a new kind of man. Indeed, travelers' reports on America impress us with their unanimity. The American is said to be shallower, freer with his money, friendlier, more uncertain of himself and his values, more demanding of approval than the European. It all adds up to a pattern which, without stretching matters too far, resembles the kind of character that a number of social scientists have seen as developing in contemporary, highly industrialized, and bureaucratic America: Fromm's "marketer," Mills's "fixer," Arnold Green's "middle class male child."[2]

It is my impression that the middle-class American of today is decisively different from those Americans of Tocqueville's writings who nevertheless strike us as so contemporary, and much of this book will be devoted to discussing these differences. It is also my impression that the conditions I believe to be responsible for other-direction are affecting increasing numbers of people in the metropolitan centers of the advanced industrial countries. My analysis of the other-directed character is thus at once an analysis of the American and of contemporary man. Much of the time I find it hard or impossible to say where one ends and the other begins. Tentatively, I am inclined to think that the other-directed type does find itself most at home in America, due to certain unique elements in American society, such as its recruitment from Europe and its lack of any feudal past. As against this, I am also inclined to put more weight on capitalism, industrialism, and urbanization — these international tendencies — than on any character-forming peculiarities of the American scene.

Bearing these qualifications in mind, it seems appropriate to treat contemporary metropolitan America as our illustration of a society — so far, perhaps, the only illustration — in which other-direction is the dominant mode of insuring conformity. It would be premature, however, to say that it is already the dominant mode in America as a whole. But since the other-directed types are to be found among the young, in the larger cities, and among the upper income groups, we may assume that, unless present trends are reversed, the hegemony of other-direction lies not far off.

If we wanted to cast our social character types into social class molds, we could say that inner-direction is the typical character of the "old" middle class — the banker, the tradesman, the small entrepreneur, the technically oriented engineer, etc. — while other-direction is becoming the typical character of the "new" middle class — the bureaucrat, the salaried employee in business, etc. Many of the economic factors associated with the recent growth of the "new" middle class are well known. They have been discussed by James Burnham, Colin Clark, Peter Drucker, and others. There is a decline in the numbers and in the proportion of the working population engaged in production and extraction — agriculture, heavy industry, heavy transport — and an increase in the numbers and the proportion engaged in

---

2. See Erich Fromm, *Man for Himself*; C. Wright Mills, "The Competitive Personality," *Partisan Review*, XIII (1946), 433; Arnold Green, "The Middle Class Male Child and Neurosis," *American Sociological Review*, XI (1946), 31. See also the work of Jurgen Ruesch, Martin B. Loeb, and co-workers on the "infantile personality."

white-collar work and the service trades. People who are literate, educated, and provided with the necessities of life by an ever more efficient machine industry and agriculture, turn increasingly to the "tertiary" economic realm. The service industries prosper among the people as a whole and no longer only in court circles.

Education, leisure, services, these go together with an increased consumption of words and images from the new mass media of communications. While societies in the phase of transitional growth step up the process of distributing words from urban centers, the flow becomes a torrent in the societies of incipient population decline. This process, while modulated by profound national and class differences, connected with differences in literacy and loquacity, takes place everywhere in the industrialized lands. Increasingly, relations with the outer world and with oneself are mediated by the flow of mass communication. For the other-directed types political events are likewise experienced through a screen of words by which the events are habitually atomized and personalized — or pseudo-personalized. For the inner-directed person who remains still extant in this period the tendency is rather to systematize and moralize this flow of words.

These developments lead, for large numbers of people, to changes in paths to success and to the requirement of more "socialized" behavior both for success and for marital and personal adaptation. Connected with such changes are changes in the family and in child-rearing practices. In the smaller families of urban life, and with the spread of "permissive" child care to ever wider strata of the population, there is a relaxation of older patterns of discipline. Under these newer patterns the peer-group (the group of one's associates of the same age and class) becomes much more important to the child, while the parents make him feel guilty not so much about violation of inner standards as about failure to be popular or otherwise to manage his relations with these other children. Moreover, the pressures of the school and the peer-group are reinforced and continued — in a manner whose inner paradoxes I shall discuss later — by the mass media: movies, radio, comics, and popular culture media generally. Under these conditions types of character emerge that we shall here term other-directed. To them much of the discussion in the ensuing chapters is devoted. *What is common to all the other-directed people is that their contemporaries are the source of direction for the individual — either those known to him or those with whom he is indirectly acquainted, through friends and through the mass media. This source is of course "internalized" in the sense that dependence on it for guidance in life is implanted early. The goals toward which the other-directed person strives shift with that guidance: it is only the process of striving itself and the process of paying close attention to the signals from others that remain unaltered throughout life.* This mode of keeping in touch with others permits a close behavioral conformity, not through drill in behavior itself, as in the tradition-directed character, but rather through an exceptional sensitivity to the actions and wishes of others.

Of course, it matters very much who these "others" are: whether they are the individual's immediate circle or a "higher" circle or the anonymous voices of the mass media; whether the individual fears the hostility of chance acquaintances or only of those who "count." But his need for approval and direction from others—and contemporary others rather than ancestors—goes beyond the reasons that lead most people in any era to care very much what others think of them. While all people want and need to be liked by some of the people some of the time, it is only the modern other-directed types who make this their chief source of direction and chief area of sensitivity . . . .[3]

THE THREE TYPES COMPARED

One way to see the structural differences that mark the three types is to see the differences in the emotional sanction or control in each type.

The tradition-directed person feels the impact of his culture as a unit, but it is nevertheless mediated through the specific, small number of individuals with whom he is in daily contact. These expect of him not so much that he be a certain type of person but that he behave in the approved way. Consequently the sanction for behavior tends to be the fear of being *shamed*.

The inner-directed person has early incorporated a psychic gyroscope which is set going by his parents and can receive signals later on from other authorities who resemble his parents. He goes through life less independent than he seems, obeying this internal piloting. Getting off course, whether in response to inner impulses or to the fluctuating voices of contemporaries, may lead to the feeling of *guilt*.

Since the direction to be taken in life has been learned in the privacy of the home from a small number of guides and since principles, rather than details of behavior, are internalized, the inner-directed person is capable of great stability. Especially so when it turns out that his fellows have gyroscopes too, spinning at the same speed and set in the same direction. But many inner-directed individuals can remain stable even when the reinforcement of social approval is not available—as in the upright life of the stock Englishman isolated in the tropics.

Contrasted with such a type as this, the other-directed person learns to respond to signals from a far wider circle than is constituted by his parents. The family is no longer a closely knit unit to which he belongs but merely part of a wider social environment to which he early becomes attentive. In these respects the other-directed person resembles the tradition-directed person: both live in a group milieu and lack the inner-directed person's capacity to go it alone. The nature of this group milieu, however, differs radically in the two cases. The other-directed person is cosmopolitan. For him the border between the familiar and the strange—a border clearly marked in the societies depending on tradition-direction—has broken down. As the family continuously absorbs the strange and reshapes itself, so the strange becomes familiar. While the inner-directed person could be

---

3. This picture of the other-directed person has been stimulated by, and developed from, Erich Fromm's discussion of the "marketing orientation" in *Man for Himself*, pp. 67–82. I have also drawn on my portrait of "The Cash Customer," *Common Sense*, XI (1942), 183.

"at home abroad" by virtue of his relative insensitivity to others, the other-directed person is, in a sense, at home everywhere and nowhere, capable of a rapid if sometimes superficial intimacy with and response to everyone.

The tradition-directed person takes his signals from others, but they come in a cultural monotone; he needs no complex receiving equipment to pick them up. The other-directed person must be able to receive signals from far and near; the sources are many, the changes rapid. What can be internalized, then, is not a code of behavior but the elaborate equipment needed to attend to such messages and occasionally to participate in their circulation. As against guilt-and-shame controls, though of course these survive, one prime psychological lever of the other-directed person is a diffuse *anxiety*. This control equipment, instead of being like a gyroscope, is like a radar.[4]

Changing Values and the Changing Teacher

Much could be said about the changing configuration of adult authorities, other than the parents, as society moves from dependence on inner-direction to dependence on other-direction. Largely for economic reasons the governess, mammy, or hired tutor, for instance, virtually disappears from middle- and upper middle-class homes. One significant consequence is that children are no longer raised by people who hold up to them the standard of a family or class. Such a standard is good training in inner-direction—in the acquisition of generalized goals; it is at the same time a partial buffer against the indiscriminate influence of the peer-group. But there is another more subtle consequence. The child who has been raised by a governess and educated by a tutor gains a very keen sense for the disparities of power in the home and in the society. When he goes off to boarding school or college he is likely to remain unimpressed by his teachers—like the upper-class mother who told the school headmaster: "I don't see why the masters can't get along with Johnny; all the other servants do." Such a child is not going to be interested in allowing his teachers to counsel him in his peer-group relations or emotional life.

Furthermore, the presence of these adults in the home—somewhat like the extended family in earlier eras—helps reduce the emotional intensity of parent-child relations. Though the child knows who is boss in the home, he

---

4. The "radar" metaphor was suggested by Karl Wittfogel.

can still play these other "officials" off against parental authority. And, indeed, the inner-directed parents, frequently not overeager for warmth from the child, are quite willing to have the child's experience of affection associated with persons of lower status. The inner-directed young man raised under these conditions learns to find emotional release with prostitutes and others of low status. He becomes capable of impersonal relations with people and sometimes incapable of any other kind. This is one of the prices he pays for his relative impermeability to the needs and wishes of his peers, and helps account for his ability, when in pursuit of some end he values, to steel himself against their indifference or hostility.

Grandmothers as authorities are almost as obsolete as governesses. There is no room for them in the modern apartment, nor can they, any more than the children themselves, find a useful economic role. Nevertheless they endure, concomitant with the increased longevity of the later population phases. The increased personalization of relationships that other-direction brings means that "strangers" in the home are less and less endurable: the inlaw problem, a standard joke in many cultures over many centuries, takes on new meaning where sensitive, highly individuated people live without characterological defenses against each other.

The elimination of the grandmother from a central role in the home is, moreover, symbolic of the rapidity of the changes we are discussing. She is two generations removed from current practices on the "frontier of consumption." While the parents try to keep up with their children, both as a means of staying young and as a means of staying influential, this is seldom possible for the grandparents. Hence their role in the formation of the other-directed character is negligible. Far from presenting the child with a relatively consistent "family portrait," standing in back of the parents and strengthening them, grandparents stand as emblems of how little one can learn from one's elders about the things that matter.

A parallel development removes another set of parent surrogates who played an important role in earlier periods: the older brothers or sisters who, like sophomores, hazed the younger in subjecting them to the family pattern of discipline. Today the older children—if there are any—are frequently more willing to earn cash as baby sitters than to supervise the training of their own younger brothers and sisters. The lure of a job may get children to work outside their homes; that still makes sense to them. But within their own home they are the privileged guests in a rather second-rate hotel, a hotel whose harassed but smiling managers they put under constant pressure for renovation.

THE TEACHER'S ROLE IN THE STAGE OF INNER-DIRECTION

One important authority, however, remains: a proxy parent whose power has probably increased as a consequence of the shift to other-direction. This is the schoolteacher, and we turn now to a fuller exploration of the change in her role.

In the period when inner-direction insures middle-class conformity, school starts relatively late—there are few nursery schools. The teacher's task is largely to train the children in decorum and in intellectual matters. The decorum may be the minimum of discipline needed to keep order in the classroom or the maximum of polish needed to decorate girls of the upper social strata. As schools become more plentiful and more readily accessible and "democratic," the obligation to train the child in middle-class speech and manners—that he may be aided in his rise above his parents' rank—falls upon the teacher. But the teacher does not work close to the child's emotional level. And the teacher regards her job as a limited one, sharply demarcated from the equally rigorous task of the home.

The physical setting in school reflects this situation. Seating is formal —all face front—and often alphabetical. The walls are decorated with the ruins of Pompeii and the bust of Caesar. For all but the few exceptional children who can transcend the dead forms of their classical education and make the ancient world come alive, these etchings and statues signify the irrelevance of the school to the emotional problems of the child.

The teacher herself has neither understanding of nor time for these emotional problems, and the child's relation to other children enters her purview only in disciplinary cases. Often she has simply no authority: she is a common scold with too large a brood. Or she manages to maintain discipline by strictures and punishments. But these absorb the emotional attention of the children, often uniting them in opposition to authority.

In the recent Swedish movie *Torment* we see this pattern still at work in the near-contemporary scene. Teachers and parents share the task of instilling inner-directed values. The villain is a harsh and overbearing, neurotic prep-school teacher. All the boys hate him; some fear him; no self-respecting boy would dream—despite the teacher's groping efforts—of being his friend. The hero is a boy who rebels, not so much because he wants to but rather because he is forced to by his teacher. He and his friends suffer, but their parents and teachers do not invade their lives, and they have privacy with each other and with girls, so long as no serious breach of decorum is evident. This rebellion itself—its success is not the issue—is part of the process of developing an inner-directed character.

An equally moving portrait is Antonia White's novel of a girl's convent school, *Frost in May*. Though the nuns at the school go quite far in "molding character" and viciously cut down signs of spontaneity and open-mindedness in the gifted heroine, they have back of them only the old-fashioned sanctions of penance and salvation. Their charges break or bend or run away or join the church—they do not open up to the nuns as friends. The universal uniforms, as in a military school, symbolize the barriers of rank and restraint that separate the authorities from the children.

We may sum all this up by saying that the school of this period is concerned largely with impersonal matters. The sexes are segregated. The focus is on an intellectual content that for most children has little emotional bite. Elocution, like female accomplishment, is impersonal, too; the child is not asked to "be himself"—nor does the school aim to be like "real life." Teachers, whether spinsterly or motherly types, do not know enough, even if they had the time and energy, to take an active hand in the socialization of tastes or of peer-group relations. While parents may permit the teachers to enforce certain rules of morality directly related to school, such as modesty of dress and honesty in examinations, and to inculcate certain rules of manners directly related to social ascent, they hardly allow interference with play groups, even in the interests of enforcing ethnic or economic democracy. The teacher is supposed to see that the children learn a curriculum, not that they enjoy it or learn group cooperation. The present practice of progressive grammar schools which decide whether or not to take a child by putting him in his putative group and seeing how he fits in would hardly have been conceivable.

Nevertheless, despite the social distance between teacher and child, the school's unquestioning emphasis on intellectual ability is profoundly important in shaping the inner-directed character. It affirms to the child that what matters is what he can accomplish, not how nice is his smile or how cooperative his attitude. And while the objectivity of the criteria for judging these skills and competences is rightfully called into question to-day—when we can see very clearly, for instance, the class bias in intelligence tests and written examinations—the inner-directed school is not aware of such biases, and hence its standards can appear unequivocal and unalterable. For this reason these standards can be internalized both by those who succeed and by those who fail. They are felt as real and given, not as somebody's whim. Thus the school reinforces the home in setting for the child goals that are clear to all and that give direction and meaning to life thereafter.

Whatever the security children gain from knowing where they stand —a security they no longer have in the other-directed progressive school —we must not forget how harshly this system bears on those who cannot make the grade: they are often broken; there is little mercy for them on psychological grounds. Brains, status, perhaps also docility, win the teacher, rather than "personality" or "problems." Some of the failures rebel. But these, too, are hammered into shape by the school—bad shape. Occasionally the frontier and other opportunities for mobility provide an exit for the academically outclassed; and, still more occasionally, the rebel returns, like a mythical hero, having lived his troubles down, to alleviate the guilt of other misfits and give them hope for their own future. By and large, however, the very unequivocality of the school's standards that gives the children a certain security also means that the standards will be internalized even by those who fail. They will carry with them the aftereffects of emotional shock whose violence lies beyond criticism—sometimes even beyond recall.

THE TEACHER'S ROLE IN THE STAGE OF OTHER-DIRECTION

Progressive education began as a movement to liberate children from the crushing of talent and breaking of will that was the fate of many, even of those whose inner-direction might have seemed to them and to the observer stable and sound enough. Its aim, and to a very considerable degree, its achievement, was to develop the individuality of the child; and its method was to focus the teacher's attention on more facets of the child than his intellectual abilities. Today, however, progressive education is often no longer progressive; as people have become more other-directed, educational methods that were once liberating may even tend to thwart individuality rather than advance and protect it. The story can be quickly told.

Progressive schools have helped lower the age of school entry; the two- to five-year-old groups learn to associate school not with forbidding adults and dreary subjects but with play and understanding adults. The latter are, increasingly, young college graduates who have been taught to be more concerned with the child's social and psychological adjustment than with his academic progress—indeed, to scan the intellectual performance for signs of social maladjustment. These new teachers are more specialized. They don't claim to "understand children" but to have studied Gesell on the "fives" or the "nines"; and this greater knowledge not only prevents the children from uniting in a wall of distrust or conspiracy against the school but also permits the teacher to take a greater hand in the socialization of spheres—consumption, friendship, fantasy—which the older-type teacher, whatever her personal desires, could not touch. Our wealthier society can afford this amount of individuation and "unnecessary" schooling.

Physical arrangements, too—in seating, age-grading, decoration—symbolize the changes in the teacher's function. The sexes are mixed. Seating is arranged "informally." That is, *alphabetic* forms disappear, often to be replaced by *sociometric* forms that bring together compeers. This often means that where to sit becomes problematical—a clue to one's location on the friendship chart. Gesell grading is as severe as intellectual grading was in the earlier era; whatever their intellectual gifts, children stay with their presumed social peers.[1] The desks change their form too; they are more apt to be movable tables with open shelves than places where one may hide things. The teacher no longer sits on a dais or struts before a blackboard but joins the family circle.

Above all, the walls change their look. The walls of the modern grade school are decorated with the paintings of the children or their montages from the class in social studies. Thus the competitive and contemporary problems of the children look down on them from walls which, like the teacher herself, are no longer impersonal. This looks progressive, looks like a salute to creativeness and individuality; but again we meet paradox. While the school de-emphasizes grades and report cards, the displays seem

---

1. Howard C. Becker ("Role and Career Problems of the Chicago Public School Teacher," unpublished Ph.D. dissertation, University of Chicago, 1951) has been observing the classroom consequences of the decline of the practice both of skipping grades and of holding children back who must repeat the grade. The teachers, faced with a group of identical age but vastly different capacities and willingnesses, meet the situation by dividing the class into two or three like-minded groups. Mobility between groups is discouraged, and children are encouraged to imitate their groupmates. The teacher herself, in the public schools, is probably inner-directed, but she is forced by her situation to promote other-direction among her charges.

The following quotation from Mr. Becker's interviews is a poignant example of how a teacher will promote other-direction in her efforts to get the children to have more interesting weekends: "Every class I have I start out the year by making a survey. I have each child get up and tell what he did over the weekend. These last few years I've noticed that more and more children get up and say, 'Saturday I went to the show, Sunday I went to the show' . . . I've been teaching twenty-five years, and it never used to be like that. Children used to do more interesting things, they would go places instead of 'Saturday I went to the show, Sunday I went to the show' . . . What I do is to give a talk on all the interesting things that could be done—like going to museums and things like that. And also things like playing baseball and going on bike rides. By the end of the term a child is ashamed if he has to get up and say, 'Saturday I went to the show, Sunday I went to the show.' All the rest of the children laugh at him. So they really try to do some interesting things."

almost to ask the children: "Mirror, mirror on the wall, who is fairest of us all?"[2]

While the children's paintings and montages show considerable imaginative gift in the pre-adolescent period, the school itself is nevertheless still one of the agencies for the destruction of fantasy, as it was in the preceding era. Imagination withers in most of the children by adolescence. What survives is neither artistic craft nor artistic fantasy but the socialization of taste and interest that can already be seen in process in the stylization of perception in the children's paintings and stories. The stories of the later progressive grades are apt to be characterized by "realism." This realism is subtly influenced by the ideals of the progressive movement. Caesar and Pompeii are replaced by visits to stores and dairies, by maps from *Life*, and by *The Weekly Reader*; and fairy tales are replaced by stories about trains, telephones, and grocery stores, and, later, by material on race relations or the United Nations or our Latin American neighbors.

These changes in arrangement and topic assist the breakdown of walls between teacher and pupil; and this in turn helps to break down walls between student and student, permitting that rapid circulation of tastes which is a prelude to other-directed socialization. Whereas the inner-directed school child might well have hidden his stories and paintings under his bed—like the adult who, as we saw, often kept a diary—the other-directed child reads his stories to the group and puts his paintings on the wall. Play, which in the earlier epoch is often an extracurricular and private hobby, shared at most with a small group, now becomes part of the school enterprise itself, serving a "realistic" purpose.

The teacher's role in this situation is often that of opinion leader. She is the one who spreads the messages concerning taste that come from the progressive urban centers. She conveys to the children that what matters is not their industry or learning as such but their adjustment in the group, their cooperation, their (carefully stylized and limited) initiative and leadership.

Especially important is the fact that the cooperation and leadership that are inculcated in and expected of the children are frequently contentless. In nursery school it is not important whether Johnny plays with a truck or in the sandbox, but it matters very much whether he involves himself with Bill—via any object at all. To be sure, there are a few, a very few, truly progressive schools where the children operating on the Dalton plan and similar plans exercise genuine choice of their program, move at their own pace, and use the teacher as a friendly reference library; here cooperation is necessary and meaningful in actual work on serious projects. Far more frequently, however, the teacher continues to hold the reins of authority in her hands, hiding her authority, like her compeer, the other-directed parent, under the cloak of "reasoning" and manipulation. She determines the program and its pace—indeed, often holding the children back because she

---

2. Still more paradoxically, it often happens that those schools that insist most strongly that the child be original and creative by this very demand make it difficult for him to be so. He dare not imitate an established master nor, in some cases, even imitate his own earlier work. Though the introduction of the arts into the school opens up the whole art world to many children, who would have no time or stimulation outside, other children are forced to socialize performances that would earlier have gone unnoticed by peers and adults.

fails to realize that children, left to themselves, are capable of curiosity about highly abstract matters. She may delay them by making arithmetic "realistic" and languages fun — as well as by substituting social studies for history. In extreme forms of this situation there is nothing on which the children have to cooperate in order to get it done. The teacher will do it for them anyway. Hence when she asks that they be cooperative she is really asking simply that they be nice.

However, though the request seems simple, it is not casually made: the teacher is very tense about it. Deprived of older methods of discipline, she is, if anything, even more helpless than the parents who can always fall back on those methods in a pinch, though guiltily and rather ineffectively. The teacher neither dares to nor cares to; she has been taught that bad behavior on the children's part implies poor management on her part. Moreover, she herself is not interested in the intellectual content of what is taught, nor is this content apt to come up in a staff meeting or PTA discussion. These adult groups are often concerned with teaching tolerance, both ethnic and economic; and the emphasis on social studies that results means that intellectual content and skill become still more attenuated. Consequently, the teacher's emotional energies are channeled into the area of group relations. Her social skills develop; she may be sensitive to cliques based on "mere friendship" and seek to break them up lest any be left out. Correspondingly, her love for certain specific children may be trained out of her. All the more, she needs the general cooperation of all the children to assure herself that she is doing her job. Her surface amiability and friendliness, coupled with this underlying anxiety concerning the children's response, must be very confusing to the children who will probably conclude that to be uncooperative is about the worst thing one can be.

Of course the teacher will see to it that the children practice cooperation in small matters: in deciding whether to study the Peruvians or the Colombians, in nominating class officers for early practice in the great contemporary rituals of electioneering and parliamenteering, and in organizing contributions for the Red Cross or a Tag Day. Thus the children are supposed to learn democracy by underplaying the skills of intellect and overplaying the skills of gregariousness and amiability. A democratically open field for talent, in fact, based on respect for ability to *do* something, tends to survive only in athletics.

There is, therefore, a curious resemblance between the role of the teacher in the small-class modern school — a role that has spread from the progressive private schools to a good number of the public schools — and the role of the industrial relations department in a modern factory. The latter is also increasingly concerned with cooperation between men and men and between men and management, as technical skill becomes less and less of a major concern. In a few of the more advanced plants there is even a pattern of democratic decision on moot matters — occasionally important because it affects piecework rates and seniority rules, but usually as trivial as the similar decisions of grammar-school government. Thus the other-directed child is taught at school to take his place in a society where the concern of the group is less with what it produces than with its internal group relations, its morale.

WILLIAM H. WHYTE, JR.

William H. Whyte, Jr., is a writer who has contributed articles to various well-known periodicals. He was for a period of time a managing editor of Fortune. *Best known for his trenchant and widely discussed study of evolving American values,* The Organization Man, *he also edited and contributed to the book* The Exploding Metropolis *(1958).*

Groupthink

A very curious thing has been taking place in this country—and almost without our knowing it. In a country where "individualism"—independence and self-reliance—was the watchword for three centuries, the view is now coming to be accepted that the individual himself has no meaning —except, that is, as a member of a group. "Group integration," "group equilibrium," "interpersonal relations," "training for group living," "group dynamics," "social interaction," "social physics"; more and more the notes are sounded—each innocuous or legitimate in itself, but together a theme that has become unmistakable.

In a sense, this emphasis is a measure of success. We have *had* to learn how to get along in groups. With the evolution of today's giant organizations—in business, in government, in labor, in education, in big cities—we have created a whole new social structure for ourselves, and one so complex that we're still trying to figure out just what happened. But the American genius for cooperative action has served us well. "Human relations" may not be an American invention, but in no country have people turned so wholeheartedly to the job of mastering the group skills on which our industrial society places such a premium.

But the pendulum has swung too far. Take, for example, the growing popularity of "social engineering" with its emphasis on the planned manipulation of the individual into the group role. Or, even more striking, the extraordinary efforts of some corporations to encompass the executive's wife in the organization—often with the willing acquiescence of the wife in the merger. And these, as we hope to demonstrate, are no isolated phenomena; recent public-opinion polls, slick-magazine fiction, current best-sellers, all document the same trend. Groupthink is becoming a national philosophy.

Groupthink being a coinage — and, admittedly, a loaded one — a working definition is in order. We are not talking about mere instinctive conformity — it is, after all, a perennial failing of mankind. What we are talking about is a *rationalized* conformity — an open, articulate philosophy which holds that group values are not only expedient but right and good as well. Three mutually supporting ideas form the underpinning: (1) that moral values and ethics are relative; (2) that what is important is the kind of behavior and attitudes that makes for the harmonious functioning of the group; (3) that the best way to achieve this is through the application of "scientific" techniques.

Once grasped, as the work of the social engineers makes clear, these principles lead us to an entirely new view of man. And what a dismal fellow he is! For the man we are now presented with is Social Man — completely a creature of his environment, guided almost totally by the whims and prejudices of the group, and incapable of any real self-determination of his destiny. Only through social engineering — i.e., applied groupthink — can he be saved. The path to salvation, social engineers explain, lies in a trained elite that will benevolently manipulate us into group harmony. And who's to be the elite? Social engineers modestly clear their throats.

THE VANISHING LAYMAN

This vision of a new elite guiding us to the integrated life has inspired some interesting speculations (e.g., Aldous Huxley's *Brave New World*, George Orwell's *Nineteen Eighty-Four*). The real danger, however, is something else again. It is not that the layman will be pushed around by the social engineers: it is that *he will become one himself*. Rather than the pawn of the experts, he will be the willing apprentice — and embrace groupthink as the road to security.

Is this coming to pass? Let's look for a moment at the direction American values are taking among the oncoming generations. There has been a rather disturbing amount of evidence that they are changing rapidly — and in a way that must warm social engineers' hearts. Every study made of the younger generation, every portrayal they make of themselves — from their dating habits to their artistic inclinations — uncovers one clear fact: our youth is the most group-minded we have ever had. Gregariousness has become a necessity. "They are parts of groups," one girl shrewdly appraises her contemporaries. "When they are alone they are bored with themselves."

While youngsters are not inclined to philosophize, their attitude toward life adds up to a fairly discernible set of values. It could be described as a "practical" relativism. The old absolute moral values are disappearing. There is still black and white, to be sure, but it is no longer determined by fixed precepts; it is determined rather by what the group thinks is black and white — and if someone does things the way his group does, well, who is to censure him for his loyalty?

The colleges furnish documentation of the drift. If recent surveys are any indication, a startling swing has taken place among students to the twin ideals of group harmony and expertism. "These men," one of their mentors says in praise, "don't question the system. Their main aim is to make it work better—to get in there and lubricate the machinery. They're not rebels; they'll be social technicians for a better society."

The registrar's records bear him out. Along with a concurrent drift from the humanities, there has been a tremendous increase in specialized courses —and of specialization within specialties. Significantly, the courses that enjoyed the most phenomenal popularity among postwar classes were those connected with personnel work. "I like people" became a universal cry, and in droves students aiming for business turned thumbs down on the idea of general, executive apprenticeship in favor of personnel work; here, with stop watch and slip stick in hand, they could measure away, safe from the doubts and intangibles of the world without. The picture was a mirage, of course, but it was only by the most strenuous efforts of placement officers and corporation personnel people that students gave it up.

Does entry into business life transform these values? Apparently not. Talk with members of the younger generation of management—and we speak not of the disaffected but of the successful—and one is struck by a curious strain of resignation that often runs through their discussion. Like the heroes of J. P. Marquand's perceptive novels, they are disturbed by a sense of individual impotence. Dispassionately, they describe themselves primarily as members of their environment—men more acted upon than acting. They are neither angry nor cynical about it; they are caught on a "treadmill" from which they will never escape, perhaps—but the treadmill is pleasant enough, they explain, and in the group role they find the emotional security they want so very badly.

So with their wives. No matter what problem they are discussing—from the possibility of advancement to the style of their living—they instinctively phrase their problems in terms of their relations with the group. The relations, they concede, are not simple—there are the girls, the gang on Ferncrest Road, Charlie's people at the office, and a host of lesser constellations to conjure with. Tough as the job may be, however, it is a job to which they have dedicated themselves.

THE SYSTEM LOVERS

Turn to the image of the good life in popular cultures and you find the same phenomenon at work. Slick-magazine fiction tells the story. It has never, of course, exactly called for a rebellion against the status quo, but back in the thirties it did present heroes and heroines who engaged in some kind of mild strife with their environment, told the boss off, or did something equally contentious. No longer. A *Fortune* analysis of 1935-36 plots and 1950-51 plots indicates that heroes and heroines have been growing remarkably submissive. Not only is the system they abide by—be it an Army camp, a business office, or a small-town environment—shown as more benevolent; in some cases the system itself becomes the *deus ex machina* that solves the problem.

So in serious fiction. More and more, writers are concerning themselves with the relationship of the individual to the group, and more and more resolving it in favor of the latter. The system—and they don't mean God or the universe—is eventually revealed to the hero as bigger than any of us, and thus it is not only foolish but wrong for him not to reconcile himself to it. From the extreme of the angry, to-hell-with-the-whole-lousy-setup tracts of the 1930's we seem to be going whole hog in the opposite direction.

Let us have a look at the current best-seller, Herman Wouk's *The Caine Mutiny*. Since it is about the Navy, the system shown has some aspects peculiar to service life. The basic question posed, however—the individual's place in the system—has great universality, and in an excitingly told tale Wouk sketches one point of view with such striking overtones that the book could almost go down as a landmark in the shift of American values.

The story tells of the terrible dilemma facing the officers of a mine sweeper; their captain, one Queeg, is a neurotic, cowardly incompetent. A typhoon brings the problem to the breaking point. Through hysteria and cowardice, Queeg is about to sink the ship. In vain, Maryk, the stolid, conventional executive officer, tries to get him to keep the ship headed into the wind. Queeg refuses. In the nick of time, Maryk makes his decision. Under Article 184 of Navy Regulations, he relieves Queeg of his command. The ship is saved.

What is the moral? Maryk, we find, shouldn't have done it. Says the author's protagonist, Lieutenant Willy Keith in a letter to his girl (p. 463): " . . . I see that we were in the wrong . . . . The idea is, once you get an incompetent ass of a skipper—and it's a chance of war—there's nothing to do but serve him as though he were the wisest and the best, cover his mistakes, keep the ship going, and bear up. So I have gone all the way around Robin Hood's barn to arrive at the old platitudes, which I guess is the process of growing up."

In other times, perhaps, this definition of maturity might have been regarded as downright parody. Obedience and discipline few could have caviled at. But would they have applauded the counseling of an obedience, so abject, so *unquestioning*, that we are asked, in effect, not only to put up with the evils of a system but to regard them as right—to reach out, as Norbert Weiner's phrase goes, and kiss the whip that lashes us? Would they have joined in censuring an act to which the only logical alternative is the passive sacrifice of several hundred lives? Hardly. The executive officer's action might well have been seen as an act of great moral courage —and one, furthermore, in true allegiance to the service; it did, after all, save the ship. The other byproduct, the withdrawal of Queeg from line command, might also have been interpreted as something less than a disaster to the system.

Not so A. D. 1952. The moral, to judge from what critics and readers have been saying about it, has struck exactly the right chord. The exec, as the dust jacket has it, was merely a well-meaning man "beyond his depth," and more to be pitied than censured. It is not for the individual to question the competence of the Queegs a system may contain. Queeg was a teacher. Queegs are necessary. We needed Queegs to win the war. So goes the assent. "It is about time that more books of this sort were written," says J. P. Marquand. "The lesson the newcomer must learn is in many ways the antithesis of democracy. It is essentially a final acceptance of the doctrine that full and unquestioning obedience must be accorded a superior officer, no matter how personally odious or stupid this individual may be—and that without this individual surrender we can never win a war."

Love that system.

THE PERMISSIVE WAY

What makes this wave of the present particularly unsettling is the surprising fact that it is in rhythm with one of the dominant currents in contemporary American academic thought. It would be a mistake, of course, to treat the connection as cause and effect; groupthink's roots go too deep to be so summarily explained. But it would be just as much of an error to dismiss the academic underpinnings, as the layman is so tempted to do, as mere ivory-tower mumbo jumbo. The ideology of groupthink is often incomprehensible to the uninitiated, but it is of great power nonetheless. Translated by its disciples in hundreds of lecture halls and papers, and by their disciples in turn, it has given a purpose and direction to the groupthink movement that it would otherwise lack.

The movement, in a sense, is an offshoot of the great academic revolt at the turn of the century against formalism. To Young Turks of the day the individualistic tradition of American thought needed redefinition. Too much attention, they felt, had been concentrated on the lone individual; as a consequence, the rigid values built up for his protection were inapplicable to the great social upheavals that were taking place. What was needed was a social view of man—man as a unit of the group—and a willingness to adapt society to his needs.

Most of the credit generally goes to John Dewey, who, with William Kilpatrick, gave "progressive" education its impetus. But there were many others—Veblen in economics, for example, and Roscoe Pound in the law ("The law is social engineering"). Like a fresh breeze, through almost every field of American thought, the new concepts swept, as converts enthusiastically fell to whacking away at the restrictions of the old absolutes. Social Man was coming of age.

When the cultural anthropologists got to work on him, his final link to the old moral absolutes was severed. From their comparisons of primitive cultures, and, later, our own, many anthropologists came to the view that the ethics of a people are relative. By this they do not mean that ethics are unimportant, but rather that they are not to be judged by any abstract conceptions of "right" or "wrong." For if we realize that other cultures and ethics are "equally valid," to use Ruth Benedict's phrase, then we will be jogged into giving up all the more readily our outworn traditions and our illusions of individual autonomy. "It is not any particular set of values," another anthropologist explains, "but a way of looking at them that is important."

A half-century has gone by and the relativistic, social view of man idea is still gaining. The appetite for cultural anthropology, for example, has been growing at such a rate that Ruth Benedict's *Patterns of Culture*, first published in 1931, has reached, after a phenomenal newsstand sale, the No. 1 best-seller spot in the Mentor paper-book series.

In several essentials, however, the nature of the movement against formalism has changed drastically. What started as a healthy revolt against dogmatism has produced an offshoot that has succeeded in becoming the new dogmatism itself. And since, like all dogmatisms, it promises respite from uncertainty, a society still shell-shocked by the upheavals of the twentieth century hasn't bothered yet to question its effects too closely. To be sure, those of the groupthink leaning customarily speak of themselves as rebels fighting an uphill battle against the enemy ("medievalists," "academicians," "absolutists") but the dog they are kicking is practically dead. They won that battle long ago.

Certainly so in one sector of education. Thanks to a strenuous academic controversy, the momentum of the militantly "progressive" brand was slowed down some time back. Groupthink, however, cannot be contained by a label, and to a formidable body of educators the basic ideal of adjustment to group values is so taken for granted that the only remaining job would appear to be working up better ways of bringing it about. "The American educator," writes one of them, Professor Stewart Cole, "[must] treat pupils as persons-in-groups-in-American-culture at every stage of their social learning." To do this the teacher should borrow from such disciplines as anthropology, the social sciences, psychology, and group dynamics. "The social interactions" of teachers and pupils should be "the primary channel of learning the good life for America."[1]

In this free, permissive atmosphere, the idea that the individual should be regarded as personally accountable for the way he behaves is, of course, old hat. And in the popular view as well. "If your young son sticks his tongue out at you and calls you a nasty old stinkpot," an article in *American Magazine* good-humoredly, but approvingly, counsels, "just ignore the insult and rejoice secretly that you have such a fine normal child. He is simply channeling his aggressive, aggrieved feelings harmlessly by verbal projection."

Where "social interaction" is the watchword, the attitude conditioning is left, in large part, to the child's peers. Even more than their elders, they are quick to reward deviance with hefty interaction; and thus in the natural distaste of the crowd for the individualist we now have a social tool. And this, the child learns from the books written for him, is as it should be. In these tales of fire engines and trains, as David Riesman has documented in his disturbing study, *The Lonely Crowd,* the neophyte groupthinker is taught that one wins by being directed by others—and that the most important thing in the world is to be a team player.

To further ensure that the child need never be a person-not-in-groups, the necessity for little groupthinkers to think as individuals *all by themselves* may soon be obviated altogether. Individual homework is now to be eliminated. Writes Amy Selwyn in the *Reader's Digest*, "Now authorities generally agree that children learn best if they do their learning in groups

---

1. Educators of this bent cannot be accused of swimming against the current. As a recent Elmo Roper poll indicates, most Americans now feel the second most important reason for sending children to high school is "to teach them to get along better with other people." (No. 1: to get them ready for a job.)

and talk out loud about lessons as they work. 'No homework' spokesmen
also say if children were not required to spend their leisure studying they
would not develop the resentment against study which often kills all incen-
tive to learn anything . . . . "

Lest the layman presume to question the drift, groupthinkers explain
that their work is rooted in the Scientific Method, and that now being a
holy phrase, it is made plain that the debate is closed to outsiders—if indeed any grounds for debate exist at all.[2] "Because this new 'doctrine' has
for its base objective findings in anthropology, social psychology, mental
hygiene, and scientific child study," Professor Alain Locke of Howard University says, "there is an authoritative consensus back of these newer educational procedures that few would care to challenge."

ON THE BRINK OF NONSENSE

He is right. Many educators have seriously questioned the excesses of educational groupthink, but a large proportion of them are curiously loath to
do it out loud right now. Criticism of the misapplications of science, they
know, will be quickly seized as an attack on science itself. To muddy matters even more, those of the extremist fringe (notably Allen Zoll) have succeeded in putting something of the kiss of death on public discussion by
their attacks on "progressive" education. They are really attacking something else, of course; their reasoning is erroneous and their motives suspect.
Nevertheless, many people who have a respectable argument to make hesitate for fear they will lose their standing as liberals. The debate, however,
cannot long be deferred—certainly so when it can be said, with some justification, that the best friend progressive education has today is Allen Zoll.

There are some signs that the wider implications of the groupthink
movement may at last provoke a counterrevolution. Significantly, some of
the most astringent critiques of groupthink are coming from the ranks of
the sociologists (cf. "The Image of Man in the Social Sciences"—Reinhard
Bendix in *Commentary*, February, 1951). In its application to the law, Roscoe
Pound himself has been led to protest the degree to which the social-utility
concept has supplanted firm values. Similarly, in England—which suffers
groupthink too—educator Sir Walter Moberly has been stirring the universities to a re-examination of the British variant.

But the best hope may well lie in the ambitions of the groupthinkers
themselves. They stand poised, finally, on the threshold of pure nonsense.
For a long time they have been growing uncomfortable over their apparent
denial of ethical relevance. As the anthropologists themselves point out,
man does need a firm sense of right and wrong, and an excessively relative
view destroys the old firmness.

This does not mean, however, that the groupthinkers are chastened.
Quite the contrary. They now propose to cure this pitfall of scientism with

---

2."I should like to see teachers and professors as sure of themselves, as confident in their training
and experience, as surgeons are, and as impatient of lay advice"—Margaret B. Pickel (Dean of
Women, Columbia University), *New York Times Magazine*, June 3, 1951.

more scientism. Ethics are to be made "a matter of scientific investigation." To some, this merely means an objective study of ethics — certainly a proper enough task. To the groupthinker, however, it means nothing less than a theoretical apparatus for the scientific determination of what is "good" or "bad." And thus "to the innermost citadel of dogmatic thinking, the realm of values," they hopefully turn. "The conquest of the field of values," as one sounds the call, "would be almost the concluding triumph." He couldn't be more correct.

ETHICS WITHOUT TEARS

Why should so despairing an ideology be so popularly contagious? In a society where the old family and community ties that so long cemented it have broken down, the impulse for association is an instinctive and healthy response. But a sense of "belonging," a sense of meaningful association with others, has never required that one sacrifice his individuality as part of the bargain. Why, then, do so many rush to embrace a philosophy that tells them it *is* necessary? Why, like the moth, do we fly to the one thing that will consume us? Why, in a country with the sort of healthy political and economic base that has historically nourished individualism, are we so pathetically eager to join up in flatulent brotherhood?

To explain this impulse is to explain our blind faith in scientism as well. For their appeal is common, and many as the variations may be, they come back, eventually, to one simple, compelling theme.

They offer us freedom from moral choice.

Through the deification of group harmony, buck-passing a moral decision becomes itself a moral act; the system — as *The Caine Mutiny* advocates — attends to these things so much better than the individual, and he might just as well relax and enjoy it.

And there is freedom in another sense as well. Moral dilemmas exist because there is uncertainty. If we can now abstract a few parts from the whole of human nature and by analysis predict objectively what will make for group harmony, the intangibles that make individual decisions so poignant may be obviated altogether. Like a general who is blessed with perfect intelligence of the enemy, we will have only one valid course of action before us. We will have finally latched on to certainty.

WHY PARTICIPATE?

Once this denial of moral relevance is made, folly must be the consequence. For groupthinkers go on to assure themselves that in groupthink itself one finds moral fulfillment. It is not put this crudely, of course; by what has now become a ritualistic explanation, our eyes are directed upward to the goal of harmony, group integration, dynamic equilibrium; upward to a golden mean in which everyone will finally attain the blessed state of — grace? No, the state of "participation."

But participation for what? As a fundamental of the democratic process, as a means of self-expression and development, participation is abundantly desirable. In this sense, *Fortune* has argued strongly for participation; it has reported its application to the problems of management and will continue to. But the word, like its blood brothers "communication" and "adjust," is assuming a sort of end-all quality. So let us put the question: *Why* participate?

In the litany of groupthink the answers describe a complete circle. One participates for the end of "social integration," for "community-centered cohesion," for better "interpersonal relations," for "group harmony," for the reduction of "social tensions," for adjustment to the environment. One participates, in other words, that he may participate. And so the end is really only a means after all. Good means, yes—but as an encompassing philosophy, somewhat less than complete.

Even as a means, participation can be a tricky concept. It is easily confused with getting a number of people to do what one did before. And in this aspect, unfortunately, it provides the resolutely pedestrian with a way of cutting down to size their up-and-coming brethren. Similarly it offers the faint of heart an alibi for ducking responsibility—if a broth is to be spoiled, it's convenient to have too many cooks participate.

Perhaps the most extraordinary aspect of groupthink is the success with which its double-talk has used the old concepts of individualism to justify their opposite. By letting others decide, one decides. By submitting oneself to the group, one becomes an individual. "It is precisely this gradual change in our mental horizon—new assumptions and hypotheses taken as factual description—that is sinister," says Lincoln Reis, professor of philosophy at Bard College. "So that while we are presented with a logical horror, we find it established and accepted widely as a fact. Nowhere vulnerable to intelligence, it is as impervious as a nightmare."

It is impervious because the ideal of unity it holds out obscures for us some disagreeable facts of life—and the necessity for facing them on moral grounds. "Communication" is a term in point. As used in its cult sense, it implies the facile premise that the conflicts that plague us are due simply to "blocks" in the communication flow, and that if we get the technical hang of it, all will be well. Up to a point this is true. But people do not always argue because they misunderstand one another; they argue because they hold different goals. These will always be a matter of debate, and attempts to evade it through "nonpartisan" communication or "education" programs simply beg the question.

UNITY—OR MONOTONY?

"Unity" is a double-edged sword. As our young corporation wife is witness, group harmony is not an unmixed blessing; conversely, neither are frustrations and tensions necessarily bad. They can be fruitful; indeed, progress is often dependent on producing rather than mitigating them. In large part, also, they stem from the scores of conflicting loyalties and allegiances we enjoy in a fluid society. Unless we forswear these in complete fealty to one embracing organization, there is no easy way to escape the moral decisions they force upon us. *Nor should there be.* The danger, as Clark Kerr points out, "is not that loyalties are divided today, but that they may become undivided tomorrow."

It is precisely this smothering of the individual that the drift to group-think seems to be making more and more imminent. Few groupthinkers, to be sure, believe themselves against the individual. But in looking so intently at man as a member of the group, they have made man seem important in this role only. There is the frequent explanation, of course, that only by group participation is the individual's potential realized. But this is only a half-truth. Individual excellence must involve something more than a re-spect for the group and a skill in working with it. "The sphere of individual action," writes Bertrand Russell, "is not to be regarded as ethically inferior to that of social duty. On the contrary, some of the best of human activities are, at least in feeling, rather personal than social . . . . Prophets, mystics, poets, scientific discoverers, are men whose lives are dominated by a vision . . . . It . . . is such men who put into the world the things that we most value."

Few of us are potential geniuses, but the constant admonition to har-monize and integrate affects us nonetheless. Each day we are faced with a multitude of decisions. Should we trust our own judgment? Or does the group's view have an inherent rightness we cannot match?

The new values would incline us to the easy harmony of the group view, for they would have us suppose that the whole is greater than the sum of the parts; that the system has a wisdom beyond the reach of ordi-nary mortals. But this is not necessarily so. Man can be greater than the group, and his lone imagination worth a thousand graphs.

He is not often a creator, but even as spectator, as "the common man," he can rise in ways his past performance would not predict. To aim at his common denominators in the name of ultimate democracy is to despise him, to perpetuate his mediocrities, and to conceive him incapable of re-sponding to anything better than the echo of his prejudices. The "equilib-rium" that is the compact to be made with this boor is inevitably static, and the trouble is not solved by sticking the adjective dynamic in front of it.

Has the individual reached a low enough estate for us to become con-cerned? When the nation's best-selling novel advocates his abject submis-sion without raising eyebrows; when some corporations make it policy not to hire honor graduates for fear they might not be good mixers; when it is seriously stated that "natural leaders" can be made obsolete, the time has come at least to think about the matter. For if the drift continues, man may soon cease to fret over such things at all. He will finally have engineered for himself that equilibrious society. Gelded into harmonious integration, he will be free from tensions and frustrations, content in the certainties of his special function, no longer tantalized by the sense of infinity. He will at last have become a complete bore.

The answer is not a return to a "rugged individualism" that never was. Nor is it a slackened interest in social science and "human relations." We need, certainly, to find ways of making this bewildering society of ours run more smoothly and we need all the illumination science can give us to do it. But we need something more. Lest man become an ethical eunuch, his autonomy sacrificed for the harmony of the group, a new respect for the individual must be kindled. A revival of the humanities, perhaps, a conscious, deliberate effort by the corporation not only to accommodate dissent but to encourage it—possible approaches to a problem so fundamental cannot easily be spelled out.

Only individuals can do it.

Education and the Organization Man

Corporations have not been setting up training schools simply because seniors want them to. Corporations started experimenting with such programs many years ago, and while the predilections of the young men have been a powerful prod, in time many corporations would have made the shift anyway. For the training schools are not simply a sugar-coating, a more attractively packaged indoctrination; they are a manifestation of a deep change in the organization's own view of what *kind* of man it wishes to achieve.

There are two divergent conceptions, and the question of which is to become dominant is still at issue. On the surface the trainee programs of most big corporations would seem very much alike. Beneath such new standardized trappings as testing, automatic rating, rotation, and the like, however, is a fundamental difference in policy.

One type of program sticks to what has been more or less the historic approach. The young man is hired to do a specific job; his orientation is usually brief in duration, and for many years what subsequent after hours training he will get will be directed at his particular job. If he proves himself executive material he may be enrolled in a management development course, but this is not likely to happen until he is in his mid-thirties.

The newer type of program is more than an intensification of the old. The company hires the young man as a potential manager and from the start he is given to thinking of himself as such. He and the other candidates are put together in a central pool, and they are not farmed out to regular jobs until they have been exposed, through a series of dry-run tasks, to the managerial view. The schooling may last as long as two years and occasionally as long as four or five.

At the risk of oversimplification, the difference can be described as that between the Protestant Ethic and the Social Ethic. In one type of program we will see that the primary emphasis is on work and on competition; in the other, on managing *others'* work and on co-operation. Needless to say, there are few pure examples of either approach; whichever way they incline, the majority of training programs have elements of both approaches, and some companies try to straddle directly over the fence. But an inclination there is, and the new training program may prove the best of introductions to the "professional manager" of the future.

To sharpen the fundamental differences, I am going to contrast two outstanding trainee programs. For an example of the first type, I am going to take the training program of the Vick Chemical Company as it was in the late thirties. There are several reasons for the choice. First, it has been one of the best-known programs in the whole personnel field. Second, though it has often been cited as a pioneer example of modern practice, it was in its fundamentals the essence of the Protestant Ethic and so undefiled by change that there was nothing in it which Henry Clews would take exception to. Third, I happen to have gone through it myself. If I grow unduly garrulous in these next pages, I bespeak the reader's indulgence; I have often pondered this odd experience, and since it furnishes so apt an illustration of certain principles of indoctrination, I would like to dwell on it at some length.

It was a school—the Vick School of Applied Merchandising, they called it. The idea, as it was presented to job-hunting seniors at the time, was that those who were chosen were not going off to a job, but to a postgraduate training institution set up by a farsighted management. In September, some thirty graduates would gather from different colleges to start a year's study in modern merchandising. There would be a spell of classroom work in New York, a continuing course in advertising, and, most important, eleven months of field study under the supervision of veteran students of merchandising and distribution. Theoretically, we should be charged a tuition, for though we understood we would do some work in connection with our studies, the company explained that its expenses far outweighed what incidental services we would perform. This notwithstanding, it was going to give us a salary of $75 a month and all traveling expenses. It would also, for reasons I was later to learn were substantial, give us an extra $25 a month to be held in escrow until the end of the course.

Let me now point out the first distinction between the Vick program and the more current type. It was not executive training or even junior-executive training. Vick's did argue that the program would help produce the leaders of tomorrow, and prominent on the walls of the office was a framed picture of a captain at the wheel, with a statement by the president that the greatest duty of management was to bring along younger men. This notwithstanding, the question of whether or not any of us would one day be executives was considered a matter that could very easily be deferred. The training was directed almost entirely to the immediate job. The only exception was an International Correspondence Schools course in advertising, one of the main virtues of which, I always felt, was to keep us so occupied during the week ends that we wouldn't have time to think about our situation.

The formal schooling we got was of the briefest character. During our four weeks in New York, we learned of Richardson's discovery of Vapo-Rub, spent a day watching the VapoRub being mixed, and went through a battery of tests the company was fooling around with to find the Vick's

WILLIAM H. WHYTE, JR.   45

type. Most of the time we spent in memorizing list prices, sales spiels, counters to objections, and the prices and techniques of Plough, Inc., whose Penetro line was one of Vick's most troublesome competitors. There was no talk about the social responsibilities of business or the broad view that I can remember, and I'm quite sure the phrase *human relations* never came up at all.

What management philosophy we did get was brief and to the point. Shortly before we were to set out from New York, the president, Mr. H. S. Richardson, took us up to the Cloud Club atop the Chrysler Building. The symbolism did not escape us. As we looked from this executive eyrie down on the skyscraper spires below, Golconda stretched out before us. One day, we gathered, some of us would be coming back up again — and not as temporary guests either. Some would not. The race would be to the swiftest.

Over coffee Mr. Richardson drove home to us the kind of philosophy that would get us back up. He posed a hypothetical problem. Suppose, he said, that you are a manufacturer and for years a small firm has been making paper cartons for your product. He has specialized so much to service you, as a matter of fact, that that's all he does make. He is utterly dependent on your business. For years the relationship has continued to be eminently satisfactory to both parties. But then one day another man walks in and says he will make the boxes for you cheaper. What do you do?

He bade each one of us in turn to answer.

But *how much* cheaper? we asked. How much time could we give the old supplier to match the new bid? Mr. Richardson became impatient. There was only one decision. Either you were a businessman or you were not a businessman. The new man, obviously, should get the contract. Mr. Richardson, who had strong views on the necessity of holding to the old American virtues, advised us emphatically against letting sentimentality obscure fundamentals. Business was survival of the fittest, he indicated, and we would soon learn the fact.

He was as good as his word. The Vick curriculum was just that — survival of the fittest. In the newer type of programs, companies will indeed fire incompetents, but a man joins with the idea that the company intends to keep him, and this is the company's wish also. The Vick School, however, was frankly based on the principle of elimination. It wouldn't make any difference how wonderful all of us might turn out to be; of the thirty-eight who sat there in the Cloud Club, the rules of the game dictated that only six or seven of us would be asked to stay with Vick. The rest would graduate to make way for the next batch of students.

Another difference between Vick's approach and that now more characteristic became very evident as soon as we arrived in the field. While the work, as the company said, was educational, it was in no sense make-work. Within a few days of our session at the Cloud Club, we were dispatched to the hinterland — in my case, the hill country of eastern Kentucky. Each of us was given a panel delivery truck, a full supply of signs, a ladder, a stock of samples, and an order pad. After several days under the eye of a senior salesman, we were each assigned a string of counties and left to shift for ourselves.

The merchandising was nothing if not applied. To take a typical day of any one of us, we would rise at 6:00 or 6:30 in some bleak boarding house or run-down hotel and after a greasy breakfast set off to squeeze in some advertising practice before the first call. This consisted of bostitching a quota of large fiber signs on barns and clamping smaller metal ones to telephone poles and trees by hog rings. By eight, we would have arrived at a general store for our exercise in merchandising. Our assignment was to persuade the dealer to take a year's supply all at once, or, preferably, more than a year's supply, so that he would have no money or shelf space left for other brands. After the sale, or no-sale, we would turn to market research and note down the amount sold him by "chiseling competitors" (i.e., competitors; there was no acknowledgment on our report blanks of any other kind).

Next we did some sampling work: "Tilt your head back, Mr. Jones," we would suddenly say to the dealer. For a brief second he would obey and we would quickly shoot a whopping dropperful of Vatronol up his nose. His eyes smarting from the sting, the dealer would smile with simple pleasure. Turning to the loungers by the stove, he would tell them to let the drummer fella give them some of that stuff. After the messy job was done, we plastered the place with cardboard signs, and left. Then, some more signposting in barnyards, and ten or twelve miles of mud road to the next call. So, on through the day, the routine was repeated until at length, long after dark, we would get back to our lodgings in time for dinner—and two hours' work on our report forms.

The acquisition of a proper frame of mind toward all this was a slow process. The faded yellow second sheets of our daily report book tell the story. At first, utter demoralization. Day after day, the number of calls would be a skimpy eight or nine, and the number of sales sometimes zero. But it was never our fault. In the large space left for explanations, we would affect a cheerful humor—the gay adventurer in the provinces—but this pathetic bravado could not mask a recurrent note of despair.[1]

To all these bids for sympathy, the home office was adamantine. The weekly letter written to each trainee would start with some perfunctory remarks that it was too bad about the clutch breaking down, the cut knee, and so on. But this spurious sympathy did not conceal a strong preoccupation with results, and lest we miss the point we were told of comrades who would no longer be with us. We too are sorry about those absent dealers, the office would say. Perhaps if you got up earlier in the morning?

As the office sensed quite correctly from my daily reports, I was growing sorry for myself. I used to read timetables at night, and often in the evening I would somehow find myself by the C & O tracks when the George Washington swept by, its steamy windows a reminder of civiliza-

---

1. I quote some entries from my own daily report forms: "They use 'dry' creek beds for roads in this country. 'Dry!' Ha! Ha! . . . Sorry about making only four calls today, but I had to go over to Ervine to pick up a drop shipment of 3/4 tins and my clutch broke down . . . . Everybody's on WPA in this county. Met only one dealer who sold more than a couple dozen VR a year. Ah, well, it's all in the game! . . . Bostitched my left thumb to a barn this morning and couldn't pick up my first call until after lunch . . . . The local brick plant here is shut down and nobody's buying anything . . . . Five, count 'em, *five* absent dealers in a row   . . . Sorry about the $20.85 but the clutch broke down again . . . . "

tion left behind. I was also sorry for many of the storekeepers, most of whom existed on a precarious credit relationship with wholesalers, and as a consequence I sold them very little of anything.

The company sent its head training supervisor to see if anything could be salvaged. After several days with me, this old veteran of the road told me he knew what was the matter. It wasn't so much my routine, wretched as this was. It was my state of mind. "Fella," he told me, "you will never sell anybody anything until you learn one simple thing. The man on the other side of the counter is the *enemy*."

It was a gladiators' school we were in. Selling may be no less competitive now, but in the Vick program, strife was honored far more openly than today's climate would permit. Combat was the ideal—combat with the dealer, combat with the "chiseling competitors," and combat with each other. There was some talk about "the team," but it was highly abstract. Our success depended entirely on beating our fellow students, and while we got along when we met for occasional sales meetings the camaraderie was quite extracurricular.

Slowly, as our sales-to-calls ratios crept up, we gained in rapacity. Somewhere along the line, by accident or skill, each of us finally manipulated a person into doing what we wanted him to do. Innocence was lost, and by the end of six months, with the pack down to about twenty-three men, we were fairly ravening for the home stretch back to the Cloud Club. At this point, the company took us off general store and grocery work and turned us loose in the rich drugstore territory.

The advice of the old salesman now became invaluable. While he had a distaste for any kind of dealer, with druggists he was implacably combative. He was one of the most decent and kindly men I have ever met, but when he gave us pep talks about this enemy ahead of us, he spoke with great intensity. Some druggists were good enough fellows, he told us (i.e., successful ones who bought big deals), but the tough ones were a mean, servile crew; they would insult you, keep you waiting while they pretended to fill prescriptions, lie to you about their inventory, whine at anything less than a 300 per cent markup, and switch their customers to chiseling competitors.

The old salesman would bring us together in batches for several days of demonstration. It was a tremendous experience for us, for though he seemed outwardly a phlegmatic man, we knew him for the artist he was. Outside the store he was jumpy and sometimes perspired, but once inside, he was composed to the point of apparent boredom. He rarely smiled, almost never opened with a joke. His demeanor seemed to say, I am a busy man and you are damned lucky I have stopped by your miserable store. Sometimes, if the druggist was unusually insolent, he would blow cigar smoke at his face. "Can't sell it if you don't have it," he would say contemptuously, and then, rather pleased with himself, glance back at us, loitering in the wings, to see if we had marked that.

Only old pros like himself could get away with that, he told us in the post-mortem sessions, but there were lots of little tricks we could pick up. As we gathered around him, like Fagin's brood, he would demonstrate how to watch for the victim's shoulders to relax before throwing the clincher;

how to pick up the one-size jar of a competitive line that had an especially thick glass bottom and chuckle knowingly; how to feign suppressed worry that maybe the deal was too big for "the smaller druggist like yourself" to take; how to disarm the nervous druggist by fumbling and dropping a pencil. No mercy, he would tell us; give the devils no mercy.

We couldn't either. As the acid test of our gall the company now challenged us to see how many drugstores we could desecrate with "flange" signs. By all the standards of the trade this signposting should have been an impossible task. Almost every "chiseling competitor" would give the druggist at least five dollars to let him put up a sign; we could not offer the druggist a nickel. Our signs, furthermore, were not the usual cardboard kind the druggist could throw away after we had left. They were of metal, they were hideous, and they were to be screwed to the druggists' cherished oak cabinets.

The trick was in the timing. When we were in peak form the procedure went like this: Just after the druggist had signed the order, his shoulders would subside, and this would signal a fleeting period of mutual bonhomie. "New fella, aren't you?" the druggist was likely to say, relaxing. This was his mistake. As soon as we judged the good will to be at full flood, we would ask him if he had a ladder. (There was a ladder out in the car, but the fuss of fetching it would have broken the mood.) The druggist's train of thought would not at that moment connect the request with what was to follow, and he would good-naturedly dispatch someone to bring out a ladder. After another moment of chatter, we would make way for the waiting customer who would engage the druggist's attention. Then, forthrightly, we would slap the ladder up against a spot we had previously reconnoitered. "Just going to get this sign up for you," we would say, as if doing him the greatest favor in the world. He would nod absent-mindedly. Then up the ladder we would go; a few quick turns of the awl, place the bracket in position, and then, the automatic screw driver. Bang! bang! Down went the sign. (If the druggist had been unusually mean, we could break the thread of the screw for good measure.) Then down with the ladder, shift it over to the second spot, and up again.

About this time the druggist would start looking up a little unhappily, but the good will, while ebbing, was still enough to inhibit him from action. *He* felt sorry for us. Imagine that young man thinking those signs are good looking! Just as he would be about to mumble something about one sign being enough, we would hold up the second one. It had a picture on it of a woman squirting nose drops up her nostrils. We would leer fatuously at it. "Just going to lay this blonde on the top of the cabinet for you, Mr. Jones," we would say, winking. We were giants in those days.

I suppose I should be ashamed, but I must confess I'm really not, and to this day when I enter a drugstore I sometimes fancy the sound of the awl biting irretrievably into the druggist's limed oak. I think the reader will understand, of course, that I am not holding up the Vick School of Applied Merchandising as an ideal model, yet I must add, in all fairness to Vick, that most of us were grateful for the experience. When we get together periodically (we have an informal alumni association), we wallow in talk about how they really separated the men from the boys then, etc. It was truly an experience, and if we shudder to recall the things we did, we must admit that as a cram course in reality it was extraordinarily efficient.

The General Electric program to which I now turn was in full force in the thirties and is actually an older one than the Vick's program. Where the latter was a late flowering of a philosophy already in the descendant, however, GE's was a harbinger of things to come. Even today, it is still somewhat ahead of its time; at this moment there are not many corporation training programs which come near General Electric's, either in the size or elaborateness of facilities or, more importantly, in consistency of principles. Yet I believe that as we take up these principal features of the General Electric program, we will be seeing what in a decade or so hence may be the middle of the road.[2]

The most immediately apparent thing about the General Electric program is the fact that it *is* a school. While the plants serve as part of the campus, the company maintains a full-time staff of 250 instructors and an educational plant complete to such details as company-published textbooks, examinations, classrooms, and alumni publications. In direct operating costs alone the company spends over five million dollars annually — a budget larger than many a medium-sized college.

The program is highly centralized. To keep this plant running, GE's corps of recruiters each year delivers between 1,000 and 1,500 college graduates, mostly engineers, to the company's Schenectady headquarters. There the trainees enter what is for them a continuation of college life. Like fraternity brothers, they live together in boarding houses and attend classes in groups. For afterhours recreation, they have the privileges of the Edison Club where, along with other GE employees with college degrees, they can meet after classes to play golf, bridge, and enjoy a planned series of parties and dances. (GE employees who haven't gone to college are eligible to join if they have achieved a supervisory rating.)

The curriculum is arranged in much the same manner as a university's. The trainee enters under one of several courses, such as engineering and accounting. All these courses will have much in common, however, for the trainee's first eighteen months are regarded as the basic part of his training. At the end of this time he will then go on to a "major." If he has been in the manufacturing training course, for example, he can elect as a major factory operations, manufacturing engineering, production and purchasing, or plant engineering.

The work the trainee does during this training is not, like Vick's applied merchandising, considered an end in itself. From time to time the trainee will work at specific jobs, but these jobs, while not mere make-work, are outside the regular cost-accounted operations of the company.

---

2. Even Vick has moved considerably in this direction. The heroic years are over; now it is "The Vick Executive Development Program," and though there has been no basic shift in underlying philosophy (Mr. Richardson is still at the helm), Vick now offers many of the material features of the GE program. Security is reasonably guaranteed; no longer are trainees "graduated" — of the roughly one hundred seniors taken in each year, all but a handful can remain as permanent employees. They are exposed to many more aspects of management and they don't have to do things like putting up flange signs.

The company considers them vehicles for training, and it rotates students from one to another on a regular schedule.

The most noteworthy feature of the General Electric approach is the emphasis on the "professional" manager. As in all training programs, the bulk of the instruction is on specifics. Unlike most, however, there is considerable study in subjects that cut across every kind of job. Trainees study personnel philosophy, labor relations, law, and, most important, the managerial viewpoint.[3]

Only a minority of the trainees will ever become managers; in ten years 1,500 to 2,000 executive slots will open up, and this means that most of the thousands of young men trained during this time will never get further than middle management. Nevertheless, it is those future executive slots that the company is thinking of, and it makes its concern plain to the trainee. On the report card form for trainees, there is a space for an evaluation as to whether the trainee is suited "for individual contribution" or whether, instead, he is suited "to manage the work of others." The company tells the trainees that it is perfectly all right for them to aim at "individual contribution," which is to say, a specialty. It would be a dull trainee, however, who did not pause before consigning himself to such a role. In one of GE's textbooks there is a picture of a man looking at two ladders. One leads up to a specialty, the other to general managing. The question before the young man, the textbook states, is: "Will I specialize in a particular field?" — or "Will I become broad-gauge, capable of effort in many fields?"

Who wants to be narrow-gauge? Trainees do not have to read too strenuously between the lines to see that one should aim to manage; as a matter of fact, they are predisposed to read a good bit more between the lines than many of their elders would like them to. Which brings us to an important point. In gauging the impact of the curriculum on the young man, his predispositions are as important as the weighting of the courses. Elders at General Electric can demonstrate that the actual amount of time devoted to the abstract arts of management is far less than the time devoted to specific skills. But the managerial part is what the trainees want to hear — and they want to hear it so much that one hour's exposure to the managerial view can be as four or five hours of something else in proportion to its effect on impressionable minds. Trainees are interested, to be sure, in how turbines are made, in the techniques of the accounting department and such, but they do not want to be *too* interested. It would make them unbalanced.

They regard specific work very much as many educators view "subject matter" courses: narrowing. As trainees play back the lesson, they see a distinction, sometimes a downright antithesis, between the qualities of the broad-gauge executive and the qualities that one must have to do a superla-

---

3. Among other things, the trainees take HOBSO. This is the course in How Our Business System Operates, originally developed by Du Pont to inoculate blue-collar employees against creeping socialism. Though GE has no reason to fear its trainees are ideologically unsound, it explains that the course will help them "detect any bad guidance they receive from union and political leaders, and even from educational and spiritual leaders."

tive piece of concrete work. Not work itself but the managing of other people's work is the skill that they aspire to. As they describe it, the manager is
a man in charge of people getting along together, and his *expertise* is relatively independent of who or what is being managed. Or why.

Not surprisingly, the part of the curriculum for which they have the
greatest affinity is the human-relations instruction. They are particularly
enthusiastic about the "Effective Presentation" course worked up by the
sales-training department. They can hardly be blamed. "YOU CAN ALWAYS
GET ANYBODY TO DO WHAT YOU WISH," the textbook proclaims. To this end
the students spend four months eagerly studying a battery of communication techniques and psychological principles which General Electric tells
them will help them to be good managers. (Sample principle. "Never say
anything controversial.")

There is nothing novel about teaching people how to manipulate other
people, and GE's scientific psychological techniques bear a strong resemblance to the how-to-be-a-success precepts standard in the U.S. for decades.
What is different about them is their justification. They are not presented on the grounds that they will help make people do what you want
them to do so that you can make more money. GE trainees see it in much
more eleemosynary terms. They do like the part about selling yourself to
others so you can get ahead, for they think a lot about this. But they don't
abide the thought of enemies on the other side of the counter; they see the
manipulative skills as something that in the long run will make other people *happy*. When in years to come the trainees are charged with the destiny
of subordinates — a possibility most take remarkably much for granted
— they will be able to achieve a stable, well-adjusted work group. They won't
drive subordinates, they explain. They will motivate them.

Trainees are also predisposed to emphasis on co-operation rather than
competition, and this they get too. The emphasis is built into the structure
of the school. For one thing, the student is given a high measure of security
from the beginning, and while there may be promotion of the fittest there
can be survival for all. There are exceptions, but one must be a very odd
ball to be one. For the first two years the trainee is part of a system in
which his salary raises will be automatic, and while later on he will be
more on his own there will be no planned elimination as there was at Vick,
nor an up-or-out policy such as the Navy's.

To get ahead, of course, one must compete — but not too much, and certainly not too obviously. While overt ambition is a bad posture for the
ambitious anywhere, the GE system has especial sanctions for the rate-
buster. The trainee is, first of all, a member of a group, and the group is
entrusted to a surprising degree with the resolution of his future. How
well, the company wants to know, does he fit in? His fellow trainees provide the answer, and in the "case study" group discussions the eager bea-
ver or the deviant is quickly exposed. And brought to heel. Trainees speak
frequently of the way close fraternity life atmosphere is valuable in ironing
out some trainees' aberrant tendencies. It may be tough on him, they concede, but better now than later. In a few years the trainee will be released
from this close association and the social character that he has perfected

will be a fundamental necessity; he will be moving from one company branch to another, and he must be able to fit into the same kind of integrated social system.

The company officially recognizes the disciplining of the group. In its periodic rating of the man, the company frequently calls on his comrades to participate in the rating. If a man is liked especially well not only by his superiors but by his peers, he may be given the job of guiding about eight or ten of his fellow trainees. He is now a "sign-up," and if he keeps on maturing he may become a "head-of-tests," the seven "sign-ups" reporting to him. Since the opinions of one's peers are so integral to advancement, this system virtually insures that the overzealous or the "knocker" type of man will not get ahead — or, at the very least, that he will successfully re-mold himself to the managerial image.

The fact that the trainee must spend so much time thinking of what other people think of him does not oppress him. Quite the opposite, the constant surveillance is one of the things the average trainee talks about most enthusiastically. The rating system is highly standardized, he explains; it is the product of *many* people rather than one, and this denominator of judgments frees him from the harshness or caprice that might result from the traditional boss-employee relationship. He is also freed from being ignored; the system insures that other people must be thinking about him quite as much as he is thinking about them, and for this reason he won't get pigeonholed. At General Electric, as one trainee remarked, not only can't you get lost, you can't even hide.

Needless to say, ambition still pulses, and I am not trying to suggest that the General Electric man is any less set on the main chance than my Vick comrades. It is quite obvious, nevertheless, that he must pursue the main chance in a much more delicate fashion. To get ahead, he must co-operate with the others — but co-operate *better* than they do.

The rules of the game do permit a few lapses, but these lapses, charac-teristically, are the display of personality. Somewhere along the line the trainees must get themselves hired into a regular job, and to do this they must attract the attention of superiors. There is a tacit understanding among trainees that it is perfectly all right to make a bald play to get on a first-name basis with superiors that might do one some good. "As soon as you know your way around a new department you start telephoning," one trainee explains, tapping the intercommunication telephone directory. "Be-lieve me, this little green book here is a man's best friend." The company encourages superiors to encourage this kind of contact. "I or anybody else," another trainee says, "can walk into a manager's office just as easily as we can each other's. By ten o'clock of the day I hit the New York office I was calling everybody by his first name."

In contrasting the General Electric type program with the old Vick's program, I have been contrasting extremes. The dividing line they illus-trate, however, is one that more and more companies are having to recog-nize. For a long time businessmen have been rather carelessly talking about the coming of the "professional manager" as if this development was merely a further refinement of the mixture as before. When executives be-gan expanding trainee programs right after the war, management literature on the subject gave no evidence that there were any policy issues involved, and the matters discussed were mainly those of the length of time men should be trained, the frequency of their rotation, and the like.

As time has gone on, however, executives have found that the trainee programs are forcing them to think a lot more than they wanted to about questions more fundamental. Was not the trainee program itself producing a rather definable type? Was this what the company wanted? And what was the company "character," anyway? For a long time executives have sensed that organizations tend to select and fashion a certain type, and while they cannot actually put their finger on it they know that, say, a Union Carbide man is somehow different from a W. R. Grace man. But they would like to leave it at that — in the realm of mystique. Now they have to analyze it.

Eventually, they would have to ponder the compatibility of the "professional manager" with the company spirit whether they put in a centralized training program or not. Times are moving fast, and from the great proselyting centers of the business schools the new man will be going forth to leave his mark on every kind of organization, traditional or otherwise. In the centralized training program, however, he does it ahead of time. It is the ideal culture for him, and though it is a case of evolution rather than revolution, the suddenness of his growth has been rather unsettling to many executives. Here, all at once, is an advance view of the man of the future, and for many a management it has proved too advanced to assimilate.

What the programs have done is accentuate the difference between generations. Ordinarily, this shift in outlook is so gradual as to be imperceptible, except in retrospect, and the company ideology can be revised without pain, or, for that matter, without anyone's knowing it's been revised at all. But not now. More consciously than other age groups before them, today's trainees see themselves as a new breed, and when you talk to them you cannot help but feel a certain premature condescension on their part for the present managers. One of the points younger men frequently make in praising their advanced training is its value to *older* men. "It brings them out of their shells," one twenty-three-year-old engineer explains. "It teaches them that there is an outside world and that there are good ideas and procedures around that the company has not come up with yet." The trainees make the same point about human-relations teaching; even if they don't need to be converted, they explain, the teaching does percolate up to the older, less progressive levels of management. "It's sad," one trainee said, "that you have to teach people how to be human in business. But the brass do need it."

Thanks to a misadventure of the Ford Motor Company, there exists a case study of what happens when this advanced view is introduced without a comparable change in the company spirit. For many reasons, including, perhaps, a certain sensitivity to charges that it was old-fashioned, shortly after the war Ford introduced an ambitious "field training program" for college graduates. Somewhat like the General Electric program, it was a centralized observation-orientation program through which incoming recruits were taken on a grand tour of the company which lasted some two years.

Ford executives now grimace at the memory of it. While no one planned it that way, the program created a cadre of "crown princes" that did not jibe at all well with the organization. As older hands were quick to remark, the trainees had gotten such a broad view of things that they had become quite confused as to what, specifically, they wanted to do in the way of actual work. Eventually they were placed in regular jobs, but to do it personnel people had to peddle them around and use a good bit of persuasion. Today the recruit gets a physical examination, a one-day orientation, and then is put to work. He is not encouraged to call the brass by their first names, and his advancement depends on what his line superior happens to think of his work.

The basic collision has been a philosophical one. Quite perceptibly, the schooling in the broad view produced a definite attitude toward work, and in Ford's case, an attitude 180 degrees away from what the company was used to. In companies like Ford — and this would include General Motors and Du Pont — the emphasis on a specific task as an end in itself shows quite readily in the way people talk about their jobs. Talk to a non-program Ford man or a Du Pont or a GM man and he will rarely dwell on abstractions that cut across the organization, but instead will talk on the concrete work he's connected with, like designing transmissions or opening new markets for paint. He may accuse himself of being too narrow, but he really doesn't worry about it — at that time, anyway — and even the highly ambitious will tend to leave to the president and the executive committee the chore of pondering the big picture. Where at General Electric a young man is likely to talk about managing, in short, at Ford he will talk about cars.

This identification with work was long regarded as the natural order of things, and it has been with some surprise that executives have found it necessary to make the reasons for it explicit. Looking back on the training program, one Ford executive summed up his complaint this way: "I always felt that human relations and getting along with people was all very important. But these trainees made me do a lot of thinking. At Ford we judge a man by results. I mean, what he gets accomplished. And I think this is the way it should be. Sure, human relations is important, but it should be subsidiary to results. Look at it this way: if the girls in a steno pool run away when a man comes around to give dictation on account of his manners, or other people hold out information on him, his results will be bad. I think that the colleges that send these men to us ought to put more emphasis on *doing things*. A lot of the young fellows I talk to think that most engineering problems are all solved and that it's just a question of human engineering. That's just not right."

Interestingly, it is management people in the thirty-five to forty-five age range who are most sensitive to the difference of viewpoint stimulated by centralized programs. Not only do they see more of the trainees than the older executives do, they expect less difference between their generation and the younger one and are surprised to find how much difference there is. Common to almost all of their criticisms is the charge that the younger men are much more sanguine than they had ever been and that the great expectations should be chastened rather than stimulated. Robert C. Landon, Industrial Relations Manager of Rohm & Haas, puts it this way: "Since the time they entered kindergarten they have spent sixteen years during which the world has been presented to them in study courses to be absorbed in an atmosphere of security. To extend this kind of thing when they reach the corporation — except for a well-founded research program — is a dangerous concept." Executives of this persuasion feel that present-day organizations are benevolent enough already. "We should let the wheel of fortune turn," one says. "It's all right for a young man to develop himself, but he shouldn't *be* developed."

I do not wish to overdraw the present distinctions. The first-rate General Electric trainee would not find it insuperable adjusting to the climate at Ford, and a first-rate Ford trainee could adapt to General Electric. Neither do I wish to suggest that a gulf is yawning between two kinds of companies. There has always been more diversity within the business creed than the nonbusinessman suspects and there always will be. But there is a problem of weighting common to all organizations, and this is my reason for dwelling on the "social character" developed by the training programs; exaggerated somewhat, here is the most likely alternative to the past. In these terms no one would choose, certainly not businessmen. The choice will be made through a multitude of day-to-day decisions which at the time will seem squarely poised over the middle way. But a shift there will be for all that.

B. F. SKINNER

B. F. Skinner is an experimental psychologist and is a major figure in American behavioristic psychology. His well-known novel Walden II *was originally published in 1948. Skinner is one of the originators and leaders in the development of teaching machines and has advanced a number of influential ideas on child rearing and infant care. Currently serving as Edgar Pierce Professor of Psychology at Harvard University, he is also the author of such works as* The Behavior of Organisms *(1938),* Science and Human Behavior *(1953),* Verbal Behavior *(1957), and* The Analysis of Behavior *(1961).*

Education in Walden II

Skinner's novel Walden II *was originally published in 1948 and is, like Orwell's* 1984 *and Huxley's* Brave New World, *a vision of a new society. Skinner's society, however, is not intended as a warning but as a promise of new and constructive things to come; and it is not set in the future but in the present. In this selection, Frazier, the originator of the ideal community of* Walden II, *shows his guests (several university professors, their students, and friends) through the educational system of his self-contained scientific community and explains some of his basic ideas about social planning.*

We assembled for an early breakfast, leaving our work clothes in our rooms for a later change. Castle had discovered himself in his coveralls in a mirror in one of the lavatories and refused to appear in public so attired unless he could carry a sign reading "Man at Work!" As it happened, we had no need for work clothes. Frazier appeared just as we were finishing breakfast and announced that we were to spend the morning visiting the schools, and that we would pick up a labor-credit or two during the afternoon.

He led the way outdoors and we skirted the flower beds in a long arc which brought us to the small picnic tables where we had rested on our first day at Walden Two. Large sheets of paper were thumbtacked to the tables, and several students, most of them ten or twelve years old but two or three certainly no older than eight, were drawing what looked like Euclidian constructions with heavy black pencils. Other children were driving pegs into the ground and running strings from one peg to another. Two surveyor's transits and a steel measuring tape were in use. So far as I could see, Euclid was getting a firsthand experimental check. Or it might have been trigonometry, I was not sure. Frazier seemed to know no more about it than the rest of us. He shrugged off Rodge's hesitant inquiry and pressed forward toward the nearest wing of the children's building. Perhaps he merely wanted to take things in order, for this proved to be the nursery.

A young woman in a white uniform met us in a small waiting room near the entrance. Frazier addressed her as Mrs. Nash.

"I hope Mr. Frazier has warned you," she said with a smile, "that we're going to be rather impolite and give you only a glimpse of our babies. We try to protect them from infection during the first year. It's especially important when they are cared for as a group."

"What about the parents?" said Castle at once. "Don't parents see their babies?"

"Oh, yes, so long as they are in good health. Some parents work in the nursery. Others come around every day or so, for at least a few minutes. They take the baby out for some sunshine, or play with it in a play room."

Mrs. Nash smiled at Frazier. "That's the way we build up the baby's resistance," she added.

She opened a door and allowed us to look into a small room, three walls of which were lined with cubicles, each with a large glass window. Behind the windows we could see babies of various ages. None of them wore more than a diaper, and there were no bedclothes. In one cubicle a small red newborn was asleep on its stomach. Some of the older babies were awake and playing with toys. Near the door a baby on all fours pressed its nose against the glass and smiled at us.

"Looks like an aquarium," said Castle.

"And very precious fish they are," said Mrs. Nash, as if the comparison were not unfamiliar.

"Which is yours?" asked Frazier.

"Over there asleep," said Mrs. Nash, pointing to a far corner. "Almost ready to graduate, too. He'll be a year old next month." She drew the door gently shut before we had satisfied our curiosity.

"I can show you one of the units in the isolation room, which isn't being used," she said, leading the way along the corridor. She opened another door and we entered. Two of the cubicles stood against the wall.

"This is a much more efficient way of keeping a baby warm than the usual practice of wrapping it in several layers of cloth," said Mrs. Nash, opening a safety-glass window to permit Barbara and Mary to look inside. "The newborn baby needs moist air at about 88 or 90 degrees. At six months, 80 is about right."

"How do you know that?" said Castle, rather belligerently.

"The baby tells us," said Mrs. Nash pleasantly, as if the question were also familiar.

"You know the story about the bath water, don't you, Mr. Castle?" Frazier interrupted. "The temperature's all right if the baby doesn't turn red or blue."

"But I hope—" Castle began.

"It's only a matter of a degree or two," said Mrs. Nash quickly. "If the baby's too warm, it does turn rather pinkish, and it usually cries. It always stops crying when we lower the temperature." She twisted the dial of a thermostat on the front of a cubicle.

"And I suppose if frost forms around the nose it's too cold," said Castle, getting himself under control.

"The baby turns rather pale," said Mrs. Nash laughing, "and takes a curious posture with its arms along its sides or slightly curled up. With a little practice we can tell at a glance whether the temperature is right or not."

"But why don't you put clothes on them?" said Barbara.

"What for? It would mean laundry for us and discomfort for the child. It's the same with sheets and blankets. Our babies lie on a stretched plastic cloth which doesn't soak up moisture and can be wiped clean in a moment."

"It looks terribly comfortable," I said. "Why don't you all sleep that way?"

"We're working on that," said Frazier, apparently quite seriously. "It would save no end of laundry, and, as you say, it would be comfortable."

"Clothing and blankets are really a great nuisance," said Mrs. Nash. "They keep the baby from exercising, they force it into uncomfortable postures—"

"When a baby graduates from our Lower Nursery," Frazier broke in, "it knows nothing of frustration, anxiety, or fear. It never cries except when sick, which is very seldom, and it has a lively interest in everything."

"But is it prepared for life?" said Castle. "Surely you can't continue to protect it from frustration or frightening situations forever."

"Of course not. But it can be prepared for them. We can build a tolerance for frustration by introducing obstacles gradually as the baby grows strong enough to handle them. But I'm getting ahead of our story. Have you any other point to make, Mrs. Nash?"

"I suppose you'd like to have them know how much work is saved. Since the air is filtered, we only bathe the babies once a week, and we never need to clean their nostrils or eyes. There are no beds to make, of course. And it's easy to prevent infection. The compartments are soundproofed, and the babies sleep well and don't disturb each other. We can keep them on different schedules, so the nursery runs smoothly. Let me see, is there anything else?"

"I think that's quite enough," said Frazier. "We have a lot of ground to cover this morning."

"Not so fast, if you please," said Castle. "I'm not satisfied yet. Aren't you raising a lot of very inadequate organisms? Controlled temperature, noiseless sleep—aren't these babies going to be completely at the mercy of a normal environment? Can you go on coddling them forever?"

"I can answer that, Mrs. Nash," said Frazier. "The answer is *no*. Our babies are especially resistant. It's true that a constant annoyance may develop a tolerance, but the commoner result is that the baby is worn down or enervated. We introduce annoyances slowly, according to the ability of the baby to take them. It's very much like inoculation."

"Another thing," said Castle. "What about mother love?"

Frazier and Mrs. Nash looked at each other and laughed.

"Are you speaking of mother love as an essence, Mr. Castle?" said Frazier.

"I am not!" said Castle, bristling. "I'm speaking of a concrete thing. I mean the love which the mother gives her baby—the affection—well, to be really concrete, the kisses, the fondling, and so on, I suppose you'd say. You can't expect me to give you the physical dimensions of mother love!" He was confused and flushed. "It's real enough to the baby, I'll bet!" he added blackly.

"Very real," said Frazier quietly. "And we supply it in liberal doses. But we don't limit it to mothers. We go in for father love, too—for everybody's love—community love, if you wish. Our children are treated with affection by everyone—and thoughtful affection too, which isn't marred by fits of temper due to overwork or careless handling due to ignorance."

"But the personal relation between the mother and the child—Isn't there some sort of patterning? I thought the whole personality could be shaped in that way?" Castle appealed to me for professional support, but I failed him.

"You mean what the Freudian calls 'identification,' I think," said Fra-

zier. "I agree that it's important, and we use it very effectively in our educational system. But unless you're a strict Freudian, we're talking in the
wrong room. Let's wait till we see another age group. Can you come to
the Upper Nursery, Mrs. Nash?"

"Let me check my staff," said Mrs. Nash. She disappeared into the
"aquarium," returned almost immediately, and led us to another wing.

The quarters for children from one to three consisted of several small playrooms with Lilliputian furniture, a child's lavatory, and a dressing and
locker room. Several small sleeping rooms were operated on the same principle as the baby-cubicles. The temperature and the humidity were controlled so that clothes or bedclothing were not needed. The cots were
double-decker arrangements of the plastic mattresses we had seen in the
cubicles. The children slept unclothed, except for diapers. There were more
beds than necessary, so that the children could be grouped according to
developmental age or exposure to contagious diseases or need for supervision, or for educational purposes.

We followed Mrs. Nash to a large screened porch on the south side of
the building, where several children were playing in sandboxes and on
swings and climbing apparatuses. A few wore "training pants"; the rest
were naked. Beyond the porch was a grassy play yard enclosed by closely
trimmed hedges, where other children, similarly undressed, were at play.
Some kind of marching game was in progress.

As we returned, we met two women carrying food hampers. They
spoke to Mrs. Nash and followed her to the porch. In a moment five or six
children came running into the playrooms and were soon using the lavatory
and dressing themselves. Mrs. Nash explained that they were being taken
on a picnic.

"What about the children who don't go?" said Castle. "What do you
do about the green-eyed monster?"

Mrs. Nash was puzzled.

"Jealousy. Envy," Castle elaborated. "Don't the children who stay
home ever feel unhappy about it?"

"I don't understand," said Mrs. Nash.

"And I hope you won't try," said Frazier, with a smile. "I'm afraid we
must be moving along."

We said good-bye, and I made an effort to thank Mrs. Nash, but she
seemed to be puzzled by that too, and Frazier frowned as if I had committed some breach of good taste.

"I think Mrs. Nash's puzzlement," said Frazier, as we left the building,
"is proof enough that our children are seldom envious or jealous. Mrs.
Nash was twelve years old when Walden Two was founded. It was a little
late to undo her early training, but I think we were successful. She's a good
example of the Walden Two product. She could probably recall the experience of jealousy, but it's not part of her present life."

"Surely that's going too far!" said Castle. "You can't be so godlike as
all that! You must be assailed by emotions just as much as the rest of us!"

"We can discuss the question of godlikeness later, if you wish," replied Frazier. "As to emotions—we aren't free of them all, nor should we

like to be. But the meaner and more annoying—the emotions which breed unhappiness—are almost unknown here, like unhappiness itself. We don't need them any longer in our struggle for existence, and it's easier on our circulatory system, and certainly pleasanter, to dispense with them."

"If you've discovered how to do that, you are indeed a genius," said Castle. He seemed almost stunned as Frazier nodded assent. "We all know that emotions are useless and bad for our peace of mind and our blood pressure," he went on. "But how arrange things otherwise?"

"We arrange them otherwise here," said Frazier. He was showing a mildness of manner which I was coming to recognize as a sign of confidence.

"But emotions are—fun!" said Barbara. "Life wouldn't be worth living without them."

"Some of them, yes," said Frazier. "The productive and strengthening emotions—joy and love. But sorrow and hate—and the high-voltage excitements of anger, fear, and rage—are out of proportion with the needs of modern life, and they're wasteful and dangerous. Mr. Castle has mentioned jealousy—a minor form of anger, I think we may call it. Naturally we avoid it. It has served its purpose in the evolution of man; we've no further use for it. If we allowed it to persist, it would only sap the life out of us. In a cooperative society there's no jealousy because there's no need for jealousy."

"That implies that you all get everything you want," said Castle. "But what about social possessions? Last night you mentioned the young man who chose a particular girl or profession. There's still a chance for jealousy there, isn't there?"

"It doesn't imply that we get everything we want," said Frazier. "Of course we don't. But jealousy wouldn't help. In a competitive world there's some point to it. It energizes one to attack a frustrating condition. The impulse and the added energy are an advantage. Indeed, in a competitive world emotions work all too well. Look at the singular lack of success of the complacent man. He enjoys a more serene life, but it's less likely to be a fruitful one. The world isn't ready for simple pacifism or Christian humility, to cite two cases in point. Before you can safely train out the destructive and wasteful emotions, you must make sure they're no longer needed."

"How do you make sure that jealousy isn't needed in Walden Two?" I said.

"In Walden Two problems can't be solved by attacking others," said Frazier with marked finality.

"That's not the same as eliminating jealousy, though," I said.

"Of course it's not. But when a particular emotion is no longer a useful part of a behavioral repertoire, we proceed to eliminate it."

"Yes, but how?"

"It's simply a matter of behavioral engineering," said Frazier.

"Behavioral engineering?"

"You're baiting me, Burris. You know perfectly well what I mean. The techniques have been available for centuries. We use them in education and in the psychological management of the community. But you're forcing my hand," he added. "I was saving that for this evening. But let's strike while the iron is hot."

We had stopped at the door of the large children's building. Frazier shrugged his shoulders, walked to the shade of a large tree, and threw himself on the ground. We arranged ourselves about him and waited.

"Each of us," Frazier began, "is engaged in a pitched battle with the rest of mankind."

"A curious premise for a Utopia," said Castle. "Even a pessimist like myself takes a more hopeful view than that."

"You do, you do," said Frazier. "But let's be realistic. Each of us has interests which conflict with the interests of everybody else. That's our original sin, and it can't be helped. Now, 'everybody else' we call 'society.' It's a powerful opponent, and it always wins. Oh, here and there an individual prevails for a while and gets what he wants. Sometimes he storms the culture of a society and changes it slightly to his own advantage. But society wins in the long run, for it has the advantage of numbers and of age. Many prevail against one, and men against a baby. Society attacks early, when the individual is helpless. It enslaves him almost before he has tasted freedom. The 'ologies' will tell you how it's done. Theology calls it building a conscience or developing a spirit of selflessness. Psychology calls it the growth of the super-ego.

"Considering how long society has been at it, you'd expect a better job. But the campaigns have been badly planned and the victory has never been secure. The behavior of the individual has been shaped according to revelations of 'good conduct,' never as the result of experimental study. But why not experiment? The questions are simple enough. What's the best behavior for the individual so far as the group is concerned? And how can the individual be induced to behave in that way? Why not explore these questions in a scientific spirit?

"We could do just that in Walden Two. We had already worked out a code of conduct—subject, of course, to experimental modification. The code would keep things running smoothly if everybody lived up to it. Our job was to see that everybody did. Now, you can't get people to follow a useful code by making them into so many jacks-in-the-box. You can't foresee all future circumstances, and you can't specify adequate future conduct. You don't know what will be required. Instead you have to set up certain behavioral processes which will lead the individual to design his own 'good' conduct when the time comes. We call that sort of thing 'self-control.' But don't be misled, the control always rests in the last analysis in the hands of society.

"One of our Planners, a young man named Simmons, worked with me. It was the first time in history that the matter was approached in an experimental way. Do you question that statement, Mr. Castle?"

"I'm not sure I know what you are talking about," said Castle.

"Then let me go on. Simmons and I began by studying the great works on morals and ethics—Plato, Aristotle, Confucius, the New Testament, the Puritan divines, Machiavelli, Chesterfield, Freud—there were scores of them. We were looking for any and every method of shaping human behavior by imparting techniques of self-control. Some techniques were obvious enough, for they had marked turning points in human history. 'Love your enemies' is an example—a psychological invention for easing the lot of an oppressed people. The severest trial of oppression is the constant rage which one suffers at the thought of the oppressor. What Jesus discovered was how to avoid these inner devastations. His technique was to *practice the opposite emotion*. If a man can succeed in 'loving his enemies' and 'taking no thought for the morrow,' he will no longer be assailed by hatred of the oppressor or rage at the loss of his freedom or possessions. He may not get his freedom or possessions back, but he's less miserable. It's a difficult lesson. It comes late in our program."

"I thought you were opposed to modifying emotions and instincts until the world was ready for it," said Castle. "According to you, the principle of 'love your enemies' should have been suicidal."

"It would have been suicidal, except for an entirely unforeseen consequence. Jesus must have been quite astonished at the effect of his discovery. We are only just beginning to understand the power of love because we are just beginning to understand the weakness of force and aggression. But the science of behavior is clear about all that now. Recent discoveries in the analysis of punishment—but I am falling into one digression after another. Let me save my explanation of why the Christian virtues—and I mean merely the Christian techniques of self-control—have not disappeared from the face of the earth, with due recognition of the fact that they suffered a narrow squeak within recent memory.

"When Simmons and I had collected our techniques of control, we had to discover how to teach them. That was more difficult. Current educational practices were of little value, and religious practices scarcely any better. Promising paradise or threatening hell-fire is, we assumed, generally admitted to be unproductive. It is based upon a fundamental fraud which, when discovered, turns the individual against society and nourishes the very thing it tries to stamp out. What Jesus offered in return for loving one's enemies was heaven *on earth*, better known as peace of mind.

"We found a few suggestions worth following in the practices of the clinical psychologist. We undertook to build a tolerance for annoying experiences. The sunshine of midday is extremely painful if you come from a dark room, but take it in easy stages and you can avoid pain altogether. The analogy can be misleading, but in much the same way it's possible to build a tolerance to painful or distasteful stimuli, or to frustration, or to situations which arouse fear, anger or rage. Society and nature throw these annoyances at the individual with no regard for the development of tolerances. Some achieve tolerances, most fail. Where would the science of immunization be if it followed a schedule of accidental dosages?

"Take the principle of 'Get thee behind me, Satan,' for example," Frazier continued. "It's a special case of self-control by altering the environment. Subclass A 3, I believe. We give each child a lollipop which has been dipped in powdered sugar so that a single touch of the tongue can be detected. We tell him he may eat the lollipop later in the day, provided it hasn't already been licked. Since the child is only three or four, it is a fairly diff____"

"Three or four!" Castle exclaimed.

"All our ethical training is completed by the age of six," said Frazier quietly. "A simple principle like putting temptation out of sight would be acquired before four. But at such an early age the problem of not licking the lollipop isn't easy. Now, what would you do, Mr. Castle, in a similar situation?"

"Put the lollipop out of sight as quickly as possible."

"Exactly. I can see you've been well trained. Or perhaps you discovered the principle for yourself. We're in favor of original inquiry wherever possible, but in this case we have a more important goal and we don't hesitate to give verbal help. First of all, the children are urged to examine their own behavior while looking at the lollipops. This helps them to recognize the need for self-control. Then the lollipops are concealed, and the children are asked to notice any gain in happiness or any reduction in tension. Then a strong distraction is arranged—say, an interesting game. Later the children are reminded of the candy and encouraged to examine their reaction. The value of the distraction is generally obvious. Well, need I go on? When the experiment is repeated a day or so later, the children all run with the lollipops to their lockers and do exactly what Mr. Castle would do—a sufficient indication of the success of our training."

"I wish to report an objective observation of my reaction to your story," said Castle, controlling his voice with great precision. "I find myself revolted by this display of sadistic tyranny."

"I don't wish to deny you the exercise of an emotion which you seem to find enjoyable," said Frazier. "So let me go on. Concealing a tempting but forbidden object is a crude solution. For one thing, it's not always feasible. We want a sort of psychological concealment—covering up the candy by paying no attention. In a later experiment the children wear their lollipops like crucifixes for a few hours."

" 'Instead of the cross, the lollipop,
About my neck was hung,' "
said Castle.

"I wish somebody had taught me that, though," said Rodge, with a glance at Barbara.

"Don't we all?" said Frazier. "Some of us learn control, more or less by accident. The rest of us go all our lives not even understanding how it is possible, and blaming our failure on being born the wrong way."

"How do you build up a tolerance to an annoying situation?" I said.

"Oh, for example, by having the children 'take' a more and more painful shock, or drink cocoa with less and less sugar in it until a bitter concoction can be savored without a bitter face."

"But jealousy or envy—you can't administer them in graded doses," I said.

"And why not? Remember, we control the social environment, too, at this age. That's why we get our ethical training in early. Take this case. A group of children arrive home after a long walk tired and hungry. They're expecting supper; they find, instead, that it's time for a lesson in self-control: they must stand for five minutes in front of steaming bowls of soup.

"The assignment is accepted like a problem in arithmetic. Any groaning or complaining is a wrong answer. Instead, the children begin at once to work upon themselves to avoid any unhappiness during the delay. One of them may make a joke of it. We encourage a sense of humor as a good way of not taking an annoyance seriously. The joke won't be much, according to adult standards — perhaps the child will simply pretend to empty the bowl of soup into his upturned mouth. Another may start a song with many verses. The rest join in at once, for they've learned that it's a good way to make time pass."

Frazier glanced uneasily at Castle, who was not to be appeased.

"That also strikes you as a form of torture, Mr. Castle?" he asked.

"I'd rather be put on the rack," said Castle.

"Then you have by no means had the thorough training I supposed. You can't imagine how lightly the children take such an experience. It's a rather severe biological frustration, for the children are tired and hungry and they must stand and look at food; but it's passed off as lightly as a five-minute delay at curtain time. We regard it as a fairly elementary test. Much more difficult problems follow."

"I suspected as much," muttered Castle.

"In a later stage we forbid all social devices. No songs, no jokes — merely silence. Each child is forced back upon his own resources — a very important step."

"I should think so," I said. "And how do you know it's successful? You might produce a lot of silently resentful children. It's certainly a dangerous stage."

"It is, and we follow each child carefully. If he hasn't picked up the necessary techniques, we start back a little. A still more advanced stage" — Frazier glanced again at Castle, who stirred uneasily — "brings me to my point. When it's time to sit down to the soup, the children count off — heads and tails. Then a coin is tossed and if it comes up heads, the 'heads' sit down and eat. The 'tails' remain standing for another five minutes."

Castle groaned.

"And you call that envy?" I asked.

"Perhaps not exactly," said Frazier. "At least there's seldom any agression against the lucky ones. The emotion, if any, is directed against Lady Luck herself, against the toss of the coin. That, in itself, is a lesson worth learning, for it's the only direction in which emotion has a surviving chance to be useful. And resentment toward things in general, while perhaps just as silly as personal aggression, is more easily controlled. Its expression is not socially objectionable."

Frazier looked nervously from one of us to the other. He seemed to be trying to discover whether we shared Castle's prejudice. I began to realize, also, that he had not really wanted to tell this story. He was vulnerable. He was treading on sanctified ground, and I was pretty sure he had not established the value of most of these practices in an experimental fashion. He could scarcely have done so in the short space of ten years. He was working on faith, and it bothered him.

I tried to bolster his confidence by reminding him that he had a professional colleague among his listeners. "May you not inadvertently teach your children some of the very emotions you're trying to eliminate?" I said. "What's the effect, for example, of finding the anticipation of a warm supper suddenly thwarted? Doesn't that eventually lead to feelings of uncertainty, or even anxiety?"

"It might. We had to discover how often our lessons could be safely administered. But all our schedules are worked out experimentally. We watch for undesired consequences just as any scientist watches for disrupting factors in his experiments.

"After all, it's a simple and sensible program," he went on in a tone of appeasement. "We set up a system of gradually increasing annoyances and frustrations against a background of complete serenity. An easy environment is made more and more difficult as the children acquire the capacity to adjust."

"But *why?*" said Castle. "Why these deliberate unpleasantnesses — to put it mildly? I must say I think you and your friend Simmons are really very subtle sadists."

"You've reversed your position, Mr. Castle," said Frazier in a sudden flash of anger with which I rather sympathized. Castle was calling names, and he was also being unaccountably and perhaps intentionally obtuse. "A while ago you accused me of breeding a race of softies," Frazier continued. "Now you object to toughening them up. But what you don't understand is that these potentially unhappy situations are never very annoying. Our schedules make sure of that. You wouldn't understand, however, because you're not so far advanced as our children."

Castle grew black.

"But what do your children get out of it?" he insisted, apparently trying to press some vague advantage in Frazier's anger.

"What do they get out of it!" exclaimed Frazier, his eyes flashing with a sort of helpless contempt. His lips curled and he dropped his head to look at his fingers, which were crushing a few blades of grass.

"They must get happiness and freedom and strength," I said, putting myself in a ridiculous position in attempting to make peace.

"They don't sound happy or free to me, standing in front of bowls of Forbidden Soup," said Castle, answering me parenthetically while continuing to stare at Frazier.

"If I must spell it out," Frazier began with a deep sigh, "what they get is escape from the petty emotions which eat the heart out of the unprepared. They get the satisfaction of pleasant and profitable social relations on a scale almost undreamed of in the world at large. They get immeasurably increased efficiency, because they can stick to a job without suffering the aches and pains which soon beset most of us. They get new horizons, for they are spared the emotions characteristic of frustration and failure. They get —" His eyes searched the branches of the trees. "Is that enough?" he said at last.

"And the community must gain their loyalty," I said, "when they discover the fears and jealousies and diffidences in the world at large."

"I'm glad you put it that way," said Frazier. "You might have said that they must feel superior to the miserable products of our public schools. But we're at pains to keep any feeling of superiority or contempt under control, too. Having suffered most acutely from it myself, I put the subject first on our agenda. We carefully avoid any joy in a personal triumph which means

the personal failure of somebody else. We take no pleasure in the sophisti-
cal, the disputative, the dialectical." He threw a vicious glance at Castle.
"We don't use the motive of domination, because we are always thinking
of the whole group. We could motivate a few geniuses that way—it was
certainly my own motivation—but we'd sacrifice some of the happiness of
everyone else. Triumph over nature and over oneself, yes. But over others,
never."

"You've taken the mainspring out of the watch," said Castle flatly.

"That's an experimental question, Mr Castle, and you have the wrong
answer."

Frazier was making no effort to conceal his feeling. If he had been riding Castle, he was now using his spurs. Perhaps he sensed that the rest of
us had come round and that he could change his tactics with a single hold-
out. But it was more than strategy, it was genuine feeling. Castle's unde-
viating skepticism was a growing frustration.

"Are your techniques really so very new?" I said hurriedly. "What
about the primitive practice of submitting a boy to various tortures before
granting him a place among adults? What about the disciplinary techniques
of Puritanism? Or of the modern school, for that matter?"

"In one sense you're right," said Frazier. "And I think you've nicely
answered Mr. Castle's tender concern for our little ones. The unhappinesses
we deliberately impose are far milder than the normal unhappinesses from
which we offer protection. Even at the height of our ethical training, the
unhappiness is ridiculously trivial—to the well-trained child.

"But there's a world of difference in the way we use these annoyances," he continued. "For one thing, we don't punish. We never administer an unpleasantness in the hope of repressing or eliminating undesirable
behavior. But there's another difference. In most cultures the child meets
up with annoyances and reverses of uncontrolled magnitude. Some are
imposed in the name of discipline by persons in authority. Some, like haz-
ings, are condoned though not authorized. Others are merely accidental.
No one cares to, or is able to, prevent them.

"We all know what happens. A few hardy children emerge, particularly
those who have got their unhappiness in doses that could be swallowed.
They become brave men. Others become sadists or masochists of varying
degrees of pathology. Not having conquered a painful environment, they
become preoccupied with pain and make a devious art of it. Others submit—and hope to inherit the earth. The rest—the cravens, the cowards
—live in fear for the rest of their lives. And that's only a single field—the reaction to pain. I could cite a dozen parallel cases. The optimist and the pessimist, the contented and the disgruntled, the loved and the unloved, the
ambitious and the discouraged—these are only the extreme products of a
miserable system.

"Traditional practices are admittedly better than nothing," Frazier
went on. "Spartan or Puritan—no one can question the occasional happy
result. But the whole system rests upon the wasteful principle of selection.
The English public school of the nineteenth century produced brave men
—by setting up almost insurmountable barriers and making the most of the
few who came over. But selection isn't education. Its crops of brave men

will always be small, and the waste enormous. Like all primitive principles, selection serves in place of education only through a profligate use of material. Multiply extravagantly and select with rigor. It's the philosophy of the 'big litter' as an alternative to good child hygiene.

"In Walden Two we have a different objective. We make every man a brave man. They all come over the barriers. Some require more preparation than others, but they all come over. The traditional use of adversity is to select the strong. We control adversity to build strength. And we do it deliberately, no matter how sadistic Mr. Castle may think us, in order to prepare for adversities which are beyond control. Our children eventually experience the 'heartache and the thousand natural shocks that flesh is heir to.' It would be the cruelest possible practice to protect them as long as possible, especially when we *could* protect them so well."

Frazier held out his hands in an exaggerated gesture of appeal.

"What alternative *had* we?" he said, as if he were in pain. "What else could we do? For four or five years we could provide a life in which no important need would go unsatisfied, a life practically free of anxiety or frustration or annoyance. What would *you* do? Would you let the child enjoy this paradise with no thought for the future—like an idolatrous and pampering mother? Or would you relax control of the environment and let the child meet accidental frustrations? *But what is the virtue of accident?* No, there was only one course open to us. We had to *design* a series of adversities, so that the child would develop the greatest possible self-control. Call it deliberate, if you like, and accuse us of sadism; there was no other course." Frazier turned to Castle, but he was scarcely challenging him. He seemed to be waiting, anxiously, for his capitulation. But Castle merely shifted his ground.

"I find it difficult to classify these practices," he said. Frazier emitted a disgruntled "Ha!" and sat back. "Your system seems to have usurped the place as well as the techniques of religion."

"Of religion and family culture," said Frazier wearily. "But I don't call it usurpation. Ethical training belongs to the community. As for techniques, we took every suggestion we could find without prejudice as to the source. But not on faith. We disregarded all claims of revealed truth and put every principle to an experimental test. And by the way, I've very much misrepresented the whole system if you suppose that any of the practices I've described are fixed. We try out many different techniques. Gradually we work toward the best possible set. And we don't pay much attention to the apparent success of a principle in the course of history. History is honored in Walden Two only as entertainment. It isn't taken seriously as food for thought. Which reminds me, very rudely, of our original plan for the morning. Have you had enough of emotion? Shall we turn to intellect?"

Frazier addressed these questions to Castle in a very friendly way and I was glad to see that Castle responded in kind. It was perfectly clear, however, that neither of them had ever worn a lollipop about the neck or faced a bowl of Forbidden Soup.

The living quarters and daily schedules of the older children furnished a particularly good example of behavioral engineering. At first sight they seemed wholly casual, almost haphazard, but as Frazier pointed out their significant features and the consequences of each, I began to make out a comprehensive, almost Machiavellian design.

The children passed smoothly from one age group to another, following a natural process of growth and avoiding the abrupt changes of the home-and-school system. The arrangements were such that each child emulated children slightly older than himself and hence derived motives and patterns for much of his early education without adult aid.

The control of the physical and social environment, of which Frazier had made so much, was progressively relaxed — or, to be more exact, the control was transferred from the authorities to the child himself and to the other members of his group. After spending most of the first year in an air-conditioned cubicle, and the second and third mainly in an air-conditioned room with a minimum of clothing and bedding, the three- or four-year-old was introduced to regular clothes and given the care of a small standard cot in a dormitory. The beds of the five- and six-year-olds were grouped by threes and fours in a series of alcoves furnished like rooms and treated as such by the children. Groups of three or four seven-year-olds occupied small rooms together, and this practice was continued, with frequent change of roommates, until the children were about thirteen, at which time they took temporary rooms in the adult building, usually in pairs. At marriage, or whenever the individual chose, he could participate in building a larger room for himself or refurnishing an old room which might be available.

A similar withdrawal of supervision, proceeding as rapidly as the child acquired control of himself, could be seen in the dining arrangements. From three through six, the children ate in a small dining room of their own. The older children, as we had observed on our first day at Walden Two, took their meals at specified times in the adult quarters. At thirteen all supervision was abandoned, and the young member was free to eat when and where he pleased.

We visited some of the workshops, laboratories, studies, and reading rooms used in lieu of classrooms. They were occupied, but it was not entirely clear that the children were actually in school. I supposed that the few adults to be seen about the building were teachers, but many of them were men, contrary to my conception of schoolteachers at that age level, and more often than not they were busy with some private business. Since Frazier had requested that we avoid questions or discussions in the presence of the children, we proceeded from one room to another in growing puzzlement. I had to admit that an enormous amount of learning was probably going on, but I had never seen a school like it before.

We inspected a well-equipped gymnasium, a small assembly room, and other facilities. The building was made of rammed earth and very simply decorated, but there was a pleasant "non-institutional" character about it. The doors and many of the windows stood open, and a fair share of the schoolwork, or whatever it was, took place outside. Children were constantly passing in and out. Although there was an obvious excitement about the place, there was little of the boisterous confusion which develops in the ordinary school when discipline is momentarily relaxed. Everyone seemed to be enjoying extraordinary freedom, but the efficiency and comfort of the whole group were preserved.

I was reminded of children on good behavior and was on the point of asking how often the pressure reached the bursting point. But there was a difference, too, and my question slowly evaporated. I could only conclude that this happy and productive atmosphere was probably the usual thing. Here again, so far as I could see, Frazier—or someone—had got things under control.

When we returned to our shade tree, I was primed with questions, and so, I am sure, was Castle. But Frazier had other plans. He had either forgotten how remarkable was the spectacle we had just witnessed, or he was intentionally allowing our wonderment and curiosity to ferment. He began from a very different point of view.

"When we discussed the economics of community life," he said, "I should have mentioned education. Teachers are, of course, workers, and I'm willing to defend all that I said about our economic advantage as specifically applied to education. God knows, the outside world is not exactly profligate in the education of its children. It doesn't spend much on equipment or teachers. Yet in spite of this penny-wise policy, there's still enormous waste. A much better education would cost less if society were better organized.

"We can arrange things more expeditiously here because we don't need to be constantly re-educating. The ordinary teacher spends a good share of her time changing the cultural and intellectual habits which the child acquires from its family and surrounding culture. Or else the teacher duplicates home training, in a complete waste of time. Here we can almost say that the school *is* the family, and vice versa.

"We can adopt the best educational methods and still avoid the administrative machinery which schools need in order to adjust to an unfavorable social structure. We don't have to worry about standardization in order to permit pupils to transfer from one school to another, or to appraise or control the work of particular schools. We don't need 'grades.' Everyone knows that talents and abilities don't develop at the same rate in different children. A fourth-grade reader may be a sixth-grade mathematician. The grade is an administrative device which does violence to the nature of the developmental process. Here the child advances as rapidly as he likes in any field. No time is wasted in forcing him to participate in, or be bored by, activities he has outgrown. And the backward child can be handled more efficiently too.

"We also don't require all our children to develop the same abilities or skills. We don't insist upon a certain set of courses. I don't suppose we have a single child who has had a 'secondary school education,' whatever that means. But they've all developed as rapidly as advisable, and they're well educated in many useful respects. By the same token we don't waste time in teaching the unteachable. The fixed education represented by a diploma is a bit of conspicuous waste which has no place in Walden Two. We don't attach an economic or honorific value to education. It has its own value or none at all.

"Since our children remain happy, energetic, and curious, we don't need to teach 'subjects' at all. We teach only the techniques of learning and thinking. As for geography, literature, the sciences — we give our children opportunity and guidance, and they learn them for themselves. In that way we dispense with half the teachers required under the old system, and the education is incomparably better. Our children aren't neglected, but they're seldom, if ever, *taught* anything.

"Education in Walden Two is part of the life of the community. We don't need to resort to trumped-up life experiences. Our children begin to work at a very early age. It's no hardship; it's accepted as readily as sport or play. And a good share of our education goes on in workshops, laboratories, and fields. It's part of the Walden Two Code to encourage children in all the arts and crafts. We're glad to spend time in instructing them, for we know it's important for the future of Walden Two and our own security."

"What about higher education?" I said.

"We aren't equipped for professional training, of course," said Frazier. "Those who want to go on to graduate study in a university are given special preparation. Entrance requirements are always tyrannical, though perhaps inevitable in a mass-production system. So far, we've been able to find graduate schools that will take our young people as special students, and as they continue to make excellent records, we expect fewer difficulties. If worse comes to worst, we shall organize as a college and get ourselves accredited. But can you imagine the stupid changes we should have to make?" Frazier snorted with impatience. "Oh, well. Tongue in cheek. Tongue in cheek."

"Don't you mean 'chin up'?" I asked.

"We'd have to set up a 'curriculum,' require a 'C average,' a 'foreign language,' 'so many years of residence,' and so on, and so on. It would be most amusing. No, 'tongue in cheek' was what I meant."

"Your people don't go to college, then?"

"We have no more reason to distinguish between college and high school than between high school and grade school. What are these distinctions, anyway, once you have separated education from the administration of education? Are there any natural breaks in a child's development? Many of our children naturally study more and more advanced material as they grow older. We help them in every way short of teaching them. We give them new techniques of acquiring knowledge and thinking. In spite of the beliefs of most educators, our children are taught to think. We give them an excellent survey of the methods and techniques of thinking, taken from logic, statistics, scientific method, psychology, and mathematics. That's all the 'college education' they need. They get the rest by themselves in our libraries and laboratories."

"But what about libraries and laboratories, though?" I said. "What can you actually provide in that line?"

"As to a library, we pride ourselves on having the best books, if not the most. Have you ever spent much time in a large college library? What trash the librarian has saved up in order to report a million volumes in the college catalogue! Bound pamphlets, old journals, ancient junk that even the shoddiest secondhand bookstore would clear from its shelves — all saved on the flimsy pretext that some day someone will want to study the 'history of a field.' Here we have the heart of a great library—not much to please the scholar or specialist, perhaps, but enough to interest the intelligent reader for life. Two or three thousand volumes will do it."

Frazier challenged me with a stare, but I did not wish to fight on such difficult terrain.

"The secret is this," he continued. "We subtract from our shelves as often as we add to them. The result is a collection that never misses fire. We all get something vital every time we take a book from the shelves. If anyone wants to follow a special interest we arrange for loans. If anyone wants to browse, we have half a barnful of discarded volumes.

"Our laboratories are good because they are real. Our workshops are really small engineering laboratories, and anyone with a genuine bent can go farther in them than the college student. We teach anatomy in the slaughterhouse, botany in the field, genetics in the dairy and poultry house, chemistry in the medical building and in the kitchen and dairy laboratory. What more can you ask?"

"And all this is just for the fun of it? You don't feel that some disciplined study is necessary?" said Castle.

"What for?" asked Frazier in unsuccessfully pretended surprise.

"To provide techniques and abilities which will be valuable later," said Castle. "For example, the study of a language."

"Why 'late'? Why not acquire a language when it's valuable? We acquire our own tongue that way! Of course, you're thinking of an educational process which comes to a dead stop sometime around the middle of June in one's last year in college. In Walden Two education goes on forever. It's part of our culture. We can acquire a technique whenever we need it.

"As to languages," Frazier continued, "you must know that even in our largest universities a language department considers itself very well off if two or three students at any one time approach fluency. We can do better than that. A member of Walden Two who once lived in France has interested several of our members, from ten to fifty years old, in the language. You may run into them during your stay. I hear them buzzing around the dining room every now and then, and they add a pleasantly cosmopolitan touch. And I'm told they're developing a good feeling for the French language and French literature. They'll never get any grades or credits, but they're getting French. Is there really any choice? Either French is worth learning, at the time you learn it, or it's not. And let's be sensible."

"I'm still skeptical," said Castle. "Of course, I'm still at a disadvantage in arguing against an accomplished fact." Frazier nodded his head violently. "But not everything has been accomplished," Castle went on. "Your pleasant schoolrooms, your industrious and contented children—these we must accept. But it would take us a long time to find out how well-educated your children really are according to our standards." Frazier made a move to speak, but Castle hurried on. "I'll admit these standards won't tell us everything. We couldn't ask your children to take our examinations, because they haven't been learning the same things, even in such a field as French. Your students would probably do no better on a second-year French examination than the average Parisian. I'll admit that, and I confess with all the humility I can muster that the kind of learning you've described is the better—if a comparison is possible. It's the ideal which every college teacher glimpses now and then when he looks up from the dance of death in which he has been caught. But I can't swallow the system you've described because I don't see what keeps the motors running. Why do your children learn anything at all? What are your substitutes for our standard motives?"

"Your 'standard motives'—exactly," said Frazier. "And there's the rub. An educational institution spends most of its time, not in presenting facts or imparting techniques of learning, but in trying to make its students learn. It has to create spurious needs. Have you ever stopped to analyze them? What are the 'standard motives,' Mr. Castle?"

"I must admit they're not very attractive," said Castle. "I suppose they consist of fear of one's family in the event of low grades or expulsion, the award of grades and honors, the snob value of a cap and gown, the cash value of a diploma."

"Very good, Mr. Castle," said Frazier. "You're an honest man. And now to answer your question—our substitute is simply the absence of these devices. We have had to *uncover* the worth-while and truly productive motives—the motives which inspire creative work in science and art outside the academies. No one asks how to motivate a baby. A baby naturally explores everything it can get at, unless restraining forces have already been at work. And this tendency doesn't die out, it's *wiped* out.

"We made a survey of the motives of the unhampered child and found more than we could use. Our engineering job was to *preserve* them by fortifying the child against discouragement. We introduce discouragement as carefully as we introduce any other emotional situation, beginning at about six months. Some of the toys in our air-conditioned cubicles are designed to build perseverance. A bit of a tune from a music box, or a pattern of flashing lights, is arranged to follow an appropriate response—say, pulling on a ring. Later the ring must be pulled twice, later still three or five or ten times. It's possible to build up fantastically perseverative behavior without encountering frustration or rage. It may not surprise you to learn that some of our experiments miscarried; the resistance to discouragement became almost stupid or pathological. One takes some risks in work of this sort, of course. Fortunately, we were able to reverse the process and restore the children to a satisfactory level.

"Building a tolerance for discouraging events proved to be all we needed," Frazier continued. "The motives in education, Mr. Castle, are the motives in all human behavior. Education should be only life itself. We don't need to create motives. We avoid the spurious academic needs you've just listed so frankly, and also the escape from threat so widely used in our civil institutions. We appeal to the curiosity which is characteristic of the unrestrained child, as well as the alert and inquiring adult. We appeal to that drive to control the environment which makes a baby continue to crumple a piece of noisy paper and the scientist continue to press forward with his predictive analyses of nature. We don't need to motivate anyone by creating spurious needs."

"I've known a few men with the kind of motivation you mean," I said.

"The contemporary culture produces a few by accident," said Frazier quickly, "just as it produces a few brave or happy men."

"But I've never understood them," I said rather faintly.

"Why should you, any more than unhappy people can understand the happy ones?"

"But isn't there a real need for the spurious satisfactions?" I said. "Little signs of personal success, money—personal domination, too, if you like. Most of what I do, I do to avoid undesirable consequences, to evade unpleasantnesses, or to reject or attack forces which interfere with my freedom."

"All the unhappy motives," said Frazier.

"Unhappy, perhaps, but powerful. I think the very thing which seems most unpromising in your system is its happiness. Your people are going to be too happy, too successful. But why won't they just go to sleep? Can we expect real achievements from them? Haven't the great men of history been essentially unhappy or maladjusted or neurotic?"

"I have little interest in conclusions drawn from history," said Frazier, "but if you must play that game, I'll play it too. For every genius you cite whose greatness seems to have sprung from a neurosis, I will undertake to cite similar acts of greatness without neurosis. Turn it around and I'll agree. A man with a touch of genius will be so likely to attack existing institutions that he'll be called unbalanced or neurotic. The only geniuses produced by the chaos of society are those who do something about it." Frazier paused, and I wondered if he were thinking of himself. "Chaos breeds geniuses. It offers a man something to be a genius about. But here, we have better things to do."

"But what about the cases where unhappiness has led to artistic or scientific achievement?" I asked.

"Oh, I daresay a few first-rate sonnets would have remained unwritten had the lady yielded," said Frazier. "But not so many, at that. Not many works of art can be traced to the lack of satisfaction of the basic needs. It's not plain sex that gives rise to art, but personal relations which are social or cultural rather than biological. Art deals with something less obvious than the satisfaction to be found in a square meal." Frazier laughed explosively, as if he had perhaps said more than he intended.

"We shall never produce so satisfying a world that there will be no place for art," he continued. "On the contrary, Walden Two has demonstrated very nicely that as soon as the simple necessities of life are obtained with little effort, there's an enormous welling up of artistic interest. And least of all do we need to fear that simple satisfactions will detract from the scientific conquest of the world. What scientist worth the name is engaged, as scientist, in the satisfaction of his own basic needs? He may be thinking of the basic needs of others, but his own motives are clearly cultural. There can be no doubt of the survival value of the inquiring spirit—of curiosity, of exploration, of the need to dominate media, of the urge to control the forces of nature. The world will never be wholly known, and man can't help trying to know more and more of it."

The topic seemed to have grown too vague to stimulate further discussion, but Castle soon offered a substitute.

"I'm torn between two questions which seem incompatible yet equally pressing," he said. "What do you do about differences among your children in intellect and talent? And what do you do to avoid producing a lot of completely standardized young people? Which question should I ask, and what's your answer?"

"They're both good questions," said Frazier, "and quite compatible." I made a move to speak and Frazier said, "I see that Mr. Burris wants to help with the answers."

"My guess is," I said, "that differences are due to environmental and cultural factors and that Mr. Frazier has no great problem to solve. Give all your children the excellent care we have just been witnessing and your differences will be negligible."

"No, you're wrong, Burris," said Frazier. "That's one question we have answered to our satisfaction. Our ten-year-olds have all had the same environment since birth, but the range of their IQ's is almost as great as in the population at large. This seems to be true of other abilities and skills as well."

"And of physical prowess, of course," said Castle.

"Why do you say 'of course'?" said Frazier, with marked interest.

"Why, I suppose because physical differences are generally acknowledged."

"All differences are physical, my dear Mr. Castle. We think with our bodies, too. You might have replied that differences in prowess have always been obvious and impossible to conceal, while other differences have customarily been disguised for the sake of prestige and family pride. We accept our gross physical limitations without protest and are reasonably happy in spite of them, but we may spend a lifetime trying to live up to a wholly false conception of our powers in another field, and suffer the pain of a lingering failure. Here we accept ourselves as we are."

"Aren't the untalented going to be unhappy?"

"But we don't go in for personal rivalry; individuals are seldom compared. We never develop a taste much beyond a talent. Our parents have little reason to misrepresent their children's abilities to themselves or others. It's easy for our children to accept their limitations — exactly as they have always accepted the gross differences which Mr. Castle called physical prowess. At the same time our gifted children aren't held back by organized mediocrity. We don't throw our geniuses off balance. The brilliant but unstable type is unfamiliar here. Genius can express itself."

We had shifted our positions from time to time to stay within the shade of our tree. We were now centered due north and crowding the trunk, for it was noon. The schoolwork in the area near the building had gradually come to an end, and the migration toward the dining room had taken place. Frazier stood up and straightened his knees with care. The rest of us also got up — except Castle, who stayed stubbornly in his place.

"I can't believe," he began, looking at the ground and apparently not caring whether he was heard or not, "I can't believe you can really get spontaneity and freedom through a system of tyrannical control. Where does initiative come in? When does the child begin to think of himself as a free agent? What is freedom, anyway, under such a plan?"

"Freedom, freedom," said Frazier, stretching his arms and neck and almost singing the words, as if he were uttering them through a yawn. "Freedom is a question, isn't it? But let's not answer it now. Let's let it ring, shall we? Let's let it ring."

GEORGE ORWELL

*George Orwell (pseudonym for Eric Blair) was for many years a prominent fig-
ure in the British labor movement. He is best remembered, however, as a novelist
and essayist. Celebrated for his political satire* Animal Farm *(1946) and for his
dire vision of a future world dominated by collectivistic totalitarianisms,* 1984
(1949), he is also the author of such well-known works as Homage to Catalonia
(1952), Down and Out in Paris and London, *and* Burmese Days.

Thinking and Learning in 1984

Orwell's well-known novel 1984 *is a vision of a future totally controlled by gi-
gantic totalitarian collectivist states. Orwell describes the society of Oceania, one
of three megastates which comprise the entire civilization of the world in the
year 1984. At one point in the novel, Orwell's hero, Winston Smith, obtains a
copy of a forbidden book purportedly written by the archenemy of the People,
Emmanuel Goldstein. The book contains this description of Oceanic civilization
in 1984.*

Given this background, one could infer, if one did not know it already, the
general structure of Oceanic society. At the apex of the pyramid comes Big
Brother. Big Brother is infallible and all-powerful. Every success, every
achievement, every victory, every scientific discovery, all knowledge, all
wisdom, all happiness, all virtue, are held to issue directly from his leadership and inspiration. Nobody has ever seen Big Brother. He is a face on the
hoardings, a voice on the telescreen. We may be reasonably sure that he will
never die, and there is already considerable uncertainty as to when he was
born. Big Brother is the guise in which the Party chooses to exhibit itself to
the world. His function is to act as a focusing point for love, fear, and reverence, emotions which are more easily felt toward an individual than toward
an organization. Below Big Brother comes the Inner Party, its numbers limited to six millions, or something less than two per cent of the population of
Oceania. Below the Inner Party comes the Outer Party, which, if the Inner

Party is described as the brain of the State, may be justly likened to the hands. Below that come the dumb masses whom we habitually refer to as "the proles," numbering perhaps eighty-five per cent of the population. In the terms of our earlier classification, the proles are the Low, for the slave populations of the equatorial lands, who pass constantly from conqueror to conqueror, are not a permanent or necessary part of the structure.

In principle, membership in these three groups is not hereditary. The child of Inner Party parents is in theory not born into the Inner Party. Admission to either branch of the Party is by examination, taken at the age of sixteen. Nor is there any racial discrimination, or any marked domination of one province by another. Jews, Negroes, South Americans of pure Indian blood are to be found in the highest ranks of the Party, and the administrators of any area are always drawn from the inhabitants of that area. In no part of Oceania do the inhabitants have the feeling that they are a colonial population ruled from a distant capital. Oceania has no capital, and its titular head is a person whose whereabouts nobody knows. Except that English is its chief lingua franca and Newspeak its official language, it is not centralized in any way. Its rulers are not held together by blood ties but by adherence to a common doctrine. It is true that our society is stratified, and very rigidly stratified, on what at first sight appear to be hereditary lines. There is far less to-and-fro movement between the different groups than happened under capitalism or even in the pre-industrial ages. Between the two branches of the Party there is a certain amount of interchange, but only so much as will ensure that weaklings are excluded from the Inner Party and that ambitious members of the Outer Party are made harmless by allowing them to rise. Proletarians, in practice, are not allowed to graduate into the Party. The most gifted among them, who might possibly become nuclei of discontent, are simply marked down by the Thought Police and eliminated. But this state of affairs is not necessarily permanent, nor is it a matter of principle. The Party is not a class in the old sense of the word. It does not aim at transmitting power to its own children, as such; and if there were no other way of keeping the ablest people at the top, it would be perfectly prepared to recruit an entire new generation from the ranks of the proletariat. In the crucial years, the fact that the Party was not a hereditary body did a great deal to neutralize opposition. The older kind of Socialist, who had been trained to fight against something called "class privilege," assumed that what is not hereditary cannot be permanent. He did not see that the continuity of an oligarchy need not be physical nor did he pause to reflect that hereditary aristocracies have always been short-lived, whereas adoptive organizations such as the Catholic Church have sometimes lasted for hundreds or thousands of years. The essence of oligarchical rule is not father-to-son inheritance, but the persistence of a certain world-view and a certain way of life, imposed by the dead upon the living. A ruling group is a ruling group so long as it can nominate its successors. The Party is not concerned with perpetuating its blood but with perpetuating itself. *Who* wields power is not important, provided that the hierarchical structure remains always the same.

All the beliefs, habits, tastes, emotions, mental attitudes that characterize our time are really designed to sustain the mystique of the Party and prevent the true nature of present-day society from being perceived. Physical rebellion, or any preliminary move toward rebellion, is at present not possible. From the proletarians nothing is to be feared. Left to themselves, they will continue from generation to generation and from century to century, working, breeding, and dying, not only without any impulse to rebel, but without the power of grasping that the world could be other than it is. They could only become dangerous if the advance of industrial technique made it necessary to educate them more highly; but, since military and commercial rivalry are no longer important, the level of popular education is actually declining. What opinions the masses hold, or do not hold, is looked on as a matter of indifference. They can be granted intellectual liberty because they have no intellect. In a Party member, on the other hand, not even the smallest deviation of opinion on the most unimportant subject can be tolerated.

A Party member lives from birth to death under the eye of the Thought Police. Even when he is alone he can never be sure that he is alone. Wherever he may be, asleep or awake, working or resting, in his bath or in bed, he can be inspected without warning and without knowing that he is being inspected. Nothing that he does is indifferent. His friendships, his relaxations, his behavior toward his wife and children, the expression of his face when he is alone, the words he mutters in sleep, even the characteristic movements of his body, are all jealously scrutinized. Not only any actual misdemeanor, but any eccentricity, however small, any change of habits, any nervous mannerism that could possibly be the symptom of an inner struggle, is certain to be detected. He has no freedom of choice in any direction whatever. On the other hand, his actions are not regulated by law or by any clearly formulated code of behavior. In Oceania there is no law. Thoughts and actions which, when detected, mean certain death are not formally forbidden, and the endless purges, arrests, tortures, imprisonments, and vaporizations are not inflicted as punishment for crimes which have actually been committed, but are merely the wiping-out of persons who might perhaps commit a crime at some time in the future. A Party member is required to have not only the right opinions, but the right instincts. Many of the beliefs and attitudes demanded of him are never plainly stated, and could not be stated without laying bare the contradictions inherent in Ingsoc.* If he is a person naturally orthodox (in Newspeak, a *goodthinker*), he will in all circumstances know, without taking thought, what is the true belief or the desirable emotion. But in any case an elaborate mental training, undergone in childhood and grouping itself round the Newspeak words *crimestop*, *blackwhite*, and *doublethink*, makes him unwilling and unable to think too deeply on any subject whatever.

A Party member is expected to have no private emotions and no respites from enthusiasm. He is supposed to live in a continuous frenzy of hatred for foreign enemies and internal traitors, triumph over victories, and self-abasement before the power and wisdom of the Party. The discontents produced by his bare, unsatisfying life are deliberately turned outwards and dissipated by such devices as the Two Minutes Hate, and the specula-

---

* The term *Ingsoc* stands for English socialism.

tions which might possibly induce a skeptical or rebellious attitude are killed in advance by his early acquired inner discipline. The first and simplest stage in the discipline, which can be taught even to young children, is called, in Newspeak, *crimestop*. *Crimestop* means the faculty of stopping short, as though by instinct, at the threshold of any dangerous thought. It includes the power of not grasping analogies, of failing to perceive logical errors, of misunderstanding the simplest arguments if they are inimical to Ingsoc, and of being bored or repelled by any train of thought which is capable of leading in a heretical direction. *Crimestop*, in short, means protective stupidity. But stupidity is not enough. On the contrary, orthodoxy in the full sense demands a control over one's own mental processes as complete as that of a contortionist over his body. Oceanic society rests ultimately on the belief that Big Brother is omnipotent and that the Party is infallible. But since in reality Big Brother is not omnipotent and the Party is not infallible, there is need for an unwearying, moment-to-moment flexibility in the treatment of facts. The key word here is *blackwhite*. Like so many Newspeak words, this word has two mutually contradictory meanings. Applied to an opponent, it means the habit of impudently claiming that black is white, in contradiction of the plain facts. Applied to a Party member, it means a loyal willingness to say that black is white when Party discipline demands this. But it means also the ability to *believe* that black is white, and more, to *know* that black is white, and to forget that one has ever believed the contrary. This demands a continuous alteration of the past, made possible by the system of thought which really embraces all the rest, and which is known in Newspeak as *doublethink*.

The alteration of the past is necessary for two reasons, one of which is subsidiary and, so to speak, precautionary. The subsidiary reason is that the Party member, like the proletarian, tolerates present-day conditions partly because he has no standards of comparison. He must be cut off from the past, just as he must be cut off from foreign countries, because it is necessary for him to believe that he is better off than his ancestors and that the average level of material comfort is constantly rising. But by far the more important reason for the readjustment of the past is the need to safeguard the infallibility of the Party. It is not merely that speeches, statistics, and records of every kind must be constantly brought up to date in order to show that the predictions of the Party were in all cases right. It is also that no change of doctrine or in political alignment can ever be admitted. For to change one's mind, or even one's policy, is a confession of weakness. If, for example, Eurasia or Eastasia (whichever it may be) is the enemy today, then that country must always have been the enemy. And if the facts say otherwise, then the facts must be altered. Thus history is continuously rewritten. This day-to-day falsification of the past, carried out by the Ministry of Truth, is as necessary to the stability of the regime as the work of repression and espionage carried out by the Ministry of Love.

The mutability of the past is the central tenet of Ingsoc. Past events, it is argued, have no objective existence, but survive only in written records and in human memories. The past is whatever the records and the memories agree upon. And since the Party is in full control of all records, and in equally full control of the minds of its members, it follows that the past is whatever the Party chooses to make it. It also follows that though the past is alterable, it never has been altered in any specific instance. For when it has been recreated in whatever shape is needed at the moment, then this new version *is* the past, and no different past can ever have existed. This holds good even when, as often happens, the same event has to be altered out of recognition several times in the course of a year. At all times the Party is in possession of absolute truth, and clearly the absolute can never have been different from what it is now. It will be seen that the control of the past depends above all on the training of memory. To make sure that all written records agree with the orthodoxy of the moment is merely a mechanical act. But it is also necessary to *remember* that events happened in the desired manner. And if it is necessary to rearrange one's memories or to tamper with written records, then it is necessary to *forget* that one has done so. The trick of doing this can be learned like any other mental technique. It *is* learned by the majority of Party members, and certainly by all who are intelligent as well as orthodox. In Oldspeak it is called, quite frankly, "reality control." In Newspeak it is called *doublethink*, although *doublethink* comprises much else as well.

Doublethink means the power of holding two contradictory beliefs in one's mind simultaneously, and accepting both of them. The Party intellectual knows in which direction his memories must be altered; he therefore knows that he is playing tricks with reality; but by the exercise of *doublethink* he also satisfies himself that reality is not violated. The process has to be conscious, or it would not be carried out with sufficient precision, but it also has to be unconscious, or it would bring with it a feeling of falsity and hence of guilt. *Doublethink* lies at the very heart of Ingsoc, since the essential act of the Party is to use conscious deception while retaining the firmness of purpose that goes with complete honesty. To tell deliberate lies while genuinely believing in them, to forget any fact that has become inconvenient, and then, when it becomes necessary again, to draw it back from oblivion for just so long as it is needed, to deny the existence of objective reality and all the while to take account of the reality which one denies —all this is indispensably necessary. Even in using the word *doublethink* it is necessary to exercise *doublethink*. For by using the word one admits that one is tampering with reality; by a fresh act of *doublethink* one erases this knowledge; and so on indefinitely, with the lie always one leap ahead of the truth. Ultimately, it is by means of *doublethink* that the Party has been able—and may, for all we know, continue to be able for thousands of years—to arrest the course of history.

All past oligarchies have fallen from power either because they ossified or because they grew soft. Either they became stupid and arrogant, failed to adjust themselves to changing circumstances, and were overthrown, or they became liberal and cowardly, made concessions when they should have used force, and once again were overthrown. They fell, that is to say, either through consciousness or through unconsciousness. It is the achievement of the Party to have produced a system of thought in which both conditions can exist simultaneously. And upon no other intellectual basis could the dominion of the Party be made permanent. If one is to rule, and to continue ruling, one must be able to dislocate the sense of reality. For the secret of rulership is to combine a belief in one's own infallibility with the power to learn from past mistakes.

It need hardly be said that the subtlest practitioners of *doublethink* are those who invented *doublethink* and know that it is a vast system of mental cheating. In our society, those who have the best knowledge of what is happening are also those who are furthest from seeing the world as it is. In general, the greater the understanding, the greater the delusion: the more intelligent, the less sane. One clear illustration of this is the fact that war hysteria increases in intensity as one rises in the social scale. Those whose attitude toward the war is most nearly rational are the subject peoples of the disputed territories. To these people the war is simply a continuous calamity which sweeps to and fro over their bodies like a tidal wave. Which side is winning is a matter of complete indifference to them. They are aware that a change of overlordship means simply that they will be doing the same work as before for new masters who treat them in the same manner as the old ones. The slightly more favored workers whom we call "the proles" are only intermittently conscious of the war. When it is necessary they can be prodded into frenzies of fear and hatred, but when left to themselves they are capable of forgetting for long periods that the war is happening. It is in the ranks of the Party, and above all of the Inner Party, that the true war enthusiasm is found. World-conquest is believed in most firmly by those who know it to be impossible. This peculiar linking-together of opposites — knowledge with ignorance, cynicism with fanaticism — is one of the chief distinguishing marks of Oceanic society. The official ideology abounds with contradictions even where there is no practical reason for them. Thus, the Party rejects and vilifies every principle for which the Socialist movement originally stood, and it chooses to do this in the name of Socialism. It preaches a contempt for the working class unexampled for centuries past, and it dresses its members in a uniform which was at one time peculiar to manual workers and was adopted for that reason. It systematically undermines the solidarity of the family, and it calls its leader by a name which is a direct appeal to the sentiments of family loyalty. Even the names of the four Ministries by which we are governed exhibit a sort of impudence in their deliberate reversal of the facts. The Ministry of Peace concerns itself with war, the Ministry of Truth with lies, the Ministry of Love with torture, and the Ministry of Plenty with starvation. These contradictions are not accidental, nor do they result from ordinary hypocrisy: they are deliberate exercises in *doublethink*. For it is only by reconciling contradictions that power can be retained indefinitely. In no other way could the ancient cycle be broken. If human equality is to be forever averted — if the High, as we have called them, are to keep their places permanently — then the prevailing mental condition must be controlled insanity.

But there is one question which until this moment we have almost ignored. It is: *why* should human equality be averted? Supposing that the mechanics of the process have been rightly described, what is the motive for this huge, accurately planned effort to freeze history at a particular moment of time?

Here we reach the central secret. As we have seen, the mystique of the Party, and above all of the Inner Party, depends upon *doublethink*. But deeper than this lies the original motive, the never-questioned instinct that first led to the seizure of power and brought *doublethink*, the Thought Police, continuous warfare, and all the other necessary paraphernalia into existence afterwards.

One of the most memorable features of the Oceanic society of 1984 is the institutionalized interval of emotional catharsis and reinforced group solidarity which is termed the "Two Minutes Hate."

It was nearly eleven hundred, and in the Records Department, where Winston worked, they were dragging the chairs out of the cubicles and grouping them in the center of the hall, opposite the big telescreen, in preparation for the Two Minutes Hate . . . .

The next moment a hideous, grinding screech, as of some monstrous machine running without oil, burst from the big telescreen at the end of the room. It was a noise that set one's teeth on edge and bristled the hair at the back of one's neck. The Hate had started.

As usual, the face of Emmanuel Goldstein, the Enemy of the People, had flashed onto the screen. There were hisses here and there among the audience. The little sandy-haired woman gave a squeak of mingled fear and disgust. Goldstein was the renegade and backslider who once, long ago (how long ago, nobody quite remembered), had been one of the leading figures of the Party, almost on a level with Big Brother himself, and then had engaged in counterrevolutionary activities, had been condemned to death, and had mysteriously escaped and disappeared. The program of the Two Minutes Hate varied from day to day, but there was none in which Goldstein was not the principal figure. He was the primal traitor, the earliest defiler of the Party's purity. All subsequent crimes against the Party, all treacheries, acts of sabotage, heresies, deviations, sprang directly out of his teaching. Somewhere or other he was still alive and hatching his conspiracies: perhaps somewhere beyond the sea, under the protection of his foreign paymasters; perhaps even—so it was occasionally rumored—in some hiding place in Oceania itself.

Winston's diaphragm was constricted. He could never see the face of Goldstein without a painful mixture of emotions. It was a lean Jewish face, with a great fuzzy aureole of white hair and a small goatee beard—a clever face, and yet somehow inherently despicable, with a kind of senile silliness in the long thin nose near the end of which a pair of spectacles was perched. It resembled the face of a sheep, and the voice, too, had a sheeplike quality. Goldstein was delivering his usual venomous attack upon the doctrines of the Party—an attack so exaggerated and perverse that a child should have been able to see through it, and yet just plausible enough to fill one with an alarmed feeling that other people, less level-headed than oneself might be taken in by it. He was abusing Big Brother, he was denouncing the dictatorship of the Party, he was demanding the immediate conclusion of peace with Eurasia, he was advocating freedom of speech, freedom of the press, freedom of assembly, freedom of thought, he was crying hysterically that the revolution had been betrayed—and all this in rapid polysyllabic speech which was a sort of parody of the habitual style of the orators of the Party, and even contained Newspeak words: more Newspeak words, indeed, than any Party member would normally use in real life. And all the while, lest one should be in any doubt as to the reality which Goldstein's specious claptrap covered, behind his head on the telescreen, there marched the endless columns of the Eurasian army—row after row of solid-looking men with expressionless Asiatic faces, who swam up to the surface of the screen and vanished, to be replaced by others exactly similar. The dull, rhythmic tramp of the soldiers' boots formed the background to Goldstein's bleating voice.

Before the Hate had proceeded for thirty seconds, uncontrollable exclamations of rage were breaking out from half the people in the room. The self-satisfied sheeplike face on the screen, and the terrifying power of the Eurasian army behind it, were too much to be borne; besides, the sight or even the thought of Goldstein produced fear and anger automatically. He was an object of hatred more constant than either Eurasia or Eastasia, since when Oceania was at war with one of these powers it was generally at peace with the other. But what was strange was that although Goldstein was hated and despised by everybody, although every day, and a thousand times a day, on platforms, on the telescreen, in newspapers, in books, his theories were refuted, smashed, ridiculed, held up to the general gaze for the pitiful rubbish that they were—in spite of all this, his influence never seemed to grow less. Always there were fresh dupes waiting to be seduced by him. A day never passed when spies and saboteurs acting under his directions were not unmasked by the Thought Police. He was the commander of a vast shadowy army, an underground network of conspirators dedicated to the overthrow of the State. The Brotherhood, its name was supposed to be. There were also whispered stories of a terrible book, a compendium of all the heresies, of which Goldstein was the author and which circulated clandestinely here and there. It was a book without a title. People referred to it, if at all, simply as *the book*. But one knew of such things only through vague rumors. Neither the Brotherhood nor *the book* was a subject that any ordinary Party member would mention if there was a way of avoiding it.

In its second minute the Hate rose to a frenzy. People were leaping up and down in their places and shouting at the tops of their voices in an effort to drown the maddening bleating voice that came from the screen. The little sandy-haired woman had turned bright pink, and her mouth was opening and shutting like that of a landed fish . . . . The dark-haired girl behind Winston had begun crying out "Swine! Swine! Swine" and suddenly she picked up a heavy Newspeak dictionary and flung it at the screen. It struck Goldstein's nose and bounced off; the voice continued inexorably. In a lucid moment Winston found that he was shouting with the others and kicking his heel violently against the rung of his chair. The horrible thing about the Two Minutes Hate was not that one was obliged to act a part, but that it was impossible to avoid joining in. Within thirty seconds any pretense was always unnecessary. A hideous ecstasy of fear and vindictiveness, a desire to kill, to torture, to smash faces in with a sledge hammer, seemed to flow through the whole group of people like an electric current, turning one even against one's will into a grimacing, screaming lunatic. And yet the rage that one felt was an abstract, undirected emotion which could be switched from one object to another like the flame of a blowlamp. Thus, at one moment Winston's hatred was not turned against Goldstein at all, but, on the contrary, against Big Brother, the Party, and the Thought Police; and at such moments his heart went out to the lonely, derided heretic on the screen, sole guardian of truth and sanity in a world of lies. And yet the very next instant he was at one with the people about him, and all that was said of Goldstein seemed to him to be true. At those moments his secret loathing of Big Brother changed into adoration, and Big Brother seemed to tower up, an invincible, fearless protector, standing like a rock against the hordes of Asia, and Goldstein, in spite of his isolation, his helplessness, and the doubt that hung about his very existence, seemed like some sinister enchanter, capable by the mere power of his voice of wrecking the structure of civilization.

It was even possible, at moments, to switch one's hatred this way or that by a voluntary act. Suddenly, by the sort of violent effort with which one wrenches one's head away from the pillow in a nightmare, Winston succeeded in transferring his hatred from the face on the screen to the dark-haired girl behind him. Vivid, beautiful hallucinations flashed through his mind. He would flog her to death with a rubber truncheon. He would tie her naked to a stake and shoot her full of arrows like Saint Sebastian. He would ravish her and cut her throat at the moment of climax. Better than before, moreover, he realized *why* it was that he hated her. He hated her because she was young and pretty and sexless, because he wanted to go to bed with her and would never do so, because round her sweet supple waist, which seemed to ask you to encircle it with your arm, there was only the odious scarlet sash, aggressive symbol of chastity.

The Hate rose to its climax. The voice of Goldstein had become an actual sheep's bleat, and for an instant the face changed into that of a sheep. Then the sheep-face melted into the figure of a Eurasian soldier who seemed to be advancing, huge and terrible, his submachine gun roaring and seeming to spring out of the surface of the screen, so that some of the people in the front row actually flinched backwards in their seats. But in the same moment, drawing a deep sigh of relief from everybody, the hostile figure melted into the face of Big Brother, black-haired, black-mustachio'd, full of power and mysterious calm, and so vast that it almost filled up the screen. Nobody heard what Big Brother was saying. It was merely a few words of encouragement, the sort of words that are uttered in the din of battle, not distinguishable individually but restoring confidence by the fact of being spoken. Then the face of Big Brother faded away again, and instead the three slogans of the Party stood out in bold capitals:

WAR IS PEACE

FREEDOM IS SLAVERY

IGNORANCE IS STRENGTH

But the face of Big Brother seemed to persist for several seconds on the screen, as though the impact that it had made on everyone's eyeballs were too vivid to wear off immediately. The little sandy-haired woman had flung herself forward over the back of the chair in front of her. With a tremulous murmur that sounded like "My Savior!" she extended her arms toward the screen. Then she buried her face in her hands. It was apparent that she was uttering a prayer.

At this moment the entire group of people broke into a deep, slow, rhythmical chant of "B-B! . . . B-B! . . . B-B!" over and over again, very slowly, with a long pause between the first "B" and the second—a heavy, murmurous sound, somehow curiously savage, in the background of which one seemed to hear the stamp of naked feet and the throbbing of tom-toms. For perhaps as much as thirty seconds they kept it up. It was a refrain that was often heard in moments of overwhelming emotion. Partly it was a sort of hymn to the wisdom and majesty of Big Brother, but still more it was an act of self-hypnosis, a deliberate drowning of consciousness by means of rhythmic noise. Winston's entrails seemed to grow cold. In the Two Minutes Hate he could not help sharing in the general delirium, but this subhuman chanting of "B-B! . . . B-B!" always filled him with horror. Of course he chanted with the rest: it was impossible to do otherwise. To dissemble your feelings, to control your face, to do what everyone else was doing, was an instinctive reaction. But there was a space of a couple of seconds during which the expression in his eyes might conceivably have betrayed him.

ALDOUS HUXLEY

Aldous Huxley was certainly one of the major literary figures of our times. His range of interests, as reflected in his published writings, extended over the entire continuum of human experience. In addition to Brave New World, *originally published in 1932, Huxley is celebrated as the author of such novels as* Antic Hay *(1923), and* Point Counter-Point *(1928). His nonfiction works include* The Perennial Philosophy *(1946),* The Doors of Perception *(1954), and* Brave New World Revisited *(1958).*

Education in the Brave New World

Huxley's novel Brave New World *was written in 1931 and has been a topic of controversy and discussion ever since. Huxley's utopia, which is projected six hundred years into the future to the year 600 A.F. (After Ford), is not a model for the future. It is, rather, a nightmarish prognosis of what could conceivably occur far sooner if certain trends—particularly trends involving future research in biology, physiology, and psychology—were to be applied to human beings on a mass social scale. As Huxley indicates:*

> The people who govern the Brave New World may not be sane (in what may be called the absolute sense of that word); but they are not madmen, and their aim is not anarchy but social stability. It is in order to achieve stability that they carry out, by scientific means, the ultimate, personal, really revolutionary revolution.

The theme of Brave New World *is the effect of scientific advances on human beings. The true revolution of the future, notes Huxley in the foreword to the 1946 edition of his novel, "is to be achieved, not in the external world, but in the souls and flesh of human beings." "The most important Manhattan projects of the future will be vast government-sponsored enquiries into what the politicians and the participating scientists will call 'the problem of happiness'—in other words, the problem of making people love their servitude."*

To bring about the Brave New World, states Huxley, we need merely to perfect the following developments:

> First, a greatly improved technique of suggestion—through infant conditioning and, later, with the aid of drugs, such as scopolamine. Second, a fully developed science of human differences, enabling government managers to assign any given individual to his or her proper place in the social and economic hierarchy. (Round pegs in square holes tend to have dangerous thoughts about the social system and to infect others with their discontents.) Third (since reality, however utopian, is something from which people feel the need of taking pretty frequent holidays), a substitute for alcohol and the other narcotics, something at once less harmful and more pleasure-giving than gin or heroin. And fourth (but this would be a long-term project, which it would take generations of totalitarian control to bring to a successful conclusion), a foolproof system of eugenics, designed to standardize the human product and so to facilitate the task of the managers.

Writing in 1946, Huxley was not optimistic about the likelihood of forestalling the kind of society which he envisions. As he stated at this time:

> Only a large-scale popular movement toward decentralization and self-help can arrest the present tendency toward statism. At present there is no sign that such a movement will take place . . . .
>
> A really efficient totalitarian state would be one in which the all-powerful executive of political bosses and their army of managers control a population of slaves who do not have to be coerced, because they love their servitude . . . .

A squat grey building of only thirty-four stories. Over the main entrance the words, CENTRAL LONDON HATCHERY AND CONDITIONING CENTRE, and, in a shield, the World State's motto, COMMUNITY, IDENTITY, STABILITY.

The enormous room on the ground floor faced towards the north. Cold for all the summer beyond the panes, for all the tropical heat of the room itself, a harsh thin light glared through the windows, hungrily seeking some draped lay figure, some pallid shape of academic goose-flesh, but finding only the glass and nickel and bleakly shining porcelain of a laboratory. Wintriness responded to wintriness. The overalls of the workers were white, their hands gloved with a pale corpse-coloured rubber. The light was frozen, dead, a ghost. Only from the yellow barrels of the microscopes did it borrow a certain rich and living substance, lying along the polished tubes like butter, streak after luscious streak in long recession down the work tables.

"And this," said the Director opening the door, "is the Fertilizing Room."

Bent over their instruments, three hundred Fertilizers were plunged, as the Director of Hatcheries and Conditioning entered the room, in the scarcely breathing silence, the absent-minded, soliloquizing hum or whistle, of absorbed concentration. A troop of newly arrived students, very young, pink and callow, followed nervously, rather abjectly, at the Director's heels. Each of them carried a notebook, in which, whenever the great man spoke, he desperately scribbled. Straight from the horse's mouth. It was a rare privilege. The D.H.C. for Central London always made a point of personally conducting his new students round the various departments.

"Just to give you a general idea," he would explain to them. For of course some sort of general idea they must have, if they were to do their work intelligently—though as little of one, if they were to be good and happy members of society, as possible. For particulars, as every one knows, make for virtue and happiness; generalities are intellectually necessary evils. Not philosophers but fretsawyers and stamp collectors compose the backbone of society.

"To-morrow," he would add, smiling at them with a slightly menacing geniality, "you'll be settling down to serious work. You won't have time for generalities. Meanwhile . . ."

Meanwhile, it was a privilege. Straight from the horse's mouth into the notebook. The boys scribbled like mad.

Tall and rather thin but upright, the Director advanced into the room. He had a long chin and big rather prominent teeth, just covered, when he was not talking, by his full, floridly curved lips. Old, young? Thirty? Fifty? Fifty-five? It was hard to say. And anyhow the question didn't arise; in this year of stability, A.F. 632, it didn't occur to you to ask it.

"I shall begin at the beginning," said the D.H.C. and the more zealous students recorded his intention in their notebooks: *Begin at the beginning*. "These," he waved his hand, "are the incubators." And opening an insulated door he showed them racks upon racks of numbered test-tubes. "The week's supply of ova. Kept," he explained, "at blood heat; whereas the male gametes," and here he opened another door, "they have to be kept at thirty-five instead of thirty-seven. Full blood heat sterilizes." Rams wrapped in theremogene beget no lambs.

Still leaning against the incubators he gave them, while the pencils scurried illegibly across the pages, a brief description of the modern fertilizing process; spoke first, of course, of its surgical introduction—"the operation undergone voluntarily for the good of Society, not to mention the fact that it carries a bonus amounting to six months' salary"; continued with some account of the technique for preserving the excised ovary alive and actively developing; passed on to a consideration of optimum temperature, salinity, viscosity; referred to the liquor in which the detached and ripened eggs were kept; and, leading his charges to the work tables, actually showed them how this liquor was drawn off from the test-tubes; how it was let out drop by drop onto the specially warmed slides of the microscopes; how the eggs which it contained were inspected for abnormalities, counted and transferred to a porous receptacle; how (and he now took them to watch the operation) this receptacle was immersed in a warm bouillon containing free-swimming spermatozoa—at a minimum concentration of one hundred thousand per cubic centimetre, he insisted; and how, after ten minutes, the container was lifted out of the liquor and its contents re-examined; how, if any of the eggs remained unfertilized, it was again immersed, and, if necessary, yet again; how the fertilized ova went back to the incubators; where the Alphas and Betas remained until definitely bottled; while the Gammas, Deltas and Epsilons were brought out again, after only thirty-six hours, to undergo Bokanovsky's Process.

"Bokanovsky's Process," repeated the Director, and the students underlined the words in their little notebooks.

One egg, one embryo, one adult—normality. But a bokanovskified egg will bud, will proliferate, will divide. From eight to ninety-six buds, and every bud will grow into a perfectly formed embryo, and every embryo into a full-sized adult. Making ninety-six human beings grow where only one grew before. Progress.

"Essentially," the D.H.C. concluded, "bokanovskification consists of a series of arrests of development. We check the normal growth and, paradoxically enough, the egg responds by budding."

Responds by budding. The pencils were busy.

He pointed. On a very slowly moving band a rack-full of test-tubes was entering a large metal box, another rack-full was emerging. Machinery faintly purred. It took eight minutes for the tubes to go through, he told them. Eight minutes of hard X-rays being about as much as an egg can stand. A few died; of the rest, the least susceptible divided into two; most put out four buds; some eight; all were returned to the incubators, where the buds began to develop; then, after two days, were suddenly chilled, chilled and checked. Two, four, eight, the buds in their turn budded; and having budded were dosed almost to death with alcohol; consequently burgeoned again and having budded—bud out of bud out of bud—were thereafter—further arrest being generally fatal—left to develop in peace. By which time the original egg was in a fair way to becoming anything from eight to ninety-six embryos—a prodigious improvement, you will agree, on nature. Identical twins—but not in piddling twos and threes as in the old viviparous days, when an egg would sometimes accidentally divide; actually by dozens, by scores at a time.

"Scores," the Director repeated and flung out his arms, as though he were distributing largesse. "Scores."

But one of the students was fool enough to ask where the advantage lay.

"My good boy!" The Director wheeled sharply round on him. "Can't you see? Can't you *see?*" He raised a hand; his expression was solemn. "Bokanovsky's Process is one of the major instruments of social stability!"

Major instruments of social stability.

Standard men and women; in uniform batches. The whole of a small factory staffed with the products of a single bokanovskified egg.

"Ninety-six identical twins working ninety-six identical machines!" The voice was almost tremulous with enthusiasm. "You really know where you are. For the first time in history." He quoted the planetary motto. "Community, Identity, Stability." Grand words. "If we could bokanovskify indefinitely the whole problem would be solved."

Solved by standard Gammas, unvarying Deltas, uniform Epsilons. Millions of identical twins. The principle of mass production at last applied to biology.

"But, alas," the Director shook his head, "we *can't* bokanovskify indefinitely."

Ninety-six seemed to be the limit; seventy-two a good average. From the same ovary and with gametes of the same male to manufacture as many batches of identical twins as possible—that was the best (sadly a second best) that they could do. And even that was difficult.

"For in nature it takes thirty years for two hundred eggs to reach maturity. But our business is to stabilize the population at this moment, here and now. Dribbling out twins over a quarter of a century—what would be the use of that?"

Obviously, no use at all. But Podsnap's Technique had immensely accelerated the process of ripening. They could make sure of at least a hundred and fifty mature eggs within two years. Fertilize and bokanovskify —in other words, multiply by seventy-two—and you get an average of nearly eleven thousand brothers and sisters in a hundred and fifty batches of identical twins, all within two years of the same age.

"And in exceptional cases we can make one ovary yield us over fifteen thousand adult individuals."

Beckoning to a fair-haired, ruddy young man who happened to be passing at the moment, "Mr. Foster," he called. The ruddy young man approached. "Can you tell us the record for a single ovary, Mr. Foster?"

"Sixteen thousand and twelve in this Centre," Mr. Foster replied without hesitation. He spoke very quickly, had a vivacious blue eye, and took an evident pleasure in quoting figures. "Sixteen thousand and twelve; in one hundred and eighty-nine batches of identicals. But of course they've done much better," he rattled on, "in some of the tropical Centres. Singapore has often produced over sixteen thousand five hundred; and Mombasa has actually touched the seventeen thousand mark. But then they have unfair advantages. You should see the way a negro ovary responds to pituitary! It's quite astonishing, when you're used to working with European material. Still," he added, with a laugh (but the light of combat was in his eyes and the lift of his chin was challenging), "still, we mean to beat them if we can. I'm working on a wonderful Delta-Minus ovary at this moment. Only just eighteen months old. Over twelve thousand seven hundred children already, either decanted or in embryo. And still going strong. We'll beat them yet."

"That's the spirit I like!" cried the Director, and clapped Mr. Foster on the shoulder. "Come along with us, and give these boys the benefit of your expert knowledge."

Mr. Foster smiled modestly. "With pleasure." They went.

In the Bottling Room all was harmonious bustle and ordered activity. Flaps of fresh sow's peritoneum ready cut to the proper size came shooting up in little lifts from the Organ Store in the sub-basement. Whizz and then, click! the lift-hatches flew open; the bottle-liner had only to reach out a hand, take the flap, insert, smooth-down, and before the lined bottle had had time to travel out of reach along the endless band, whizz, click! another flap of peritoneum had shot up from the depths, ready to be slipped into yet another bottle, the next of that slow interminable procession on the band.

Next to the Liners stood the Matriculators. The procession advanced; one by one the eggs were transferred from their test-tubes to the larger containers; deftly the peritoneal lining was slit, the morula dropped into place, the saline solution poured in . . . and already the bottle had passed, and it was the turn of the labellers. Heredity, date of fertilization, membership of Bokanovsky Group—details were transferred from test-tube to bottle. No longer anonymous, but named, identified, the procession marched slowly on; on through an opening in the wall, slowly on into the Social Predestination Room.

"Eighty-eight cubic metres of card-index," said Mr. Foster with relish, as they entered.

"Containing *all* the relevant information," added the Director.

"Brought up to date every morning."

"And co-ordinated every afternoon."

"On the basis of which they make their calculations."

"So many individuals, of such and such quality," said Mr. Foster.

"Distributed in such and such quantities."

"The optimum Decanting Rate at any given moment."

"Unforeseen wastages promptly made good."

"Promptly," repeated Mr. Foster. "If you knew the amount of overtime I had to put in after the last Japanese earthquake!" He laughed goodhumouredly and shook his head.

"The Predestinators send in their figures to the Fertilizers."

"Who give them the embryos they ask for."

"And the bottles come in here to be predestined in detail."

"After which they are sent down to the Embryo Store."

"Where we now proceed ourselves."

And opening a door Mr. Foster led the way down a staircase into the basement.

The temperature was still tropical. They descended into a thickening twilight. Two doors and a passage with a double turn insured the cellar against any possible infiltration of the day.

"Embryos are like photograph film," said Mr. Foster waggishly, as he pushed open the second door. "They can only stand red light."

And in effect the sultry darkness into which the students now followed him was visible and crimson, like the darkness of closed eyes on a summer's afternoon. The bulging flanks of row on receding row and tier above tier of bottles glinted with innumerable rubies, and among the rubies moved the dim red spectres of men and women with purple eyes and all the symptoms of lupus. The hum and rattle of machinery faintly stirred the air.

"Give them a few figures, Mr. Foster," said the Director, who was tired of talking.

Mr. Foster was only too happy to give them a few figures.

Two hundred and twenty metres long, two hundred wide, ten high. He pointed upwards. Like chickens drinking, the students lifted their eyes towards the distant ceiling.

Three tiers of racks: ground floor level, first gallery, second gallery.

The spidery steel-work of gallery above gallery faded away in all directions into the dark. Near them three red ghosts were busily unloading demijohns from a moving staircase.

The escalator from the Social Predestination Room.

Each bottle could be placed on one of fifteen racks, each rack, though you couldn't see it, was a conveyor traveling at the rate of thirty-three and a third centimetres an hour. Two hundred and sixty-seven days at eight metres a day. Two thousand one hundred and thirty-six metres in all. One circuit of the cellar at ground level, one on the first gallery, half on the second, and on the two hundred and sixty-seventh morning, daylight in the Decanting Room. Independent existence—so called.

"But in the interval," Mr. Foster concluded, "we've managed to do a lot to them. Oh, a very great deal." His laugh was knowing and triumphant.

"That's the spirit I like," said the Director once more. "Let's walk around. You tell them everything, Mr. Foster."

Mr. Foster duly told them.

Told them of the growing embryo on its bed of peritoneum. Made them taste the rich blood-surrogate on which it fed. Explained why it had to be stimulated with placentin and thyroxin. Told them of the *corpus luteum* extract. Showed them the jets through which at every twelfth metre from zero to 2040 it was automatically injected. Spoke of those gradually increasing doses of pituitary administered during the final ninety-six metres of their course. Described the artificial maternal circulation installed in every bottle at Metre 112; showed them the reservoir of blood-surrogate, the centrifugal pump that kept the liquid moving over the placenta and drove it through the synthetic lung and waste product filter. Referred to the embryo's troublesome tendency to anaemia, to the massive doses of hog's stomach extract and foetal foal's liver with which, in consequence, it had to be supplied.

Showed them the simple mechanism by means of which, during the last two metres out of every eight, all the embryos were simultaneously shaken into familiarity with movement. Hinted at the gravity of the so-called "trauma of decanting," and enumerated the precautions taken to minimize, by a suitable training of the bottled embryo, that dangerous shock. Told them of the test for sex carried out in the neighborhood of Metre 200. Explained the system of labelling—a T for the males, a circle for the females and for those who were destined to become freemartins a question mark, black on a white ground.

"For of course," said Mr. Foster, "in the vast majority of cases, fertility is merely a nuisance. One fertile ovary in twelve hundred—that would really be quite sufficient for our purposes. But we want to have a good choice. And of course one must always have an enormous margin of safety. So we allow as many as thirty per cent of the female embryos to develop normally. The others get a dose of male sex-hormone every twenty-four metres for the rest of the course. Result: they're decanted as freemartins—structurally quite normal (except," he had to admit, "that they *do* have the slightest tendency to grow beards), but sterile. Guaranteed sterile. Which brings us at last," continued Mr. Foster, "out of the realm of mere slavish imitation of nature into the much more interesting world of human invention."

He rubbed his hands. For of course, they didn't content themselves with merely hatching out embryos: any cow could do that.

"We also predestine and condition. We decant our babies as socialized human beings, as Alphas or Epsilons, as future sewage workers or future . . ." He was going to say "future World controllers," but correcting himself, said "future Directors of Hatcheries," instead.

The D.H.C. acknowledged the compliment with a smile.

They were passing Metre 320 on Rack 11. A young Beta-Minus mechanic was busy with screw-driver and spanner on the blood-surrogate pump of a passing bottle. The hum of the electric motor deepened by fractions of a tone as he turned the nuts. Down, down . . . A final twist, a glance at the revolution counter, and he was done. He moved two paces down the line and began the same process on the next pump.

"Reducing the number of revolutions per minute," Mr. Foster explained. "The surrogate goes round slower; therefore passes through the lung at longer intervals; therefore gives the embryo less oxygen. Nothing like oxygen-shortage for keeping an embryo below par." Again he rubbed his hands.

"But why do you want to keep the embryo below par?" asked an ingenuous student.

"Ass!" said the Director, breaking a long silence. "Hasn't it occurred to you that an Epsilon embryo must have an Epsilon environment as well as an Epsilon heredity?"

It evidently hadn't occurred to him. He was covered with confusion.

"The lower the caste," said Mr. Foster, "the shorter the oxygen." The first organ affected was the brain. After that the skeleton. At seventy per cent of normal oxygen you got dwarfs. At less than seventy eyeless monsters.

"Who are no use at all," concluded Mr. Foster.

Whereas (his voice became confidential and eager), if they could discover a technique for shortening the period of maturation what a triumph, what a benefaction to Society!

"Consider the horse."

They considered it.

Mature at six; the elephant at ten. While at thirteen a man is not yet sexually mature; and is only full-grown at twenty. Hence, of course, that fruit of delayed development, the human intelligence.

"But in Epsilons," said Mr. Foster very justly, "we don't need human intelligence."

Didn't need and didn't get it. But though the Epsilon mind was mature at ten, the Epsilon body was not fit to work till eighteen. Long years of superfluous and wasted immaturity. If the physical development could be speeded up till it was as quick, say, as a cow's, what an enormous saving to the Community!

"Enormous!" murmured the students. Mr. Foster's enthusiasm was infectious.

He became rather technical; spoke of the abnormal endocrine coordination which made men grow so slowly; postulated a germinal mutation to account for it. Could the effects of this germinal mutation be undone? Could the individual Epsilon embryo be made a revert, by a suitable technique, to the normality of dogs and cows? That was the problem. And it was all but solved.

Pilkington, at Mombasa, had produced individuals who were sexually mature at four and full-grown at six and a half. A scientific triumph. But socially useless. Six-year-old men and women were too stupid to do even Epsilon work. And the process was an all-or-nothing one; either you failed to modify at all, or else you modified the whole way. They were still trying to find the ideal compromise between adults of twenty and adults of six. So far without success. Mr. Foster sighed and shook his head.

Their wanderings through the crimson twilight had brought them to the neighborhood of Metre 170 on Rack 9. From this point onwards Rack 9 was enclosed and the bottles performed the remainder of their journey in a kind of tunnel, interrupted here and there by openings two or three metres wide.

"Heat conditioning," said Mr. Foster.

Hot tunnels alternated with cool tunnels. Coolness was wedded to discomfort in the form of hard X-rays. By the time they were decanted the embryos had a horror of cold. They were predestined to emigrate to the tropics, to be miners and acetate silk spinners and steel workers. Later on their minds would be made to endorse the judgment of their bodies. "We condition them to thrive on heat," concluded Mr. Foster. "Our colleagues upstairs will teach them to love it."

"And that," put in the Director sententiously, "that is the secret of happiness and virtue—liking what you've *got* to do. All conditioning aims at that: making people like their unescapable social destiny."

In a gap between two tunnels, a nurse was delicately probing with a long fine syringe into the gelatinous contents of a passing bottle. The students and their guides stood watching her for a few moments in silence.

"Well, Lenina," said Mr. Foster, when at last she withdrew the syringe and straightened herself up.

The girl turned with a start. One could see that, for all the lupus and the purple eyes, she was uncommonly pretty.

"Henry!" Her smile flashed redly at him—a row of coral teeth.

"Charming, charming," murmured the Director and, giving her two or three little pats, received in exchange a rather deferential smile for himself.

"What are you giving them?" asked Mr. Foster, making his tone very professional.

"Oh, the usual typhoid and sleeping sickness."

"Tropical workers start being inoculated at Metre 150," Mr. Foster explained to the students. "The embryos still have gills. We immunize the fish against the future man's diseases." Then, turning back to Lenina, "Ten to five on the roof this afternoon," he said, "as usual."

"Charming," said the Director once more, and, with a final pat, moved away after the others.

On Rack 10 rows of next generation's chemical workers were being trained in the toleration of lead, caustic soda, tar, chlorine. The first of a batch of two hundred and fifty embryonic rocket-plane engineers was just passing the eleven hundred metre mark on Rack 3. A special mechanism kept their containers in constant rotation. "To improve their sense of balance," Mr. Foster explained. "Doing repairs on the outside of a rocket in mid-air is a ticklish job. We slacken off the circulation when they're right way up, so that they're half starved, and double the flow of surrogate when they're upside down. They learn to associate topsy-turvydom with well-being; in fact, they're only truly happy when they're standing on their heads.

"And now," Mr. Foster went on, "I'd like to show you some very interesting conditioning for Alpha Plus Intellectuals. We have a big batch of them on Rack 5. First Gallery level," he called to two boys who had started to go down to the ground floor.

"They're round about Metre 900," he explained. "You can't really do any useful intellectual conditioning till the foetuses have lost their tails. Follow me."

But the Director had looked at his watch. "Ten to three," he said. "No time for the intellectual embryos, I'm afraid. We must go up to the Nurseries before the children have finished their afternoon sleep."

Mr. Foster was disappointed. "At least one glance at the Decanting Room," he pleaded.

"Very well then." The Director smiled indulgently. "Just one glance."

Mr. Foster was left in the Decanting Room. The D.H.C. and his students stepped into the nearest lift and were carried up to the fifth floor.

INFANT NURSERIES. NEO-PAVLOVIAN CONDITIONING ROOMS, announced the notice board.

The Director opened a door. They were in a large bare room, very bright and sunny; for the whole of the southern wall was a single window. Half a dozen nurses, trousered and jacketed in the regulation white viscose-linen uniform, their hair aseptically hidden under white caps, were engaged in setting out bowls of roses in a long row across the floor. Big bowls, packed tight with blossom. Thousands of petals, ripe-blown and silkily smooth, like the cheeks of innumerable little cherubs, but of cherubs, in that bright light, not exclusively pink and Aryan, but also luminously Chinese, also Mexican, also apoplectic with too much blowing of celestial trumpets, also pale as death, pale with the posthumous whiteness of marble.

The nurses stiffened to attention as the D.H.C. came in.

"Set out the books," he said curtly.

In silence the nurses obeyed his command. Between the rose bowls the books were duly set out—a row of nursery quartos opened invitingly each at some gaily coloured image of beast or fish or bird.

"Now bring in the children."

They hurried out of the room and returned in a minute or two, each pushing a kind of tall dumb-waiter laden, on all its four wire-netted shelves, with eight-month-old babies, all exactly alike (a Bokanovsky Group, it was evident) and all (since their caste was Delta) dressed in khaki.

"Put them down on the floor."

The infants were unloaded.

"Now turn them so that they can see the flowers and books."

Turned, the babies at once fell silent, then began to crawl towards those clusters of sleek colours, those shapes so gay and brilliant on the white pages. As they approached, the sun came out of a momentary eclipse behind a cloud. The roses flamed up as though with a sudden passion from within; a new and profound significance seemed to suffuse the shining pages of the books. From the ranks of the crawling babies came little squeals of excitement, gurgles and twitterings of pleasure.

The Director rubbed his hands. "Excellent!" he said. "It might almost have been done on purpose."

The swiftest crawlers were already at their goal. Small hands reached out uncertainly, touched, grasped, unpetaling the transfigured roses, crumpling the illuminated pages of the books. The Director waited until all were happily busy. Then, "Watch carefully," he said. And, lifting his hand, he gave the signal.

The Head Nurse, who was standing by a switchboard at the other end of the room, pressed down a little lever.

There was a violent explosion. Shriller and ever shriller, a siren shrieked. Alarm bells maddeningly sounded.

The children started, screamed; their faces were distorted with terror.

"And now," the Director shouted (for the noise was deafening), "now we proceed to rub in the lesson with a mild electric shock."

He waved his hand again, and the Head Nurse pressed a second lever. The screaming of the babies suddenly changed its tone. There was something desperate, almost insane, about the sharp spasmodic yelps to which they now gave utterance. Their little bodies twitched and stiffened; their limbs moved jerkily as if to the tug of unseen wires.

"We can electrify that whole strip of floor," bawled the Director in explanation. "But that's enough," he signalled to the nurse.

The explosions ceased, the bells stopped ringing, the shriek of the siren died down from tone to tone into silence. The stiffly twitching bodies relaxed, and what had become the sob and yelp of infant maniacs broadened out once more into a normal howl of ordinary terror.

"Offer them the flowers and the books again."

The nurses obeyed; but at the approach of the roses, at the mere sight of those gaily-coloured images of pussy and cock-a-doodle-doo and baa-baa black sheep, the infants shrank away in horror; the volume of their howling suddenly increased.

"Observe," said the Director triumphantly, "observe."

Books and loud noises, flowers and electric shocks—already in the infant mind these couples were compromisingly linked; and after two hundred repetitions of the same or a similar lesson would be wedded indissolubly. What man has joined, nature is powerless to put asunder.

"They'll grow up with what the psychologists used to call an 'instinctive' hatred of books and flowers. Reflexes unalterably conditioned. They'll be safe from books and botany all their lives." The Director turned to his nurses. "Take them away again."

Still yelling, the khaki babies were loaded on to their dumb-waiters and wheeled out, leaving behind them the smell of sour milk and a most welcome silence.

One of the students held up his hand; and though he could see quite well why you couldn't have lower-caste people wasting the Community's time over books, and that there was always the risk of their reading something which might undesirably decondition one of their reflexes, yet . . . well, he couldn't understand about the flowers. Why go to the trouble of making it psychologically impossible for Deltas to like flowers?

Patiently the D.H.C. explained. If the children were made to scream at the sight of a rose, that was on grounds of high economic policy. Not so very long ago (a century or thereabouts), Gammas, Deltas, even Epsilons, had been conditioned to like flowers—flowers in particular and wild nature in general. The idea was to make them want to be going out into the country at every available opportunity, and so compel them to consume transport.

"And didn't they consume transport?" asked the student.

"Quite a lot," the D.H.C. replied. "But nothing else."

Primroses and landscapes, he pointed out, have one grave defect: they are gratuitous. A love of nature keeps no factories busy. It was decided to abolish the love of nature, at any rate among the lower classes; to abolish the love of nature, but *not* the tendency to consume transport. For of course it was essential that they should keep on going to the country, even though they hated it. The problem was to find an economically sounder reason for consuming transport than a mere affection for primroses and landscapes. It was duly found.

"We condition the masses to hate the country," concluded the Director. "But simultaneously we condition them to love all country sports. At the same time, we see to it that all country sports shall entail the use of elaborate apparatus. So that they consume manufactured articles as well as transport. Hence those electric shocks."

"I see," said the student, and was silent, lost in admiration.

There was a silence; then, clearing his throat, "Once upon a time," the Director began, "while our Ford was still on earth, there was a little boy called Reuben Rabinovitch. Reuben was the child of Polish-speaking parents." The Director interrupted himself. "You know what Polish is, I suppose?"

"A dead language."

"Like French and German," added another student, officiously showing off his learning.

"And 'parent'?" questioned the D.H.C.

There was an uneasy silence. Several of the boys blushed. They had not yet learned to draw the significant but often very fine distinction between smut and pure science. One, at last, had the courage to raise a hand.

"Human beings used to be . . ." he hesitated; the blood rushed to his checks. "Well, they used to be viviparous."

"Quite right." The Director nodded approvingly.

"And when the babies were decanted . . ."

" 'Born,' " came the correction.

"Well, then they were the parents—I mean, not the babies, of course; the other ones." The poor boy was overwhelmed with confusion.

"In brief," the Director summed up, "the parents were the father and the mother." The smut that was really science fell with a crash into the boys' eye-avoiding silence. "Mother," he repeated loudly rubbing in the science; and, leaning back in his chair, "These," he said gravely, "are unpleasant facts; I know it. But then most historical facts *are* unpleasant."

He returned to Little Reuben—to Little Reuben, in whose room, one evening, by an oversight, his father and mother (crash, crash!) happened to leave the radio turned on.

("For you must remember that in those days of gross viviparous reproduction, children were always brought up by their parents and not in State Conditioning Centres.")

While the child was asleep, a broadcast programme from London suddenly started to come through; and the next morning, to the astonishment of his crash and crash (the more daring of the boys ventured to grin at one another), Little Reuben woke up repeating word for word a long lecture by that curious old writer ("one of the very few whose works have been permitted to come down to us"), George Bernard Shaw, who was speaking, according to a well-authenticated tradition, about his own genius. To Little Reuben's wink and snigger, this lecture was, of course, perfectly incomprehensible and, imagining that their child had suddenly gone mad, they sent for a doctor. He, fortunately, understood English, recognized the discourse as that which Shaw had broadcasted the previous evening, realized the significance of what had happened, and sent a letter to the medical press about it.

"The principle of sleep-teaching, or hypnopædia, had been discovered." The D.H.C. made an impressive pause.

The principle had been discovered; but many, many years were to elapse before that principle was usefully applied.

"The case of Little Reuben occurred only twenty-three years after Our Ford's first T-Model was put on the market." (Here the Director made a sign of the T on his stomach and all the students reverently followed suit.) "And yet . . ."

Furiously the students scribbled. *"Hypnopædia, first used officially in A. F. 214. Why not before? Two reasons. (a) . . ."*

"These early experimenters," the D.H.C. was saying, "were on the wrong track. They thought that hypnopædia could be made an instrument of intellectual education . . ."

(A small boy asleep on his right side, the right arm stuck out, the right hand hanging limp over the edge of the bed. Through a round grating in the side of a box a voice speaks softly.

"The Nile is the longest river in Africa and the second in length of all the rivers of the globe. Although falling short of the length of the Mississippi-Missouri, the Nile is at the head of all rivers as regards the length of its basin, which extends through 35 degrees of latitude . . ."

At breakfast the next morning, "Tommy," some one says, "do you know which is the longest river in Africa?" A shaking of the head. "But don't you remember something that begins: The Nile is the . . ."

"The - Nile - is - the - longest - river - in - Africa - and - the - second - in - length - of - all - the - rivers - of - the - globe . . ." The words come rushing out. "Although - falling - short - of . . ."

"Well now, which is the longest river in Africa?"

The eyes are blank. "I don't know."

"But the Nile, Tommy."

"The - Nile - is - the - longest - river - in - Africa - and - second . . ."

"Then which river is the longest, Tommy?"

Tommy burst into tears. "I don't know," he howls.)

That howl, the Director made it plain, discouraged the earliest investigators. The experiments were abandoned. No further attempt was made to teach children the length of the Nile in their sleep. Quite rightly. You can't learn a science unless you know what it's all about.

"Whereas, if they'd only started on *moral* education," said the Director, leading the way towards the door. The students followed him, desperately scribbling as they walked and all the way up in the lift. "Moral education, which ought never, in any circumstances, to be rational."

"Silence, silence," whispered a loud speaker as they stepped out at the fourteenth floor, and "Silence, silence," the trumpet mouths indefatigably repeated at intervals down every corridor. The students and even the Director himself rose automatically to the tips of their toes. They were Alphas, of course; but even Alphas have been well conditioned. "Silence, silence." All the air of the fourteenth floor was sibilant with the categorical imperative.

Fifty yards of tiptoeing brought them to a door which the Director cautiously opened. They stepped over the threshold into the twilight of a shuttered dormitory. Eighty cots stood in a row against the wall. There was a sound of light regular breathing and a continuous murmur, as of very faint voices remotely whispering.

A nurse rose as they entered and came to attention before the Director.

"What's the lesson this afternoon?" he asked.

"We had Elementary Sex for the first forty minutes," she answered. "But now it's switched over to Elementary Class Consciousness."

The Director walked slowly down the long line of cots. Rosy and relaxed with sleep, eighty little boys and girls lay softly breathing. There was a whisper under every pillow. The D.H.C. halted and, bending over one of the little beds, listened attentively.

"Elementary Class Consciousness, did you say? Let's have it repeated a little louder by the trumpet."

At the end of the room a loud speaker projected from the wall. The Director walked up to it and pressed a switch.

". . . all wear green," said a soft but very distinct voice, beginning in the middle of a sentence, "and Delta Children wear khaki. Oh no, I don't want to play with Delta children. And Epsilons are still worse. They're too stupid to be able to read or write. Besides they wear black, which is such a beastly colour. I'm *so* glad I'm a Beta."

There was a pause; then the voice began again.

"Alpha children wear grey. They work much harder than we do, because they're so frightfully clever. I'm really awfully glad I'm a Beta, because I don't work so hard. And then we are much better than the Gammas and Deltas. Gammas are stupid. They all wear green, and Delta children wear khaki. Oh no, I *don't* want to play with Delta children. And Epsilons are still worse. They're too stupid to be able . . ."

The Director pushed back the switch. The voice was silent. Only its thin ghost continued to mutter from beneath the eighty pillows.

"They'll have that repeated forty or fifty times more before they wake; then again on Thursday, and again on Saturday. A hundred and twenty times three times a week for thirty months. After which they go on to a more advanced lesson."

Roses and electric shocks, the khaki of Deltas and a whiff of asafœtida — wedded indissolubly before the child can speak. But wordless conditioning is crude and wholesale; cannot bring home the finer distinctions, cannot inculcate the more complex courses of behaviour. For that there must be words, but words without reason. In brief, hypnopædia.

"The greatest moralizing and socializing force of all time."

The students took it down in their little books. Straight from the horse's mouth.

Once more the Director touched the switch.

". . . so frightfully clever," the soft, insinuating, indefatigable voice was saying, "I'm really awfully glad I'm a Beta, because . . ."

Not so much like drops of water, though water, it is true, can wear holes in the hardest granite; rather, drops of liquid sealing-wax, drops that adhere, incrust, incorporate themselves with what they fall on, till finally the rock is all one scarlet blob.

"Till at last the child's mind *is* these suggestions, and the sum of the suggestions *is* the child's mind. And not the child's mind only. The adult's

mind too—all his life long. The mind that judges and desires and decides
—made up of these suggestions. But all these suggestions are *our* suggestions!'' The Director almost shouted in his triumph. ''Suggestions from the
State.'' He banged the nearest table. ''It therefore follows . . .''

A noise made him turn round.

''Oh, Ford!'' he said in another tone, ''I've gone and woken the children.''

Outside, in the garden, it was playtime. Naked in the warm June sunshine,
six or seven hundred little boys and girls were running with shrill yells
over the lawns, or playing ball games, or squatting silently in twos and
threes among the flowering shrubs. The roses were in bloom, two nightin-
gales soliloquized in the boskage, a cuckoo was just going out of tune
among the lime trees. The air was drowsy with the murmur of bees and
helicopters.

The Director and his students stood for a short time watching a game
of Centrifugal Bumble-puppy. Twenty children were grouped in a circle
round a chrome steel tower. A ball thrown up so as to land on the platform
at the top of the tower rolled down into the interior, fell on a rapidly re-
volving disk, was hurled through one or other of the numerous apertures
pierced in the cyclindrical casing, and had to be caught.

''Strange,'' mused the Director, as they turned away, ''strange to think
that even in Our Ford's day most games were played without more apparatus than a ball or two and a few sticks and perhaps a bit of netting. Imagine
the folly of allowing people to play elaborate games which do nothing
whatever to increase consumption. It's madness. Nowadays the Controllers
won't approve of any new game unless it can be shown that it requires at
least as much apparatus as the most complicated of existing games.'' He
interrupted himself.

''That's a charming little group,'' he said, pointing.

In a little grassy bay between tall clumps of Mediterranean heather,
two children, a little boy of about seven and a little girl who might have
been a year older, were playing, very gravely and with all the focussed attention of scientists intent on a labour of discovery, a rudimentary sexual
game.

''Charming, charming!'' the D.H.C. repeated sentimentally.

''Charming,'' the boys politely agreed. But their smile was rather pa-
tronizing. They had put aside similar childish amusements too recently to
be able to watch them now without a touch of contempt. Charming? but it
was just a pair of kids fooling about; that was all. Just kids.

''I always think,'' the Director was continuing in the same rather maud-
lin tone, when he was interrupted by a loud boo-hooing.

From a neighbouring shrubbery emerged a nurse, leading by the hand
a small boy, who howled as he went. An anxious-looking little girl trotted
at her heels.

''What's the matter?'' asked the Director.

The nurse shrugged her shoulders. ''Nothing much,'' she answered.
''It's just that this little boy seems rather reluctant to join in the ordinary

erotic play. I'd noticed it once or twice before. And now again to-day. He started yelling just now . . ."

"Honestly," put in the anxious-looking little girl, "I didn't mean to hurt him or anything. Honestly."

"Of course you didn't, dear," said the nurse reassuringly. "And so," she went on, turning back to the Director, "I'm taking him in to see the Assistant Superintendent of Psychology. Just to see if anything's at all abnormal."

"Quite right," said the Director. "Take him in. You stay here, little girl," he added, as the nurse moved away with her still howling charge. "What's your name?"

"Polly Trotsky."

"And a very good name too," said the Director. "Run away now and see if you can find some other little boy to play with."

The child scampered off into the bushes and was lost to sight.

"Exquisite little creature!" said the Director, looking after her. Then, turning to his students, "What I'm going to tell you now," he said, "may sound incredible. But then, when you're not accustomed to history, most facts about the past *do* sound incredible."

He let out the amazing truth. For a very long period before the time of Our Ford, and even for some generations afterwards, erotic play between children had been regarded as abnormal (there was a roar of laughter); and not only abnormal, actually immoral (no!): and had therefore been rigorously suppressed.

A look of astonished incredulity appeared on the faces of his listeners. Poor little kids not allowed to amuse themselves? They could not believe it.

"Even adolescents," the D.H.C. was saying, "even adolescents like yourselves . . ."

"Not possible!"

"Barring a little surreptitious auto-erotism and homosexuality — absolutely nothing."

"*Nothing?*"

"In most cases, till they were over twenty years old."

"Twenty years old?" echoed the students in a chorus of loud disbelief.

"Twenty," the Director repeated. "I told you that you'd find it incredible."

"But what happened?" they asked. "What were the results?"

"The results were terrible." A deep resonant voice broke startlingly into the dialogue.

They looked around. On the fringe of the little group stood a stranger —a man of middle height, black-haired, with a hooked nose, full red lips, eyes very piercing and dark. "Terrible," he repeated.

The D.H.C. had at that moment sat down on one of the steel and rubber benches conveniently scattered through the gardens; but at the sight of the stranger, he sprang to his feet and darted forward, his hand outstretched, smiling with all his teeth, effusive.

"Controller! What an unexpected pleasure! Boys, what are you thinking of? This is the Controller; this is his fordship, Mustapha Mond."

In the latter part of the novel, the Savage, a native of the "uncivilized" world of Indians and half-breeds who live in an isolated area reserved for those allowed to preserve such "repulsive habits and customs" as marriage, Christianity, and traditional liberal education, is granted an interview with the Controller of the utopia, his fordship, Mustapha Mond. The following dialogue ensues:

The Savage was silent for a little. "All the same," he insisted obstinately, "*Othello's* good, *Othello's* better than those feelies."*

"Of course it is," the Controller agreed. "But that's the price we have to pay for stability. You've got to choose between happiness and what people used to call high art. We've sacrificed the high art. We have the feelies and the scent organ instead."

"But they don't mean anything."

"They mean themselves; they mean a lot of agreeable sensations to the audience."

"But they're . . . they're told by an idiot."

The Controller laughed. "You're not being very polite to your friend, Mr. Watson. One of your most distinguished Emotional Engineers." . . .

The Savage shook his head. "It all seems to me quite horrible."

"Of course it does. Actual happiness always looks pretty squalid in comparison with the over-compensations for misery. And, of course, stability isn't nearly so spectacular as instability. And being contented has none of the glamour of a good fight against misfortune, none of the picturesqueness of a struggle with temptation, or a fatal overthrow by passion or doubt. Happiness is never grand . . . .

"I see you don't like our Bokanovsky Groups; but, I assure you, they're the foundation on which everything else is built. They're the gyroscope that stabilizes the rocket plane of state on its unswerving course." The deep voice thrillingly vibrated; the gesticulating hand implied all space and the onrush of the irresistible machine. Mustapha Mond's oratory was almost up to synthetic standards.

"I was wondering," said the Savage, "why you had them at all—seeing that you can get whatever you want out of those bottles. Why don't you make everybody an Alpha Double Plus while you're about it?"

Mustapha Mond laughed. "Because we have no wish to have our throats cut," he answered. "We believe in happiness and stability. A society of Alphas couldn't fail to be unstable and miserable. Imagine a factory staffed by Alphas—that is to say by separate and unrelated individuals of good heredity and conditioned so as to be capable (within limits) of making a free choice and assuming responsibilities. Imagine it!" he repeated.

The Savage tried to imagine it, not very successfully.

"It's an absurdity. An Alpha-decanted, Alpha-conditioned man would go mad if he had to do Epsilon Semi-Moron work—go mad, or start smash-

---

*The "feelies" are movies augmented with stereoscopic vision, stereophonic sound, and appropriate sorts of sensory-kinesthetic stimulation. They are usually accompanied by synchronized stimulation from the scent organ, an instrument designed to interweave the appropriate odors and blends of odors to the action at hand.

ing things up. Alphas can be completely socialized—but only on condition that you make them do Alpha work. Only an Epsilon can be expected to make Epsilon sacrifices, for the good reason that for him they aren't sacrifices; they're the line of least resistance. His conditioning has laid down rails along which he's got to run. He can't help himself; he's foredoomed. Even after decanting, he's still inside a bottle—an invisible bottle of infantile and embryonic fixations. Each one of us, of course," the Controller meditatively continued, "goes through life inside a bottle. But if we happen to be Alphas, our bottles are, relatively speaking, enormous. We should suffer acutely if we were confined in a narrower space. You cannot pour upper-caste champagne-surrogate into lower-caste bottles. It's obvious theoretically. But it has also been proved in actual practice. The result of the Cyprus experiment was convincing."

"What was that?" asked the Savage.

Mustapha Mond smiled. "Well, you can call it an experiment in rebottling if you like. It began in A.F. 473. The Controllers had the island of Cyprus cleared of all its existing inhabitants and re-colonized with a specially prepared batch of twenty-two thousand Alphas. All agricultural and industrial equipment was handed over to them and they were left to manage their own affairs. The result exactly fulfilled all the theoretical predictions. The land wasn't properly worked; there were strikes in all the factories; the laws were set at naught, orders disobeyed; all the people detailed for a spell of low-grade work were perpetually intriguing for high-grade jobs, and all the people with high-grade jobs were counter-intriguing at all costs to stay where they were. Within six years they were having a first-class civil war. When nineteen out of the twenty-two thousand had been killed, the survivors unanimously petitioned the World Controllers to resume the government of the island. Which they did. And that was the end of the only society of Alphas that the world has ever seen."

The Savage sighed, profoundly.

"The optimum population," said Mustapha Mond, "is modelled on the iceberg—eight-ninths below the water line, one-ninth above."

"And they're happy below the water line?"

"Happier than above it. Happier than your friend here, for example." He pointed.

"In spite of that awful work?"

"Awful? *They* don't find it so. On the contrary, they like it. It's light, it's childishly simple. No strain on the mind or the muscles. Seven and a half hours of mild, unexhausting labour, and then the *soma*† ration and games and unrestricted copulation and the feelies. What more can they ask for? True," he added, "they might ask for shorter hours. And of course we could give them shorter hours. Technically, it would be perfectly simple to reduce all lower-caste working hours to three or four a day. But would they be any the happier for that? No, they wouldn't. The experiment was tried, more than a century and a half ago. The whole of Ireland was put on to the four-hour day. What was the result? Unrest and a large increase in the consumption of *soma*; that was all. Those three and a half hours of extra leisure were

---

†"*Soma*" is a combination tranquilizer and euphoric drug which is used as a central instrument for social control in the Brave New World.

so far from being a source of happiness, that people felt constrained to take a holiday from them. The Inventions Office is stuffed with plans for labour-saving processes. Thousands of them." Mustapha Mond made a lavish gesture. "And why don't we put them into execution? For the sake of the labourers; it would be sheer cruelty to afflict them with excessive leisure. It's the same with agriculture. We could synthesize every morsel of food, if we wanted to. But we don't. We prefer to keep a third of the population on the land. For their own sakes—because it takes *longer* to get food out of the land than out of a factory. Besides, we have our stability to think of. We don't want to change. Every change is a menace to stability. That's another reason why we're so chary of applying new inventions. Every discovery in pure science is potentially subversive; even science must sometimes be treated as a possible enemy. Yes, even science. . . .

"Yes," Mustapha Mond was saying, "that's another item in the cost of stability. It isn't only art that's incompatible with happiness; it's also science. Science is dangerous; we have to keep it most carefully chained and muzzled. . . .

"I'm interested in truth, I like science. But truth's a menace, science is a public danger. As dangerous as it's been beneficent. It has given us the stablest equilibrium in history. China's was hopelessly insecure by comparison; even the primitive matriarchies weren't steadier than we are. Thanks, I repeat, to science. But we can't allow science to undo its own good work. That's why we so carefully limit the scope of its researches. We don't allow it to deal with any but the most immediate problems of the moment. All other enquiries are most sedulously discouraged. It's curious," he went on after a little pause, "to read what people in the time of Our Ford used to write about scientific progress. They seemed to have imagined that it could be allowed to go on indefinitely, regardless of everything else. Knowledge was the highest good, truth the supreme value; all the rest was secondary and subordinate. True, ideas were beginning to change even then. Our Ford himself did a great deal to shift the emphasis from truth and beauty to comfort and happiness. Mass production demanded the shift. Universal happiness keeps the wheels steadily turning; truth and beauty can't. And, of course, whenever the masses seized political power, then it was happiness rather than truth and beauty that mattered. Still, in spite of everything, unrestricted scientific research was still permitted. People still went on talking about truth and beauty as though they were the sovereign goods. Right up to the time of the Nine Years' War. *That* made them change their tune all right. What's the point of truth or beauty or knowledge when the anthrax bombs are popping all around you? That was when science first began to be controlled—after the Nine Years' War. People were ready to have even their appetites controlled then. Anything for a quiet life. We've gone on controlling ever since. It hasn't been very good for truth, of course. But it's been very good for happiness. One can't have something for nothing. Happiness has got to be paid for . . . ."

"What about self-denial, then? If you had a God, you'd have a reason for self-denial."

"But industrial civilization is only possible when there's no self-denial. Self-indulgence up to the very limits imposed by hygiene and economics. Otherwise the wheels stop turning."

"You'd have a reason for chastity!" said the Savage, blushing a little as he spoke the words.

"But chastity means passion, chastity means neurasthenia. And passion and neurasthenia mean instability. And instability means the end of civilization. You can't have a lasting civilization without plenty of pleasant vices."

"But God's the reason for everything noble and fine and heroic. If you had a God . . ."

"My dear young friend," said Mustapha Mond, "civilization has absolutely no need of nobility or heroism. These things are symptoms of political inefficiency. In a properly organized society like ours, nobody has any opportunities for being noble or heroic. Conditions have got to be thoroughly unstable before the occasion can arise. Where there are wars, where there are divided allegiances, where there are temptations to be resisted, objects of love to be fought for or defended—there, obviously, nobility and heroism have some sense. But there aren't any wars nowadays. The greatest care is taken to prevent you from loving any one too much. There's no such thing as a divided allegiance; you're so conditioned that you can't help doing what you ought to do. And what you ought to do is on the whole so pleasant, so many of the natural impulses are allowed free play, that there really aren't any temptations to resist. And if ever, by some unlucky chance, anything unpleasant should somehow happen, why, there's always soma to give you a holiday from the facts. And there's always soma to calm your anger, to reconcile you to your enemies, to make you patient and long-suffering. In the past you could only accomplish these things by making a great effort and after years of hard moral training. Now, you swallow two or three half-gramme tablets, and there you are. Anybody can be virtuous now. You can carry at least half your mortality about in a bottle. Christianity without tears—that's what soma is." . . .

"What you need," the Savage went on, "is something with tears for a change. Nothing costs enough here."

("Twelve and a half million dollars," Henry Foster had protested when the Savage told him that. "Twelve and a half million—that's what the new Conditioning Centre cost. Not a cent less.")

"Exposing what is mortal and unsure to all that fortune, death and danger dare, even for an eggshell. Isn't there something in that?" he asked, looking up at Mustapha Mond. "Quite apart from God—though of course God would be a reason for it. Isn't there something in living dangerously?"

"There's a great deal in it," the Controller replied. "Men and women must have their adrenals stimulated from time to time."

"What?" questioned the Savage, uncomprehending.

"It's one of the conditions of perfect health. That's why we've made the V.P.S. treatments compulsory."

"V.P.S.?"

"Violent Passion Surrogate. Regularly once a month. We flood the whole system with adrenin. It's the complete physiological equivalent of fear and rage. All the tonic effects of murdering Desdemona and being murdered by Othello, without any of the inconveniences."

HAROLD ROSENBERG

Harold Rosenberg's essays have appeared in various literary and art periodicals. His interests are extensive and deal with such disparate topics as politics, poetry, and painting. His book The Tradition of the New *is a collection of nineteen of his critical essays which have appeared separately.*

The Orgamerican Phantasy

America masks its terrors behind patterns of fact. Here the intolerable discloses its presence not in the grimaces of comedy or tragedy but in the bland citations of the scientific report. Since the War, no novel or play has given body to the larger disturbances of the American consciousness. Literature, one hears, is dead, or too enfeebled to risk arduous adventures. Nevertheless, documents keep appearing that touch upon apprehensions equal to any in the history of men: computations of the daily incidence of outlawed sex in America's bedrooms; records of scientific sadism practiced by governments and their programs to transform the will of individuals; estimates by atomic technicians of the flimsiness of the earth and of the natural shape of the human body. When phenomena of this order are explored in a work of the imagination, its author tends to be exiled to the colony of "morbid intellectuals." Given the form of the report or survey, and authorized by the rhetoric of the professions, the most alarming topics overcome the handicap of their profundity and enter into the conversation of solid men of affairs.

Among the grand metaphysical themes of this decade, the one that has proved perhaps most fascinating and persistent has been that of "alienation"—the loss by the individual of personal identity through the operation of social processes. The tone of the post-war imagination was set by Orwell's *1984*; since the appearance of that work, "the dehumanized collective that so haunts our thoughts" (as Mr. William H. Whyte, Jr. calls it in *The Organization Man*) has been a topic for the best-seller lists.

Orwell's melodrama of the pulverized ego was a work of fiction. But Orwell was a Briton; besides *1984* could be read as a description of life in Stalin's Russia or in a future Labor Party England, rather than of the destiny of America. Of U.S. storytellers who essayed to raise the same spectre, none achieved large public impact. Americans awoke to the menace of robotization when it passed from the fiction-writer's yarn to the testimony of the sociologist and cultural anthropologist. Riesman's *The Lonely Crowd*, with its "other-directed" hero-victims of automobile showrooms and PTA meetings, left no doubt that the familiar feeling of being someone else was not a mere after-effect of seeing the wrong movie. Spectorsky's *The Exurbanites*, Whyte's *The Organization Man*, Mills' *White Collar*, Packard's *The Hidden Persuaders* filled in important details of personnel, locale and method. Like The Man With The Bomb That Can Blow Up The World, The Creature That Lost Himself ceased to be a reflection of the dream-maker's art, or a literary construction of the philosophical moralist, and emerged as a statistical probability from the file-cards of the social scientist.

It goes without saying that the Other-Directed Man, The Exurbanite, the Organization Man, is a *type*, that is to say, the personification of a behavior system, on the order of, say, Sinclair Lewis' Babbitt. In this respect the difference between the sociologist and the novelist reduces itself to the fact that Riesman explains that he is writing about "social characters" and devotes his book to analyzing what they do, while Lewis trots Babbitt out on the stage and has him do it.

The type or character is deficient in individuality *by definition*. Said Strindberg: "The word 'character' . . . became the middle-class expression for the automaton. An individual who had once for all become fixed in his natural disposition, or had adapted himself to some definite role in life —who, in fact, had ceased to grow—was called a character . . . This middle-class conception of the immobility of the soul was transferred to the stage, where the middle class has always ruled."

Since the immobility or eternal fixedness of the present-day American social type—let us nickname him the Orgman—is presented as something new, in contrast to the dynamism and inwardness of the Inner-Directed Man (Riesman) or the Protestant Ethic Person (Whyte) of the nineteenth century, let us keep in mind Strindberg's point that the image of the person who is identical with his social role has been with us for centuries.

Automata of manners are a feature of traditional literature, as the true automaton, the Golem, Homunculus, Frankenstein, is a familiar figure of mythology and folklore. Most interesting with regard to the type presented by the new American sociology in his relation to the "mechanical man" image conceived by last-century writers as associated with the effects upon human beings of the new machine culture. Poe, in "The Man Who Was Made Up," imagined a person put together from fabricated parts; while Marx built his political philosophy upon the misery and triumph of that human "product of modern industry," the proletariat.

In the current writings, the type that displaces the human person also originates in the productive and distributive machinery of society. The Orgman is further identified with the older literature of industrial alienation by the part of science in his drama. In Marx the key force in historical progress is, of course, science; and it is the scientist of revolution who releases the proletariat upon the world; in *1984* the scientist reappears as the personality-crushing interrogator. Says *The Organization Man*: "The first denominator is scientism;" and goes on to demonstrate the presence in all American institutions of the traditional creator of the mannikin, the "mad scientist," now wearing the guise of the personnel expert, the motivational researcher or some other "soul engineer."

Blood brother to the inhuman "double," the Mr. Hyde, of romantic literature, on the one hand, and to the proletarian of revolutionary socialism, on the other, the Orgman belongs to the latest episode in the saga of the conquest of society by hordes of faceless *directed* men.

Yet the new literature is neither romantic nor revolutionary, and in this lie its most striking characteristics. One no longer hears the metallic lockstep coming closer, like the rising of swarms of beetles or crabs. The enemy of this decade does not come from below. His is neither the face of the ogre over the edge, nor of the ghost behind the window pane. In the muted melodrama of the current sociology, the inhuman does not *invade*. It sits in the living room twisting the TV dial or takes the family for a ride in the two-tone hard-top. It is you.

Recoiling from the outerworld of society's monsters, outcasts, and victims, the analysts of contemporary America center their interest on the majority that benefits from the existing social process. With this shift of attention the spectre has shifted too. The alienated man has left the company town for the suburb; the factory for the office, the drafting room, the lecture hall. The presence within him of the socially constructed Other is, by the testimony of each of our authors, the mark of "the new middle class" man. It is to the absorption of this alter-ego that all his education and training are directed. Says Riesman: "The mass media ask the child to see the world as 'the' child — that is, the other child — sees it." To be inhabited by the abstract social person is what is currently meant by the terms "normal" and "socially adjusted."

The charge that all our social behavior stands as a power over and against us *is a more extreme accusation of existing American society than that of the preceding radicalism.* Implicating *everyone,* without distinction as to social class or function, in a single deepening process of dehumanization, such works as *The Lonely Crowd, The Organization Man, The Hidden Persuaders,* communicate in atmosphere, if not in stated concept, the sinister overtones of a developing totalitarianism from which there is no escape. In this literature with its subdued manners of scientific analysis Orwell keeps springing up like a red devil. *The Hidden Persuaders* features Big Brother on the jacket and promises the reader "a slightly chilly feeling along the spine"; an effect which the blurb for Whyte's volume has already delivered through billing its hero as the man who "not only works for the Organization: he belongs to it." The smiling credit manager you spoke to this morning is a piece of company apparatus like the filing case from which he extracts the card that is you; his human appearance is a disguise and his real name isn't Brown but Agent F-362.

With Marx the conversion of the individual's "living time" into lifeless commodities was restricted to the routine of the wage worker. In the current studies no one who participates in any capacity in the system of production and distribution can escape the vampire that drains him of himself. Differences in class functions have ceased to matter. Even the division between labor and leisure has lost its meaning; for the psychic mortification of the individual takes place not only in and through his work but by means of his participation in any form, public or private, of social life, from churchgoing, to cocktail parties, to his relations with his wife and children. Whyte and Mills put the major emphasis on the job as the ground of estrangement; Spectorsky gives mode of employment and style of leisure about equal play, seeing one as the extension (laboratory?) of the other; Riesman regards the externally controlled psyche as a phenomenon of "the consumer age" — and is supported by the evidence of *The Hidden Persuaders* concerning supermarket penetration-assaults and the cold war against the customer by means of the new psycho-sales weapons. All our authors are at one in conceiving the flattening of personality in America as a universal effect of our interrelated economic and social practices.

What the Orgman-critics expose is not a flaw in society but the injurious realities of its normal everyday life. These, however, are presented in a perspective that denudes them of radical implications. Here "scientific objectivity" has become the disguise of a philosophy of fatalism. The emergence of the Orgman is conceived in terms far more deterministic than those of the "historical materialists." Neither Riesman's "age of consumption" nor Whyte's "Organization" was brought into being by the choice, nor even the need, of anyone, whether individual, class, or nation. The "other-directed society" of the first is a manifestation of the population-curve; the new corporate "collectivism" of the second, of an immanent process of expansion and stratification. The vocabularies chosen by Riesman and Whyte of themselves exclude human intervention, in the future as in the past: you cannot re-direct an other-directed period, any more than you can refill an Orgman with "Protestant Ethic." Even if you could, there would be no point in doing so, since other-direction and the ubiquity of the Organization are necessities of our time.

In any case, the histrionic effect of the new criticism is unmistakable: the bland deadpan of the Objective Observer has definitely replaced the scowl of the radical accuser. For him such words as "capitalist," "class conflict," "profits," "depression" are at once too bulky and needlessly exciting. Since they draw from the same storehouse of material and cultural consumers' goods, all Americans have become "capitalists"; since they are changed into directed beings by their work and social consumption, all have become "proletarianized." On both counts, there is no cause for conflict and a unanimity of interest prevails. All of us, Whyte thinks, will have to revolt. But whatever basis there was for Marx's conception of a metaphysico-political uprising of human machine parts against a minority of opulent personalities has vanished in the universal estrangement.

In the new Organization America there are no fundamental issues, though some old-fashioned people may not yet have gotten rid of the habit of taking sides. To "moralize the flow of words," says Riesman, through which events are apprehended today is a tendency of "the inner-directed person who remains still extant in this period" — which is a marvellously ironical way of saying that you know what is happening only through what you're told about it in the mass media, and that if you care one way or another you merely define yourself as a relic. The deadpan, apparently, is a requisite not only of the analyst of society but of all of us. If Riesman's irony goes unnoticed, as Whyte complains his has, it is because his language is too consistently detached from his subject matter to admit any sense of contrast: Orgprose, too, is deadpan.

Evoking the sinister concept of man as a tool and as an object, the new writing does so in an oddly disembodied and unpainful way. Its tone is one of injury but of injury unsuffered. It would seem that among the "groups," particularly the better-paid ones, that have replaced the classes in Orgamerica, the substitution of a corporate identity for one's own is not the unmixed deprivation it might have been for the twelve-hour-a-day factory hand or for the citizen of the slave state. Before the Orgman can feel put upon, it is only fair that he consider the advantages gained. "It is not," explains Whyte, "the evils of the organization that puzzle him, but its very beneficence." Strange literature which, assembling the proof of society's subversion of both the will and the intelligence of its members, cries out, like the man in the joke, "But good. But good."

When the fear of the unreal becomes mixed with an idyllic dependence on it, a kind of mythic euphoria ensues which is related to the essence of the comic. Chinese folklore is full of the pranks of demons who have shed their awfulness and sit on window-sills and above doorways minding one's business like so many other-directed neighbors. These every-day fiends may be as spiteful on occasion as one of Whyte's integration-specialists, but their troublemaking only adds gaiety to the way the "system" to which they belong achieves its generous aims. The tale of the Orgman has as much in common with dream farce as with the Orwellian torture phantasy. If its hero suffers, it is in the drugged world of *A Midsummer Night's Dream* laden with bodily pleasures and tremors, where, in the words of *The Organization Man*, "the demands for his surrender are constant and powerful, and the more he has come to like the organization the more difficult does he find it to resist these demands, or even to recognize them."

For both radicalism and conservatism, history is a struggle of winners and losers. In the new American scene, everyone has won a fairytale luxury and lost himself. The drama of history has been replaced by a pantomime in which, freed of individual or mass conflicts, bewildered, adjusted beings respond as in a narcosis to mysterious signs, whispers, hints and shocks, which each receives on his Riesman "radar mechanism." The scientific wand-wielder responsible for these psychological pinches and tweaks which inject dream anxieties into their physical serenity is a kind of affable Puck; for even the scientist, since he is necessary, is no longer a real villain; the evil lies rather in his abstract double, "scientism." Riesman and Whyte construct their shadowplay in such a way as to leave no point of resistance. As in Whyte's description quoted above, any struggle against surrender on the part of the individual constitutes a wrestle in a dream. Neither Whyte nor Riesman indicates any direction in which the American person can realize himself in the actual world.

Yet disregarding the nature of the type or "character" as automaton, each holds out the hope that the alter-ego he is describing may some day develop into a human individual. This empty happy-ending is excellent as finale in a farce like *The Three Penny Opera;* as a substitute for protest or for tragic pathos in a portrayal of actual life, such sudden optimism arouses the suspicion of an attempt at ingratiation. Whyte looks forward to a time when "men partially liberated might be tantalized into demanding more" — no doubt by means of mass-persuasion techniques. As for Riesman, he can lift his consumer type out of the trap of "belongingness" only by attaching to him the time-fuse of a self-transforming process: "these developments [the mass distribution of art and literature] suggest to me that the process of taste-exchanging holds the promise of transcending itself and becoming something quite different, and of signally contributing to the development of autonomy in other-directed men." As if one could go from the abstract to the concrete, the automaton to the organism. Our sociologists' remedy for alienation is not "scientism" — it is sorcery.

Extremist but neither radical nor conservative, the Organization criticism is inspired not by a passion for social correction but by nostalgia. A sigh over the lost person mars the phantasy of American unanimity which has supplanted the ideological Passion Plays of Marxian condemnation and conflict. Whyte's memoir on his training in the Vicks Vaporub rugged individualist sales force of "the old days" (the late 'thirties) is the most eloquent and touching passage in this entire literature. The Age of the Giants — alas, gone forever. With Vicks' Richardson extinct, every human degradation may be logically anticipated. Today, the Orgman, the "dominant member of society," still lives among the relics of older types. Tomorrow he will tread the stage alone, in conflict only with himself.

It is the business type of yesterday whom the new social criticism has generalized into its "inner-directed" and "Protestant Ethic" abstraction, and in the name of which it fires its barrages against present-day tendencies. If it takes some daring to bury the boss, it takes less if one also bewails him in public. Especially in a situation where he had much to gain by playing dead. In Whyte's indictment of the human exactions of the Corporation, one hears the voice of the Founder deploring "the drift toward socialization."

Loosed from action, for which it can see no aim, the post-radical criticism often exaggerates its complaints, producing a worse impression of conditions than is warranted by the facts, at the same time that it seeks remedies in the wrong direction. For example, Mills, the most emotionally authentic of these writers, undervalues the personal and social expression of the white-collar worker on the job, with an effect of melancholy that seems unreal when one looks at actual men and women coming out of an office building. On the other hand, the salvation through improvement of taste proposed by Riesman, or through a psychic resistance based on private life (far more impoverished for the clerk than his job) suggested by Whyte, are, as we have seen, equally unreal.

But there is more to the conception of the Orgman than regret for an older social type. As the representative of the new post-War employed intelligentsia, the post-radical critic suffers also a nostalgia for himself as an independent individual. For his former abstract sympathy with a nominal working class, the intellectual of this decade has substituted an examination in the mirror of his own social double as insider of the Organization and the Community. It is what he sees there that has caused him to project a morbid image of society compared with which the old "class struggle" America seems not only naïf but as relatively healthy as a war with rifles and cannons.

For in regard to the misery of alienation, who is a greater victim of what Whyte calls the split "between the individual as he is and the role he is called upon to play" than the member of the intellectual caste newly enlisted *en masse* in carrying out society's functions? As writer, artist, social scientist, he is one with his talents and his education for creative work; in playing his part in the service of the Organization he must eliminate any thought of functioning for himself. Through his personal inventiveness he has in the past fifteen years achieved prosperity and social prestige, yet he is the most dependent of wage earners and the most anxiously conscious of his dependence — *The Exurbanites* chronicles this dependence and anxiety to the last installment dollar. (Applying itself to the narrower spectrum of the commercialized intellectuals, *The Exurbanites* is the most realistic of the works we have been considering.)

The intellectual employee also accepts a more total identification with his role than other workers, in that the editorial director, the designer, the copywriter, etc., sells himself more completely in terms of both psychic energy expended and number of hours worked. With him the division between work and leisure, discipline and freedom, has truly been erased. If the free artist or the founder of a great enterprise builds his life exclusively out of the substance of his work, today's intellectual unbuilds his life in order to live his job.[1]

Besides being the prime victim and exemplar of self-loss in contemporary society, the "organized" professional cannot escape a conviction of guilt for his part in depriving others of their individuality. He has consented to use his capacities as a tool and to approve in practice the proposition recorded by Whyte that "all the great ideas have already been discovered." His skills tend to relate to human management, e.g., writing, image-making, program-forming; even if his specialty is in engineering or the physical sciences, the results of his work directly augment the force by which society is controlled. The intellectual cannot function as Organization Man without also functioning as Organization-Man moulder; as human object he must also affect others as objects; as manipulated act as manipulator. Thus he cannot help but feel himself to be a betrayer of humanity as of his own mind. Helpless to change anything, he is yet the chief culprit of the alienation drama, the driven "scientist," who directs the undermining of the raw individual, whether as motivational expert, inventor of personnel tests, or as preacher of despairing acceptance.

Self-displacement through one's acts is the innermost problem of life in America as of that in all civilized countries. The Social Type has always been among us, of course, despite Riesman's effort to distinguish today's

---

1. The rule quoted by Whyte for corporation executives generally, "You promote the guy who takes his problem home with him," becomes for the intellectual, "You hire the guy who takes his problem to bed with him." His job has a creative side in which his preconscious must also collaborate. Take this into account in computing his average salary, and the difference between the wage-earner of the suburb and of the company town becomes largely a matter of overtime pay. At $2.50 an hour the totally employed intellectual would earn more than $20,000 a year.

other-directed man from his nineteenth-century counterpart. Tolstoy's Ivan Ilych, who decorated his house entirely according to his own original ideas only to have it turn out exactly like all other houses of his class, is as good an example of automatic "radared" taste-exchanging (Riesman) as can be found in Fairfield County. Tolstoy explicitly insisted that Ilych was a socially made-up man, an "object" guided by public opinion, an example of "dead" living.

In the United States nineteenth-century literature, whether in the popular stage comedies of manners or in the symbolism of the romantics, centers on society's human abstractions. We mentioned above Poe's hero who owed to industry his movable parts. A contemporary of this invention was the ubiquitous Salesman-Preacher, whom Melville, writing in a less unctuous age than ours, named the Confidence Man. Like Whyte, Spectorsky and Packard, Melville saw in this professional who supplied his countrymen with things, ideas and feeling, the outstanding specimen of man as social artifice. As his complement, he set up the brooding inner-directed Indian Fighter, paranoiac Ahab of the prairies; while from the silent recesses of the office files, he drew forth the white-collared tomb deity, Bartleby.

What is new in America is not the socially reflexive person but the presence of a self-conscious intellectual caste whose disillusionment has induced its members to volunteer for the part. The predicament in which these individuals find themselves is what casts a bar sinister over their image of America. The fear-augury that the Orgman will become everyone in a quiet, unopposable totalitarianism is not a conclusion based on social analysis but a projection of the fate they have chosen for themselves. The American landscape has by no means been re-made by the "Social Ethic" compression machine into an electrified Eden set out on porcelain grass. Except in the new suburbs, the physical condition of America's cities, towns and villages is of itself proof enough that decay, shiftlessness, egotism and other forms of popular expressionism are more than holding their own against other-direction. Granted that the growth of the supercorporation and the absorption and standardization of small business has changed the independent operator into an agent, at the same time that mechanization has been turning the workman into a technician; granted that Whyte's notation that "the collectivization so visible in the corporation has affected almost every field of work" is indisputable; and that today Orgmen reproduce themselves like fruit flies in whatever is organized, whether it be a political party or a museum of advanced art; given this groundwork for the conquest of America by this "type," still the contention that the nation is, or even might be, subordinated to such a master is at least as ludicrous as it is alarming. The increasing concentration of control and the standardization of work present well-known alternatives which we need not discuss here; but for the individual, the last voice in the issue of being or not being himself is still his own.

The inhabitant of the sacred groves has, however, surrendered all choices. Having accepted self-alienation in trade for social place the post-radical intellectual can see nothing ahead but other-direction and a corporately styled personality. For him the Orgworld has closed for good. Within these limits the deploring of "conformity" is simply an expression of self-pity. The strategy of fighting the organization through secret resistance behind the outer-shaped mask (Whyte) is, by the measure of the ancient intellectual tradition of denunciation or self-exile, only a dreary professional's ruse for holding on to the best of both worlds. That such a proposal should seem relevant is another proof that the Orgman is, with necessary additions and disguise, none else than the new intellectual talking about himself. Certainly the deft management of the corporate Look which solves things for Whyte would be of no help to the farmer or to the workingman, nor would the boss need to make use of it. The "what to do about it" part of the studies of Whyte and Riesman are clearly sermons for their milieu rather than challenges to history in the name of mankind.

The critics of the new America are disheartened by a revolution won —their revolution, which can go no farther than the ending of the underground life of the American intellectual mass through economic recognition of the services it has to offer. With his own success achieved the only issue the intellectual can see as remaining for society is "personality." Somehow, this seems unattainable in "the dehumanized collective" in the building of which he is taking a leading part. The result is depression—and it is by the power of the depression it generates, in contrast to the smugness of the old-time boosting, that the present sociology is a force against a more radical and realistic understanding of American life.

Part 2

ALIENATION, AUTONOMY, AND EDUCATION

Introduction

Closely associated with the various criticisms and analyses directed at the real or imagined shift occurring in American cultural values there has been a growing concern with the problem of alienation—the sense of acute emotional disaffection with the established norms of our culture which seems to be affecting increasing numbers of people. In Part Two a variety of different individuals, representing a variety of different backgrounds, address themselves to the intimately related questions of what alienation *is* and how it *functions* within the context of formal education.

Erich Fromm, in the initial selection "The Sick Individual and the Sick Society," presents the Marxist point of view, which holds that "alienation" occurs when the individual "does not experience himself as the subject of his own acts, as a thinking, feeling, loving person, but he experiences himself only in the things he has created, as the object of the externalized manifestations of his powers. He is in touch with himself only by surrendering himself to the products of his creation."[1] From this point of view, of course, alienation is primarily a social problem. In an "insane society," states Fromm,

> the man who has . . . become subject to his alienated needs is [notes Marx] "a mentally and physically dehumanized being . . . the self-conscious and self-acting commodity." This commodity-man knows only one way of relating himself to the world outside, by having it and by consuming (using) it. The more alienated he is, the more the sense of having and using constitutes his relationship to the world. "The less you are [notes Marx] the less you express your life, the more you have, the greater is your alienated life and the greater is the saving of your alienated being."[2]

All alienation, charges Fromm, is a form of idolatry, a displacement of the real self into objects or idols. "Modern man, in industrial society, has changed the form and intensity of idolatry. He has become the object of blind economic forces which rule his life."[3]

Still another type of alienation is that which arises out of religious idolatry. As Fromm remarks,

> the essential difference between monotheism and polytheism is not one of the numbers of gods, but lies in the fact of alienation . . . . Idolatrous man bows down to the work of his own hands. The idol represents his own life-forces in an alienated form.

---

1. Erich Fromm, *Beyond the Chains of Illusion* (New York: Trident Press, Inc., 1962), p. 44.
2. *Ibid.*, p. 51.
3. *Ibid.*, p. 59.

> *The principle of monotheism, in contrast, is that man is infinite, that there is no partial quality in him which can be hypostatized into the whole. God, in the monotheistic concept, is unrecognizable and undefinable; God is not a "thing."*[4]

Theologian Paul Tillich, in his article "The Person in a Technical Society," is concerned primarily with this latter, or religious, type of alienation as it is reflected in the existentialist rebellion of the subjective self against the depersonalizing forces of modern civilization. "Western technical society," states Tillich,

> *has produced methods of adjusting persons to its demands in production and consumption which are less brutal, but in the long run, more effective than totalitarian suppression. They depersonalize not by commanding but by providing—providing, namely, what makes individual creativity superfluous.*[5]

Elements of both Marxist and existentialist thought can be detected in the writings of anthropologist Jules Henry. "The school," states Henry in his selection "Golden Rule Days: American Schoolrooms," "is an institution for drilling children in cultural orientations."[6] The schools have never been the place for stimulating young minds.

> *The function of education has never been to free the mind and the spirit of man, but to bind them; and to the end that the mind and spirit of his children should never escape* Homo sapiens *has employed praise, ridicule, admonition, accusation, mutilation, and even torture to chain them to the culture pattern. Throughout most of his historic course* Homo sapiens *has wanted from his children acquiescence, not originality . . . . It stands to reason that were young people truly creative the culture would fall apart, for originality, by definition, is different from what is given, and what is given is the culture itself. From the endless, pathetic, "creative hours" of kindergarten to the most abstruse problems in sociology and anthropology, the function of education is to prevent the truly creative intellect from getting out of hand . . . .*

> *Creativity is the last thing wanted in any culture because of its potentialities for disruptive thinking; . . . the primordial dilemma of all education derives from the necessity of training the mighty brain of* Homo sapiens *to be stupid . . . .*

> *The early schooling process is not successful unless it has accomplished in the child an acquiescence in its criteria, unless the child*

---

4. *Ibid.* p. 58.
5. Paul Tillich, "The Person in a Technical Society," in *Christian Faith and Social Action*, ed. John A. Hutchison (New York: Charles Scribner's Sons, 1953), p. 150.
6. Jules Henry, *Culture Against Man* (New York: Random House, Inc., 1963), p. 283.

*wants to think the way school has taught him to think. He must
have accepted alienation as a rule of life . . . .*

*School metamorphoses the child, giving it the kind of Self the
school can manage, and then proceeds to minister to the Self it
has made . . . .*

*In a society where competition for the basic cultural goods is a pivot
of action, people cannot be taught to love one another, for those
who do cannot compete with one another, except in play . . . .*

*School is . . . a training for later life not because it teaches the 3
Rs (more or less), but because it instills the essential cultural nightmare fear of failure, envy of success, and absurdity . . . .*

*Hardboiled critics of the educational system concentrate on curricu-
lum. The teachers know better; the* real, *the persisting subject matter
is noise.*[7]

An educator who appears to be in substantial agreement with Jules Henry
is John Holt. In the selection entitled "Education for Failure," taken from
his book *How Children Fail*, Holt discusses the way in which American education is structured to preclude real success and satisfaction. "The true test
of intelligence," comments Holt, "is not how much we know how to do,
but how we behave when we don't know what to do."[8] True education is
not a product of formal knowledge, the outcome of the usual sort of academic processes. It is basically the outgrowth of proper attitudes, a capacity
to be *psychologically present* to the world. "Nobody starts off stupid," notes
Holt. "What happens is that [the natural capacity for learning and intellectual growth] is destroyed, and more than by any other one thing, by the
process that we misname education—a process that goes on in most homes
and schools."[9]

*We kill, not only their curiosity, but their feeling that it is a good
and admirable thing to be curious, so that by the age of ten most of
them will not ask questions, and will show a good deal of scorn for
the few who do . . . .*

*We turn the vast majority of our students into the kind of people for
whom all symbols are meaningless; who cannot use symbols as a
way of learning about and dealing with reality . . . . The minority,
the able and successful students, we are very likely to turn
into . . . the kind of people who can manipulate words and symbols fluently while keeping themselves largely divorced from the reality for which they stand . . . .*

---

7. *Ibid.,* pp. 286, 288, 291, 292, and 305.
8. John Holt, *How Children Fail* (New York: Dell Publishing Co., Inc., Delta Books, 1964), p. 165.
9. *Ibid.,* p. 167.

When you have acres of paper to fill up with pencil marks, you have no time to waste on the luxury of thinking. By such means children are firmly established in the habit of using only a small part of their thinking capacity. They feel that school is a place where they must spend most of their time doing dull tasks in a dull way. Before long they are deeply settled in a rut of unintelligent behavior from which most of them could not escape even if they wanted to . . . .

The alternative . . . is to have schools and classrooms in which each child in his own way can satisfy his curiosity, develop his abilities and talents, pursue his interests, and from the adults and older children around him get a glimpse of the great variety and richness of life. In short, the school should be a great smörgåsbord of intellectual, artistic, creative, and athletic activities, from which each child could take whatever he wanted, and as much as he wanted, or as little.[10]

In much the same vein, sociologist Edgar Z. Friedenberg, in the selection "An Ideology of School Withdrawal," indicts the schools for encouraging a bland mediocre consensus imposed by authority. At the secondary level of instruction, states Friedenberg, "compulsory school attendance appears as a gross violation of civil liberty: a bill of attainder against a specific age group that guarantees no compensation in return."[11] The high school and junior high school curriculum, he continues, "serves . . . exactly the same purpose as . . . responsive reading."[12]

The function of the school becomes essentially liturgical, not epistemological. It isn't supposed to make sense. It is not appropriate to believe, disbelieve, or test what one is taught in school. Instead, one relates to it; one tries to figure out why this line has been taken rather than another, to figure out what response is expected, and give it.

The result is a peculiar kind of moral vacuity; a limitation of responsible perception, and therefore, of moral behavior, to situations that are wholly concrete and immediate. The public school is not primarily an educational institution. I have forgotten who first said that most Christians would feel equal consternation at hearing Christianity denounced and at seeing it practiced; it ought, presumably, to have been Mary. But I am quite sure that this could justly be said of most Americans with respect to public education. In many ways, the relationship of the school to the community is like that of a TV station that carries mostly network programs but that is largely dependent on local advertising for support. Like the TV station, the

---

10. *Ibid.*, pp. 168, 169, 170, and 180.
11. Edgar Z. Friedenberg, *The Dignity of Youth and Other Atavisms* (Boston: Beacon Press, 1965), p. 137.
12. *Ibid.*, p. 138.

school has its own technical staff, and such autonomy as it possesses is derived from their custody of the mysteries and the records, rather than from any considerable measure of popular deference to their authority. The entertainment provided is frequently high quality and shrewdly geared to the public taste. Concessions to the intellect and culture, provided as a public service, tend to be more ponderous, conventional, and unconvincing. Though the staff likes to boast about how much of this sort of thing they program, they are self-conscious about it, and rather fearful. The commercials for the local way of life are interminable, boring, and egregiously dishonest, and the audience knows it. But they are hard to change, for they are the real basis for the support the school receives. And they are effective, as good commercials are, not so much in stimulating an active desire for the product as in convincing the audience that only a social misfit would be without it.[13]

In this plight, the school people are partly the victims of their own past complicity in the American social order. The American public school and its leadership have, by and large, reflected the anti-intellectualism of their local constituency and have regarded it as their pleasure as well as their clear duty to give the community what those of its members who were in a position to express their wishes in politically effective terms wanted. What they wanted, by and large, was economic advancement and job security; the school was expected to get some youngsters into college and others into jobs, certifying them as loyal, competent, and trouble-free. It also served willingly as the community's trusted and ubiquitous Sitter, and al-tered its conception of the Sitter's role to suit the community's atti-tudes toward youngsters of different ages. The elementary school sits with children and the high school on "teenagers." If this all adds up to a rather limited professional function, the community has seldom demanded more and the profession has seldom challenged it by in-sisting on specifically educational goals of its own.[14]

Still another contemporary thinker who shares many of these misgivings about contemporary American education is teacher-scholar Paul Goodman. In his book *Compulsory Mis-Education*, Goodman takes the position that "education is a natural community function and occurs inevitably . . . ."[15] Our schools are not merely out-of-date, they are "crucially irrelevant." It may well be that the existing schools not only *fail* to educate but even *pre-vent* real education from occurring. We should, states Goodman, abolish

---

13. Edgar Z. Friedenberg, "The School As a Social Environment," *College Admissions 10: The Behavioral Sciences and Education* (New York: College Entrance Examination Board), pp. 25–26. Reprinted by permission.
14. Edgar Z. Friedenberg, "Intimations of Mortality in the Literature of Public Education," *Social Problems*, XI (1964), p. 315. Reprinted by permission.
15. Paul Goodman, *Compulsory Mis-Education* (New York: Random House, Inc., Vintage Books, 1956), p. 16.

compulsory class attendance altogether. "The schools less and less represent *any* human values, but simply adjustment to a mechanical system."[16] "Rather than bourgeois, our schools have become petty-bourgeois, bureaucratic, time-serving, gradgrind-practical, timid, and *nouveau riche* climbing. In the upper grades and colleges, they often exude a cynicism that belongs to rotten aristocrats."[17]

> *With the movies, TV, and radio that the illiterate also share, there is certainly no lack of "communications." We cannot say that as humanities or science, the reading-matter of the great majority is in any way superior to the content of these other media . . . .*

> *Perhaps in the present dispensation we should be as well off if it were socially acceptable for large numbers not to read. It would be harder to regiment people if they were not so well "informed"; as Norbert Wiener used to point out, every repetition of a cliché only increases the noise and* prevents *communication . . . .*

> *Given the amount of exposure that any urban child gets, any normal animal should spontaneously catch on to the code. What prevents? It is almost demonstrable that, for many children, it is precisely going to school that prevents—because of the school's alien style, banning of spontaneous interest, extrinsic rewards and punishments. (In many underprivileged schools, the I.Q. steadily falls the longer they go to school.) Many of the backward readers might have had a better chance on the streets.*[18]

Two educators whose radical ideas about education and child-rearing have elicited widespread comment and generated vast controversy are Mario Montessori, the son of the celebrated Italian educational reformer Dr. Maria Montessori and one of the best-known contemporary spokesmen for the Montessori method, and A. S. Neill, the celebrated headmaster of the progressive English boarding school Summerhill. In the selection "A Discussion of Schools and Child Rearing," these two famous educators discuss their respective positions about the way to rear and educate children.

The Montessori approach is based on the principle of freedom in a prepared environment and features special didactic materials. It focuses on the essential differences between the child and the adult and seeks to maximize spontaneous self-activity which encourages the child to teach himself through guided learning experiences. In the Montessori method strong emphasis is placed on following the natural inner rhythm and tempo of the child's life, and special attention is directed to laying a strong sensorial foundation for later cognitive development.

---

16. *Ibid.*, p. 21.
17. *Ibid.*, p. 22.
18. *Ibid.*, pp. 24, 25, and 26.

Neill's Summerhill is based on the regulatory principle that the child should be allowed total freedom to act as he pleases and therefore to learn whatever he likes providing that this freedom does not degenerate into license which subverts the freedom of others or threatens the physical well-being of the child himself. "Children do not need teaching," states Neill, "as much as they need love and understanding."[19] "The whole idea of Summerhill is release: allowing a child to live out his natural interests."[20] "Our whole educational system," states Neill, "is full of lies, our schools hand on the lie that obedience and industry are virtues, that history and French are education."[21] The time has come for a new kind of education based on new ideas: "Abolish authority. Let the child be himself. Don't push him around. Don't teach him. Don't lecture him. Don't elevate him. Don't force him to do anything."[22]

Central to much of the "new progressivism" in education which is often associated with such individuals as Henry, Holt, Friedenberg, and Neill are a series of radical new ideas that have developed out of contemporary philosophy — particularly existentialism — and out of the philosophical frontiers of contemporary psychology — particularly in the areas of psychotherapy and personality theory. Psychologists Carl R. Rogers and Abraham Maslow discuss some of these ideas in their selections.

Psychotherapist Carl R. Rogers, in his brief article entitled "Personal Thoughts on Teaching and Learning," is fully as radical as A. S. Neill and, in certain respects, perhaps even more so. *"The outcomes of teaching,"* states Rogers, *"are either unimportant or hurtful."*[23] It would be best to do away with teaching altogether. "People would get together if they wished to learn."[24] In the following selection, "Carl R. Rogers and Non-Directive Teaching," educator and philosopher Samuel Tenenbaum discusses his personal reactions to participating in one of Dr. Rogers' "non-directive" classes.

In the realm of speculative psychology — an area which has largely replaced traditional epistemology as the basis for many new developments in philosophy and religion — a thinker who has had a dramatic impact on the intellectual frontiers of modern education is psychologist Abraham Maslow. In the selection "Deficiency Motivation and Growth Motivation," Maslow develops a radical new approach to the motivation dynamics behind human behavior. There are, states Maslow, not one but two basic types of human motivation, deficiency motivation and growth motivation. Using terms adapted from Fromm, he distinguishes between scarcity-pleasure,

---

19. A. S. Neill, *Summerhill: A Radical Approach to Child-Rearing* (New York: Hart Publishing Co., 1960), p. 118.
20. *Ibid.,* p. 114.
21. *Ibid.,* p. 147.
22. *Ibid.,* p. 297.
23. Carl R. Rogers, *On Becoming a Person* (Boston: Houghton Mifflin Company, 1961), p. 276.
24. *Ibid.,* p. 277.

"the 'lower' pleasure of satiation of a need," and abundance-pleasure, "the 'higher' pleasure of production, creation and growth of insight."[25]

> *The psychological life of the person, in many of its aspects, is lived out differently when he is deficiency-need-gratification-bent and when he is growth-dominated or "metamotivated" or growth-motivated or self-actualizing.*[26]

"The deficit-motivated man," continues Maslow,

> *is far more dependent upon other people than is the man who is predominantly growth-motivated. He is more "interested," more needful, more attached, more desirous.*
>
> *This dependency colors and limits interpersonal relations . . . .*
>
> *Fully disinterested, desireless, objective and holistic perception of another human being becomes possible only when nothing is needed from him, only when he is not needed. Idiographic, aesthetic perception of the whole person is far more possible for self-actualizing people (or in moments of self-actualization), and furthermore approval, admiration, and love are based less upon gratitude for usefulness and more upon the objective, intrinsic qualities of the perceived person.*[27]

The second selection by Maslow presents his controversial report "Self-Actualizing People: a Study of Psychological Health." In this selection Maslow takes the position that it is possible, in certain instances, for people to transcend deficiency motivation and to become fully functioning on a higher level of activity. Individuals who go beyond normal "coping" behavior are termed "self-actualizing."

> *Such people become far more self-sufficient and self-contained. The determinants which govern them are now primarily inner ones, rather than social or environmental. They are the laws of their own inner nature, their potentialities and capacities, their talents, their latent resources, their creative impulses, their needs to know themselves and to become more and more integrated and unified, more and more aware of what they really are, of what they really want, of what their call or vocation or fate is to be.*
>
> *Since they depend less on other people, they are less ambivalent about them, less anxious and also less hostile, less needful of their praise*

---

25. Abraham Maslow, *Toward a Psychology of Being* (Princeton, N.J.: Van Nostrand Co., Inc., 1962), p. 30.
26. *Ibid.*, p. 25.
27. *Ibid.*, pp. 33–34.

*and their affection. They are less anxious for honors, prestige and
rewards.*[28]

Perhaps the primary characteristic of self-actualizing people is that they
have a "more efficient perception of reality and more comfortable relation
with it."[29]

> *The self-actualizing person sees reality more clearly: our subjects
> see human nature as it is and not as they would prefer it to be. Their
> eyes see what is before them without being strained through specta-
> cles of various sorts to distort or shape or color the reality.*[30]

> *The neurotic is not only emotionally sick — he is cognitively* wrong!
> *If health and neurosis are, respectively, correct and incorrect per-
> ceptions of reality, propositions of fact and propositions of value
> merge in this area, and in principle, value propositions should then
> be empirically demonstrable rather than merely matters of taste or
> exhortation.*[31]

As a result of this enhanced perceptual acuity, self-actualizing people tend
to be autonomous — "ruled by the laws of their own character rather than
by the rules of society."[32]

---

28. *Ibid.,* p. 32.
29. Abraham Maslow, *Motivation and Personality* (New York: Harper and Brothers, 1954), p. 203.
30. *Ibid.,* p. 207.
31. *Ibid.,* p. 204.
32. *Ibid.,* p. 227.

ERICH FROMM

Erich Fromm is a well-known psychologist and writer. Born in Frankfurt, Germany, Fromm is now an American citizen. He has lectured at a number of prominent universities and colleges, including Yale, Bennington, Michigan State, and the National University of Mexico. His books include Escape from Freedom *(1941),* Man for Himself *(1947),* The Sane Society *(1955),* Beyond the Chains of Illusion *(1963), and* Marx's Concept of Man *(1962).*

The Sick Individual
and the Sick Society

What is the concept of psychic pathology in Freud and in Marx? Freud's concept is well-known. It assumes that if man fails to solve his Oedipus complex, or to put it differently, if man does not overcome his infantile strivings and develop a mature genital orientation, he is torn between the desires of the child within himself and the claims which he makes as a grown-up person. The neurotic symptom represents a compromise between infantile and grown-up needs, while the psychosis is that form of pathology in which the infantile desires and phantasies have flooded the grown-up ego, and thus there is no more compromise between the two worlds.

Marx, of course, never developed a systematic psychopathology, yet he speaks of one form of psychic crippledness which to him is the most fundamental expression of psychopathology and which to overcome is the goal of socialism: *alienation.*[1]

What does Marx mean by alienation (or "estrangement")? The essence of this concept, which was first developed by Hegel, is that the world (nature, things, others, and he himself) have become alien to man. He does not

1. The concept of alienation has become increasingly the focus of the discussion of Marx's ideas in England, France, Germany, and the U. S. A., as well as in Yugoslavia and Poland. The majority of those involved in this debate which includes Protestant and Catholic theologians, as well as humanist socialists take a position that alienation and the task of overcoming it is the center of Marx's socialist humanism and the aim of socialism; furthermore that there is a complete continuity between the young and the mature Marx, in spite of changes in terminology and emphasis (to this group belong, to mention only a few, Rubel, Goldman, Bottomore, Fromm, Petrovic, Markovic, Vranicki, Bloch, Lukacs). Other authors like D. Bell, L. Feuer, and to some extent C. W. Mills have taken the position that alienation is either not a useful, or a central theme in Marx.

experience himself as the subject of his own acts, as a thinking, feeling, loving person, but he experiences himself only in the things he has created, as the object of the externalized manifestations of his powers. He is in touch with himself only by surrendering himself to the products of his creation.

Hegel, taking God as the subject of history, had seen God in man, in a state of self-alienation and in the process of history God's return to himself.

Feuerbach turned Hegel upside down; God, so he thought, represented man's own powers transferred from man, the owner of these powers, to a being outside of him, so that man is in touch with his own powers only by his worship of God; the stronger and richer God is, the weaker and poorer becomes man.

Marx was deeply stirred and influenced by Feuerbach's thought. In his introduction to the *Critique of Hegel's Philosophy of Right* (written toward the end of 1843) he followed Feuerbach in his analysis of alienation. In his *Economic-Philosophical Manuscripts* (1844) Marx proceeded from the phenomenon of *religious alienation* to that of the *alienation of labor*. Parallel to Feuerbach's analysis of religious alienation Marx wrote: "The worker becomes poorer, the more wealth he produces and the more his production increases in power and extent."[2] And a few paragraphs later he wrote: "All these consequences follow from the fact that the worker is related to the *product of his labor* as to an *alien* object. For it is clear on this presupposition that the more the worker expends himself in work, the more powerful becomes the world of objects which he creates in face of himself, the poorer he becomes in his inner life and the less he belongs to himself; it is just the same as in religion. The more of himself man attributes to God the less he has left in himself. The worker puts his life into the object and his life then belongs no longer to himself but to the object. The greater his activity, therefore, the less he possesses . . . . The *alienation* of the worker in his product means not only that his labor becomes an object, assumes an external existence, but that it exists independently, outside himself that it stands opposed to him as an autonomous power. The life which he has given to the object sets itself against him as an alien and hostile force."[3] But, so Marx goes on to say, the worker is not only alienated from the products which he creates; "alienation appears not only in the result, but also in the *process*, of production, within *productive activity* itself."[4] And again he returns to the analogy of alienation in labor with alienation in religion, "Just as in religion the spontaneous activity 'Selbsttaetigkeit' of human fantasy, of the human brain and heart, reacts independently as an alien activity of gods and devils upon the individual, so the activity of the worker is not his own spontaneous activity."[5]

From the concept of alienated work, Marx proceeds to the concept of

---

2. *Economic and Philosophical Manuscripts,* p. 95. It may not be too farfetched to speculate that Marx was influenced in his erroneous theory of the increasing impoverishment of the worker in the process of capitalistic evolution by this analogy between religious and economic alienation even though his economic assumption *seems* to be nothing but the logical outcome of his economic theory of labor, value, and other factors.

3. *Ibid.,* pp. 95–96.

4. *Ibid.,* p. 99.

5. *Ibid.,* p. 101.

man's alienation from himself, his fellowman, and from nature. He defines labor in its original and nonalienated form as "life activity, productive life 'Lebenstaetigkeit, das produktiv Leben,'" and then proceeds to define the species character of man as "free, conscious activity." ("freie bewusste Taetigkeit") In alienated labor the free and conscious activity of man becomes distorted into alienated activity and thus "Life itself appears only as a *means of life*."[6]

As the previous statement shows, Marx is by no means only concerned with the alienation of man from his product nor only with the alienation of work. He is concerned with man's alienation from life, from himself, and from his fellowman. This idea is expressed in the following: "Thus alienated labor turns the *species life of man*, and also nature as his mental species-property, into an *alien* being and into a *means* for his *individual existence*. It alienates from man his own body, external nature, his mental life, and his *human* life. A direct consequence of the alienation of man from the product of his labor from his life activity and from the species life is that man is *alienated* from other *men*. When man confronts himself he also confronts *other* men. What is true of man's relationship to his work, to the product of his work, and to himself, is also true of his relationship to other men, to their labor, and to the objects of their labor. In general, the statement that man is alienated from his species life means that each man is alienated from others, and that each of the others is likewise alienated from human life."[7]

I must add to this presentation of Marx's concept of alienation as he expressed it in his *Economic and Philosophical Manuscripts* that the concept, although not the word, remains of central significance throughout his whole later main work, including *The Capital*. In the *German Ideology* Marx wrote: "As long as a cleavage exists between the particular and the common interest man's own deed becomes an alien power opposed to him, which enslaves him instead of being controlled by him."[8] And later: "This crystallization of social activity, this consolidation of what we ourselves produce into an objective power above us, growing out of our control, thwarting our expectations, bringing to naught our calculations, is one of the chief factors in historical development up to now."[9] Here follow some of the many statements in *Capital* dealing with alienation: "In handicraft and manufacture, the workman makes use of a tool; in the factory the machine makes use of him. There the movements of the instruments of labor proceed from him; here it is the movement of the machines that he must follow. In manufacture, the workmen are part of a living mechanism; in the factory, we have a lifeless mechanism, independent of the workman, who becomes its mere living appendage."[10] Or (education of the future will) "combine productive labor with instruction and gymnastics, not only as one of the methods of adding to the efficiency of production, but as the only method of producing *fully developed human beings*."[11] Or: "Modern Indus-

---

6. *Ibid.*, p. 101.
7. *Ibid.*, p. 103.
8. *German Ideology*, p. 220.
9. *Ibid.*, pp. 22–23.
10. *Capital I*, pp. 461–462.
11. *Capital I*, pp. 529–533 (My italics, E.F.).

try, indeed, compels society, on the penalty of death, to replace the detail-worker of today, *crippled* by lifelong repetition of one and the same trivial operation, and thus reduced to the mere *fragment* of a man, by the *fully developed* individual . . . to whom the different social functions he performs are but so many *modes of giving free scope to his own natural and acquired powers.*"[12] Alienation then, is, for Marx, *the* sickness of man. It is not a new sickness, since it starts necessarily with the beginning of division of labor, that is, of civilization transcending primitive society; it is most strongly developed in the working class yet it is a sickness from which everybody suffers. The sickness can be cured only when it has reached its peak; only the totally alienated man can overcome the alienation — he is forced to overcome his alienation since he cannot live as a totally alienated man and remain sane. Socialism is the answer; it is a society in which man becomes the conscious subject of history, experiences himself as the subject of his powers and thus emancipates himself from the bondage to things and circumstances. Marx gave expression to this idea of socialism and the realization of freedom in the following passage at the end of the third volume of *Capital:* "In fact, the realm of freedom does not commence until the point is passed where labor under the compulsion of necessity and of external utility is required. In the very nature of things it lies beyond the sphere of material production in the strict meaning of the term. Just as the savage must wrestle with nature, in order to satisfy his wants, in order to maintain his life and reproduce it, so civilized man has to do it, and he must do it in all forms of society and under all possible modes of production. With his development the realm of natural necessity expands, because his wants increase; but at the same time the forces of production increase, by which these wants are satisfied. The freedom in this field cannot consist of anything else but of the fact that *socialized man, the associated producers, regulate their interchange with nature rationally, bring it under their common control, instead of being ruled by it as by some blind power;* that they accomplish their task with the least expenditure of energy and under conditions most adequate to their human nature and most worthy of it. *But it always remains a realm of necessity.* Beyond it begins that development of human power, which is its own end, the true realm of freedom, which, however, can flourish only upon that realm of necessity as its basis."[13]

We come closer to the problem of alienation as a moral and a psychological problem if we consider statements which Marx made in these two respects. For Marx alienation corrupts and perverts all human values. By making economic activities and the values inherent in them, like "gain, work, thrift and sobriety,"[14] the supreme value of life, man fails to develop the truly moral values of humanity, "the riches of a good conscience, of virtue, etc., but how can I be virtuous if I am not alive and how can I have a good conscience if I am not aware of anything?"[15] In a state of alienation, each sphere of life, the economic and the moral, is independent from the

12. *Loc. cit.*, p. 534.
13. *Capital III*, p. 954.
14. *Ibid.*, p. 146. Incidentally, these values are not only those of nineteenth-century capitalism, but they are the main values in contemporary Soviet Russia.
15. *Economic and Philosophical Manuscripts*, p. 146.

other, "each is concentrated upon a specific area of alienated activity and is itself alienated from the other."[16]

Marx foresaw with amazing clarity how the needs of man in an alienated society would be perverted into true weaknesses. In capitalism, as Marx sees it, "Every man speculates upon creating a *new* need in another in order to force him to a new sacrifice, to place him in a new dependence, and to entice him into a new kind of pleasure and thereby into economic ruin. Everyone tries to establish over others an *alien* power in order to find there the satisfaction of his own egoistic need. With the mass of objects, therefore, there also increases the realm of alien entities to which man is subjected. Every new product is a new *potentiality* of mutual deceit and robbery. Man becomes increasingly poor as a man; he has increasing need of *money* in order to take possession of the hostile being. The power of *money* diminishes directly with the growth of the quantity of production, i.e., his need increases with the increasing *power* of money. The need for money is therefore the real need created by the modern economy, and the only need which it creates. The *quantity* of money becomes increasingly its only important quality. Just as it reduces every entity to its abstraction, so it reduces itself in its own development to a *quantitative* entity. Excess and immoderation become its true standard. This is shown subjectively, partly in the fact that the expansion of production and of needs becomes an *ingenious* and always *calculating* subservience to inhuman, depraved, unnatural, and *imaginary* appetites. Private property does not know how to change crude need into *human* need; its *idealism* is *fantasy*, *caprice* and *fancy*. No eunuch flatters his tyrant more shamefully or seeks by more infamous means to stimulate his jaded appetite, in order to gain some favor, than does the eunuch of industry, the entrepreneur, in order to acquire a few silver coins or to charm the gold from the purse of his dearly beloved neighbor. (Every product is a bait by means of which the individual tries to entice the essence of the other person, his money. Every real or potential need is a weakness which will draw the bird into the line. As every imperfection of man is a bond with heaven, a point at which his heart is accessible to the priest, so every want is an opportunity for approaching one's neighbor with the air of friendship, and saying, 'Dear friend, I will give you what you need, but you know the *conditio sine qua non*. You know what ink you must use in signing yourself over to me. I shall swindle you while providing your enjoyment.' All this constitutes a universal exploitation of human communal life.) The entrepreneur accedes to the most depraved fancies of his neighbor, plays the role of pander between him and his needs, awakens unhealthy appetites in him, and watches for every weakness in order, later, to claim the remuneration for this labor of love."[17] The man who has thus become subject to his alienated needs is "a *mentally* and *physically* dehumanized being . . . the *self-conscious* and *self-acting* commodity."[18] This commodity-man knows only one way of relating himself to the world outside, by having it and by consuming (using) it. The more

16. *Ibid.*
17. *Economic and Philosophical Manuscripts,* pp. 140–142.
18. *Ibid.,* p. 111.

alienated he is, the more the sense of having and using constitutes his relationship to the world. "The less you *are*, the less you express your life, the more you *have*, the greater is your *alienated* life and the greater is the saving of your alienated being."[19]

Discussing Marx's concept of alienation, it might be of some interest to point to the close connection between the phenomenon of alienation and the phenomenon of transference which is one of the most fundamental concepts in Freud's system. Freud had observed that the psychoanalytic patient tended to fall in love with the analyst, to be afraid of him, or to hate him, and all this quite without regard to the reality of the analyst's personality. Freud believed that he had found the theoretical explanation to this phenomenon by the assumption that the patient transferred the feelings of love, fear, hate, he had experienced as a child toward father and mother, to the person of the analyst. In the "transference," so Freud reasoned, the child in the patient relates himself to the person of the analyst as to his father or mother. Undoubtedly, Freud's interpretation of the transference phenomenon has much truth in it, and is supported by a good deal of evidence. Yet it is not a complete interpretation. The grown-up patient *is not* a child, and to talk about the child in him, or "his" unconscious, is using a topological language which does not do justice to the complexity of the facts. The neurotic, grown-up patient is an alienated human being, he does not feel strong, he is frightened and inhibited because he does not experience himself as the subject and originator of his own acts and experiences. He is neurotic *because* he is alienated. In order to overcome his sense of inner emptiness and impotence, he chooses an object onto whom he projects all his own human qualities: his love, intelligence, courage, etc. By submitting to this object, he feels in touch with his own qualities; he feels strong, wise, courageous, and secure. To lose the object means danger of losing himself. This mechanism, idolatric worship of an object, based on the fact of the individual's alienation, is the central dynamism of transference, that which gives transference its strength and intensity. The less alienated person may also transfer some of his infantile experience to the analyst, but there would be little intensity in it. The alienated patient, in search for and in need of an idol, finds the analyst and usually endows him with the qualities of his father and mother as the two powerful persons he knew as a child. Thus the *content* of transference is usually related to infantile patterns while its *intensity* is the result of the patient's alienation. Needless to add that the transference phenomenon is not restricted to the analytic situation. It is to be found in all forms of idolization of authority figures, in political, religious, and social life.

Transference is not the only phenomenon of psychopathology which can be understood as an expression of alienation. Indeed, it is not accidental that *aliéné* in French, and *alienado* in Spanish, are older words for the psychotic, and the English "alienist" refers to a doctor who cares for the insane, the absolutely alienated person.

Alienation as a sickness of the self can be considered to be the core of the psychopathology of modern man even in those forms which are less

---

19. *Ibid.*, p. 144.

extreme than psychosis. Some clinical examples may serve to illustrate the process. The most frequent and obvious case of alienation is perhaps the false "great love." A man has fallen enthusiastically in love with a woman; after she had responded at first, she is beset by increasing doubts and breaks off the relationship. He is overcome by a depression which brings him close to suicide. Life, he feels, has no more meaning to him. Consciously he explains the situation as a logical result of what happened. He believes that for the first time he has experienced what real love is, that with this woman, and only with her, could he experience love and happiness. If she leaves him, there will never be anyone else who can arouse the same response in him. Losing her, so he feels, he has lost his one chance to love. Hence it is better to die. While all this sounds convincing to himself, his friends may ask some questions: Why is it that a man who thus far seemed less capable of loving than the average person is now so completely in love that he would rather die than live without his beloved? Why is it that although he is so completely in love he seems to be unwilling to make any concessions, to give up certain demands which conflict with those of the woman he loves? Why is it that while he speaks of his loss, he mainly speaks about himself and what has happened to him, and shows relatively little interest in the feelings of the woman he loves so much? If one speaks to the unhappy man himself, at greater length, one need not be surprised to hear him say at one point that he feels completely empty, so empty in fact as if he had left his heart with the girl he lost. If he can understand the meaning of his own statement he can understand that his predicament is one of alienation. He never was capable of loving actively, of leaving the magic circle of his own ego, and of reaching out to and becoming one with another human being. What he did was to transfer his longings for love to the girl and to feel that being with her he experiences his "loving" when he really experiences only the illusion of loving. The more he endows her not only with his longing for love but also for aliveness, happiness, and so on, the poorer he becomes, and the emptier he feels if he is separated from her. He was under the illusion of loving, when actually he had made the woman into an idol, the goddess of love, and believed that by being united with her he experienced love. He had been able to initiate a response in her but he had not been able to overcome his own inner muteness. Losing her is not, as he thinks, losing the person he loves, but losing himself as a potentially loving person.

Alienation of thought is not different from alienation of the heart. Often one believes he has thought through something, that his idea is the result of his own thinking activity; the fact is that he has transferred his brain to the idols of public opinion, the newspapers, the government or a political leader. He believes that they express his thoughts while in reality he accepts their thoughts as his own, because he has chosen them as his idols, his gods of wisdom and knowledge. Precisely for this reason he is dependent on his idols and incapable of giving up his worship. He is their slave because he has deposited his brain with them.

Another example of alienation is the alienation of hope, in which the future is transformed into an idol. This idolatry of history can be clearly seen in Robespierre's views. "O posterity, sweet and tender hope of humanity, thou art not a stranger to us; it is for thee that we brave all the blows of tyranny; it is thy happiness which is the price of our painful struggles: often discouraged by the obstacles that surround us, we feel the need of thy consolations; it is to thee that we confide the task of completing our labors, and the destiny of all the unborn generations of men! . . . Make haste, O posterity, to bring to pass the hour of equality, of justice, of happiness!"[20] Similarly, a distorted version of Marx's philosophy of history has often been used in the same sense by Communists. The logic of this argument is: whatever is in accord with the historical trend is necessary, hence good and vice versa. In this view, whether in the form of Robespierre's or the communist argument, it is not man who makes history but history that makes man. It is not man who hopes and has faith in the future but the future judges him and decides whether he had the right faith. Marx expressed very succinctly the opposite view of history to the alienated one I just quoted. "History," he wrote in *The Holy Family*, "does *nothing*, it possesses no colossal riches, it fights *no* battles! It is rather man, actual and living man, who does all this; 'history' does not use man as a means for *its* purposes as though it were a person apart; it is *nothing* but the activity of man pursuing his ends."

The phenomenon of alienation has other clinical aspects, which I can discuss only briefly. Not only are all forms of depression, dependence and idol worship (including the "fanatic") direct expressions of, or compensations for, alienation; the phenomenon of the failure to experience one's identity which is a central phenomenon at the root of psychopathological phenomena is also a result of alienation. Precisely because the alienated person has transformed his own functions of feeling and thought to an object outside he is not himself, he has no sense of "I," of identity. This lack of a sense of identity has many consequences. The most fundamental and general one is that it prevents integration of the total personality, hence it leaves the person disunited within himself, lacking either capacity "to will one thing" or if he seems to will one thing his will lacks authenticity.

In the widest sense, every neurosis can be considered an outcome of alienation; this is so because neurosis is characterized by the fact that one passion (for instance, for money, power, women, etc.) becomes dominant and separated from the total personality, thus becoming the ruler of the person. This passion is his idol to which he submits even though he may rationalize the nature of his idol and give it many different and often well-sounding names. He is ruled by a partial desire, he transfers all he has left to this desire, he is weaker the stronger "it" becomes. He has become alienated from himself precisely because "he" has become the slave of a part of himself.

Seeing alienation as a pathological phenomenon must, however, not obscure the fact that Hegel and Marx considered it a *necessary* phenomenon, one which is inherent in human evolution. This is true with regard to the alienation of reason as well as of love. Only when I can distinguish between the world outside and myself, that is, only if the world outside

20. Quoted by Carl L. Becker, *The Heavenly City of the Eighteenth-Century Philosophers* (Yale University Press, 1932), pp. 142–143.

becomes an *object*, can I grasp it and make it my world, become one with it again. The infant, for whom the world is not yet conceived as "object," can also not grasp it with his reason and reunite himself with it. Man has to become alienated in order to overcome this split in the activity of his reason. The same holds true for love. As long as the infant has not separated himself from the world outside he is still part of it, and hence cannot love. In order to love, the "other" must become a stranger, and in the act of love, the stranger ceases to be a stranger and becomes me. Love presupposes alienation — and at the same time overcomes it. The same idea is to be found in the prophetic concept of the Messianic Time and in Marx's concept of socialism. In Paradise man still is one with nature, but not yet aware of himself as separate from nature and his fellowman. By his act of disobedience man acquires self-awareness, the world becomes estranged from him. In the process of history, according to the prophetic concept, man develops his human powers so fully that eventually he will acquire a new harmony with men and nature. Socialism, in Marx's sense, can only come, once man has cut off all primary bonds, when he has become completely alienated and thus is able to reunite himself with men and nature without sacrificing his integrity and individuality.

The concept of alienation has its roots in a still earlier phase of the Western tradition, in the thought of the Old Testament prophets, more specifically in their concept of *idolatry*. The prophets of monotheism did not denounce heathen religions as idolatrous primarily because they worshiped several gods instead of one. The essential difference between monotheism and polytheism is not one of the *numbers* of gods, but lies in the fact of alienation. Man spends his energy, his artistic capacities on building an idol, and then he worships this idol, which is nothing but the result of his own human effort. His life forces have flowed into a "thing," and this thing, having become an idol, is not experienced as a result of his own productive effort, but as something apart from himself, over and against himself, which he worships and to which he submits. As the prophet Hosea says (XIV, 8): "Assur shall not save us; we will not ride upon horses; neither will we say any more to the work of our hands, you are our gods; for in thee the fatherless finds love." Idolatrous man bows down to the work of his own hands. *The idol represents his own life-forces in an alienated form.*

The principle of monotheism, in contrast, is that man is infinite, that there is no partial quality in him which can be hypostatized into the whole. God, in the monotheistic concept, is unrecognizable and indefinable; God is not a "thing." Man being created in the likeness of God is created as the bearer of infinite qualities. In idolatry man bows down and submits to the projection of one partial quality in himself. He does not experience himself as the center from which living acts of love and reason radiate. He becomes a thing, his neighbor becomes a thing, just as his gods are things. "The idols of the heathen are silver and gold, the work of men's hands. They have mouths but they speak not; eyes have they, but they see not; they have ears but they hear not; neither is there any breath in their mouths. They that make them are like them; so is everyone that trusts in them." (Psalm 135)

Modern man, in industrial society, has changed the form and intensity of idolatry. He has become the object of blind economic forces which rule his life. He worships the work of his hands, he transforms himself into a thing. Not the working class alone is alienated (in fact, if anything, the skilled worker seems to be less alienated than those who manipulate men and symbols) but everybody is. This process of alienation which exists in the European-American industrialized countries, regardless of their political structure, has given rise to new protest movements. The renaissance of socialist humanism is one symptom of this protest. Precisely because alienation has reached a point where it borders on insanity in the whole industrialized world, undermining and destroying its religious, spiritual, and political traditions and threatening general destruction through nuclear war, many are better able to see that Marx had recognized the central issue of modern man's sickness; that he had not only seen, as Feuerbach and Kierkegaard had, this "sickness" but that he had shown that contemporary idolatry is rooted in the contemporary mode of production and can be changed only by the complete change of the economic-social constellation together with the spiritual liberation of man.

Surveying the discussion of Freud's and Marx's respective views on mental illness, it is obvious that Freud is primarily concerned with individual pathology, and Marx is concerned with the pathology common to a society and resulting from the particular system of that society. It is also clear that the content of psychopathology is quite different for Marx and for Freud. Freud sees pathology essentially in the failure to find a proper balance between the Id and Ego, between instinctual demands and the demands of reality; Marx sees the essential illness, as what the nineteenth century called *la maladie du siècle*, the estrangement of man from his own humanity and hence from his fellow man. Yet it is often overlooked that Freud by no means thought exclusively in terms of individual pathology. He speaks also of a "social neurosis." "If the evolution of civilization," he writes, "has such a far-reaching similarity with the development of an individual, and if the same methods are employed in both, would not the diagnosis be justified that many systems of civilization—or epochs of it—possibly even the whole of humanity—have become 'neurotic' under the pressure of civilizing trends? To analytic dissection of these neuroses, therapeutic recommendations might follow which could claim a great practical interest. I would not say that such an attempt to apply psychoanalysis to civilized society would be fanciful or doomed to fruitlessness. But it behooves us to be very careful, not to forget that after all we are dealing only with analogies, and that it is dangerous, not only with men but also with concepts, to drag them out of the region where they originated and have matured. The diagnosis of *collective neuroses*, moreover, will be confronted by a special difficulty. In the neurosis of an individual we can use as a starting point the contrast presented to us between the patient and his environment which we assume to be 'normal.' No such background as this would be available for any society similarly affected; it would have to be supplied in some other way. And with regard to any therapeutic application of our knowledge, what would be the use of the most acute analysis of social neuroses, since no one possesses the power to compel the community to adopt the therapy? In spite of all these difficulties, we may expect that one day someone will venture upon this *research into the pathology of civilized communities.*"[21]

But it spite of Freud's interest in the "social neuroses," one fundamental difference between Freud's and Marx's thinking remains: Marx sees man as formed by his society, and hence sees the root of pathology in specific qualities of the social organization. Freud sees man as primarily formed by his experience in the family group; he appreciates little that the family is only the representative and agent of society, and he looks at various societies mainly in terms of the *quantity* of repression they demand, rather than the *quality* of their organization and of the impact of this social quality on the quality of the thinking and feeling of the members of a given society.

This discussion of the difference between Marx's and Freud's views on psychopathology, brief as it is, must mention one more aspect in which their thinking follows the same method. For Freud the state of primary narcissism of the infant, and the later oral and anal stages of libido development, are "normal" inasmuch as they are necessary stages in the process of evolution. The dependent, greedy infant is not a sick infant. Yet the dependent, greedy adult, who has been "fixated" on, or who has "regressed" to, the oral level of the child is a sick adult. The main needs and strivings are the same in the infant and in the adult; why then is the one healthy and the other sick? The answer lies quite obviously in the concept of evolution. What is normal at a certain stage is pathological at another stage. Or, to put it differently: what is *necessary* at one stage is also normal or rational. What is *unnecessary*, seen from the standpoint of evolution, is irrational and pathological. The adult who "repeats" an infantile stage at the same time does not and cannot repeat it, precisely because he is no longer a child.

Marx following Hegel, employs the same method in viewing the evolution of man in society. Primitive man, medieval man, and the alienated man of industrial society are sick and yet not sick, because their stage of development is a necessary one. Just as the infant has to mature physiologically in order to become an adult, so the human race has to mature sociologically in the process of gaining mastery of nature and of society in order to become fully human. All irrationality of the past, while regrettable, is rational inasmuch as it was necessary. But when the human race stops at a stage of development which it should have passed, when it finds itself in contradiction with the possibilities which the historical situation offers, then its state of existence is irrational or, if Marx had used the term, pathological. Both Marx's and Freud's concepts of pathology can be understood fully only in terms of their evolutionary concept of individual and human history.

---

21. S. Freud, *Civilization and Its Discontents*, translated from the German by J. Riviere (London: The Hogarth Press, Ltd., 1953), pp. 141–142 (My italics, E.F.).

PAUL TILLICH

Paul Tillich is generally accorded to have been one of the great contemporary Protestant theologians. Dismissed from his post as professor of philosophy at the University of Frankfurt-am-Main in Germany in 1933, he came to the United States and taught for many years at Union Theological Seminary in New York. In later years he was a member of the divinity schools at Harvard University and the University of Chicago. The author of over twenty-five books relating religion to philosophy, psychology, sociology, art, and politics, his most important contribution is the voluminous Systematic Theology. *Tillich is also the author of such works as* The Protestant Era *(1948),* The Shaking of the Foundations *(1948),* The Courage to Be *(1952), and* The Dynamics of Faith *(1958).*

The Person in a Technical Society

It is my understanding of the movement which is called Existentialism and which is at least one hundred years old that it rebels in the name of personality against the depersonalizing forces of technical society. For the sake of my special subject as well as in the spirit of this volume, I want to begin with some references to the earlier history of Existentialism. This history, going on since the middle of the nineteenth century, has determined the fate of the twentieth century in all spheres of human existence. The immense tragedy of our political as well as the creative chaos of our spiritual situation are foreshadowed and deeply influenced by the Existentialist rebels of the nineteenth century. Moreover, the tradition, out of which this book is written and out of which he to whom it is dedicated has worked, is rooted in the protest of the lonely prophets of the nineteenth century against the threatening destruction of humanity and personality by technical society. Finally, it is my conviction that the new beginning, of which this volume is supposed to be a symbol, should be and, I hope, will be a continuation of this tradition under new conditions and with new means. But the aim should be what it was in the preceding movements of protest: a fight for humanity, which includes both community and personality, against the dehumanizing power of modern society.

I. KIERKEGAARD AND EXISTENTIALISM

It is usual to refer to Kierkegaard as the instigator of Existentialism. For the theologians especially this is the natural start. Historically, however, this is incorrect, since people like Pascal, Schelling and others had raised the Existentialist protest before Kierkegaard. They had done it for the same reason and with the same purpose as Kierkegaard: to resist a world in which everything was transformed into a thing, a means, an object of scientific calculation, psychological and political management. Kierkegaard saw that, in spite of many romantic elements in Hegel and in spite of his doctrine of freedom as the purpose of history, *this* was the meaning of his attempt to subject all reality to a system of logical forms: The existing individual was swallowed, the deciding personality was eliminated. The world-process, playing with the individual, gave him the feeling that he was deciding for himself, while the process, governed by dialectical necessity, had already decided about him. Kierkegaard's metaphor of the "leap" embodying his protest against Hegel's logically determined world process is the idealistic mirror of the realities of the modern world. This was its greatness and this was the reason why the revolt against our world found its most successful expression in the protest against this mirror. Kierkegaard made his protest on the basis of classical Protestantism. But classical Protestantism had ceased to be an immediate reality. It had been lost and had to be regained. How? By being put in its place in the whole of the dialectical process, answered Hegel. By being reached through the leap of faith, answered Kierkegaard. Hegel's answer makes classical Protestantism a useful element within the frame of technical society; Kierkegaard's answer asks the individual to break away from this society in order to save his existence as a person. Therefore Kierkegaard's loneliness, therefore the pathological traits in his dealing with marriage, vocation and Church, therefore the lack of any effect in his own time. All this is understandable if the existing person can only be saved by a leap. Our own period, in which Kierkegaard has shaped philosophy as well as theology in the Existentialist direction, has shown this clearly. Philosophical Existentialism demands the leap of the individual out of all traditions and social obligations into the freedom of normless decisions. Theological Existentialism demands the leap of the individual out of his given cultural and intellectual situation into the acceptance of a sacred tradition formulated hundreds of years ago. The leap liberates, but does it not enslave again? The personalities of Sartre's novels have absolute freedom, but it is actually the freedom of falling under the compulsion of the internal or external situation of the moment. And the Neo-Orthodox Christian subjects himself through the leap of faith to traditional ecclesiastical dogmas. He is free in the moment of his leap. But his leap into freedom involves the sacrifice of his freedom. The power of technical society is manifest in this conflict between rational necessity and the leap of freedom. The person is lost if rational necessity prevails. He tried to save himself by the leap which, however, leads to new forms of servitude, natural or supranatural ones. Only if we face realistically this situation, which even more than Hegel's and Kierkegaard's is our own situation, can we realize the seriousness of the problem: "The person in a technical society."

II. MARX AS EXISTENTIALIST

While Hegel provided the idealistic mirror of technical society, Marx gave
its realistic description. This accounts for his ambiguous relation to Hegel,
his opposition to him, insofar as the idealistic side is concerned, his dependence on him, with respect to the dialectical analysis of present day society. Marx saw much more clearly than Kierkegaard that it is not a system
of thought, but the reality of modern society which is responsible for the
reduction of the person to a commodity. His famous descriptions of the dehumanizing effects of economy in the industrial age center around the
proletariat, but they are meant for all groups of society. Everyone, insofar as
he is drawn into the all-embracing mechanism of production and consumption, is enslaved to it, loses his character as person and becomes a thing.
Marx did not think that it is the technical method of production as such
which destroys personal freedom, but that the social structure of the class
society is responsible for it. He believed in possibilities of humanizing the
technical process, but he did not believe that this could happen within
the frame of the class society. Therefore he became a political rebel against the
social and economic structure of bourgeois society and a tremendous historical force, not only in the countries which became "Marxist"—at least in
pretense—but also in those which avoided a radical transformation by fulfilling demands of the Marxist movements within the framework of bourgeois society. This latter fact should not be forgotten by those who are still
interested in an unprejudiced, scientific criticism of Marx. The way in
which Marx envisages the salvation of the person in technical society
unites in an highly ambiguous way dialectical necessity with political decision. Marx, the sociologist, follows Hegel's method of structural analysis
and derives from it not what Hegel did, a systematic glorification of the
present, but a necessary, calculable development into a glorious future. At
the same time he appeals to the action of the proletariat, especially the vanguard which consists of proletarians and people from other groups who
have joined them. Appeal is senseless without the presupposition that it
can be accepted or rejected. He did not believe that the "person" in the
proletarian was extinguished to such a degree that political appeals would
be meaningless. This view is supported by the two concepts which characterize Marx's view of man, the concept of "dehumanization" and the concept of "real humanism." Both presuppose that man can be distorted by
social conditions in such a way that his humanity is lost, and both presuppose that there will be a state of things in which his community is reestab-
lished. Both show that Marx is concerned with the loss and the salvation
of the "person" in the technical society as he experienced it.

But again, as in the case of Kierkegaard, the power of this society became manifest as soon as the question was: how can one break away from
it? The answer seems to be easy: through the dialectical process and the
revolution it will bring about. But social dialectics and revolution occur
through human beings, and this introduces alternatives which are as difficult as those we found in Kierkegaard's doctrine of the leap. If those in a
state of complete depersonalization are carried by the dialectical process
into the "realm of freedom," how can they use it without radical transfor-

mation from thing to person? But if they are still persons they introduce an incalculable element into the situation. The proletarians may not see their real interest or their enemies may be unexpectedly strong or groups may become active who do not fit the simple class scheme, or the proletarians may carry through their demands to such a degree that they cease to be proletarians in the genuine sense of the word. All this has actually happened and has produced two contradictory reactions. The one is the reaction by what is called today "the free world," namely, the attempt to save the person within the frame of the bourgeois-capitalistic society by methods of reforms (whatever they may be called). The other is the reaction by what is called today Communism, namely, the attempt to save the person in a future state of history by removing in the present those personal elements which might endanger the future. This has led to the establishment of the communist system in which all technical refinements are used to eliminate the risks involved in personal resistance against the system. A type of technical society has been created in which the person of the present is completely sacrificed for the sake of the expected person of the future. A movement which started with a passionate fight against depersonalization has turned into one of the greatest powers of depersonalization in all history.

III. NIETZSCHE'S PROTEST

The fight of Existentialism against the dangers of the technical society was done, at the same time, on a third front, on that front which determines more than the two others the present fight against depersonalization. It was in the name of life that Nietzsche fought against the "nihilism" of the technical culture. Many followed him in all spheres of spiritual creativity. He and the movement of which he is the most conspicuous symbol saw more sharply than Kierkegaard and Marx the deepest roots of the dehumanizing and depersonalizing implications of modern society. Technical society — this is the message of all adherents of the "philosophy of life" (whether philosophers or poets or writers or artists) — destroys the creative power of life. Man becomes, according to Nietzsche, a cog in the all-embracing machine of production and consumption. This self whose center is the will to realize itself has nothing to will any more, and, therefore, it wills the "nothing." Only a new beginning of the will which wills itself can save life from a complete disintegration. This will (misleadingly called by Nietzsche the "will to power") is the self-affirmation of life as life against everything which transforms it into an object, a thing, a tool. Only a small group of people are the bearers of this new beginning, persons acting in the sense of heroic self-affirmation. They are the saviors of personal existence, through whom the power of life will reappear. On this basis the philosophers of life denounce the technical mass civilization, the egalitarian ideals, the subjection to the system of values which are accepted in this civilization, including the Christian values insofar as they are amalgamated with the ideals of the modern society. Only a few romanticists amongst the philosophers of life attacked the technical development as such (just as a few ecstatics amongst the socialists, and a few pietists amongst the followers of Kierke-gaard). Generally speaking the technical world was accepted as a meaningful creation of life. But the way in which this creation turns against its creator produces the wrath of all philosophers of life. They want to restitute the integrity of creative life by looking for something below the split into sub-ject and object. On their way they meet the depth-psychology, the empha-sis on the unconscious, or the instincts, or the demonic, or the unreflected and unbroken self-realization. From the beginning in the early nineteenth century to their full development at the end of the nineteenth and the first half of the twentieth century depth-psychology, philosophy of life and Ex-istentialism were intimate allies. Their common enemy was and is the ob-jectifying, depersonalizing power of technical society. They do not look for the religious liberation through the leap of faith as did Kierkegaard, nor to the political liberation through the social dialectics as did Marx, but they look at the liberation which comes out of the depth of the personal life it-self, his unconscious ground, his drives and instincts, his unity with na-ture, his self-affirming will. Sometimes they look back into the past, not in order to return to it, but in order to discover in it examples of undistorted life, e.g., in the Middle Ages, or in the archaic periods of the ancient cul-tures, or in the so-called primitives. Some go even beyond this and use the unreflected animal life to symbolize the ideal they put against the realities of technical society (note the use of animal symbols in Nietzsche's *Zara-thustra*).

IV. CONTEMPORARY PROTESTS

Again the protest is profound and forceful. But is it able to pierce the walls of the society and its depersonalizing magic? Obviously not. It is driven to fateful self-contradiction. It has to fight the state of reflection with the tools of reflection. Politically the fight against the intelligentsia, and for the prim-itive and the genuine—in its extreme form for "blood and soil"—has produced the most sophisticated and technically elaborated tools for sup-pressing every genuine expression of life which did not fit the demands of the political system. Man in this society was pressed into a scheme of thought, action and daily behavior which reminds more of machine parts than of human beings. Even the faces of the storm troopers, for example, were as stereotyped as normal industrial tools. Any indication of personality and individuality was removed. The attempt, made in the name of life, to overcome the rule of depersonalized things, has produced the complete removal of humanity in the supporters of this attempt. And its victims (in-cluding many followers) were transformed by terror into slaves, not less obedient than the slave which is called machine. The only way in which the original emphasis on life was maintained was the unrestricted realiza-tion of formerly repressed drives toward power, pleasure and destruction. This was done in the name of vitality, against rationality. But the result was a mutilated, self-destroying vitality united with bestiality and absurdity. The power of the technical world proved again to be overwhelming.

Recent Existentialism (Sartre) tried to break its power by isolating the individual from the embracing structure of technical civilization. It tries to save the person by asking him to create himself without norms, laws and principles, without anybody else or anything else. True humanism is declared to be the message of the individual making himself. Since "man's essence is his existence" no criteria are given to him for his self-creating activity. The will willing itself, the decision deciding for the sake of deciding and not for the sake of a content, the freedom maintaining itself by the rejection of any obligation and devotion — all these descriptions of the existential situation express the protest of Existentialism against our technical world. They are in analogy to Kierkegaard's "leap"; and their freedom is as much a leap into the dark as Kierkegaard's leap would have been without his participation in the Christian Lutheran tradition. By surrendering all norms they deliver the person to the contingencies of the situation, they depersonalize him.

Much more successful in saving the person from the dehumanizing power of technical society seems to be the third ally in the fight for genuine life, the depth-psychology, especially in its latest development in which all emphasis is put on the analysis and synthesis of the personal life. "Personality" has become the central concept of the post-Freudian psychotherapeutic development. The analytic attempt to liberate the unconscious from the repressions, forced upon it by the society, to liberate the Ego from the authoritarian representatives of the "Superego," to liberate the person from the compulsive drives which subdue the personal center and eliminate its power of making personal decisions — all this seems to be the way to the salvation of the person in the technical society. Many people believe that it is, and feel that their own experiences support this belief. So we must ask: Is psychotherapy the way to break through the otherwise unconquerable fortress of technical society? Is it the way to save the person from becoming a thing amongst things? Or is there a similar problem as that in the other attempts to save personal existence, namely the problem of transition, "the leap," the breaking away from the tyranny of the technical civilization. For two reasons it seems to me that the situation is not essentially different: first, because the individual person is not isolated; second, because the method of liberating him may strengthen that from which it tries to liberate. The first reason points back to Marx, the second to Nietzsche. A philosophical analyst once said to me: "What is the use of my work with my patients even if most successful, when I have to send them back into *this* society?" More and more psychotherapists have discovered that the conflicts of their patients are partly and often largely conditioned by the social situation in which they live, the competitive, technical, post-puritan society with the repressions, the anxiety, and the compulsions it produces. This, however, means a limit to the healing power of analysis and the demand for a social transformation for the sake of the person and his salvation from the depersonalizing forces.

But psychoanalysis has not only its "Marxist" problem, it has also its "Nietzschean" problem. It is the question: can a method, a technically elaborated procedure, save the person from technical society? Two answers can be given to this question. The one would say that psychotherapy is indeed a technique and works like every technique through adequate means towards a definite end. The end is healing of pathological states of mind; the means are determined by their methodological adequacy to their end. If this answer is accepted, the psychoanalyst no more saves the person than does the internist in bodily medicine. The opposite answer would say that within the psychotherapeutic method elements are present which transcend the mere technical sphere, above all a person-to-person relationship which may be saving for the patient as person. If this answer is accepted it means that the analyst implicitly and indirectly exercises priestly functions. This is quite possible and certainly very often real. But then it is not a psychotherapy as psychotherapy which saves the person, but the spiritual substance in which both the analyst and the patient participate. And the question remains: What is this saving power?

V. TWO SHORTCUTS

The result of all this seems to be quite negative. It seems that the Existential revolts against technical society have been futile. From Kierkegaard to present-day psychotherapy, the problem of transition is decisive for the failure to save the person within the technical society. The "leap" in all its variations is more an expression of despair than an answer. Nevertheless, the Existentialist revolt is the decisive event, theoretical and practical, of the last one hundred years. It has shown the problem and it has given different solutions, each of which proved the superiority of the technical society over all those who attacked it. But the attack itself was and is most significant. Whether victorious or not, it kept alive the consciousness that technical society is the great threat against the person. This is the reason why almost all important creations of the last decades were creations by those who belong to the movement of rebellion against the technical society.

These attacks have led to attitudes and systems of life and thought which challenge the contemporary bourgeois society. What, then, about this society and the attitude toward it by groups who largely agree with the criticism made by the one hundred years of Existentialist protest and who, at the same time, are aware of the tragic self-contradictions into which the protesting ideas were driven when they succeeded politically or spiritually? It seems to me that such groups, *e.g.*, the contributors of this volume and the movement they represent, must avoid two shortcuts, the one to return, in a state of disappointment, to a full affirmation of present-day technical society, the other, to use the Christian message as a *deus ex machina*, which solves all problems, unsolved by the other movements!

The first shortcut is an understandable reaction to the chaos of disintegration and the horrors of attempted reintegration which we have experienced in our period. A conservative mood today pervades, not only the disappointed members of the older generation, but also the younger people who without a revolutionary impetus and without visions concerning the future adapt themselves, in a matter-of-fact way, to the concrete demands of the given reality. It is a practical positivism, but without the forward looking enthusiasm of the earlier positivism. It is a realism of resignation. One hardly can resist this mood in a world in which small groups under the protection of political and military secrecy rule mankind; and in which the dependence on production of a highly technical character subjects everybody more and more to a new kind of fate—as incalculable and threatening as that towards the end of the ancient world. Nevertheless, one can resist this mood, not by closing one's eyes to this actual situation, not by glorifying our own reality because it is not as bad as the reality else-where—certainly it is better, yet the threat is the same—not by pointing to the improvements of the social situation in the western world—certainly there are improvements, yet the conflict between person and industrial so-ciety is not removed—but by transcending the whole situation and seeing it from a point beyond it.

This point, however, is not the Christian Church and her traditional message. To say this would be another shortcut. One must ask, especially on Christian ground, why the Church and her message are so powerless in their fight against the depersonalizing forces of the present world. The rea-son cannot be that they are in themselves without power. The opposite is true, not only for the vision of faith, but also for sociological and psycho-logical observation. The reason that the Church and her message are unable to resist the progressive annihilation of the person within industrial society is something else. It is the unintended participation of the Church in the essential structure of industrial society. Step by step, the Church, including the way she has shaped and communicated her message, has been deter-mined by the categories of life and thought which characterizes the indus-trial society. The Church became a section of that against which she was supposed to defend the person. The process of depersonalization has caught up even with the churches and their members. One should not close his eyes in face of this situation, and one should not glorify the churches as more protected against depersonalization. Certainly, they are more protected in principle, namely, by their foundation, their message, their commu-nity—but this is not a necessary protection in the actual churches. They have means of resisting depersonalization in their traditions, their sym-bols, their rites—but these means can be transformed into powerful tools of dehumanization. They emphasize the infinite value of the individual per-son—but they are in danger of depersonalizing the person in order to pre-serve his infinite value. One must transcend not only society but also that section in the society which is taken by the churches, in order to see the situation in its threatening power. Only from "beyond," can industrial so-ciety and its dehumanizing forces be resisted and finally overcome.

VI. MAN AND THE NEW REALITY

Two shortcuts have been rejected: the conservative acceptance of the state of things within the so-called "free world," and the ecclesiastical accept-ance of the churches as the means of saving the person in the industrial society. It is obvious that the widespread combination of the two shortcuts does not provide for the right way. What, then, is the direction in which we must look for the right way? It is the Christian message of the New Reality, seen in the light of the Existentialist criticism of the old reality, and

of its special expression in the industrial society. This, it seems to me, must
be the program of a group as that which is represented by this volume. It is
now possible to point to some basic implications of this idea.

The first critical statement to be derived from it is directed against the
reality of such a thing as "Industrial Society." Its meaning is a society
whose character is determined by man's industrial activity. Man certainly
is *homo faber*, industrial man. The being which invented the first tool *as* a
tool for permanent use transcends by this act everything given and was
potentially the creator of a world beyond the given world. The importance
of this fact can hardly be exaggerated in a theological or philosophical doctrine of man. But this power of transcending the given is not an isolated
element in man's nature. It is interdependent with many other elements
within a total structure. The industrial man is at the same time the man
who is able to speak because he has universals, and he is social man because he is able to have I-Thou relations, and he is theoretical man because
he is able to ask and to receive answers, and he is moral man because he
is able to make responsible decisions, and he is religious man because he is
able to be aware of his finitude and of the infinite to which he belongs at
the same time. Man is all this because of the basic structure of being which
is complete in him; he has a centered self in correlation with a structured
world. He looks at both of them, he is free from and for both of them, and
he can transcend them both.

If one element in this structure is developed in isolation and put into
control over the others, not only the whole structure is distorted, but the
special element itself loses its power and its meaning. If, for instance, industrial society transforms the universities into places of research for
industrial purposes, not only the universities lose their function of asking
radically for the truth, but the technical development itself will be stopped
in the long run — the danger of present-day America. On the other hand, if
the universities isolate their function of asking for man's existential concern,
e.g., the social, they lose their significance and fall victims to unanalyzed
ideologies — the danger of past Germany. Many similar examples about the
self-destructive consequences of the isolation and imperialism of a special
function of the human mind can easily be given. In all of them the result is
depersonalization, for the person is a centered whole to which all his functions are subjected. As soon as one function is separated from the others
and put into control over the whole, the person is subjected to this function
and through it to something which is not itself. It *becomes* this function.
This is even true of religion. The abominable word "religionist" implies
that a man has dissolved his personality into the religious function, that he
is, for example, not free to ask radically even for the truth of religion, that
he cannot transcend his functional limits — an implication which is not in
vocational names as artist, economist, statesman, bishop. If religion makes
"religionists," it destroys the person as much as industry by producing an
industrial age. Not industry but the isolation and imperialism of industry
is the threat for the person in our age.

Homo faber, the industrial man, makes tools; this is the only thing he
can "make." The "world above" the "world" he produces is the world of
means, leaving open the question of the ends. One previous consideration

has shown that the person is either the end for which everything else is means, or the person becomes a means and then not only the person but also the end is lost. There is no end in the chain of means and ends except the person. And if the person himself becomes a means, an endless chain of means-and-ends-and-means is established which crushes purpose, meaning and person. But one may ask the question: Is it not the person for whose comfort and well-being the whole technical world is produced; and even more, is not the creation and the use of tools, from the hammer to the artificial brain in itself an expression of man's power over nature and a confirmation of his personal superiority? To this one must answer that, certainly, only man as a person is able to produce this "second world," but that is doing so he can become himself a tool for the production of tools, spiritually as well as economically, centered in "gadgets" and considered as a part of the production and consumption power. And although the tool serves the comfort of the person, it cannot serve the person as person, that which makes him a person. It can make communication easier. But that which makes the person is the content of what is communicated, and it may well be that the ease and the content of the communication are inversely proportional. Another question could be raised, namely, whether the person is the end which cannot become means without being destroyed. Is not the glory of God or the Kingdom of God or, in more secular terms the realization of values, the ultimate end for which everything must become means, even the person? But such a question is self-contradictory. The meaning of, for instance, Kingdom of God is not the unity of things or functions, but it is the unity of persons including their relationship to the whole non-personal realm. Through persons, *i.e.*, through beings who can decide for or against them, values and the glory of God are actualized. To say that God is the ultimate end is saying that the person is the ultimate end.

VII. CONFORMITY VERSUS MAN

Western technical society has produced methods of adjusting persons to its demands in production and consumption which are less brutal, but in the long run, more effective than totalitarian suppression. They depersonalize not by commanding but by providing — providing, namely, what makes individual creativity superfluous. If one looks around at the methods which produce conformity one is astonished that still enough individual creativity is left even to produce these refined methods. One discovers that man's spiritual life has a tremendous power of resistance against a reduction to prescribed patterns of behavior. But one also sees that this resistance is in a great danger of being worn down by the ways in which adjustment is forced upon him in the industrial society. It starts with the education of "adjustment" which produces conformity just by allowing for more spontaneity of the child than any pre-industrial civilization. But the definite frame within which this spontaneity is quietly kept, leads to a spontaneous adjustment which is more dangerous for creative freedom than any openly deterministic influence. At the same time, and throughout his whole life, other powerful means of adjustment are working upon the person in the technical society; the newspapers which choose the facts worth reporting and suggest their interpretation, the radio programs which eliminate non-conformist contents and interpreters, television which replaces the visual imagination by selected pictorial presentations, the movie which for commercial and censorship reasons has to maintain in most of its productions a conscious mediocrity, adjusting itself to the adjusted taste of the masses, the patterns of advertisement which permeate all other means of public communication, and have an inescapable omnipresence. All this means that more people have more occasions to encounter the cultural contents of past and present than in any pre-industrial civilization. But it also means that these contents become cultural "goods," sold and bought after they have been deprived of the ultimate concern they represented when originally created. They cease to be a matter of *to be or not to be* for the person. They become matters of entertainment, sensation, sentimentality, learning, weapons of competition or social prestige, and lose in this way the power of mediating a spiritual center to the person. They lose their potential dangers for the conformity which is needed for the functioning of the technical society. And by losing their dangers they also lose their creative power, and the person without a spiritual center disintegrates.

VIII. THE STRUGGLE FOR PERSONS

To struggle for the right of the person under the conditions of technical society should not become a fight against the technical side of mass communications; it should not even become a fight against their adjusting power. The technical development is irreversible and adjustment is necessary in every society, especially in a mass society. The person as a person can preserve himself only by a *partial nonparticipation in* the objectifying structures of technical society. But he can withdraw even partially only if he has a place to which to withdraw. And this place is the New Reality to which the Christian message points, which transcends Christianity as well as non-Christianity, which is anticipated everywhere in history, and which has found its criterion in the picture of Jesus as the Christ. But the place of the withdrawal is at the same time, the starting point for the attack on the technical society and its power of depersonalization.

It is the task of the Church, especially of its theology, to describe the place of withdrawal, mainly the "religious reservation." It is the task of active groups within and on the boundary line of the Church to show the possibilities of attack, to participate in it wherever it is made and to be ready to lead it if necessary.

Looking back at the three great movements of protest against the dehumanization in the technical society, we can say that he who fights today for the person has to become an heir of all three of them. He must join in the rebellion of creative life against the degradation of person into an object. This is the first frontier of a Christian action today. Together with the philosophers of life, the Existentialists, the depth-psychologists, and whatever new allies appear, it must show how the "structure of objectivation" (transforming life and person partly into a thing, partly into a calculating machine), penetrates all realms of life and all spiritual functions. It must show especially how even the religious symbols have been misinterpreted as statements about facts and events within the whole of objectivity, thus losing their inborn power to transcend this realm of the subjective-objective, and to mediate visions of that level of reality in which life and personality are rooted. Christian action must be as daring as that of the Existentialists in their analysis of the human situation generally and the present cultural and religious situation especially. It must be as conscious of the infinite complexity of the human soul as that of the depth-psychologists, fully aware of the fact that religion is responsible as much for the complexities and conflicts of the mind as it can contribute to the solution of the conflicts. Christian action today must, like the philosophers of life, have the courage to join the rebellion of life against internal repression and external suppression—in spite of the risk of chaos. But in joining these allies, Christian action must show that it comes from a place of withdrawal where it has received a criterion and a power able to overcome the danger of losing the person while attempting to save him.

And Christian action today must be aware of the second front: together with all movements for social justice whether they are called socialist or not, it must show how the competitive society produces patterns of existence which destroy personality because they destroy community, and which increase that all pervading anxiety which characterizes our century. Christian action today must preserve, in spite of political and social odds against it, the tradition of social criticism which runs from the enthusiasts of the Reformation period through the bourgeois revolutionaries of the eighteenth century to the social critics of the nineteenth century of whom Marx was the most passionate, the most profound and the most dangerous. In alliance with all these movements Christian action must attack wherever social patterns become visible by which persons are treated as means or transferred into things or deprived of their freedom to decide and to create, or thrown into anxiety or bitterness or hate or tragic guilt. But in joining these allies, Christian action must show that it comes from a place of withdrawal where it has received a criterion and a power able to overcome the danger of sacrificing the person in order to save him.

And Christian action today must be aware of the third front: Together with all the movements within and outside Christianity which have rediscovered, partly in dependence on Kierkegaard, man's existential situation and the ultimate conflict which underlies all other conflicts, his estrangement from the ground of his being and meaning, Christian action must point to the ultimate roots of personal being. It must show that man can maintain his nature and dignity as a person only by a personal encounter with the ground of everything personal. In this encounter, which is the living center of religion and which, against rational as well as mystical criticism, has been defended by Christianity, the person is established. In showing this, Christian action shows also the place to which it withdraws from the technical society in order to attack this society. This place is that which transcends every place, even the Christian Churches. It is the New Reality which is manifest in Christ and against which even technical society and its power of destroying the person as person cannot prevail. Only out of the ground of the personal can the personal be saved. Only those who withdraw from action can receive the power to act. Christian action today rests on two poles, the one which transcends the structure of technical society—the new reality of which Christianity is the witness; the other which is present within the structure of technical society—the movements which struggle, from different sides, against its depersonalizing power. In the correlation of these two poles Christian action must find a way to save the person in the industrial society.

JULES HENRY

Jules Henry is a professor of anthropology and sociology at Washington University in St. Louis. He has long been interested in the educational and emotional problems of children and worked for some time as a research associate with Bruno Bettelheim at the Sonia Shankman Orthogenic School in Chicago. His best-known work is Culture Against Man.

Golden Rule Days: American Schoolrooms

School is an institution for drilling children in cultural orientations. Educationists have attempted to free the school from drill, but have failed because they have gotten lost among a multitude of phantasms—always choosing the most obvious "enemy" to attack. Furthermore, with every enemy destroyed, new ones are installed among the old fortifications — the enduring contradictory maze of the culture. Educators think that when they have made arithmetic or spelling into a game; made it unnecessary for children to "sit up straight"; defined the relation between teacher and children as democratic; and introduced plants, fish, and hamsters into schoolrooms, they have settled the problem of drill. They are mistaken.

EDUCATION AND THE HUMAN CONDITION

Learning to Learn

The paradox of the human condition is expressed more in education than elsewhere in human culture, because learning to learn has been and continues to be *Homo sapiens'* most formidable evolutionary task. Although it is true that mammals, as compared to birds and fishes, have to learn so much that it is difficult to say by the time we get to chimpanzees what behavior is inborn and what is learned, the learning task has become so enormous for man that today learning — education — along with survival, constitutes a major preoccupation. In all the fighting over education we are simply saying that we are not yet satisfied — after about a million years of struggling to become human — that we have mastered the fundamental human task, learning. It must also be clear that we will never quite learn how to learn, for since *Homo sapiens* is self-changing, and since the *more* culture changes the *faster* it changes, man's methods and rate of learning will never quite keep pace with his need to learn. This is the heart of the problem of "cultural lag," for each fundamental scientific discovery presents man with an incalculable number of problems which he cannot foresee. Who, for example, would have anticipated that the discoveries of Einstein would have presented us with the social problems of the nuclear age, or that information theory would have produced unemployment and displacement in world markets?

Fettering and Freeing

Another learning problem inherent in the human condition is the fact that we must conserve culture while changing it; that we must always be *more* sure of surviving than of adapting — *as we see it*. Whenever a new idea appears our first concern as *animals* must be that it does not kill us; then, and only then, can we look at it from other points of view. While it is true that we are often mistaken, either because we become enchanted with certain modes of thought or because we cannot anticipate their consequences, this tendency to look first at survival has resulted in fettering the capacity to learn new things. In general, primitive people solved this problem simply by walling their children off from new possibilities by educational methods that, largely through fear (including ridicule, beating, and mutilation) so narrowed the perceptual sphere that other than traditional ways of viewing the world became unthinkable. Thus throughout history the cultural pattern has been a device for binding the intellect. Today, when we think we wish to free the mind so it will soar, we are still, nevertheless, bound by the ancient paradox, for we must hold our culture together through clinging to old ideas lest, in adopting new ones, we literally cease to exist.

In searching the literature on the educational practices of other civilizations I have found nothing that better expresses the need to teach and to fetter than the following, from an account by a traveler along the Niger River in Africa in the fourteenth century:

> Their zeal for learning the Koran by heart [is so great that] they put their children in chains if they show any backwardness in memorizing it, and they are not set free until they have it by heart. I visited the qadi in his house on the day of the festival. His children were chained up, so I said to him, "Will you not let them loose?" He replied, "I shall not do so until they learn the Koran by heart."[1]

Perhaps the closest material parallel we have to this from our own cultural tradition is the stocks in which ordinary English upper-class children were forced to stand in the eighteenth century while they pored over their lessons at home. The fettering of the mind while we "set the spirit free" or the fettering of the spirit as we free the mind is an abiding paradox of "civilization" in its more refined dimensions. It is obvious that chimpanzees are incapable of this paradox. It is this capacity to pass from the jungles of the animal world into the jungle of paradox of the human condition that, more than anything else, marks off human from animal learning. It is this jungle that confronts the child in his early days at school, and that seals his destiny — if it has not previously been determined by poverty — as an eager mind or as a faceless learner.

Since education is always against some things and for others, it bears the burden of the cultural obsessions. While the Old Testament extols without cease the glory of the One God, it speaks with equal emphasis against the gods of the Philistines; while the children of the Dakota Indians learned loyalty to their own tribe, they learned to hate the Crow; and while our children are taught to love our American democracy, they are taught contempt for totalitarian regimes. It thus comes about that most educational systems are imbued with anxiety and hostility, that they are against as many things as they are for. Because, therefore, so much anxiety inheres in any human educational system — anxiety that it may free when it should fetter; anxiety that it may fetter when it should free; anxiety that it may teach sympathy when it should teach anger; anxiety that it may disarm where it should arm — our contemporary education system is constantly under attack. When, in anxiety about the present state of our world, we turn upon the schools with even more venom than we turn on our government, we are "right" in the sense that it is in the schools that the basic binding and freeing processes that will "save" us will be established. But being

---

1. Ibn Battuta, *Travels in Asia and Africa* (London: Broadway House, Carter Lane, 1957), p. 330. (Translated and selected by H. A. R. Gibb, from the original written in 1325–1354.)

"right" derives not so much from the faults of our schools but from the fact that the schools are the central conserving force of the culture. The Great Fear thus turns our hostility unerringly in the direction of the focus of survival and change, in the direction of education.

Creativity and Absurdity

The function of education has never been to free the mind and the spirit of man, but to bind them; and to the end that the mind and spirit of his children should never escape *Homo sapiens* has employed praise, ridicule, admonition, accusation, mutilation, and even torture to chain them to the culture pattern. Throughout most of his historic course *Homo sapiens* has wanted from his children acquiescence, not originality. It is natural that this should be so, for where every man is unique there is no society, and where there is no society there can be no man. Contemporary American educators think they want creative children, yet it is an open question as to what they expect these children to create. And certainly the classrooms — from kindergarten to graduate school — in which they expect it to happen are not crucibles of creative activity and thought. It stands to reason that were young people truly creative the culture would fall apart, for originality, by definition, is different from what is given, and what is given is the culture itself. From the endless, pathetic, "creative hours" of kindergarten to the most abstruse problems in sociology and anthropology, the function of education is to prevent the truly creative intellect from getting out of hand. Only in the exact and the biological sciences do we permit unlimited freedom, for we have (but only since the Renaissance, since Galileo and Bruno underwent the Inquisition) found a way — or *thought* we had found a way — to bind the explosive powers of science in the containing vessel of the social system.

American classrooms, like educational institutions anywhere, express the values, preoccupations, and fears found in the culture as a whole. School has no choice; it must train the children to fit the culture as it is. School can give training in skills; it cannot teach creativity. All the American school can conceivably do is nurture creativity when it appears. And who has the eyes to see it? Since the creativity that is conserved and encouraged will always be that which seems to do the most for the culture, which seems at the moment to do the most for the obsessions and the brutal preoccupations and anxieties from which we all suffer, schools nowadays encourage the child with gifts in mathematics and the exact sciences. But the child who has the intellectual strength to see through social shams is of no consequence to the educational system.

Creative intellect is mysterious, devious, and irritating. An intellectually creative child may fail, for example, in social studies, simply because he cannot understand the stupidities he is taught to believe as "fact." He may even end up agreeing with his teachers that he is "stupid" in social studies. Learning social studies is, to no small extent, whether in elementary school or the university, learning to be stupid. Most of us accomplish this task before we enter high school. But the child with a socially creative imagination will not be encouraged to play among new social systems, values, and relationships; nor is there much likelihood of it, if for no other reason than that the social studies teachers will perceive such a child as a poor student. Furthermore, such a child will simply be unable to fathom the absurdities that seem transparent *truth* to the teacher. What idiot believes in the "law of supply and demand," for example? But the children who do tend to *become* idiots, and learning to be an idiot is part of growing up! Or, as Camus put it, learning to be *absurd*. Thus the child who finds it impossible to learn to think the absurd the truth, who finds it difficult to accept absurdity as a way of life, the intellectually creative child whose mind makes him flounder like a poor fish in the net of absurdities flung around him in school, usually comes to think himself stupid.

The schools have therefore never been places for the stimulation of young minds. If all through school the young were provoked to question the Ten Commandments, the sanctity of revealed religion, the foundations of patriotism, the profit motive, the two-party system, monogamy, the laws of incest, and so on, we would have more creativity than we could handle. In teaching our children to accept fundamentals of social relationships and religious beliefs without question we follow the ancient highways of the human race, which extend backward into the dawn of the species, and indefinitely into the future. There must therefore be more of the caveman than of the spaceman about our teachers.

Up to this point I have argued that learning to learn is man's foremost evolutionary task, that the primary aim of education has been to fetter the mind and the spirit of man rather than to free them, and that nowadays we confront this problem in our effort to stimulate thought while preventing the mind of the child from going too far. I have also urged that since education, as the central institution for the training of the young in the ways of the culture, is thus burdened with its obsessive fears and hates, contemporary attacks upon our schools are the reflection of a nervousness inherent in the school as a part of the central obsession. Finally, I argued that creativity is the last thing wanted in any culture because of its potentialities for disruptive thinking; that the primordial dilemma of all education derives from the necessity of training the mighty brain of *Homo sapiens* to be stupid; and that creativity, when it is encouraged (as in science in our culture), occurs only after the creative thrust of an idea has been tamed and directed toward socially approved ends. In this sense, then, creativity can become the most obvious conformity. In this sense we can expect scientists—our cultural maximizers—to be socially no *more* creative than the most humble elementary school teacher, and probably less creative socially than a bright second-grader.

COMMUNICATION

Much of what I have to say . . . pivots on the inordinate capacity of a human being to learn more than one thing at a time. Although it is true that all the higher orders of animals can learn several things at a time, this capacity for polyphasic learning reaches unparalleled development in man.

A child writing the word "August" on the board, for example, is not only learning the word "August" but also how to hold the chalk without making it squeak, how to write clearly, how to keep going even though the class is tittering at his slowness, how to appraise the glances of the children in order to know whether he is doing it right or wrong, et cetera. If the spelling, arithmetic, or music lesson were only what it appeared to be, the education of the American child would be much simpler; but it is all the things the child learns *along with* his subject matter that really constitute the drag on the educational process as it applies to the curriculum.

A classroom can be compared to a communications system, for certainly there is a flow of messages between teacher (transmitter) and pupils (receivers) and among the pupils; contacts are made and broken, messages can be sent at a certain rate of speed only, and so on. But there is also another interesting characteristic of communications systems that is applicable to classrooms, and that is their inherent tendency to generate *noise*. *Noise*, in communications theory, applies to all those random fluctuations of the system that cannot be controlled. They are the sounds that are not part of the message: the peculiar quality communicated to the voice by the composition of the telephone circuit, the static on the radio, and so forth. In a classroom lesson on arithmetic, for example, such *noise* would range all the way from the competitiveness of the students, the quality of the teacher's voice ("I remember exactly how she sounded when she told me to sit down"), to the shuffling of the children's feet. The striking thing about the child is that along with his arithmetic—his "messages about arithmetic"—he learns all the noise in the system also. It is this inability to avoid *learning the noise with the subject matter* that constitutes one of the greatest hazards for an organism so prone to polyphasic learning as man. It is this that brings it about that an objective observer cannot tell which is being learned in any lesson, the *noise* or the formal subject matter. But—and mark this well—it is *not* primarily the message (let us say, the arithmetic or the spelling) that constitutes the most important subject matter to be learned, but the noise! The most significant cultural learnings—primarily the cultural drives—are communicated as *noise*.

Let us take up these points by studying selected incidents in some of the suburban classrooms my students and I studied over a period of six years.

THE REALM OF SONG

> It is March 17 and the children are singing songs from Ireland and her neighbors. The teacher plays on the piano, while the children sing. While some children sing, a number of them hunt in the index, find a song belonging to one of Ireland's neighbors, and raise their hands in order that they may be called on to name the next song. The singing is of that pitchless quality always heard in elementary school classrooms. The teacher sometimes sings through a song first, in her off-key, weakishly husky voice.

The usual reason for having this kind of a song period is that the children are broadened, while they learn something about music and singing.

It is true that the children learn something about singing, but what they learn is to sing like everybody else, in the standard, elementary school pitchlessness of the English-speaking world—a phenomenon impressive enough for D. H. Lawrence to have mentioned it in *Lady Chatterly's Lover*. The difficulty in achieving true pitch is so pervasive among us that missionaries carry it with them to distant jungles, teaching the natives to sing hymns off key. Hence on Sundays we would hear our Pilagá Indian friends, all of them excellent musicians in the Pilagá scale, carefully copy the missionaries by singing Anglican hymns, translated into Pilagá, off key exactly as sharp or as flat as the missionaries sang. Thus one of the first things a child with a good ear learns in elementary school is to be musically stupid; he learns to doubt or to scorn his innate musical capacities.

But possibly more important than this is the use to which teacher and pupils put the lesson in ways not related at all to singing or to Ireland and her neighbors. To the teacher this was an opportunity to let the children somehow share the social aspects of the lesson with her, to democratically participate in the selection of the songs. The consequence was distraction from singing as the children hunted in the index and raised their hands to have their song chosen. The net result was to activate the competitive, achievement, and dominance drives of the children, as they strove with one another for the teacher's attention, and through her, to get the class to do what they wanted it to do. In this way the song period on Ireland and her neighbors was scarcely a lesson in singing but rather one in extorting the maximal benefit for the Self from *any* situation. The first lesson a child has to learn when he comes to school is that lessons are not what they seem. He must then forget this and act as if they were. This is the first step toward "school mental health"; it is also the first step in becoming absurd. In the first and second grades teachers constantly scold children because they do not raise their hands enough—the prime symbol of having learned what school is all about. After that, it is no longer necessary; the kids have "tumbled" to the idea.

The second lesson is to put the teachers' and students' criteria in place of his own. He must learn that the proper way to sing is tunelessly and not the way *he* hears the music; that the proper way to paint is the way the teacher says, not the way he sees it; that the proper attitude is not pleasure but competitive horror at the success of his classmates, and so on. And these lessons must be so internalized that he will fight his parents if they object. The early schooling process is not successful unless it has accomplished in the child an acquiescence in its criteria, unless the child *wants* to think the way school has taught him to think. He must have accepted alienation as a rule of life. What we see in the kindergarten and the early years of school is the pathetic surrender of babies. How could it be otherwise?

Now, if children are taught to adopt alienation as a way of life, it follows that they must have feelings of inadequacy, for nothing so saps self-confidence as alienation from the Self. It would follow that school, the chief agent in the process, must try to provide the children with "ego support," for culture tries to remedy the ills it creates.

Hence the effort to give recognition; and hence the conversion of the songfest into an exercise in Self-realization. That anything essential was nurtured in this way is an open question, for the kind of individuality that was recognized as the children picked titles out of the index was mechanical, without a creative dimension, and under the strict control of the teacher. Let us conclude this discussion by saying that *school metamorphoses the child, giving it the kind of Self the school can manage, and then proceeds to minister to the Self it has made.*

Perhaps I have put the matter grossly, appearing to credit the school with too much formative power. So let us say this: let us grant that American children, being American, come to school on the first day with certain potentialities for experiencing success and failure, for enjoying the success of their mates or taking pleasure in their failure, for competitiveness, for cooperation, for driving to achieve or for coasting along, et cetera. But school cannot handle variety, for as an institution dealing with masses of children it can manage only on the assumption of a homogeneous mass. Homogeneity is therefore accomplished by defining the children in a certain way and by handling all situations uniformly. In this way no child is directly coerced. It is simply that the child must react in terms of the institutional definitions or he fails. The first two years of school are spent not so much in learning the rudiments of the three Rs, as in learning definitions.

It would be foolish to imagine that school, as a chief molder of character, could do much more than homogenize the children, but it does do more — it sharpens to a cutting edge the drives the culture needs.

If you bind or prune an organism so it can move only in limited ways, it will move rather excessively in that way. If you lace a man into a strait jacket so he can only wiggle his toes, he will wiggle them *hard.* Since in school children are necessarily constrained to limited human expression, under the direction of the teacher, they will have a natural tendency to do with exaggerated enthusiasm what they are permitted to do. They are like the man in the strait jacket. In class children are usually not permitted to talk much, to walk around much, to put their arms around each other during lessons, to whistle or sing. But they are permitted to raise their hands and go to the pencil sharpener almost at will. Thus hand-raising, going to the pencil sharpener, or hunting in the back of a song book for a song for the class to sing are not so much activities stemming from the requirements of an immediate situation as expressions of the intensified need of the organism for relief from the five-hour-a-day pruning and confining process. This goes under the pedagogical title of "release of tension"; but in our view the issue is that what the children are at length permitted — and invited — to do, and what they therefore often throw themselves into with the enthusiasm of multiple pent-up feelings, are cultural drive-activities narrowly construed by the school. In that context the next example is not only an expression by the children of a wish to be polite, but an inflated outpouring of contained human capacities, released enthusiastically into an available — because approved — cultural channel.

ON HANGING UP A COAT

The observer is just entering her fifth-grade classroom for the observation period. The teacher says, "Which one of you nice, polite boys

would like to take [the observer's] coat and hang it up?" From the
waving hands, it would seem that all would like to claim the title.
The teacher chooses one child, who takes the observer's coat. The
teacher says, "Now, children, who will tell [the observer] what we
have been doing?"

The usual forest of hands appears, and a girl is chosen to
tell . . . . The teacher conducted the arithmetic lessons mostly by
asking, "Who would like to tell the answer to the next problem?"
This question was usually followed by the appearance of a large and
agitated forest of hands, with apparently much competition to answer.

What strikes us here are the precision with which the teacher was able
to mobilize the potentialities in the boys for proper social behavior, and the
speed with which they responded. One is impressed also with the fact that
although the teacher could have said, "Johnny, will you please hang up
[the observer's] coat?" she chose rather to activate all the boys, and thus
give *them* an opportunity to activate their Selves, in accordance with the
alienated Selfhood objectives of the culture. The children were thus given
an opportunity to exhibit a frantic willingness to perform an act of uninvolved solicitude for the visitor; in this way each was given also a chance to
communicate to the teacher his eagerness to please her "in front of company."

The mere appearance of the observer in the doorway sets afoot a kind
of classroom destiny of self-validation and actualization of pupil-teacher
communion, and of activation of the cultural drives. In the observer's simple act of entrance the teacher perceives instantly the possibility of exhibit-
ing her children and herself, and of proving to the visitor, and once again
to herself, that the pupils are docile creatures, eager to hurl their "company"
Selves into this suburban American tragicomedy of welcome. From behind this scenery of mechanical values, meanwhile, the most self-centered
boy might emerge a *papier maché* Galahad, for what he does is not for
the benefit of the visitor but for the gratification of the teacher and of his
own culturally molded Self. The large number of waving hands proves that
most of the boys have already become absurd; but they have no choice.
Suppose they sat there frozen?

From this question we move to the inference that the skilled teacher
sets up many situations in such a way that *a negative attitude can be construed only as treason.* The function of questions like, "Which one of you
nice polite boys would like to take [the observer's] coat and hang it up?" is
to bind the children into absurdity—to compel them to acknowledge that
absurdity is existence, to acknowledge that it is better to exist absurd than
not to exist at all.

It is only natural, then, that when the teacher next asks, "Now who will
tell what we have been doing?" and "Who would like to tell the answer to
the next problem?" there should appear "a large and agitated forest of
hands," for failure to raise the hand could be interpreted only as an act of
aggression. The "arithmetic" lesson, transformed by the teacher, had become an affirmation of her matriarchal charisma as symbol of the system.

The reader will have observed that the question is not put, "Who *has*
the answer to the next problem?" but "Who *would like to tell*" it? Thus,

what at one time in our culture was phrased as a challenge to skill in arithmetic, becomes here an invitation to group participation. What is sought is a sense of "groupiness" rather than a distinguishing of individuals. Thus, as in the singing lesson an attempt was made to deny that it was a group activity, in the arithmetic lesson the teacher attempts to deny that it is an individual one. The essential issue is that *nothing is but what it is made to be by the alchemy of the system.*

In a society where competition for the basic cultural goods is a pivot of action, people cannot be taught to love one another, for those who do cannot compete with one another, except in play. It thus becomes necessary for the school, without appearing to do so, to teach children how to hate, without appearing to do so, for our culture cannot tolerate the idea that babes should hate each other. How does the school accomplish this ambiguity? Obviously through competition itself, for what has greater potential for creating hostility than competition? One might say that this is one of the most "creative" features of school. Let us consider an incident from a fifth-grade arithmetic lesson.

AT THE BLACKBOARD

> *Boris had trouble reducing "12/16" to the lowest terms, and could only get as far as "6/8". The teacher asked him quietly if that was as far as he could reduce it. She suggested he "think." Much heaving up and down and waving of hands by the other children, all frantic to correct him. Boris pretty unhappy, probably mentally paralyzed. The teacher, quiet, patient, ignores the others and concentrates with look and voice on Boris. She says, "Is there a bigger number than two you can divide into the two parts of the fraction?" After a minute or two, she becomes more urgent, but there is no response from Boris. She then turns to the class and says, "Well, who can tell Boris what the number is?" A forest of hands appears, and the teacher calls Peggy. Peggy says that four may be divided into the numerator and the denominator.*

Thus Boris' failure has made it possible for Peggy to succeed; his depression is the price of her exhilaration; his misery the occasion for her rejoicing. This is the standard condition of the American elementary school, and is why so many of us feel a contraction of the heart even if someone we never knew succeeds merely at garnering plankton in the Thames: because so often somebody's success has been bought at the cost of our failure. To a Zuñi, Hopi, or Dakota Indian, Peggy's performance would seem cruel beyond belief, for competition, the wringing of success from somebody's failure, is a form of torture foreign to those noncompetitive redskins. Yet Peggy's action seems natural to us; and so it is. How else would you run our world? And since all but the brightest children have the constant experience that others succeed at their expense they cannot but develop an inherent tendency to hate—to hate the success of others, to hate others who are successful, and to be determined to prevent it. Along with this, naturally, goes the hope that others will fail. This hatred masquerades under the euphemistic name of "envy."

Looked at from Boris' point of view, the nightmare at the blackboard was, perhaps, a lesson in controlling himself so that he would not fly shrieking from the room under the enormous public pressure. Such experiences imprint on the mind of every man in our culture the *Dream of Failure*, so that over and over again, night in, night out, even at the pinnacle of success, a man will dream not of success, but of failure. *The external nightmare is internalized for life.* It is this dream that, above all other things, provides the fierce human energy required by technological drivenness. It was not so much that Boris was learning arithmetic, but that he was learning the *essential nightmare. To be successful in our culture one must learn to dream of failure.*

From the point of view of the other children, of course, they were learning to yap at the heels of a failure. And why not? Have they not dreamed the dream of flight themselves? If the culture does not teach us to fly from failure or to rush in, hungry for success where others have failed, who will try again where others have gone broke? Nowadays, as misguided teachers try to soften the blow of classroom failure, they inadvertently sap the energies of success. The result will be a nation of chickens unwilling to take a chance.

When we say that "culture teaches drives and values" we do not state the case quite precisely. One should say, rather, that culture (and especially the school) provides the occasions in which drives and values are *experienced in events* that strike us with *overwhelming and constant force.* To say that culture "teaches" puts the matter too mildly. Actually culture invades and infests the mind as an obsession. If it does not, culture will not "work," for only an obsession has the power to withstand the impact of critical differences; to fly in the face of contradiction; to engulf the mind so that it will see the world only as the culture decrees that it shall be seen; to compel a person to be absurd. The central emotion in obsession is fear, and the central obsession in education is fear of failure. In order not to fail most students are willing to believe anything and to care not whether what they are told is true or false. Thus one becomes absurd through being afraid; but paradoxically, *only by remaining absurd can one feel free from fear.* Hence the immovableness of the absurd.

In examining education as a process of teaching the culture pattern, I have discussed a singing lesson, an arithmetic lesson, and the hanging up of a coat. Now let us consider a spelling lesson in a fourth-grade class.

"SPELLING BASEBALL"

The children form a line along the back of the room. They are to play "spelling baseball," and they have lined up to be chosen for the two teams. There is much noise, but the teacher quiets it. She has selected a boy and a girl and sent them to the front of the room as team captains to choose their teams. As the boy and girl pick the children to form their teams, each child chosen takes a seat in orderly succession around the room. Apparently they know the game well. Now Tom, who has not yet been chosen, tries to call attention to himself in order to be chosen. Dick shifts his position to be more in the direct line of vision of the choosers, so that he may not be overlooked. He seems quite anxious. Jane, Tom, Dick, and one girl whose name the observer does not know, are the last to be chosen. The teacher even has to remind the choosers that Dick and Jane have not been chosen . . . .

The teacher now gives out words for the children to spell, and they write them on the board. Each word is a pitched ball, and each correctly spelled word is a base hit. The children move around the room from base to base as their teammates spell the words correctly. With some of the words the teacher gives a little phrase: "Tongue, watch your tongue, don't let it say things that aren't kind; butcher, the butcher is a good friend to have; dozen, twelve of many things; knee, get down on your knee; pocket, keep your hand out of your pocket, and anybody else's. No talking! Three out!" The children say, "Oh, oh!"

The outs seem to increase in frequency as each side gets near the children chosen last. The children have great difficulty spelling "August." As they make mistakes, those in the seats say, "No!" The teacher says, "Man on third." As a child at the board stops and thinks, the teacher says, "There's a time limit; you can't take too long, honey." At last, after many children fail on "August" one child gets it right and returns, grinning with pleasure, to her seat . . . . The motivation level in this game seems terrific. All the children seem to watch the board, to know what's right and wrong, and seem quite keyed up. There is no lagging in moving from base to base. The child who is now writing "Thursday" stops to think after the first letter, and the children snicker. He stops after another letter. More snickers. He gets the the word wrong. There are frequent signs of joy from the children when their side is right.

Since English is not pronounced as it is spelled, "language skills" are a disaster for educators as well as for students. We start the problem of "spelling baseball" with the fact that the spelling of English is so mixed up and contradictory and makes such enormous demands on the capacity for being absurd that nowadays most people cannot spell. "Spelling baseball" is an effort to take the "weariness, the fever, and the fret" out of spelling by absurdly transforming it into a competitive game. Over and over again it has seemed to our psychologist designers of curriculum scenery that the best way to relieve boredom is to transmute it into competition. Since children are usually good competitors, though they may never become good spellers, and although they may never learn to *spell* "success" (which really should be written *sukses*), they know what it *is*, how to go after it, and how it feels not to have it. A competitive game is indicated when children are failing, because the drive to succeed in the *game* may carry them to victory over the *subject matter*. At any rate it makes spelling less boring for the teacher and the students, for it provides the former with a drama of excited children, and the latter with a motivation that transports them out of the secular dreariness of classroom routine. "Spelling baseball" is thus a major effort in the direction of making things seem not as they are. But once a spelling lesson is cast in the form of a game of baseball a great variety of *noise* enters the system, because the sounds of *baseball* (the baseball "messages") cannot but be *noise* in a system intended to communicate *spelling*. Let us therefore analyze some of the baseball noise that has entered this spelling system from the sandlots and the bleachers.

We see first that a teacher has set up a choosing-rejecting system directly adopted from kid baseball. I played ball just that way in New York. The two best players took turns picking out teammates from the bunch, coldly selecting the best hitters and fielders first; as we went down the line it didn't make much difference who got the chronic muffers (the kids who couldn't catch a ball) and fanners (the kids who couldn't hit a ball). I recall that the kids who were not good players danced around and called out to the captains, "How about me, Slim? How about me?" Or they called attention to themselves with gestures and intense grimaces, as they pointed to their chests. It was pretty noisy. Of course, it didn't make any difference because the captains knew whom they were going to try to get, and there was not much of an issue after the best players had been sorted out to one or the other team. It was an honest jungle and there was nothing in it that didn't belong to the high tension of kid baseball. But nobody was ever left out; and even the worst were never permitted to sit on the sidelines.

"Spelling baseball" is thus sandlot baseball dragged into the school-room and bent to the uses of spelling. If we reflect that one could not settle a baseball game by converting it into a spelling lesson, we see that baseball is bizarrely *irrelevant* to spelling. If we reflect further that a kid who is a poor speller might yet be a magnificent ballplayer, we are even further impressed that learning spelling through baseball is learning by absurd association. In "spelling baseball" words become detached from their real significance and become assimilated to baseballs. Thus a spelling game that promotes absurd associations provides an indispensable bridge between the larger culture, where doubletalk is supreme, and the primordial meaningfulness of language. It provides also an introduction to those associations of mutually irrelevant ideas so well known to us from advertising — girls and vodka gimlets, people and billiard balls, lipstick and tree-houses, et cetera.

In making spelling into a baseball game one drags into the classroom whatever associations a child may have to the impersonal sorting process of kid baseball, and in this way some of the *noise* from the baseball system enters spelling. But there are differences between the baseball world and the "spelling baseball" world also. Having participated in competitive athletics all through my youth, I seem to remember that we sorted ourselves by skills, and we recognized that some of us were worse than others. In baseball I also seem to remember that if we struck out or muffed a ball we hated ourselves and turned flips of rage, while our teammates sympathized with our suffering. In "spelling baseball" one experiences the sickening sensation of being left out as others are picked — to such a degree that the teachers even have to remind team captains that some· are unchosen. One's failure is paraded before the class minute upon minute, until, when the worst spellers are the only ones left, the conspicuousness of the failures has been enormously increased. Thus the *noise* from baseball is amplified by a *noise* factor specific to the classroom.

It should not be imagined that I "object" to all of this, for in the first place I am aware of the indispensable social functions of the spelling game, and in the second place, I can see that the rendering of failure conspicuous, the forcing of it on the mind of the unchosen child by a process of creeping extrusion from the group, cannot but intensify the quality of the essential nightmare, and thus render an important service to the culture. Without nightmares human culture has never been possible. Without hatred competition cannot take place.

One can see from the description of the game that drive is heightened in a complex competitive interlock: each child competes with every other to get the words right; each child competes with all for status and approval among his peers; each child competes with the other children for the approval of the teacher; and, finally, each competes as a member of a team. Here failure will be felt doubly because although in an ordinary spelling lesson one fails alone, in "spelling baseball" one lets down the children on one's team. Thus though in the game the motivation toward spelling is heightened so that success becomes triumph, so does failure become disaster. The greater the excitement the more intense the feeling of success and failure, and the importance of spelling or failing to spell "August" becomes exaggerated. But it is in the nature of an obsession to exaggerate the significance of events.

We come now to the *noise* introduced by the teacher. In order to make the words clear she puts each one in a sentence: "Tongue: watch your tongue; don't let it say things that aren't kind." "Butcher: the butcher is a good friend to have." "Dozen: twelve of many things." "Knee: get down on your knee." "Pocket: keep your hand out of your pocket, and anybody else's." More relevant associations to the words would be, "The leg bends at the knee." "A butcher cuts up meat." "I carry something in my pocket," etc. What the teacher's sentences do is introduce a number of her idiosyncratic cultural preoccupations, without clarifying anything; for there is no *necessary* relation between butcher and friend, between floor and knee, between pocket and improperly intrusive hands, and so on. In her way, therefore, the teacher establishes the same irrelevance between words and associations as the game does between spelling and baseball. She amplifies the *noise* by introducing ruminations from her own inner communication system.

CARPING CRITICISM

The unremitting effort by the system to bring the cultural drives to a fierce pitch must ultimately turn the children against one another; and though they cannot punch one another in the nose or pull each other's hair in class, they can vent some of their hostility in carping criticism of one another's work. Carping criticism is so destructive of the early tillerings of those creative impulses we cherish, that it will be good to give the matter further review.

Few teachers are like Miss Smith in this sixth-grade class:

> *The Parent-Teachers Association is sponsoring a school frolic, and the children have been asked to write jingles for publicity. For many of the children, the writing of a jingle seems painful. They are restless, bite their pencils, squirm in their seats, speak to their neighbors, and from time to time pop up with questions like, "Does it have to rhyme, Miss Smith?" At last she says, "Alright, let's read some of the jingles now." Child after child says he "couldn't get one," but some have succeeded. One girl has written a very long jingle, obviously the best in the class. However, instead of using "Friday" as the frolic day, she used "Tuesday," and several protests were heard from the children. Miss Smith defended her, saying, "Well, she made a mistake. But you are too prone to criticize. If you could only do so well!"*

In our six years of work, in hundreds of hours of observation in elementary and high schools, Miss Smith is unique in that she scolded the children for tearing down the work of a classmate. Other teachers support such attacks, sometimes even somewhat against their will.

"For many of the children, the writing of a jingle seems painful" says the record. "They are restless, bite their pencils, squirm in their seats . . . ." What are they afraid of but failure? This is made clear by Miss Smith's angry defense of the outstanding child as she says to her critics, "If only *you* could do so well!"

In a cooperative society carping is less likely to occur. Spiro says of the *kibbutz:*

> *The emphasis on group criticism can potentially engender competitive, if not hostile feelings among the children. Frequently, for example, the children read their essays aloud, and the others are then asked to comment. Only infrequently could we detect any hostility in the criticisms of the students, and often the evaluations were filled with praise.*[2]

But in Miss Smith's class, because the children have failed while one of their number has succeeded, they carp. And why not? However we may admire Miss Smith's defense of the successful child, we must not let our own "inner Borises" befog our thinking. A competitive culture endures by tearing people down. Why blame the children for doing it?

Let us now consider two examples of carping criticism from a fifth-grade class as the children report on their projects and read original stories.

> *Bill has given a report on tarantulas. As usual the teacher waits for volunteers to comment on the child's report.*
>
> *Mike: The talk was well illustrated and well prepared.*
> *Bob: Bill had a piece of paper [for his notes] and teacher said he should have them on cards . . . .*

---

2. Melford Spiro, *Children of the Kibbutz* (Cambridge, Mass.: Harvard University Press, 1958), p. 261.

Bill says he could not get any cards, and the teacher says he should tear the paper the next time he has no cards.

Bob: He held the paper behind him. If he had had to look at it, it wouldn't have been very nice.

The children are taking turns reading to the class stories they have made up. Charlie's is called The Unknown Guest.

"One dark, dreary night, on a hill a house stood. This house was forbidden territory for Bill and Joe, but they were going in anyway. The door creaked, squealed, slammed. A voice warned them to go home. They went upstairs. A stair cracked. They entered a room. A voice said they might as well stay and find out now; and their father came out. He laughed and they laughed, but they never forgot their adventure together."

Teacher: Are there any words that give you the mood of the story?
Lucy: He could have made the sentences a little better. . . .
Teacher: Let's come back to Lucy's comment. What about his sentences?
Gert: They were too short.

Charlie and Jeanne have a discussion about the position of the word "stood" in the first sentence.

Teacher: Wait a minute; some people are forgetting their manners. . . .
Jeff: About the room: the boys went up the stairs and one "cracked," then they were in the room. Did they fall through the stairs, or what?

The teacher suggests Charlie make that a little clearer . . . .

Teacher: We still haven't decided about the short sentences. Perhaps they make the story more spooky and mysterious.
Gwynne: I wish he had read with more expression instead of all at one time.
Rachel: Not enough expression.
Teacher: Charlie, they want a little more expression from you. I guess we've given you enough suggestions for one time. [Charlie does not raise his head, which is bent over his desk as if studying a paper.] Charlie! I guess we've given you enough suggestions for one time, Charlie, haven't we? [Charlie half raises his head, seems to assent grudgingly.]

It stands to reason that a competitive system must do this; and adults, since they are always tearing each other to pieces, should understand that children will be no different. School is indeed a training for later life not because it teaches the 3 Rs (more or less), but because it instills the essential cultural nightmare fear of failure, envy of success, and absurdity.

We pass now from these horrors to gentler aspects of school: impulse release and affection.

IMPULSE RELEASE AND AFFECTION

The root of life is impulse, and its release in the right amount, at the proper time and place, and in approved ways, is a primary concern of culture. Nowadays, however, in the era of impulse release and fun, the problem of impulse release takes on a special character because of the epoch's commitment to it. This being the case, teachers have a task unique in the history of education: the fostering of impulse release rather than, as in past ages, the installation of controls. Everywhere controls are breaking down, and firmness with impulse is no part of contemporary pedagogy of "the normal child." Rather impulse release, phrased as "spontaneity," "life adjustment," "democracy," "permissiveness," and "mothering," has become a central doctrine of education. It persists, despite protests from tough-minded critics from the Eastern Seaboard. In this sense education, often attacked for being "soft," is, as so often the case, far ahead of its detractors. Hardboiled critics of the educational system concentrate on curriculum. The teachers know better; the *real*, the persisting subject matter is noise.

How can a teacher face the whelming impulse life of children and yet discharge the task this period of history has assigned her? How can she release children's emotions without unchaining chaos? How can she permit the discharge of impulse and yet teach subject matter? How can she permit so much *noise* and not lose the message? Were they alive, the teachers I had in P.S. 10 and P.S. 186 in New York City, where we had to sit rigid and absolutely silent with our hands behind our backs or clasped before us on the desk, would say that chaos does prevail in many modern classrooms and that the message *is* lost. But then, each age has its own criteria of order, and what seems reasonable order to us nowadays might look and sound like chaos to them . . . .

Today our emphasis on impulse release, spontaneity, and creativity goes hand in hand with culture-weariness, a certain tiredness and disillusionment with impulse restraint, and a feeling that the Self has been sold down the river. In these circumstances permissiveness has invaded many phases of work with children, so that in some schools there is a great relaxation of controls, the essential nightmare is impaired, and the teacher most highly regarded is the one who lets children be free. Of course, it is the *adult* Self that is really straining to be free; and when Mr. Jeffries says that a child held in tight rein may break loose and "stomp" on somebody, the racehorse tearing at the halter is his own inner Self.

It is hard for us to see, since we consider most people inherently replaceable, that there is anything remarkable in a parent-figure like a teacher showering the symbols of affection on a child for a year and then letting him walk out of her life, to be replaced next year and the next and the next by different children. However, this is almost unheard of outside the stream of Western civilization; and even in the West it is not common. As a matter of fact, the existence of *children* willing to accept such demonstrations is in itself an interesting phenomenon, based probably on the obsolescence of the two-parent family. The fact that a teacher can be thus demonstrative without inflicting deep wounds on *herself* implies a character structure having strong brakes on involvement. Otherwise how could the teacher not go to pieces? If she became deeply involved in the children in her classes she would have to give up teaching, for the hurt inflicted on her as she lost her beloved children each year would be too severe. It must be, then, that the expressions of tenderness imply also, "So far and no far- ther"; over the years, children must come to recognize this. It is a kind of mutual conspiracy of affectivity in which children and teacher hold them- selves aloof, neither giving nor demanding more than the tacit rules permit. If this were not so children would have to be dragged shrieking from grade to grade, for they would become too deeply attached to teachers. This is one of the first lessons a child has to learn in kindergarten or the first grade. From this regular replacement-in-affection they learn that the affection- giving figure, the teacher, is replaceable also. In this way children are drilled in uninvolvement: they are affectively weaned from the social sys- tem. Meanwhile they learn the symbols of affectivity; that they can be used ambiguously, and that they are not binding—that they can be scattered upon the world without commitment. Classroom demonstrativeness is a phantom commitment on which no one can collect.

The reader should not imagine I am "against" affectionate classrooms. They are a necessary adjunct to contemporary childhood and to the sociali- zation of parenthood at this stage of our culture. They are also an indispens- able training ground for the release of impulse and for the buddy-buddy relations of contemporary business, government, and university.

A FINAL NOTE ON LEARNING AND CREATIVITY

In some areas of modern education theory (especially inside the heads of my education majors) democracy, permissiveness, originality, spontaneity, impulse release, learning, thinking, and adjustment to life are all mixed up together, so that, without any historic perspective at all, students come to me with the conviction that criticism of permissiveness is an attack on democracy itself. They have not been taught that the schoolrooms in which the originators of our American democracy received instruction were places of strict discipline. During the eighteenth and nineteenth centuries, when England was creating the industrial revolution and adding to her great lit- erature, schools were anything but models of permissiveness. Although German schools have been among the most "authoritarian" in Europe, Germany was one of the most creative nations in the West—and also, be- fore Hitler, a great political democracy. China is unparalleled in the tyranny with which schoolmasters ruled, yet China has given the world great poetry, drama, painting, and sculpture. France is one of the most turbulent and creative democracies of modern times, yet her classrooms are strict—much stricter, for example, than those of Czechoslovakia.

What, then, is the central issue? The central issue is love of knowledge for its own sake, not as the creature of drive, exploited largely for survival and for prestige. When knowledge is loved for itself, *noise* is at a minimum and never endangers the subject matter. Creative cultures have loved the "beautiful person"—meditative, intellectual, and exalted. As for the crea- tive individual, the history of the great civilizations seems to reveal little about creativity except that it has had an obstinate way of emerging only in gifted individuals, and that it has never appeared in the mass of the people. Loving the beautiful person more we might alter this.

·

SUMMARY

The twentieth century is the period in history when man has at last set himself to thoroughly investigate the process of learning; his study has produced an enormous mass of literature. *Homo sapiens* has finally come consciously to grips with his most essential evolutionary task; for as his culture swept him on he discovered that he was moving rapidly in the current of new knowledge but yet had no efficient way of understanding its full implications or communicating its enormous mass to his children.

As he acquires new knowledge, modern man becomes perplexed by the fact that old ideas and preoccupations bind; that in the process of teaching his children he acts in ancient ways, fettering mind and spirit. But while acknowledging that this hampers the capacity to move, man is yet afraid that unchaining the young intellect will cause overthrow and chaos. Meanwhile culture, which must be impressed upon the young mind so that traditional ways will not be thrust aside by youthful rebellion or new ideas, has to have obsessive power, and convey its antagonisms and sympathies during learning. Thus education is burdened with the weight of cultural anxieties and hatreds to the degree, indeed, that what it *loves* is often obscured, and originality is thrust aside.

Children everywhere have been trained to fit culture as it exists; and to the end that they should not fail to fit, man has used the great ingenuity of which he is capable. As a device for teaching what was necessary and preventing deviation, education became an instrument for narrowing the perceptual sphere, thus defining the human condition of being absurd; of learning to be stupid; of learning to alienate one's Self from inner promptings.

Turning to the contemporary school we see it as a place where children are drilled in cultural orientations, and where subject matter becomes to a very considerable extent the instrument for instilling them. This comes about, however, not only because school, as the heartbeat of the culture, naturally embodies and expresses the central preoccupations, but also because schools deal with masses of children, and can manage therefore only by reducing them all to a common definition. Since it is in the nature of things that the definition should be determined by the cultural preoccupations, school creates what I have called the *essential nightmare*. The nightmare must be dreamed in order to provide the fears necessary to drive people away from something (in our case, failure) and toward something (success). In this way children, instead of loving knowledge become embroiled in the nightmare.

In this situation a modern trend to make school the habitat of impulse release and fun is an expected development. It is a therapy for the cultural obsession — educators' expression of their own disenchantment with the cultural nightmares — and they have made the trend synonymous with democracy itself. That a vital democracy can be the product of a disciplined and intelligent population only; that disorder and laxity are poison to democracy, they naturally cannot see because they are just as obsessed with destroying the nightmare as an older generation was with creating it.

JOHN HOLT

John Holt is a mathematics teacher in the intermediate grades at a private school. His book How Children Fail *is essentially a collection of entries from a journal which he kept to record his children's responses to classroom teaching over a period of three years. He has recently published a second book entitled* How Children Learn *(1968).*

Education for Failure

When we talk about intelligence, we do not mean the ability to get a good score on a certain kind of test, or even the ability to do well in school; these are at best only indicators of something larger, deeper, and far more important. By intelligence we mean a style of life, a way of behaving in various situations, and particularly in new, strange, and perplexing situations. The true test of intelligence is not how much we know how to do, but how we behave when we don't know what to do.

The intelligent person, young or old, meeting a new situation or problem, opens himself up to it; he tries to take in with mind and senses everything he can about it; he thinks about *it*, instead of about himself or what it might cause to happen to him; he grapples with it boldly, imaginatively, resourcefully, and if not confidently at least hopefully; if he fails to master it, he looks without shame or fear at his mistakes and learns what he can from them. This is intelligence. Clearly its roots lie in a certain feeling about life, and one's self with respect to life. Just as clearly, unintelligence is not what most psychologists seem to suppose, the same thing as intelligence only less of it. It is an entirely different style of behavior, arising out of an entirely different set of attitudes.

Years of watching and comparing bright children and the not-bright, or less bright, have shown that they are very different kinds of people. The bright child is curious about life and reality, eager to get in touch with it, embrace it, unite himself with it. There is no wall, no barrier between him and life. The dull child is far less curious, far less interested in what goes on and what is real, more inclined to live in worlds of fantasy. The bright child likes to experiment, to try things out. He lives by the maxim that there is more than one way to skin a cat. If he can't do something one way, he'll try another. The dull child is usually afraid to try at all. It takes a good deal of urging to get him to try even once; if that try fails, he is through.

The bright child is patient. He can tolerate uncertainty and failure, and will keep trying until he gets an answer. When all his experiments fail, he can even admit to himself and others that for the time being he is not going to get an answer. This may annoy him, but he can wait. Very often, he does not want to be told how to do the problem or solve the puzzle he has struggled with, because he does not want to be cheated out of the chance to figure it out for himself in the future. Not so the dull child. He cannot stand uncertainty or failure. To him, an unanswered question is not a challenge or an opportunity, but a threat. If he can't find the answer quickly, it must be given to him, and quickly; and he must have answers for everything. Such are the children of whom a second-grade teacher once said, "But my children *like* to have questions for which there is only one answer." They did; and by a mysterious coincidence, so did she.

The bright child is willing to go ahead on the basis of incomplete understanding and information. He will take risks, sail uncharted seas, explore when the landscape is dim, the landmarks few, the light poor. To give only one example, he will often read books he does not understand in the hope that after a while enough understanding will emerge to make it worth while to go on. In this spirit some of my fifth graders tried to read *Moby Dick*. But the dull child will go ahead only when he thinks he knows exactly where he stands and exactly what is ahead of him. If he does not feel he knows exactly what an experience will be like, and if it will not be exactly like other experiences he already knows, he wants no part of it. For while the bright child feels that the universe is, on the whole, a sensible, reasonable, and trustworthy place, the dull child feels that it is senseless, unpredictable, and treacherous. He feels that he can never tell what may happen, particularly in a new situation, except that it will probably be bad.

Nobody starts off stupid. You have only to watch babies and infants, and think seriously about what all of them learn and do, to see that, except for the most grossly retarded, they show a style of life, and a desire and ability to learn that in an older person we might well call genius. Hardly an adult in a thousand, or ten thousand, could in any three years of his life learn as much, grow as much in his understanding of the world around him, as every infant learns and grows in his first three years. But what happens, as we get older, to this extraordinary capacity for learning and intellectual growth?

What happens is that it is destroyed, and more than by any other one thing, by the process that we misname education—a process that goes on in most homes and schools. We adults destroy most of the intellectual and creative capacity of children by the things we do to them or make them do. We destroy this capacity above all by making them afraid, afraid of not doing what other people want, of not pleasing, of making mistakes, of failing, of being *wrong*. Thus we make them afraid to gamble, afraid to experiment, afraid to try the difficult and the unknown. Even when we do not create children's fears, when they come to us with fears ready-made and built-in, we use these fears as handles to manipulate them and get them to do what we want. Instead of trying to whittle down their fears, we build them up, often to monstrous size. For we like children who are a little afraid of us, docile, deferential children, though not, of course, if they are so obviously afraid that they threaten our image of ourselves as kind, lovable people whom there is no reason to fear. We find ideal the kind of "good" children who are just enough afraid of us to do everything we want, without making us feel that fear of us is what is making them do it.

We destroy the disinterested (I do *not* mean *un*interested) love of learning in children, which is so strong when they are small, by encouraging and compelling them to work for petty and contemptible rewards—gold stars, or papers marked 100 and tacked to the wall, or A's on report cards, or honor rolls, or dean's lists, or Phi Beta Kappa keys—in short, for the ignoble satisfaction of feeling that they are better than someone else. We encourage them to feel that the end and aim of all they do in school is nothing more than to get a good mark on a test, or to impress someone with what they seem to know. We kill, not only their curiosity, but their feeling that it is a good and admirable thing to be curious, so that by the age of ten most of them will not ask questions, and will show a good deal of scorn for the few who do.

In many ways, we break down children's convictions that things make sense, or their hope that things may prove to make sense. We do it, first of all, by breaking up life into arbitrary and disconnected hunks of subject matter, which we then try to "integrate" by such artificial and irrelevant devices as having children sing Swiss folk songs while they are studying the geography of Switzerland, or do arithmetic problems about rail-splitting while they are studying the boyhood of Lincoln. Furthermore, we continually confront them with what is senseless, ambiguous, and contradictory; worse, we do it without knowing that we are doing it, so that, hearing nonsense shoved at them as if it were sense, they come to feel that the source of their confusion lies not in the material but in their own stupidity. Still further, we cut children off from their own common sense and the world of reality by requiring them to play with and shove around words and symbols that have little or no meaning to them. Thus we turn the vast majority of our students into the kind of people for whom all symbols are meaningless; who cannot use symbols as a way of learning about and dealing with reality; who cannot understand written instructions; who, even if they read books, come out knowing no more than when they went in; who may have a few new words rattling around in their heads, but whose mental models of the world remain unchanged and, indeed, impervious to change. The minority, the able and successful students, we are very likely to turn into something different but just as dangerous: the kind of people who can manipulate words and symbols fluently while keeping themselves largely divorced from the reality for which they stand; the kind of people who like to speak in large generalities but grow silent or indignant if someone asks for an example of what they are talking about; the kind of people who, in their discussions of world affairs, coin and use such words as megadeaths and megacorpses, with scarcely a thought to the blood and suffering these words imply.

We encourage children to act stupidly, not only by scaring and confusing them, but by boring them, by filling up their days with dull, repetitive tasks that make little or no claim on their attention or demands on their intelligence. Our hearts leap for joy at the sight of a roomful of children all slogging away at some imposed task, and we are all the more pleased and satisfied if someone tells us that the children don't really like what they are doing. We tell ourselves that this drudgery, this endless busywork, is good preparation for life, and we fear that without it children would be hard to "control." But why must this busywork be so dull? Why not give tasks that are interesting and demanding? Because, in schools where every task must be completed and every answer must be right, if we give children more demanding tasks they will be fearful and will instantly insist that we show them how to do the job. When you have acres of paper to fill up with pencil marks, you have no time to waste on the luxury of thinking. By such means children are firmly established in the habit of using only a small part of their thinking capacity. They feel that school is a place where they must spend most of their time doing dull tasks in a dull way. Before long they are deeply settled in a rut of unintelligent behavior from which most of them could not escape even if they wanted to.

* * *

School tends to be a dishonest as well as a nervous place. We adults are not often honest with children, least of all in school. We tell them, not what we think, but what we feel they ought to think; or what other people feel or tell us they ought to think. Pressure groups find it easy to weed out of our classrooms, texts, and libraries whatever facts, truths, and ideas they happen to find unpleasant or inconvenient. And we are not even as truthful with children as we could safely be, as the parents, politicians, and pressure groups would let us be. Even in the most non-controversial areas our teaching, the books, and the textbooks we give children present a dishonest and distorted picture of the world.

The fact is that we do not feel an obligation to be truthful to children. We are like the managers and manipulators of news in Washington, Moscow, London, Peking, and Paris, and all the other capitals of the world. We think it our right and our duty, not to tell the truth, but to say whatever will best serve our cause — in this case, the cause of making children grow up into the kind of people we want them to be, thinking whatever we want them to think. We have only to convince ourselves (and we are very easily convinced) that a lie will be "better" for the children than the truth, and we will lie. We don't always need even that excuse; we often lie only for our own convenience.

Worse yet, we are not honest about ourselves, our own fears, limitations, weaknesses, prejudices, motives. We present ourselves to children as if we were gods, all-knowing, all-powerful, always rational, always just, always right. This is worse than any lie we could tell about ourselves. I have more than once shocked teachers by telling them that when kids ask me a question to which I don't know the answer, I say, "I haven't the faintest idea"; or that when I make a mistake, as I often do, I say, "I goofed again"; or that when I am trying to do something I am no good at, like paint in water colors or play a clarinet or bugle, I do it in front of them so they can see me struggling with it, and can realize that not all adults are good at everything. If a child asks me to do something that I don't want to do, I tell him that I won't do it because I don't want to do it, instead of giving him a list of "good" reasons sounding as if they had come down from the Supreme Court. Interestingly enough, this rather open way of dealing with children works quite well. If you tell a child that you won't do something because you don't want to, he is very likely to accept that as a fact which he cannot change; if you ask him to stop doing something because it drives you crazy, there is a very good chance that, without further talk, he will stop, because he knows what that is like.

We are, above all, dishonest about our feelings, and it is this sense of dishonesty of feeling that makes the atmosphere of so many schools so unpleasant. The people who write books that teachers have to read say over and over again that a teacher must love all the children in a class, all of them equally. If by this they mean that a teacher must do the best he can for every child in a class, that he has an equal responsibility for every child's welfare, an equal concern for his problems, they are right. But when they talk of love they don't mean this; they mean feelings, affection, the kind of pleasure and joy that one person can get from the existence and company of another. And this is not something that can be measured out in little spoonfuls, everyone getting the same amount.

In a discussion of this in a class of teachers, I once said that I liked some of the kids in my class much more than others and that, without saying which ones I liked best, I had told them so. After all, this is something that children know, whatever we tell them; it is futile to lie about it. Naturally, these teachers were horrified. "What a terrible thing to say!" one said. "I love all the children in my class exactly the same." Nonsense; a teacher who says this is lying, to herself or to others, and probably doesn't like any of the children very much. Not that there is anything wrong with that; plenty of adults don't like children, and there is no reason why they should. But the trouble is they feel they should, which makes them feel guilty, which makes them feel resentful, which in turn makes them try to work off their guilt with indulgence and their resentment with subtle cruelties — cruelties of a kind that can be seen in many classrooms. Above all, it makes them put on the phony, syrupy, sickening voice and manner, and the fake smiles and forced, bright laughter that children see so much of in school, and rightly resent and hate.

As we are not honest with them, so we won't let children be honest with us. To begin with, we require them to take part in the fiction that school is a wonderful place and that they love every minute of it. They learn early that not to like school or the teacher is *verboten*, not to be said, not even to be thought. I have known a child, otherwise healthy, happy, and wholly delightful, who at the age of five was being made sick with worry by the fact that she did not like her kindergarten teacher. Robert Heinemann worked for a number of years with remedial students whom ordinary schools were hopelessly unable to deal with. He found that what choked up and froze the minds of these children was above all else the fact that they could not express, they could hardly even acknowledge the fear, shame, rage, and hatred that school and their teachers had aroused in them. In a situation in which they were and felt free to express these feelings to themselves and others, they were able once again to begin learning. Why can't we say to children what I used to say to fifth graders who got sore at me, "The law says you have to go to school; it doesn't say you have to like it, and it doesn't say you have to like me either." This might make school more bearable for many children.

Children hear all the time, "Nice people don't say such things." They learn early in life that for unknown reasons they must not talk about a large part of what they think and feel, are most interested in, and worried about. It is a rare child who, anywhere in his growing up, meets even one older person with whom he can talk openly about what most interests him, concerns him, worries him. This is what rich people are buying for their troubled kids when for $25 per hour they send them to psychiatrists. Here is someone to whom you can speak honestly about whatever is on your mind, without having to worry about his getting mad at you. But do we have to wait until a child is snowed under by his fears and troubles to give him this chance? And do we have to take the time of a highly trained professional to hear what, earlier in his life, that child might have told anybody who was willing to listen sympathetically and honestly? The workers in a project called Streetcorner Research, in Cambridge, Mass., have found that nothing more than the opportunity to talk openly and freely about themselves and their lives, to people who would listen without judging, and who were interested in them as human beings rather than as problems to be solved or disposed of, has totally remade the lives and personalities of a number of confirmed and seemingly hopeless juvenile delinquents. Can't we learn something from this? Can't we clear a space for honesty and openness and self-awareness in the lives of growing children? Do we have to make them wait until they are in a jam before giving them a chance to say what they think?

*   *   *

Behind much of what we do in school lie some ideas, that could be expressed roughly as follows: (1) Of the vast body of human knowledge, there are certain bits and pieces that can be called essential, that everyone should know; (2) the extent to which a person can be considered educated, qualified to live intelligently in today's world and be a useful member of society, depends on the amount of this essential knowledge that he carries about with him; (3) it is the duty of schools, therefore, to get as much of this essential knowledge as possible into the minds of children. Thus we find ourselves trying to poke certain facts, recipes, and ideas down the gullets of every child in school, whether the morsel interests him or not, even if it frightens him or sickens him, and even if there are other things that he is much more interested in learning.

These ideas are absurd and harmful nonsense. We will not begin to have true education or real learning in our schools until we sweep this nonsense out of the way. Schools should be a place where children learn what they most want to know, instead of what we think they ought to know. The child who wants to know something remembers it and uses it once he has it; the child who learns something to please or appease someone else forgets it when the need for pleasing or the danger of not appeasing is past. This is why children quickly forget all but a small part of what they learn in school. It is of no use or interest to them; they do not want, or expect, or even intend to remember it. The only difference between bad and good students in this respect is that the bad students forget right away, while the good students are careful to wait until after the exam. If for no other reason, we could well afford to throw out most of what we teach in school because the children throw out almost all of it anyway.

The notion of a curriculum, an essential body of knowledge, would be absurd even if children remembered everything we "taught" them. We don't and can't agree on what knowledge is essential. The man who has trained himself in some special field of knowledge or competence thinks, naturally, that his specialty should be in the curriculum. The classical scholars want Greek and Latin taught; the historians shout for more history; the mathematicians urge more math and the scientists more science; the modern language experts want all children taught French, or Spanish, or Russian; and so on. Everyone wants to get his specialty into the act, knowing that as the demand for his special knowledge rises, so will the price that he can charge for it. Who wins this struggle and who loses depends not on the real needs of children or even of society, but on who is most skillful in public relations, who has the best educational lobbyists, who best can capitalize on events that have nothing to do with education, like the appearance of Sputnik in the night skies.

The idea of the curriculum would not be valid even if we could agree what ought to be in it. For knowledge itself changes. Much of what a child learns in school will be found, or thought, before many years, to be untrue. I studied physics at school from a fairly up-to-date text that proclaimed that the fundamental law of physics was the law of conservation of matter — matter is not created or destroyed. I had to scratch that out before I left school. In economics at college I was taught many things that were not true of our economy then, and many more that are not true now. Not for many years after I left college did I learn that the Greeks, far from being a detached and judicious people surrounded by chaste white temples, were hot-tempered, noisy, quarrelsome, and liked to cover their temples with gold leaf and bright paint; or that most of the citizens of Imperial Rome, far from living in houses in which the rooms surrounded an atrium, or central court, lived in multi-story tenements, one of which was perhaps the largest building in the ancient world. The child who really remembered everything he heard in school would live his life believing many things that were not so.

Moreover, we cannot possibly judge what knowledge will be most needed forty, or twenty, or even ten years from now. At school, I studied Latin and French. Few of the teachers who claimed then that Latin was essential would make as strong a case for it now; and the French might better have been Spanish, or better yet, Russian. Today the schools are busy teaching Russian; but perhaps they should be teaching Chinese, or Hindi, or who-knows-what? Besides physics, I studied chemistry, then perhaps the most popular of all science courses; but I would probably have done better to study biology, or ecology, if such a course had been offered (it wasn't). We always find out, too late, that we don't have the experts we need, that in the past we studied the wrong things; but this is bound to remain so. Since we can't know what knowledge will be most needed in the future, it is senseless to try to teach it in advance. Instead, we should try to turn out people who love learning so much and learn so well that they will be able to learn whatever needs to be learned.

How can we say, in any case, that one piece of knowledge is more important than another, or indeed, what we really say, that some knowledge is essential and the rest, as far as school is concerned, worthless? A child who wants to learn something that the school can't and doesn't want to teach him will be told not to waste his time. But how can we say that what he wants to know is less important than what we want him to know? We must ask how much of the sum of human knowledge anyone can know at the end of his schooling. Perhaps a millionth. Are we then to believe that one of these millionths is so much more important than another? Or that our social and national problems will be solved if we can just figure out a way to turn children out of schools knowing two millionths of the total, instead of one? Our problems don't arise from the fact that we lack experts enough to tell us what needs to be done, but out of the fact that we do not and will not do what we know needs to be done now.

Learning is not everything, and certainly one piece of learning is as good as another. One of my brightest and boldest fifth graders was deeply interested in snakes. He knew more about snakes than anyone I've ever known. The school did not offer herpetology; snakes were not in the curriculum; but as far as I was concerned, any time he spent learning about snakes was better spent than in ways I could think of to spend it; not least of all because, in the process of learning about snakes, he learned a great deal more about many other things than I was ever able to "teach" those unfortunates in my class who were not interested in anything at all. In another fifth-grade class, studying Romans in Britain, I saw a boy trying to read a science book behind the cover of his desk. He was spotted, and made to put the book away, and listen to the teacher; with a heavy sigh he did so. What was gained here? She traded a chance for an hour's real learning about science for, at best, an hour's temporary learning about history —much more probably no learning at all, just an hour's worth of daydreaming and resentful thoughts about school.

It is not subject matter that makes some learning more valuable than others, but the spirit in which the work is done. If a child is doing the kind of learning that most children do in school, when they learn at all—swallowing words, to spit back at the teacher on demand—he is wasting his time, or rather, we are wasting it for him. This learning will not be permanent, or relevant, or useful. But a child who is learning naturally, following his curiosity where it leads him, adding to his mental model of reality whatever he needs and can find a place for, and rejecting without fear or guilt what he does not need, is growing—in knowledge, in the love of learning, and in the ability to learn. He is on his way to becoming the kind of person we need in our society, and that our "best" schools and colleges are *not* turning out, the kind of person who, in Whitney Griswold's words, seeks and finds meaning, truth, and enjoyment in everything he does. All his life he will go on learning. Every experience will make his mental model of reality more complete and more true to life, and thus make him more able to deal realistically, imaginatively, and constructively with whatever new experience life throws his way.

We cannot have real learning in school if we think it is our duty and our right to tell children what they must learn. We cannot know, at any moment, what particular bit of knowledge or understanding a child needs most, will most strengthen and best fit his model of reality. Only he can do this. He may not do it very well, but he can do it a hundred times better than we can. The most we can do is try to help, by letting him know roughly what is available and where he can look for it. Choosing what he wants to learn and what he does not is something he must do for himself.

There is one more reason, and the most important one, why we must reject the idea of school and classroom as places where, most of the time, children are doing what some adult tells them to do. The reason is that there is no way to coerce children without making them afraid, or more afraid. We must not try to fool ourselves into thinking that this is not so. The would-be progressives, who until recently had great influence over most American public school education, did not recognize this—and still do not. They thought, or at least talked and wrote as if they thought, that there were good ways and bad ways to coerce children (the bad ones mean, harsh, cruel, the good ones gentle, persuasive, subtle, kindly), and that if they avoided the bad and stuck to the good they would do no harm. This was one of their greatest mistakes, and the main reason why the revolution they hoped to accomplish never took hold.

The idea of painless, non-threatening coercion is an illusion. Fear is the inseparable companion of coercion, and its inescapable consequence. If you think it your duty to make children do what you want, whether they will or not, then it follows inexorably that you must make them afraid of what will happen to them if they don't do what you want. You can do this in the old-fashioned way, openly and avowedly, with the threat of harsh words, infringement of liberty, or physical punishment. Or you can do it in the modern way, subtly, smoothly, quietly, by withholding the acceptance and approval which you and others have trained the children to depend on; or by making them feel that some retribution awaits them in the future, too vague to imagine but too implacable to escape. You can, as many skilled teachers do, learn to tap with a word, a gesture, a look, even a smile, the great reservoir of fear, shame, and guilt that today's children carry around inside them. Or you can simply let your own fears, about what will happen to you if the children don't do what you want, reach out and infect them. Thus the children will feel more and more that life is full of dangers from which only the goodwill of adults like you can protect them, and that this goodwill is perishable and must be earned anew each day.

The alternative—I can see no other—is to have schools and classrooms in which each child in his own way can satisfy his curiosity, develop his abilities and talents, pursue his interests, and from the adults and older children around him get a glimpse of the great variety and richness of life. In short, the school should be a great smörgåsbord of intellectual, artistic, creative, and athletic activities, from which each child could take whatever he wanted, and as much as he wanted, or as little. When Anna was in the sixth grade, the year after she was in my class, I mentioned this idea to her. After describing very sketchily how such a school might be run, and what the children might do, I said, "Tell me, what do you think of it? Do you think it would work? Do you think the kids would learn anything?" She said, with utmost conviction, "Oh, yes, it would be wonderful!" She was silent for a minute or two, perhaps remembering her own generally unhappy schooling. Then she said thoughtfully, "You know, kids really like to learn; we just don't like being pushed around."

No, they don't; and we should be grateful for that. So let's stop pushing them around, and give them a chance.

EDGAR Z. FRIEDENBERG

Sociologist Edgar Z. Friedenberg has written a number of provocative articles and books dealing with education and the problems of adolescence. He is the author of The Vanishing Adolescent *(1962),* Coming of Age in America *(1967), and* The Dignity of Youth and Other Atavisms *(1966). Friedenberg is currently a professor of sociology and education at the University of Buffalo.*

An Ideology of School Withdrawal

Compulsory school attendance in the United States has been justified from the beginning as essential to democratic polity. Everyone knows Madison's statement to the effect that popular government without popular education is the prelude to a tragedy, or a farce, or both. We have had both, continuously ever since. I have just finished Theodore White's *The Making of the President, 1960;* and I think this book is the strongest indictment of American public education I have ever seen, though Mr. White does not discuss the issue directly. Still, the laws are on the books. Within a century, with the Kalamazoo decision (1874), the legal basis had been laid for what Madison thought so necessary.

And, be it noted, for the reasons he gave. So far as I know, public support of education in this country has never been justified on the grounds that education was beneficial to the individual student, except to the extent that this pertained to equality of opportunity. It is logical to argue that the individuals who share the responsibilities of citizenship must learn what they have to know in order to discharge them. I wouldn't say the logic was water-tight. In Louisiana, where I was raised, we have never regarded either ignorance or lunacy as a bar to high public office; and this liberalism has permitted us to enjoy unusually creative leadership. But, on the whole, the point is well taken. If public education can be justified on the grounds that it is essential to citizenship, it can also claim, for that reason, to be good for the future citizens themselves.

School attendance laws, however, are a very distorted reflection of the purpose implicit in Madison's phrase. They are not *licensing* laws. They do not require attendance until a specified minimum level of competence deemed essential to the conduct of adult life has been attained; this would mean a life sentence for some. Nor are they *contractual:* they do not assure the student any outcome or even any minimum standard of educational service or decent treatment in exchange for his obligation to attend. Other laws, to be sure, do set up such standards, but the student has no remedy against their breach. Even if he can establish that the school is sub-standard and that he personally is mistreated there, he cannot legally withdraw; he can only try to force the school authorities to make improvements which, usually, they would already have made long ago if they possibly could.

From this point of view, compulsory school attendance appears as a gross violation of civil liberty: a bill of attainder against a specific age group that guarantees no compensation in return. The school may, indeed, benefit the child; but it doesn't have to in order to earn the right to retain him. In talking about the youngsters who drop out, therefore, I am not going to start with the assumption that they ought to be retained. My hunch is that a large proportion of the dropouts may be doing what is best for themselves under the atrocious circumstances that exist. But I do want to analyze those circumstances, and see why the schools have so little to offer these youngsters.

In the small Southern Methodist college I attended, we had chapel services twice a week; and after the opening hymn there was a responsive reading. The Dean—it was a poor school and could only afford one—would read a portion of Scripture aloud; and the students, assembled as a congregation, would read the following portion: his in light-faced type, ours in bold. There was one of these that I liked especially well, and I remember fragments of it distinctly—not accurately, but distinctly. It began:

> DEAN: *Whereof from a young man's fancy shall he wend his way?*
> STUDENTS: *By taking heed unto the Lord, and the firmament thereof.*

This responsive reading, in the version in which I recall it, is admirably suited to its purpose. The first line reveals real evidence of poetic influence. It ties in with the culture, showing that we share in its heritage, and it alludes to the necessity for progress and achievement; while the second line asserts the necessity of basing these on a sound moral imperative. By saying it over together we experienced a feeling of mutuality and belonging, of being the same kind. Yet we ran no risk of binding ourselves to too literal an interpretation of its mandate, because it doesn't actually make any sense at all.

For the types of students it is designed for, the public high school and junior high school curriculum serves, I believe, exactly the same purpose as this responsive reading. Its function is liturgical. This is not as true of elementary school, because the basic skills really work. If you read as you are taught there, you will understand at least the words; if you write, your words will be understood; if you follow the rules of arithmetic, your calculations will check out and your books will balance, though you may never have the remotest conception of mathematics.

High school, however, is another matter. What would happen to the businessman, or just citizen, who attempted to apply what he was taught in high-school civics to the actual power structure of his community or his country? Who learns to love reading, or to find the kind of reading he can love among the classics and the bitty anthologies of the high-school English course? High-school history, by and large, is not even propaganda, because nobody is expected to believe it or to be moved by it; it is received as official myth. We tell youngsters that the Pilgrims came to New England searching for religious freedom not in order to give them an understanding of the actual root values of Colonial New England, but in order to provide them with the relevant cliché about the relation of church and state in America, and to let them know that a good middle-class American thinks of "my religious affiliation" or "the faith of my choice." This keeps the youngsters from getting hung up on religion, like an Italian peasant or rural Southerner. As for high-school science, it has, since Sputnik, increased its work load enormously and often tries to duplicate the content of college science courses. But essentially, it serves not as an introduction to science but to legitimate the American middle-class epistemology; science proves that Truth is an aggregate of general principles induced from empirical data that observers can agree on. The function of science is to protect people from odd-balls by setting up the rules so that subjective feeling is discounted. The scientific method, then, becomes a way of separating ends and means. When we want to win an election, or spy on the Soviet Union, or redevelop a slum, we go about it scientifically—i.e., by defining what we are trying to do as a technical problem. Naturally, we care about the feelings of the people affected; people's emotions are a very important factor. That's why we have psychologists on our team.

It is even truer than the progressives have always maintained that there is no valid distinction between the curriculum and the extra-curriculum. What counts is the total experience of the student, and what he learns in both the classroom and the playing field is a posture, a pattern of anxieties and a pattern of responses for dealing with it. There is seldom any pleasure in scholarship or ideas as such; the classroom and the playing field alike are places where you try to make it, and learn the techniques for making it that alienate you least from your peers. The over-all rules are the same in both: learn the ropes; don't get hung up; always be friendly, sincere, and creative. And win!

The important thing about this familiar picture is that it is a picture of a totally instrumental institution. Nothing about the institution is meant to be valuable, here and now, for its own sake. I don't mean that high-school students don't have any fun. Of course they do; in the suburbs, at least, the high school is a "fun place." But this sort of fun is a part of the social pattern to be learned; being "fun" helps you to make it as well or better than anything, and it takes a great deal of social skill which American adolescents, notably, do learn.

We have never had much interest in what education means and feels like to the youngsters who are subjected to it; only in what it might help them to make of themselves. Even the Supreme Court, in its decision against segregation, could not rest on the moral obloquy and insult that segregation imposes on Negro children; that was not enough. It had to support its position further by pointing out that a major reason why separate schools could not be equal even if they were identical was that the Negro students couldn't make the same contacts there that white students could in their school, and that this was what people really go to school for.

So it is: the Court has done our motives no discredit, but merely reaffirmed our tradition. The public school gives poor boys a chance to develop their potentialities, both by formal education and by providing an opportunity to mingle with and learn from their social superordinates. The commonwealth is then the richer for the skills they later contribute, which would otherwise have been forever lost. This is exactly the opportunity our dropouts need, and which they ought presumably to welcome. So what has gone wrong?

What has gone wrong is pretty complicated; but basically I think one might locate it in the schools' perennial assumptions about the nature of what they have had to offer the children of the poor. These assumptions were probably never valid; but both the school and the poor once believed them. Now, only the school continues to assert them, though no longer with much conviction.

The schools assumed that in order to get ahead in America the student had to learn not only a body of skills, but also a set of social conventions, increasingly subtle and refined as he climbed up the ladder. In school he was taught techniques for handling things and manners for getting along with people. The teachers were the transmitters of an alien culture—alien to them, too. Social mobility was a process like preparing to get a job as a rice farmer in China or a coffee-grower in Brazil. There was a strange language to be learned—from instructors who didn't speak it too well themselves; a strange body of techniques to be mastered—from teachers who had never practiced them at first hand. It would all have to be learned over again when he got there; but at the time it seemed relevant, and made the student feel that he was well on his way.

Now, there are three important ways in which this situation differs from the condition in the high school today. In the first place, the problem of dropouts did not then exist. Most of the students who drop out today would never have been in high school fifty years ago; the school-leaving age has risen irregularly over the past decades, and a more rigid and self-confident school policy would not have hesitated to keep students in grade school until they reached it, whatever it was, if they did not pass. A good many of these dropped out, and took unskilled jobs, which existed; and that was the last anyone thought of them till election day six or seven years later. They weren't a dropout problem; they were the working class.

But those who didn't drop out, even though they came from a working-class background, did not feel at the time that they were losing their identity. This happened later, after they had made it, in the classical discovery of the loneliness of the long-distance runner. In school you were still you: *striving* didn't separate you from other poor, immigrant boys; it was exactly what poor, immigrant boys were supposed to do. There was no intimation at the time that you were leaving yourself behind. It wasn't that you were becoming a different person; the old *you* was learning new tricks. Education was instrumental, all right—it has always been that in America —but the instruments were thought to be in the curriculum. The student didn't have to learn to think of *himself* as one.

And finally, nobody doubted what the norms were. It seemed very clear that the people in the next stratum up were the ones who knew what the student had to learn; he had to be able to do what they did. This wouldn't make them accept him willingly; but it would allow him to work his way in even if they didn't.

I don't mean to imply that the school actually delivered the social mobility it promised; sometimes it did, more often it didn't. But this was the way it was supposed to work, and why there was so little controversy over whether compulsory school attendance was good for the individual as well as for the commonwealth. As long as the students who stayed in school believed in education naïvely, it served—much better than religion could have in this heterogeneous country—as the opiate of the people. And opium vendors don't have dropout problems.

Apparently, however—to judge by the present situation—they can: the American poor are getting over their addiction.[1] It takes more and more education every year to invoke the same dream; and reality breaks through too often, leaving them sick, mean, and edgy. The educational establishment, fearful of losing popular support, is naturally much concerned with the possibilities of a *rapprochement,* of which two have already been tried. The simplest of these is an effort to beef up the traditional, but paradoxically faltering, economic appeal of education. Students are reminded over and over that today, more than ever, you need a high-school diploma to get any sort of job and a college degree to get a good one. They are given the statistics on the fabulous return education, as an investment, brings in over a lifetime in increments of annual income. The unemployment data on adolescents and unskilled labor are stressed so that the youngsters will understand how hopeless things will be for them if they drop out of school. If they and their teacher are sophisticated enough, the demographic shift in job-type may be explained: how unskilled and blue-collar work has fallen off, while service and white-collar jobs, demanding a higher level of school achievement, have enormously increased in proportion.

All this is true enough, but the implication is false. It does not follow that most of the students now dropping out would have a better chance, even economically, if they stayed in school. As S. M. Miller and Frank Riessman have pointed out in a recent WBAI broadcast, the illusory success of some of these school-retention efforts in leading students to better jobs is based on the fact that they made hardly a dent in the number of school dropouts; if the programs had been successful in reaching the students they would inevitably have failed in delivering the jobs. In our economy, the demonstrable economic value of an education is partly a consequence of its scarcity. The blue-collar-white-collar figures are relative, and one loses sight of how much smaller the white-collar one was to begin with. The absolute increase in white-collar opportunity does not compensate for the absolute loss in blue-collar jobs—a discrepancy which is rapidly increasing in magnitude as automation proceeds. Today's dropouts are, perhaps fortunately, pretty skeptical kids; if they all believed that the school could deliver them to a brighter economic future we would soon have unemployed IBM operators and technicians hanging around the way India and Africa have lawyers.

The other, and more sophisticated, *rapprochement* is represented by the

---

1. Thus, in her recent study of the schools in Big City, Patricia Sexton reports dropout rates even in *elementary school* of 15.5 per 10,000 children from families earning from $3,000–5,000 annually, falling to 3 children per 10,000 for families earning $5,000–7,000. For families making more than $9,000, the rate was less than 1 child per 10,000. In high schools, of course, the rate is enormously greater, but follows the same pattern. There is no high school in Big City whose median family income is less than $5,000. For schools with median family incomes ranging from $5,000–5,999, Sexton found a dropout rate of 19.2 per cent of the total registration falling to 7.9 per cent for schools whose students had a median family income of $7,000–7,999, and to 3.6 per cent for the school whose students came from families having median incomes above $9,000. (*Education and Income*, Viking, 1961, pp. 97 and 202.)

Higher Horizons Program, about which I wish I could bring myself to be less doubtful, for it is a program that seems to me characterized by much intelligence, ingenuity, enthusiasm, and sheer good will. Its appeal, moreover, is not purely economic. I understand it to be an attempt to convey to students that middle-class culture, *in toto*, is not beyond their grasp. It can be theirs, if only they do their work. As the title implies, the Higher Horizons approach seeks to make education appear more worthwhile to the student, and encourages him to remain in school to develop his potentialities, by raising his level of aspiration not just economically but culturally. As the boy lifts himself to gaze beyond the slum there comes into view the Museum of Modern Art.

It is heartening to find the middle class so generously willing to share its resources, and, for once, apparently confident of their value. It is also obvious that if the middle class cannot somehow make public education acceptable to the poor on its terms rather than theirs, middle-class dominance of public education — a long established fact of American life — is doomed. But if the effort is successful, it will remind me of a story that a very intelligent, very British, very working-class hospital orderly used to tell, in a sensitive effort to ease his middle-class patients' embarrassment at the services he was obliged to perform for them. This story concerned a small pharmaceutical firm that was facing bankruptcy. It had an established reputation as Britain's most reputable manufacturer of suppositories. But respect for craftsmanship, as is well known, was declining; their customers, apparently, were turning to other sources for satisfaction. Things looked black. Then the firm consulted one of Madison Avenue's most resourceful advertising agencies. And the agency, after much brainstorming, came up with a slogan that at once opened vast markets to the company by motivating the very segment of the population which had hitherto most successfully resisted its appeal. The slogan was, very simply, "If you don't like our suppositories, you know what you can do with them!"

The dropouts, by and large, don't like middle-class culture; and they know quite well what we can do with it. Dropping out is one way of telling us, and it is about time we turned our attention to the things about the school that are bugging them. The school is the arena in which these youngsters encounter middle-class life; this is where the dropouts fight the ten-year's ideological war that ends in their defeat and rout. In this warfare the core values of their culture and the values the school represents are at issue, and any one that we start by considering will lead to the others. I think the most fruitful might be the familiar question of deferred gratification, or impulse control, which is the source of so much conflict with the school authorities.

We all know the school's side of the question; and know that lower-class youngsters act out their conflicts. Retention programs try to face up to this by helping the youngsters learn more self-control and giving them some valid experience of being rewarded for it, so that they will discover for themselves that certain very desirable goals exist that can only be achieved by people who plan, save, and give a soft answer to wrath-provoking circumstances. In this way the kids learn that there may be more desirable rewards than the immediate pleasure of blowing up and shooting your bolt. "Now, Dionysus, let's think about what we're really trying to get done here," friendly Apollo is always urging; and of course he is right. The difficulty lies in getting Dionysus to listen.

Or does it? Let me return for a moment to Mr. White's account of the 1960 election, and the Apollonian behavior it elicited from the Republican candidate.

> *And this, finally, was the only summary one could make of the campaign that Richard M. Nixon had so valiantly waged, under such personal suffering: that there was neither philosophy nor structure to it, no whole picture either of the man or of the future he offered. One could perceive neither in this last climactic proposal nor in his prepared speeches nor in his personal discourses any shape of history, any sense of the stream of time or flow of forces by which America had come to this point in history and might move on. Nixon's skill in politics was enormous, his courage unquestioned, his endurance substantial. But they were the skills, courage, and endurance of the sailor who knows the winds and can brave the storm and recognize the tide. There was missing in him always the direction of the navigator . . . . Thus, it is impossible to distinguish, from his campaign performance, what Nixon's personal political attitude was to the arrest of Martin Luther King when that hero figure of American Negroes was arrested in the last days of the campaign . . . . On the afternoon of the sentencing of Martin Luther King to four months of hard labor in Georgia, the Department of Justice — at the suggestion of a wise yet shrewd Republican Deputy Attorney-General — composed a draft statement to support the application for release of the imprisoned Negro minister. Two copies of the draft were sent out immediately for approval — one to the White House, one to Mr. Nixon's traveling headquarters. No one has yet revealed who killed this draft statement that was so critically important in the tense politics of civil rights. Either President Eisenhower or Vice-President Nixon could have acted — yet neither did. However obscure Eisenhower's motivations were, Nixon's are more perplexing, for he was the candidate. He had made the political decision at Chicago to court the Negro vote in the North; only now, apparently, he felt it quite possible that Texas, South Carolina, and Louisiana might all be won to him by the white vote and he did not wish to offend that vote. So he did not act — there was no whole philosophy of politics to instruct him.*
>
> *There could never be any doubt of the Vice-President's pugnacity or innate courage; yet it was a pugnacity and courage committed without a framing strategy to make them effective.*

The terms of Mr. White's criticism are as interesting as the incident itself. No philosophy of politics? No framing strategy? On the contrary, he was all strategy. What he lacked was heart and a sense of outrage: the capacity to make moral judgments. Yet, Mr. White cannot say this because his whole book, though very sensitive to moral factors in the contest, shares the assumption that a candidate's first duty is to get elected. Nixon lost, and the figures do indeed show that his expediency on this issue may have cost him the election. But to infer from this fact that the worst thing about Mr. Nixon's behavior was that it didn't work is to share his posture.

Earlier on, Mr. White describes the situations in the campaign that found Mr. Nixon at his best:

> One had to see Nixon entering a small Iowa village—the streets lined with school children, all waving American flags until it seemed as if the cavalcade were entering a defile lined by fluttering, peppermint-striped little banners—then see him stop at a Harvest Festival (in Red Oaks)—where on the festival tables lay the ripened ears of field corn . . . to see him at his best. For in such small towns he found an echo. These people were his natural constituency, his idiom their idiom . . . . He woke in Marietta, Ohio, on Monday, October 25th, to begin his last "peak" effort, and it was clear from his first speech of the day that he was at one with his audience as he had not been since he had passed through the corn fields of Iowa in the first week of the campaign. A sign outside the courthouse of Marietta, Ohio, read: HIGH SCHOOL DEBATERS GREET WORLD DEBATER—the sign was apropos and of the essence of this last trip as he revived. For he was a high-school debater, the boy who had some thirty years before won a Los Angeles Times prize for his high-school oration on the Constitution. He was seeking not so much to score home a message as to win the hearts of his little audiences; his style was homestyle and during the next two weeks told much about him.

In Red Oaks and Marietta they don't have much of a dropout problem. Good, solid communities, with woodsheds ample to the needs of youth, they turn out clean-cut boys and girls among whom Mr. Nixon is right at home. It was the urban proletariat, and overwhelmingly the Negroes, who refused to take part in his Harvest Festival, though the corn be ripe and the harvest long overdue.

To carry this illustration further would not make my point clearer; in any case, it is simple enough. I think the youngsters who drop out are probably, in many ways, a more promising moral resource than those who stay in, and I think they are driven out in part by moral revulsion from the middle-class life of the school. They could never, themselves, identify their feelings as moral repugnance because they view morality as being on the side of the enemy and therefore square; they imagine they dislike morality and have never been allowed to realize that they have morals of their own. They don't have a complete moral *system*, because they are not systematic; they are unprincipled in their behavior, because principles are too abstract for them to handle. But in a concrete situation they can be trusted more safely than their middle-class peers who are trying to make it.

Mr. Nixon and his silent superior are symbols, too; and I am not naïve enough to attribute the lower-class response to them solely to the revulsion they arouse in the breast of the noble savage. The opposition was well-organized and well-manipulated. But there are natural affinities and polarities in politics that set limits to what manipulation can achieve, and these, among other things, are reflected in the class structure of American society. Officially, American society is, however, middle-class and opportunistic — in the Land of Opportunity these are the values that receive official support and that in fact prevail. It is surely fair enough to take Mr. Eisenhower, and Nr. Nixon at the zenith of his presidential aspirations, as representative of what is most American. But one need not be wholly partisan. President Kennedy has also stated emphatically that we need technical rather than ideological or philosophical approaches to the problems that confront us.

This moral attitude dominates our life. We are caught in it in crisis after crisis: in the U-2 incident, the Cuban invasion, the presence of our observers in Vietnam organizing the forced evacuation of peasants so that their farms can be burned, and helping the government see to it that the Viet Cong guerrillas don't get any antibiotics. Time after time the world finds a nice, friendly American standing in the middle of somebody else's ruins, with no more to say for himself than a rueful "It shoulda worked, but somebody must have goofed!"

I have a name for this boy. I call him Edsel, and I think it is time we withdrew him from production and got out a more responsive and less hazardous model. Even the practical-minded may not have much use for him any more; the locals seem to be getting pretty tired of Edsel and are about ready to get him out of there, with a hammer and sickle if necessary. But if we are to grow anything better, the dropouts are the kids to start with, for they have come part way on their own, against heavy opposition, already. They are ill-disciplined. They have no basic skills. They are so sore that any place you touch them hurts, and when they are hurt they hurt back. They are extremely parochial, limited in their experience of the world to a few city blocks of desolate slum, and therefore both gullible and suspicious about anything beyond it. They are sometimes homeless, and never have any quiet place to study and think. They are inconveniently aware of their own sexuality and inconveniently skilled at bringing it to the attention of others. They live, their teachers sometimes say, like animals; and as they say it, a ghost sobs, harshly. But if these youngsters are trapped, it is not in their apprehensions of pseudo-events. They are not alienated from themselves. They still have access to their sense-data, and, on their own terms, they are accustomed to fidelity.

These are the qualities that, I believe, we hoped to preserve and continually renew by building an open society in which a sensitive, compulsively masculine boy could become an Ernest Hemingway and a poor but beautiful waif a Marilyn Monroe. But at this juncture, less fatal alternatives to mediocrity are needed. Can a school geared to success and social mobility help formulate them? Its traditions are against it, its staff is against it, its relationship to the community power structure is against it.

To reach the dropouts and give them a reason for staying, the school would have to start by accepting their *raison d'être*. It would have to take lower-class life seriously as a condition and a pattern of experience — not just as a contemptible and humiliating set of circumstances that every decent boy or girl is anxious to escape from. It would have to accept their language, and their dress, and their values as a point of departure for disciplined exploration, to be understood, not as a trick for luring them into the middle class, but as a way of helping them to explore the meaning of their own lives. This is the way to encourage and nurture potentialities from *whatever* social class. Talent, and genius, when real, are expressions of individual experience and the inner life. But success and higher status are not the first goals to which talent or genius is devoted—though they are sometimes the last.

I do not mean to imply that I accept Sitwell's Fallacy: that the poor are happier in their station in life and should be left to enjoy it. Most lower-class people of whatever age hate lower-class life, I am sure: the noise, and the filth, and the crowding, and the vulnerability to the police and illness; never feeling quite well or quite rested. Worst of all, perhaps, is the constant din of the mass media—including the school—telling them that if they were any good at all they would be middle-class like everybody else, and live in loveliness in Larchmont. But the fact that they have reason to hate their life of fear and deprivation does not give us the right to force ours on them as the only acceptable alternative to it. This is something they must work out for themselves, and the school's job is to help them understand most fully the meaning and nature of what they have to work with. Basically, the problem of reaching the dropout is analogous to that faced by the Peace Corps in reaching the peoples of underdeveloped countries. Can we—do we even really wish to—help them deal with their situation on their terms with our resources, while leaving our way of life aside till somebody asks for it?

Frankly, I doubt it. This is not how the teachers I know approach lower-status youngsters. They are afraid of them, for one thing. The principal is afraid of disorder which looks bad in his record and in the records of his teachers, and they each have their careers to think of, too. So they learn early to keep the kids in line; this comes first. Order *is* helpful to learning, but it doesn't come first, it grows out of the common task; and teachers who put it first are not enthusiastic allies in keeping disorderly youngsters in school till a basis for order can be created. Order is not, to be sure, the central issue, but it will serve to symbolize the sharpness of the issue between those whose security depends on the suppression of impulse, and those who depend on its expression.

In the urban public school today, the former predominate, and I don't think they can be easily changed, within the limits of personality and bureaucracy that characterize the school. If they can be, there is no fundamental reason why the kinds of youngsters who now drop out may not be well served. But this is a big *if*, for the public school, as it is, is profoundly expressive of our culture. And the fate of the "dropouts" is just one more expression of their actual status in our democracy.

The answer, then, may be "No; this plant makes only Edsels." But if it is, I see no dropout problem. Let them go, let them go, God bless them. They may pop up again. St. James (or Santiago, as this chiliastic figure is known in Spanish) is not merely more merciful than the school system; he is far more flexible and versatile. He can accommodate a wider range of talent; he has a great Court, as well as an Infirmary, and though no familiar avenue bears his name, he has, like James Madison, been thus honored by the inhabitants of certain cities. The nearest, unfortunately, in Cuba.

PAUL GOODMAN

Paul Goodman is one of the most controversial figures in contemporary American education. Currently a professor of philosophy at Brandeis University, Goodman has written extensively, and his books range from novels and poetry to studies in city planning. Of particular interest to educators are Compulsory Mis-Education *(1966),* The Community of Scholars *(1966), and* Growing Up Absurd *(1960). Goodman is also co-author (with Frederick Perls and Ralph F. Hefferline) of the book* Gestalt Therapy *(1951). He is a frequent contributor to such journals as* Commentary, The Partisan Review, *and* The Kenyon Review.

The Universal Trap

I

A conference of experts on school drop-outs will discuss the background of poverty, cultural deprivation, race prejudice, family and emotional troubles, neighborhood uprooting, urban mobility. It will explore ingenious expedients to counteract these conditions, though it will not much look to remedying them — that is not its business. And it will suggest propaganda — e.g., no school, no job — to get the youngsters back in school. It is axiomatic that they ought to be in school.

After a year, it proves necessary to call another conference to cope with the alarming fact that more than 75% of the drop-outs who have been cajoled into returning, have dropped out again. They persist in failing; they still are not sufficiently motivated. What curricular changes must there be? how can the teachers learn the life-style of the underprivileged?

Curiously muffled in these conferences is the question that puts the burden of proof the other way: What are they drop-outs from? Is the schooling really good for them, or much good for anybody? Since, for many, there are such difficulties with the present arrangements, might not some better arrangements be invented? Or bluntly, since schooling undertakes to be compulsory, must it not continually review its claim to be useful? Is it the only means of education? Isn't it unlikely that *any* single type of social institution could fit almost every youngster up to age 16 and beyond? (It is predicted that by 1970, 50% will go to college.)

But conferences on drop-outs are summoned by school professionals, so perhaps we cannot hope that such elementary questions will be raised. Yet neither are they raised by laymen. There is a mass superstition, under-written by additional billions every year, that adolescents must continue going to school. The middle-class *know* that no professional competence —i.e., status and salary—can be attained without many diplomas; and poor people have allowed themselves to be convinced that the primary remedy for their increasing deprivation is to agitate for better schooling. Neverthe-less, I doubt that, *at present or with any reforms that are conceivable under present school administration*, going to school is the best use for the time of life of the majority of youth.

II

Education is a natural community function and occurs inevitably, since the young grow up on the old, toward their activities, and into (or against) their institutions; and the old foster, teach, train, exploit, and abuse the young. Even neglect of the young, except physical neglect, has an educa-tional effect—not the worst possible.

Formal schooling is a reasonable auxiliary of the inevitable process, whenever an activity is best learned by singling it out or special attention with a special person to teach it. Yet it by no means follows that the com-plicated artifact of a school system has much to do with education, and cer-tainly not with good education.

Let us bear in mind the way in which a big school system might have nothing to do with education at all. The New York system turns over $700 millions annually, not including capital improvements. There are 750 schools, with perhaps 15 annually being replaced at an extra cost of $2 to $5 millions each. There are 40,000 paid employees. This is a vast vested inter-est, and it is very probable that—like much of our economy and almost all of our political structure, of which the public schools are a part—it goes on for its own sake, keeping more than a million people busy, wasting wealth, and pre-empting time and space in which something else could be going on. It is a gigantic market for textbook manufacturers, building contractors, and graduate-schools of Education.

The fundamental design of such a system is ancient, yet it has not been altered although the present operation is altogether different in scale from what it was, and therefore it must have a different meaning. For example, in 1900, 6% of the 17-year-olds graduated from high school, and less than ½% went to college; whereas in 1963, 65% graduated from high school and 35% went on to something called college. Likewise, there is a vast differ-ence between schooling intermitted in life on a farm or in a city with plenty of small jobs, and schooling that is a child's only "serious" occupation and often his only adult contact. Thus, a perhaps outmoded institution has become almost the only allowable way of growing up. And with this pre-empting, there is an increasing intensification of the one narrow experi-ence, e.g., in the shaping of the curriculum and testing according to the in-creasing requirements of graduate schools far off in time and place. Just as our American society as a whole is more and more tightly organized, so its school system is more and more regimented as part of that organization.

In the organizational plan, the schools play a non-educational and an educational role. The non-educational role is very important. In the tender grades, the schools are a baby-sitting service during a period of collapse of the old-type family and during a time of extreme urbanization and urban mobility. In the junior and senior high school grades, they are an arm of the police, providing cops and concentration camps paid for in the budget under the heading "Board of Education." The educational role is, by and large, to provide — at public and parents' expense — apprentice-training for corporations, government, and the teaching profession itself, and also to train the young, as New York's Commissioner of Education has said (in the Worley case), "to handle constructively their problems of adjustment to authority."

The public schools of America have indeed been a powerful, and beneficent, force for the democratizing of a great mixed population. But we must be careful to keep reassessing them when, with changing conditions, they become a universal trap and democracy begins to look like regimentation.

III

Let me spend a page on the history of the compulsory nature of the school systems. In 1961, in *The Child, the Parent, and the State,* James Conant mentions a possible incompatibility between "individual development" and "national needs"; this, to my mind, is a watershed in American philosophy of education and puts us back to the ideology of Imperial Germany, or on a par with contemporary Russia.

When Jefferson and Madison conceived of compulsory schooling, such an incompatibility would have been unthinkable. They were in the climate of the Enlightenment, were strongly influenced by Congregational (town-meeting) ideas, and were of course makers of a revolution. To them, "citizen" meant society-*maker*, not one "participating in" or "adjusted to" society. It is clear that they regarded themselves and their friends as citizens existentially, so to speak; to make society was their breath of life. But obviously such conceptions are worlds removed from, and diametrically opposed to, our present political reality, where the ground rules and often the score are pre-determined.

For Jefferson, people had to be taught in order to multiply the sources of citizenly initiative and to be vigilant for freedom. Everybody had to become literate and study history, in order to make constitutional innovations and be fired to defend free institutions, which was presumably the moral that history taught. And those of good parts were to study a technological natural philosophy, in order to make inventions and produce useful goods for the new country. By contrast, what are the citizenly reasons for which we compel everybody to be literate, etc.? To keep the economy expanding, to understand the mass-communications, to choose between indistinguishable Democrats and Republicans. Planning and decision-making are lodged in top managers; rarely, and at most, the electorate serves as a pressure-group.

There is a new emphasis on teaching science — we will discuss this in another context — but the vast majority will never use this knowledge and will forget it; they are consumers.

Another great impulse for compulsory education came from the new industrialism and urbanism during the three or four decades after the Civil War, a time also of maximum immigration. Here the curricular demands were more mundane: in the grades, literacy and arithmetic; in the colleges, professional skills to man the expanding economy. But again, no one would have spoken of an incompatibility between "individual development" and "national needs," for it was considered to be an open society, abounding in opportunity. Typically, the novels of Horatio Alger, Jr., treat schooling as morally excellent as well as essential for getting ahead; and there is no doubt that the immigrants saw education-for-success as also a human value for their children. Further, the school-system was not a trap. The 94% who in 1900 did not finish high school had other life opportunities, including making a lot of money and rising in politics. But again, by and large this is not our present situation. There is plenty of social mobility, opportunity to rise — except precisely for the ethnic minorities who are our main concern as drop-outs — but the statuses and channels are increasingly stratified, rigidified, cut and dried. Most enterprise is parceled out by feudal corporations, or by the state; and these determine the requirements. Ambition with average talent meets these rules or fails; those without relevant talent, or with unfortunate backgrounds, cannot even survive in decent poverty. The requirements of survival are importantly academic, attainable only in schools and universities; but such schooling is ceasing to have an initiating or moral meaning.

We do not have an open economy; even when jobs are not scarce, the corporations and state dictate the possibilities of enterprise. General Electric swoops down on the high schools, or IBM on the colleges, and skims off the youth who have been pre-trained for them at public or private expense. (Private college tuition runs upward of $6000, and this is estimated as a third or less of the actual cost for "education and educational administration.") Even a department store requires a diploma for its salespeople, not so much because of the skills they have learned as that it guarantees the right character: punctual and with a smooth record. And more generally, since our powers-that-be have opted for an expanding economy with a galloping standard of living, and since the powers of the world are in an arms and space race, there *is* a national need for many graduates specifically trained. Thus, even for those selected, the purpose is irrelevant to citizenly initiative, the progress of an open society, or personal happiness, and the others have spent time and effort in order to be progressively weeded out. Some drop out.

IV

It is said that our schools are geared to "middle-class values," but this is a false and misleading use of terms. The schools less and less represent *any* human values, but simply adjustment to a mechanical system.

Because of the increasing failure of the schools with the poor urban mass, there has developed a line of criticism—e.g., Oscar Lewis, Patricia Sexton, Frank Riessman, and even Edgar Friedenberg—asserting that there is a "culture of poverty" which the "middle-class" schools do not fit, but which has its own virtues of spontaneity, sociality, animality. The implication is that the "middle-class," for all its virtues, is obsessional, prejudiced, prudish.

Pedagogically, this insight is indispensable. A teacher must try to reach each child in terms of what he brings, his background, his habits, the language he understands. But if taken to be more than technical, it is a disastrous conception. The philosophic aim of education must be to get each one out of his isolated class and into the one humanity. Prudence and responsibility are not middle-class virtues but human virtues; and spontaneity and sexuality are not powers of the simple but of human health. One has the impression that our social-psychologists are looking not to a human community but to a future in which the obsessionals will take care of the impulsives!

In fact, some of the most important strengths that have historically belonged to the middle class are flouted by the schools: independence, initiative, scrupulous honesty, earnestness, utility, respect for thorough scholarship. Rather than bourgeois, our schools have become petty-bourgeois, bureaucratic, time-serving, gradgrind-practical, timid, and *nouveau riche* climbing. In the upper grades and colleges, they often exude a cynicism that belongs to rotten aristocrats.

Naturally, however, the youth of the poor and of the middle class respond differently to the petty bourgeois atmosphere. For many poor children, school is orderly and has food, compared to chaotic and hungry homes, and it might even be interesting compared to total deprivation of toys and books. Besides, the wish to improve a child's lot, which on the part of a middle-class parent might be frantic status-seeking and pressuring, on the part of a poor parent is a loving aspiration. There is here a gloomy irony. The school that for a poor Negro child might be a great joy and opportunity is likely to be dreadful; whereas the middle-class child might be better off *not* in the "good" suburban school he has.

Other poor youth, herded into a situation that does not fit their disposition, for which they are unprepared by their background, and which does not interest them, simply develop a reactive stupidity very different from their behavior on the street or ball field. They fall behind, play truant, and as soon as possible drop out. If the school situation is immediately useless and damaging to them, their response must be said to be life-preservative. They thereby somewhat diminish their chances of a decent living, but we shall see that the usual propaganda—that schooling is a road to high salaries—is for most poor youth a lie; and the increase in security is arguably not worth the torture involved.

The reasonable social policy would be not to have these youth in school, certainly not in high school, but to educate them otherwise and provide opportunity for a decent future in some other way. How? I shall venture some suggestions later; in my opinion, the wise thing would be to have our conferences on *this* issue, and omit the idea of drop-out altogether.

But the brute fact is that our society isn't really interested; the concern for the drop-outs is mainly because they are a nuisance and a threat and can't be socialized by the existing machinery.

Numerically far more important than these overt drop-outs at 16, however, are the children who conform to schooling between the ages of 6 to 16 or 20, but who drop out internally and day-dream, their days wasted, their liberty caged and scheduled. And there are many such in the middle class, from backgrounds with plenty of food and some books and art, where the youth is seduced by the prospect of money and status, but even more where he is terrified to jeopardize the only pattern of life he knows.

It is in the schools and from the mass media, rather than at home or from their friends, that the mass of our citizens in all classes learn that life is inevitably routine, depersonalized, venally graded; that it is best to toe the mark and shut up; that there is no place for spontaneity, open sexuality, free spirit. Trained in the schools, they go on to the same quality of jobs, culture, politics. This *is* education, mis-education, socializing to the national norms and regimenting to the national "needs."

John Dewey used to hope, naïvely, that the schools could be a community somewhat better than society and serve as a lever for social change. In fact, our schools reflect our society closely, except that they *emphasize* many of its worst features, as well as having the characteristic defects of academic institutions of all times and places.

V

Let us examine realistically half a dozen aspects of the school that is dropped out *from*.

(a) There is widespread anxiety about the children not learning to read, and hot and defensive argument about the methods of teaching reading. Indeed, reading deficiency is an accumulating scholastic disadvantage that results in painful feeling of inferiority, truancy, and drop-out. Reading is crucial for school success — all subjects depend on it — and therefore for the status-success that the diploma is about. Yet in all the anxiety and argument, there is no longer any mention of the freedom and human cultivation that literacy is supposed to stand for.

In my opinion, there is something phony here. For a change, let us look at this "reading" coldly and ask if it is really such a big deal except precisely in the school that is supposed to teach it and is sometimes failing to do so.

With the movies, TV, and radio that the illiterate also share, there is certainly no lack of "communications." We cannot say that as humanities or science, the reading-matter of the great majority is in any way superior to the content of these other media. And in the present stage of technology and economy, it is probably *less* true than it was in the late nineteenth century — the time of the great push to universal literacy and arithmetic — that the mass-teaching of reading is indispensable to operate the production and clerical system. It is rather our kind of urbanism, politics, and buying and selling that require literarcy. These are not excellent.

Perhaps in the present dispensation we should be as well off if it were socially acceptable for large numbers not to read. It would be harder to regiment people if they were not so well "informed"; as Norbert Wiener used to point out, every repetition of a cliché only increases the noise and *prevents* communication. With less literacy, there would be more folk culture. Much suffering of inferiority would be avoided if youngsters did not have to meet a perhaps unnecessary standard. Serious letters could only benefit if society were less swamped by trash, lies, and bland verbiage. Most important of all, *more* people might become genuinely literate if it were understood that reading is not a matter-of-course but a *special useful art with a proper subject-matter, imagination and truth,* rather than a means of communicating top-down decisions and advertising. (The advertising is a typical instance: when the purpose of advertising was to give information—"New shipment of salt fish arrived, very good, foot of Barclay Street"—it was useful to be able to read; when the point of advertising is to create a synthetic demand, it is better not to be able to read.)

(b) Given their present motives, the schools are not competent to teach authentic literacy, reading as a means of liberation and cultivation. And I doubt that most of us who seriously read and write the English language ever learned it by the route of "Run, Spot, Run" to *Silas Marner.* Rather, having picked up the rudiments either in cultured homes or in the first two grades, we really learned to read by our own will and free exploration, following our bent, generally among books that are considered inappropriate by school librarians!

A great neurologist tells me that the puzzle is not how to teach reading, but why some children fail to learn to read. Given the amount of exposure that any urban child gets, any normal animal should spontaneously catch on to the code. What prevents? It is almost demonstrable that, for many children, it is precisely going to school that prevents—because of the school's alien style, banning of spontaneous interest, extrinsic rewards and punishments. (In many underprivileged schools, the I.Q. steadily falls the longer they go to school.) Many of the backward readers might have had a better chance on the streets.

But let me say something, too, about the "successful" teaching of reading and writing in the schools. Consider, by contrast, the method employed by Sylvia Ashton-Warner in teaching little Maoris. She gets them to ask for their *own* words, the particular gut-word of fear, lust, or despair that is obsessing the child that day; this is written for him on strong cardboard; he learns it instantaneously and never forgets it; and soon he has an exciting, if odd, vocabulary. From the beginning, writing is by demand, practical, magical; and of course it is simply an extension of speech—it is the best and strongest speech, as writing should be. What is read is what somebody is importantly trying to tell. Now what do our schools do? We use tricks of mechanical conditioning. These do positive damage to spontaneous speech, meant expression, earnest understanding. Inevitably, they create *in the majority* the wooden attitude toward "writing," as entirely different from speech, that college-teachers later try to cope with in Freshman Composition. And reading inevitably becomes a manipulation of signs, e.g., for test-passing, that has no relation to experience.

(Until recently, the same discouragement by schoolteachers plagued children's musical and plastic expression, but there have been attempts to get back to spontaneity—largely, I think, because of the general revolution in modern art and musical theory. In teaching science, there is just now a strong movement to encourage imagination rather than conditioned "answers." In teaching foreign languages, the emphasis is now strongly on vital engagement and need to speak. Yet in teaching reading and writing, the direction has been the contrary; even progressive education has gone back to teaching spelling. These arts are regarded merely as "tools.")

(c) The young rightly resist animal constraint. But, at least in New York where I have been a school-board Visitor, most teachers—and the principals who supervise their classes—operate as if progressive education had not proved the case for noise and freedom of bodily motion. (Dewey stresses the salutary alternation of boisterousness and tranquility.) The seats are no longer bolted to the floor, but they still face front. Of course, the classes are too large to cope with without "discipline." Then make them smaller, or don't wonder if children escape out of the cage, either into truancy or baffled daydream. Here is a typical case: an architect replacing a Harlem school is forbidden by the Board to spend money on soundproofing the classrooms, even though the principal has called it a necessity for the therapy of pent-up and resentful children. The resentment, pent-up hostility, is a major cause of reactive stupidity; yet there is usually an absolute ban on overt expression of hostility, or even of normal anger and aggression.

Again, one has to be blind not to see that, from the onset of puberty, the dissidence from school is importantly sexual. Theoretically, the junior high school was introduced to fit this change of life; yet astoundingly, it is sexless. My own view, for what it's worth, is that sexuality is lovely, there cannot be too much of it, it is self-limiting if it is satisfactory, and satisfaction diminishes tension and clears the mind for attention and learning. Therefore, sexual expression should be approved in and out of season, also in school, and where necessary made the subject of instruction. But whether or not this view is correct, it certainly is more practical than the apparent attempt of the schools to operate as if sexual drives simply did not exist. When, on so crucial an issue, the schools act a hundred years out of date, they are crucially irrelevant.

But the following *is* something new:

> "*Trenton, May 24 (AP)—A state health official believes some overanxious New Jersey parents are dosing their children with tranquilizers before sending them to school . . . the Health Department pediatrician assigned to the State Education Department said the parents apparently are trying to protect the children from cracking under pressure for good grades.*"

(d) Terrible damage is done to children simply by the size and standardization of the big system. Suppose a class size of 20 is good for average purposes; it does *not* follow that 35 is better than nothing. Rather, it is likely to be positively harmful, because the children have ceased to be persons and the teacher is destroyed as a teacher. A teacher with a 10-year-old class reading at 7-year level will have to use the content as well as the vocabulary of *Dick and Jane* since that is the textbook bought by the hundred thousands. The experience of a wise principal is that the most essential part of his job is to know every child's name and be an available "good father," so he wants a school for 400. Yet the city will build the school for 2000, because only that is practical, even though the essence is entirely dissipated. The chief part of learning is in the community of scholars, where classwork and social life may cohere; yet social engineers like Dr. Conant will, for putative efficiencies, centralize the high schools—the "enriched" curriculum with equipment is necessary for the national needs.

A program—e.g., to prevent drop-out—will be, by an attentive teacher, exquisitely tailored to the children he works with; he will have a success. Therefore his program must be standardized, watered down, for 75 schools—otherwise it cannot be financed—although now it is worthless. But here is an unbeatable anecdote: An architect is employed to replace a dilapidated school but is forbidden to consult the principal and teachers of the school about their needs, since his building must conform to uniform plans at headquarters, the plans being two generations out of date. As a functionalist, the architect demurs, and it requires an *ad hoc* assembly of all the superintendents to give him special permission.

Presumably all this is administratively necessary, but then it is also necessary for bruised children to quit. Our society makes a persistent error in metaphysics. We are so mesmerized by the operation of a system with the appropriate name, for instance "Education," that we assume that it *must* be working somewhat, though admittedly not perfectly, when perhaps it has ceased to fulfill its function altogether and might even be preventing the function, for instance education.

(e) Especially today, when the hours of work will sharply diminish, the schools are supposed to educate for the satisfaction of life and for the worthwhile use of leisure. Again, let us try to be realistic, as a youngster is. For most people, I think, a candid self-examination will show that their most absorbing, long, and satisfactory hours are spent in activities like friendly competitive sports, gambling, looking for love and love-making, earnest or argumentative conversation, political action with signs and sit-ins, solitary study and reading, contemplation of nature and cosmos, arts and crafts, music, and religion. Now none of these requires much money. Indeed, elaborate equipment takes the heart out of them. Friends use one another as resources. God, nature, and creativity are free. The media of the fine arts are cheap stuff. Health, luck, and affection are the only requirements for good sex. Good food requires taking pains more than spending money.

What is the moral for our purposes? Can it be denied that in some respects the drop-outs make a wiser choice than many who go to school, not to get real goods but to get money? Their choice of the "immediate"—their notorious "inability to tolerate delay"—is not altogether impulsive and neurotic. The bother is that in our present culture, which puts its entire emphasis on the consumption of expensive commodities, they are so nagged by inferiority, exclusion, and despair of the future that they cannot enjoy their leisure with a good conscience. Because they know little, they are deprived of many profound simple satisfactions and they never know what to do with themselves. Being afraid of exposing themselves to awkwardness and ridicule, they just hang around. And our urban social arrangements—e.g., high rent—have made it impossible for anybody to be decently poor on a "low" standard. One is either in the rat-race or has dropped out of society altogether.

(f) As a loyal academic, I must make a further observation. Mainly to provide Ph.D.'s, there is at present an overwhelming pressure to gear the "better" elementary schools to the graduate-universities. This is the great current reform, genre of Rickover. But what if the top of the ladder is corrupt and corrupts the lower grades? On visits to 70 colleges everywhere in the country, I have been appalled at how rarely the subjects are studied in a right academic spirit, for their truth and beauty and as part of humane international culture. The students are given, and seek, a narrow expertise, "mastery," aimed at licenses and salary. They are indoctrinated with a national thoughtlessness that is not even chauvinistic. Administrators sacrifice the community of scholars to aggrandizement and extramurally sponsored research.

Conversely, there is almost never conveyed the sense in which learning is truly practical, to enlighten experience, give courage to initiate and change, reform the state, deepen personal and social peace. On the contrary, the entire educational system itself creates professional cynicism or the resigned conviction that Nothing Can Be Done. If this is the University, how can we hope for aspiring scholarship in the elementary schools? On the contrary, everything will be grades and conforming, getting ahead not in the subject of interest but up the ladder. Students "do" Bronx Science in order to "make" M.I.T. and they "do" M.I.T. in order to "make" Westinghouse; some of them have "done" Westinghouse in order to "make" jail.

VI

What then? The compulsory system has become a universal trap, and it is no good. Very many of the youth, both poor and middle class, might be better off if the system simply did not exist, even if they then had no formal schooling at all. (I am extremely curious for a philosophic study of Prince Edward County in Virginia, where for some years schooling did not exist for Negro children.)

But what would become of these children? For very many, both poor and middle class, their homes are worse than the schools, and the city streets are worse in another way. Our urban and suburban environments are precisely not cities or communities where adults naturally attend to the young and educate to a viable life. Also, perhaps especially in the case of the overt drop-outs, the state of their body and soul is such that we must give them refuge and remedy, whether it be called school, settlement house, youth worker, or work camp.

There are thinkable alternatives. Throughout this little book, as occasion arises, I shall offer alternative proposals that I as a single individual have heard of or thought up. Here are half a dozen directly relevant to the subject we have been discussing, the system as compulsory trap. In principle, when a law begins to do more harm than good, the best policy is to alleviate it or try doing without it.

i. Have "no school at all" for a few classes. These children should be selected from tolerable, though not necessarily cultured, homes. They should be neighbors and numerous enough to be a society for one another and so that they do not feel merely "different." Will they learn the rudiments anyway? This experiment cannot do the children any academic harm, since there is good evidence that normal children will make up the first seven years school-work with four to seven months of good teaching.

ii. Dispense with the school building for a few classes; provide teachers and use the city itself as the school—its streets, cafeterias, stores, movies, museums, parks, and factories. Where feasible, it certainly makes more sense to teach using the real subject-matter than to bring an abstraction of the subject-matter into the school-building as "curriculum." Such a class should probably not exceed 10 children for one pedagogue. The idea—it is the model of Athenian education—is not dissimilar to Youth gang work, but not applied to delinquents and not playing to the gang ideology.

iii. Along the same lines, but both outside and inside the school building, use appropriate *unlicensed* adults of the community—the druggist, the storekeeper, the mechanic—as the proper educators of the young into the grown-up world. By this means we can try to overcome the separation of the young from the grown-up world so characteristic in modern urban life, and to diminish the omnivorous authority of the professional school-people. Certainly it would be a useful and animating experience for the adults. (There is the beginning of such a volunteer program in the New York and some other systems.)

iv. Make class attendance not compulsory, in the manner of A. S. Neill's Summerhill. If the teachers are good, absence would tend to be eliminated; if they are bad, let them know it. The compulsory law is useful to get the children away from the parents, but it must not result in trapping the children. A fine modification of this suggestion is the rule used by Frank Brown in Florida: he permits the children to be absent for a week or a month to engage in any worthwhile enterprise or visit any new environment.

v. Decentralize an urban school (or do not build a new big building) into small units, 20 to 50, in available store-fronts or clubhouses. These tiny schools, equipped with record-player and pin-ball machine, could combine play, socializing, discussion, and formal teaching. For special events, the small units can be brought together into a common auditorium or gymnasium, so as to give the sense of the greater community. Correspondingly, I think it would be worthwhile to give the Little Red Schoolhouse a spin under modern urban conditions, and see how it works out: that is, to combine all the ages in a little room for 25 to 30, rather than to grade by age.

vi. Use a pro rata part of the school money to send children to economically marginal farms for a couple of months of the year, perhaps 6 children from mixed backgrounds to a farmer. The only requirement is that the farmer feed them and not beat them; best, of course, if they take part in the farm-work. This will give the farmer cash, as part of the generally desirable program to redress the urban-rural ratio to something nearer to 70% to 30%.

(At present, less than 8% of families are rural.) Conceivably, some of the urban children will take to the other way of life, and we might generate a new kind of rural culture.

I frequently suggest these and similar proposals at teachers colleges, and I am looked at with an eerie look—do I really mean to *diminish* the state-aid grant for each student-day? But mostly the objective is that such proposals entail intolerable administrative difficulties.

Above all, we must apply these or any other proposals to particular individuals and small groups, without the obligation of uniformity. There is a case for uniform standards of achievement, lodged in the Regents, but they *cannot* be reached by uniform techniques. The claim that standardization of procedure is more efficient, less costly, or alone administratively practical, is often false. Particular inventiveness requires thought, but thought does not cost money.

MARIO MONTESSORI
A. S. NEILL

Mario Montessori is the son of the celebrated Italian educational reformer Maria Montessori. A well-known educator in his own right, he is active throughout the world as a proponent of updated and enlightened instructional methods. He is one of the foremost spokesmen for the Montessori point of view.

Educator and writer A. S. Neill is founder and headmaster of Summerhill, an extremely progressive coeducational, self-governing boarding school at Leiston, in Suffolk, about one hundred miles from London. In addition to Summerhill, *Neill has written a number of other works about education including* The Problem Child *(1926),* The Problem Parent *(1932),* Hearts Not Heads in the School *(1945), and* The Free Child *(1953). His most recent book to be published in the United States is* Freedom and License *(1967).*

A Discussion of Schools
and Child Rearing

Less than five years ago a book by A. S. Neill, an elderly English school-master, was published in America under the title *Summerhill — A Radical Approach to Child Rearing*. It was what book publishers call a sleeper. Attracting little attention at first, the book ignited a conversation here, a controversy there, soon the beginnings of a small nationwide cult, until in almost any informed discussion of children and education, someone was almost sure to ask, "Have you read *Summerhill?*"

At about the same time, in Greenwich, Connecticut, a group of parents organized an extraordinary school based on another education method, widely admired in America 50 years ago but since then almost forgotten. It had been developed by Dr. Maria Montessori, Italy's first woman physician, after many years of experimenting with children in the slums of Rome.

Summerhill School in England and Montessori schools around the world start with the premise that a child has a deep urge to "create himself" into an able, constructive adult; he does this best when he is freest from the influence or interference of parents and teachers.

Summerhill students, ranging in age from six to fifteen, are permitted to stay away from classes for months at a time if they wish. All rules of the school are set by student vote. The main purpose of Summerhill is not to compel young people to study, but to help them develop emotional health, happiness and self-reliance. Yet Summerhill students are, for the most part, eager students with developed curiosities. They seem unusually free of rebelliousness, and are remarkably confident in dealing with adults. Despite the absence of rules requiring study — or perhaps because of it — a number of students have attained prominence in the fields of engineering, mathematics, handicrafts, art and teaching.

Montessori Method pupils, on the other hand, who begin school as early as three years of age, work in a "prepared environment" that emphasizes formal learning. Each child, however, works at his own pace. He chooses a self-teaching device that engages his curiosity at a given moment, working with it alone or with a group, as he wishes. When his interest turns to something else, he is free to return the device to its proper place — order is emphasized in a Montessori class — and select another. The belief is that emotional health naturally follows fulfillment of a child's inborn urge to learn. Almost never does a Montessori teacher (usually called a directress) call a class to attention so that she can instruct. Montessori pupils commonly do arithmetic, including multiplying and dividing, by the age of four; reading and writing by four or five; square and cube roots by six or seven. Although supervision is at a minimum, antisocial behavior is almost nonexistent in Montessori classrooms.

In recent months several starts have been made toward establishing American private schools modeled after Summerhill, including one now being organized in New York by the actor-comedian Orson Bean. In the past five years, more than 50 schools claiming to use the Montessori Method have sprung up from New England to California.

There appears to be an appreciable revival of the feeling that a good education should grow out of more individual freedom and self-development than our schools presently allow. Yet the advocates of Summerhill, on the one hand, and the Montessori Method, on the other, have deep disagreements as to how children should be set free. (To read further about Summerhill and the Montessori Method, see *Summerhill*, by A. S. Neill, Hart Publishing Co.; *Maria Montessori, Her Life and Work*, by E. M. Standing, published in paperback by Mentor-Omega; and various books by Maria Montessori. A good lending library will have most of them.)

REDBOOK recently arranged for the first face-to-face meeting between the leading spokesmen of the two controversial methods. A. S. Neill, 80 years old, agreed to journey 100 miles from Leiston, England, to London to meet Mario Montessori, who flew from his home near Amsterdam, Holland. Mario Montessori, in his early 60's, is the only child of Dr. Maria Montessori, who died in 1951. He directs the International Montessori Association, devoted to promoting interest in his mother's work. The two men met in an office of the University of London. They greeted each other with cordial reserve and noticeable wariness.

Neill (*With a characteristic twinkle*): What'll we fight about?
Montessori (*Smiling*): I have no intention of fighting with you. You're probably a very hard fighter. You've been fighting all your life — for your cause, I mean.
Neill: My dear man, you're dealing with a profoundly ignorant person. I've never read John Dewey. I've been accused of being a follower of Rousseau but I've never read the man. Many years ago I bought the Montessori books. Then I visited a Montessori school in London and got a shock. There was a lady there who — Signorina Maccheroni was her name————
Montessori: That's right. She's still there.
Neill: We were watching some children, and one boy was building a long stair out of special blocks and he began to use it as a train, puffing across the room, and she got frightfully annoyed and went and took the train away from him. And I said, "What the devil did you do that for?" She says, "He's using the apparatus for the wrong purpose." I said, "Well, if a child can't use his fantasy in play, if that's Montessorianism, I don't like it." Why must you make him stick to the long stair? What's the answer to that? Mind you, it was long ago, fifty years ago. But was she right or wrong?
Montessori: First of all, Mr. Neill, I————
Neill: Don't call me *Mister* Neill.
Montessori: All right, Neill; first of all, I would like to say that I am much more ignorant than you are. Now, getting to your question, Dr. Montessori

started her observations with very poor children. They were very disorderly, you might say. In fact, if it is possible to have gangsters of three and four years of age, they were that kind. Then, through the experience she gave them with certain learning apparatus, their behavior changed. She didn't understand why it changed until many years later, not until she was your age. But in her effort to understand how these destructive elements were replaced by something positive, she tried for a while to preserve the conditions of that first school. That was why, in the beginning, she was quite rigid. Now, when a child is born, he certainly is new to the world, isn't he?

Neill: What?

Montessori: New to the world. And one of his unconscious tasks is to classify his environment, to be able to recognize different objects—their size, qualities. In other words, he starts to classify. The "long stair" was part of the apparatus to help train a child to recognize different dimensions, and so forth. During a certain sensitive period very early in life he is attracted by nature to building such experience. If the child cannot fulfill his natural urges, he escapes into fantasy. The aim is not to stop him from escaping into fantasy but to try to bring him back—to implement his natural urges toward coordination, self-control, intelligence. As for your criticism of the apparatus, Dr. Montessori used to say, You are free to give the children anything. You can have a train if you want a train. If you want bricks you can have bricks. But if you use a microscope for riding horseback, it's useless to have a microscope. And that was why that distinction was made.

Neill: The Montessorians talk so much about education. You know, I don't care a darn for education. What do you call education?

Montessori: Well, everybody considers education reading and writing and mathematics. It is absolutely not that. That's one disagreement Dr. Montessori had and I'm having with some schools that call themselves Montessori, particularly in the United States right now. They stress how to teach the children to teach themselves. What Dr. Montessori was interested in was the construction of harmonious personalities in children so that they will not come into conflict with themselves and into conflict with adults.

Neill: She must have been frightfully handicapped by her parents.

Montessori: By whose parents?

Neill: By the parents of her pupils. She hadn't any boarding schools, had she? The children must have been under terrific conflict.

Montessori: Quite—quite. The parents were casual workers. Some of them had criminal records. They were dirty, and the mothers never combed their hair. In fact, the slovenliness was such that if you asked a woman after she had married, "Why don't you take care of yourself any more?" she'd say, "After all, I have a husband now; I don't need to." That was the attitude, and it certainly must have influenced the children. But surprisingly, the children then began to transform the parents. When these children came home all clean and began putting things in order, the mothers seemed ashamed, and they too became more clean and tidy.

Neill: Yes, yes.

Montessori: Yes, and these mothers, after the children learned how to read and to write, they came to Dr. Montessori and said, "I'm so terribly

ashamed. My child knows how to write and I do not. Please teach me."
That is a positive influence from children four and five years old.

Neill: This is beyond me. It's beyond me.

Montessori: Why should this be beyond you?

Neill: It's beyond me because you're talking about education, the three R's and science, and I'm thinking about the dynamics of life, the dynamic in a child, how we're going to prevent that child from becoming a Gestapo, or becoming a color hater and all these things. The sickness of the world. I'm interested in what we're going to do *for* children to stop them from being haters, to stop them from being anti-life. The methods, I don't think————

Montessori: How do you feel that children can be saved from this kind of thing?

Neill: Well, the first thing is to be loved. I mean, the only child I've ever had in my school I couldn't do very much with was the child who had no love as a baby. [*Pausing.*] There was a terrifying film on the BBC about a year ago about some nursery school in France where the nurses or nuns, or whoever they were, only gave physical attention and no love; and every child in the room was sitting rocking like that—and the journalist gave one a teddy bear and she just looked at it indifferently. They were all dead faces, all dead eyes. It was a terrible picture of what happens when a child doesn't get loved. And so I go from the point of view that the first thing a child wants is to be loved from the very beginning, and I don't care whether they learn reading by look-say or by the phonetic method. In fifty years it won't matter. At Summerhill we don't try to mold children in any way. I mean, we let them live and govern themselves. It's not so easy when they're four or five years old. We don't get them till they're five or six, and then they gradually sit at all the self-government meetings and talk, very often talk sensibly when they're five. Fundamentally, I think, that's the idea of Summerhill anyhow, that the child must be free from the very beginning to be itself without being told how to live. Mind you, it *is* told how to live by living in the community. It's *got* to adapt itself.

Montessori: I agree with you absolutely. I will give another example much stronger than you have given me. There was a Dutch doctor, in about 1923 or 1924, who had a nursery for orphans where some working mothers also left children in the day. But many of the orphans died.

Neill: The orphans what?

Montessori: By the time they were six months the orphans began to perish, die. They had the most perfect hygienic conditions. The nurses treated each child the same, orphan or not. The children of the working mothers were from poor people, who were dirty, who lived in unfavorable conditions, hygienically speaking. Yet these children flourished. The doctor saw that the only difference was that when a mother came, she took the child and began to kiss him and fondle him and things like that, and the orphans, those poor devils, had nothing of this kind. So the doctor told the nurses, do as the mothers do, start making love to the children. And what happened? The phenomenon of the orphans' dying disappeared. So the need for love is tremendous in children. The only trouble comes in allowing mothers, as you say, to indoctrinate the children for things which they are not at the age to do. It goes against the guidance of nature, and that's where the trouble comes. You read in Dr. Montessori's first books that she considered adults to be the first enemy of the child, among them the mother and father. They did not understand the natural process of growth, and they saw the child doing something, trying to touch something—"That you cannot touch, this you cannot do, that you cannot do." And therefore there is the conflict the child finds himself in—the conflict between this driving energy that asks him to become a capable person and the parent's or the educator's ideas which tell him, "No, you must not do that, because I think it is not right."

Neill: Yes, but mind you, in actual practice, you can't avoid a little of that. If a mother's cooking the dinner, she can't allow the child to go up and put his hands on the stove. She's got to say no, you see.

Montessori: Of course, of course. That is common sense.

Neill: That's another matter, yes.

Montessori: But, at the time, for instance, if the child wanted to play with something of his father's, the mother would slap it—"Leave it alone because that's for Papa." And if he tried to get a plate, "Leave it alone because you are going to break it." Then they would give them idle toys and unbreakable things. As soon as the child gets a breakable thing it would smash it down. Naturally. But afterward, as I say, when Dr. Montessori gave them a chance to grow in their own way, all this aggression and destructiveness disappeared. That was what converted Dr. Montessori, this disappearance of hatred and violence.

Neill: Well, I'm all on the side of any system that minimizes hatred, of course I am. By the way, when I used to treat the children in analysis—I was more or less Freudian in those days—I got one of my staff to make a family of father and mother and brother and sister—dolls with sexual organs and, of course, different clothes—and I just left them lying about in my office. I had to renew the mother every six weeks. She was kicked to death and the father wasn't. It seemed to disprove completely Freud's theory about the father. It was the mother who was hated all the time.

Montessori: What age were the children?

Neill: Oh, up to twelve.

Montessori: Up to twelve. Well there, at that age, a lot of violence appears. I suppose that if it was at the age of three and four, it would be just the opposite.

Neill: I'm trying to link up what you say about education and reading and writing with what I think is important—freeing a child from guilt. Freedom from the idea of sin, freedom from the idea that the sexual parts are wicked. That's the sort of thing I'm interested in, freedom from guilt feelings, and I don't see how this is fitting in.

Montessori: Well, it fits in the sense that if children are not permitted to have constructive experiences, they will find less desirable ones. Dr. Montessori had an expression, a little vulgar. She'd say, "If these hands want to do things with objects [*motioning out in the air*] and the hands are forbidden, where do they go? Naturally, they go down here."

Neill: No, no, no, I think that's wrong. That fits in with the public [British private] school idea that the more you give the boys games, the less they'll masturbate.

Montessori: No, no, no, not games, not games, not games. I find the child, in building himself into a person, has a hunger for certain things, not games. At the age I mean there are certain experiences which he prefers to games, so much so that he leaves toys. If you want to learn to swim, how can you develop your coordination if you're stopped from trying? And if you are not allowed to develop your coordination, you will seek satisfaction elsewhere. In the same way, mentally, if you're stopped from acquiring certain experiences, then you'll find compensation somewhere else. One way a child may go is toward masturbation. But this disappeared, my dear sir, disappeared when the children were permitted to do the things they really wanted and needed to do. It was not a question of repression.

Neill: I never see it in my school either. I haven't seen one of my children masturbating in forty years, but I wouldn't think it healthy if masturbation disappeared.

Montessori: But you agree with me that it is not something natural? After all, the organs are created, and when they are mature they will develop the inclination to function. But in the premature age, if they are brought into use then, it means there is something lacking.

Neill: Not so much lacking—a fear of "You mustn't do that." I believe it begins in the cradle, myself, this reacting to adults. I don't agree, by the way, that masturbation is unnatural. Maybe there's too much attempt by the Montessorians to impose adult patterns. I feel that way without the evidence. I don't know enough about it, you see. I just feel there's a sort of adult pattern coming out of it, somehow.

Montessori: Our essence, our central aim, is to serve the child for the sake of life, not for the sake of the three R's. But if society requests that the child learn the three R's for the advancement of the individual, not knowing them will be a handicap. It is not we who teach the child the three R's. We merely put before him the apparatus through which he gets a certain experience which is attractive to him. Working with this apparatus, each child gathers his own knowledge of the three R's. Again it is self-creation, not imposition.

Neill: When it comes to his learning things on his own, I can't think of any boy we've ever had who hasn't learned to use his hands. Some of them make their own furniture. They fantasy a thing and then turn it into something constructive. I think free children are very constructive, in the main.

Montessori: Well, now, would you agree that if the child wants to do something with, let us say, carpentry—a box or anything like that—he would need to know the use of tools? Doesn't he need the self-discipline of learning the proper way to use them?

Neill: Yes, but I have something to say about that. Some years ago I went to see a big school noted for its handwork, and I saw about twenty-four boys all planing, and I said to the teacher, how many of these boys will carry this on as a hobby when they leave? And he said, not one. And I didn't say it to him, but I think the reason was that they were only learning techniques or learning how to make joints instead of making a thing. I think the opposite way is the right way. In my school, for example, a child wants to make a box. He gets a saw and then he saws wood and nails it together roughly, and then next time he maybe puts screw nails in, and not always, but usually, when he gets older he says, I don't like this. How do I make a joint? So then is the time to tell him. *When he wants to do it, you see.* I think that's where our handwork teaching is all wrong. It begins at the wrong end.

Montessori: Absolutely. Absolutely.

Neill: I had to drop a theory I've had for years. I've written about it. My theory was, you see, that children won't make a thing unless they can attach a fantasy to it. He makes a boat, he makes an airplane, he makes a sword. I used to have a hobby of hammering copper or brass, making brass bowls or trays. The children used to look at me with a slight superiority —look at old Neill, you see—and they didn't want to hammer brass because you can't attach a fantasy to a brass bowl. You can't fly the world with it. You can't go under the sea with it. But I had to modify my theory because my stepson was trained by the best potter in England. Then my boy started teaching pottery and he's getting some marvelous things out of small pupils. They're making teapots and things that look practical and professional. And so my theory goes out the window like that. Children will indeed make things without fantasy.

Montessori: Is it your idea that as children grow up among adults, their fantasy is crushed?

Neill: Oh, the fantasy is destroyed. That's why it's so evil to send missionaries to convert the heathen. It's not right to destroy anybody's fantasy. You've no right to do it. I'd think myself a criminal if I were to go to somebody who's deeply religious and I tried to destroy his religious beliefs; and I think it would be criminal. Of course it would. And the same with a child.

Montessori: Well, you think, then, that it is possible to crush fantasy?

Neill: You can distort it. That may be one of the bases of the sickness of the world. The arresting of fantasy and the perversion of fantasy. You see, religion has *become* a fantasy. It's become perverted, and nobody is a Christian today. As Nietzsche said, Christ was the first and last Christian. Jesus was real, but today I think our idea of Christianity is pure fantasy. Otherwise all the bishops would be sitting in Trafalgar Square against the H-bomb or something, instead of leaving it to an atheist like Bertrand Russell. Well, I'm wandering a bit. I'm wandering.

Montessori: Well, you were saying that playing games—red Indians or something like that—is fantasy. I used to take children camping with me, a place in a wood where there was a stream. One day when they were playing red Indians they saw me absorbed with a plant which grew bent like that, instead of growing straight up, and I told them this was so because the plant was looking for light. They said, "What? The plant looks for light?" Then they became interested, little by little, in other aspects of nature. Soon, in class, they began to do vegetable physiology in a scientific way. Now, this led them, on their next camping trips, to observe the botanical situation, the geological situation, to recognize the work of a stream—erosion and deposition—things like that. Their outings, instead of being occasions for fantasy, such as playing Indians, became a sort of continuous exploratory journey. One time we had a lunch ready but couldn't get them to lunch because they were so interested in their scientific studies.

Neill: How does this fit in with trying to guarantee that these children aren't going to beat their children or tell their children lies or try to control their children's lives, their emotions? Because I'm convinced that none of my old pupils will ever beat a child or tell them lies about anything or mold their opinions or characters in any way; and that's all I want. That's all. That satisfies me, and I'm wondering how much this fits in with the other things.

Montessori: Well, when one grows up as I am describing, you don't need to tell lies. You don't tell lies. Dr. Montessori showed that we have hardly begun to discover the possibilities for developing honest, decent, happy human beings.

Neill: We agree about that. The question is, how are you going to get there?

Montessori: Well, I think she did what you also do—giving children freedom. But she also investigated how children go through sensitive periods.

Neill: Sensitive periods?

Montessori: Sensitive periods that unconsciously lead the child toward learning experiences and emotional equilibrium. These sensitive periods change from age to age. For instance, who is it that teaches a child to talk? When I studied English, I had books, I had teachers, I had help, I had professors. But I could never acquire the English of a child born in England. That child does it just by himself. There is nobody who teaches him. How is that possible at so young an age? The child starts his first syllables at six months, when there is no organized intelligence, no possibility of instructing him. Yet the child acquires the language so perfectly in its pronunciation and structure that it becomes the mother tongue.

Neill: Yes, but he acquires balance and walking without any instruction, too.

Montessori: Exactly, exactly. Speech is not the only thing. So in this process, evidently there is tremendous attraction felt by the child for the spoken word, for the way people talk. One will even acquire the subtle patterns of the gestures of the Chinese, and another the gestures of Italians. Dr. Montessori called this the absorbent mind of the child, the photographic mind, which acts not only through the intellect but also the emotions. At a certain stage of development, seeing others write, he starts writing. I think there is where the majority of educators do not consider the real feelings of the child. In most places, despite the child's demonstrated inclinations, it is forbidden by law for a child to learn to read or to write before he is six or seven.

Neill: Where, in Italy?

Montessori: In many countries. In many countries. In Italy, yes. In Switzerland it is forbidden. In France, the United States and elsewhere children are forbidden to learn until long after they have shown they are ready to do so. But Dr. Montessori had intercommunicating classes of children from three to six, for instance, in one room, and then from six to nine in another, each child working on his own level. Certain children would see older children, for instance, working, with a teacher's guidance, on the decimal system. Who could imagine something like that to be attractive to a child of four? But children of four and a half in her classes had such an intense interest that they actually appropriated the material for learning such things—and their interest lasted! Yet children of seven and eight were only mildly—only briefly interested. If you introduced reading and writing at seven years of age, it became something so terribly boring that the children hated it. Whereas the children of four, four and a half, they explode into writing. We've had the experience in several countries of Europe and Asia and America that a favorable age for learning reading and writing is between four and a half and five. Some people learn before. Three and a half. So in that sense the freedom that Dr. Montessori gave was not the so-called freedom of *not* having to do these things because they were too young, but to give them the opportunity to do them and see what the result was. That's why Dr. Montessori called it free choice. Whether it was learning to write or learning arithmetic.

Neill: To hell with arithmetic . . . .

Montessori: Why do you say to hell with arithmetic?

Neill: That's partly personal. You see, I spent four years at Edinburgh University taking an Honours English degree and then I went to found a school in Germany in 1921, and suddenly I found I had to sit silent and listen to people talking about art and philosophy and music. I didn't learn a thing about them, and it struck me then what a miserably narrow thing any university education is. And it's true, I think, all of that stuff you learn at school, most of it, flies away. I once could read Homer in Greek; I can't now. I once could read Latin. I can't read Latin today. So much of that has gone, so that I discounted it as being relatively unimportant.

Montessori: It is relatively unimportant.

Neill: I've often had critics say to me, "Is it fair to keep a child away from music? It's not that they have to know music, but look at the joy they get." But look at the millions of good, happy people who don't learn music. Look at the millions who don't know anything about astronomy and things like that. So many things to know. But I find that children simply follow what they can. One boy with not much gray matter has just left our school. He's a carpenter, quite a good one and quite happy. Four other boys are university professors—or at least lecturers. I had a boy of seventeen who left Summerhill unable to read or write. He's now a very successful engineer.

Montessori: He couldn't read or write at the age of seventeen?

Neill: No, he couldn't. He learned because he found that without reading he couldn't read engineering plans. That was a complicated case, because he had a grandmother who tried to make him read the Bible at three, I think. My daughter learned to read and write without any teaching at all, really, at five or six.

Montessori: If one is interested, he will go to the effort of reading and writing, no matter at what age. We had one child who absolutely didn't want to read or write. No interest at all. Then he became intensely interested in biology. We had illustrated books in the class. He kept begging a friend to read him bits from them. His friend did it for three or four days, but finally he said, "Look, I have to do my own work. You go away." And then the first boy went to his teacher and said, "Please teach me how to read." And he learned very quickly.

Neill: One drawback, I think, was the invention of the talkie cinema. In the early days when my children went to the old silents, with the printed words, one kid would ask, "What does that say?" and the other would say, "Oh, shut up. I'm watching." So they had to learn to read for themselves, you see.

Montessori: They're actually doing that for adults in Indonesia now—did you know that? Movies are free, but only for those who know how to read. It seems to be a great success. But the sensitive period means that there is a natural interest for certain things at certain times of life. For instance, the question of square and cube root. These were very difficult in Dr. Montessori's day for children of thirteen and fourteen, just as they are today. But very funnily—she found them an immense joy for children of eight.

Neill: Well, I believe that that isn't the important thing. The important thing is being yourself.

Montessori: I agree.

Neill: You hear all this talk about teaching social studies to make good citizens. I don't care about *teaching* social studies. I'm interested in *living* social studies. And the only way to do that is to let them govern themselves.

Montessori: How does your self-government work?

Neill: Well, self-government. You see, we meet every Saturday night and make our own laws. The chairman's always one of the children. And they pass laws and everybody has one vote. Because I'm headmaster it doesn't mean that what I propose is carried. What the group passes becomes law that everybody must observe. No minority rights. But the minority accepts them, as a general rule. They're quite sensible laws, you see. Now, remember we're a residence school. You couldn't very well have self-government in a day school. There's nothing to govern about. In our meetings you don't hear anything about lessons. What's brought up is So-and-so disturbed the community last night by making a row after lights-out time. Somebody rode my bicycle. Somebody swore in public down at the cinema. It's a social thing. Tell me, what happens when a child swears in a Montessori school? Do they swear at Montessori schools?

Montessori: If they want to, yes.

Neill: With the approval of the teacher?

Montessori: Well, yes, with the approval of the teacher. Look, you must not—you had your experience long ago at a Montessori———

Neill: I had the wrong experience———

Montessori: But if you want to know what I'm doing in my old age, I'm trying to destroy the idea that Montessori schools are the perfect answer for all children—a view held by the perfectionist, rigid Montessorians. They have taken a grasp of only certain aspects of Montessorianism and sometimes condemn those who do not agree. They even condemned Dr. Montessori! Once she was trying something new, different from the way it was written in her book, and a teacher objected, "You cannot do that. That way is not Montessori." So if you bring me an example of something bad in a Montessori school, I can bring you much worse examples.

Neill: Look at Freud and what they do in his name. Look at those American Summerhill schools. I sent a letter to the *Greenwich Village Voice*, in New York, disclaiming any affiliation with any American school that calls itself a Summerhill school. I've heard so many rumors about them. It's one thing to use freedom. Quite another to use license. I haven't visited regular American schools, but more than half the young people now in my school are Americans. There is a difference between American children and English children. The Americans are accustomed more to license than freedom, I think. In America I visited the home of a psychologist, or someone like that, hoping to have a chat with him. But his wife and two kids were in the room. The children monopolized the conversation. In another case visitors came with a new Cadillac. They had a boy of thirteen. The boy was bored with talking, and he said, "Dad, give me the car keys; I'm going for a ride." Dad says, "Okay, Son." A boy of thirteen with a Cadillac! I don't know if that's usual in America, but that's the impression I got. At Summerhill we've had difficulties with American children coming over. They've read my book, you see. They say, "This is a free school; we'll do what we like." And when they find they're up against self-government and they can't do what they like, they object.

Montessori: How would you distinguish between freedom and license?

Neill: Well, freedom in my school is, do what you like as long as you don't interfere with somebody else. Put it this way. If a child doesn't want to study mathematics, it's nobody's business; it's his own. But if he wants to play a trumpet when other people are sleeping, that's everybody's business. That's license.

Montessori: I agree. Absolutely.

CARL R. ROGERS

Carl R. Rogers is an outstanding figure in contemporary American psychology. A clinical psychologist, Rogers is perhaps best known for his innovative work in the area of what he terms "client-centered therapy." Until recently a professor of psychology and psychiatry at the University of Wisconsin, Rogers is presently a resident fellow at the Western Behavioral Sciences Institute in La Jolla, California. His major works in the field of psychotherapy and counseling theory include Counseling and Psychotherapy *(1942),* Client-Centered Therapy *(1951), and* On Becoming a Person *(1961).*

Personal Thoughts
on Teaching and Learning

This brief selection by Rogers was originally delivered at a conference organized by Harvard University on "Classroom Approaches to Influencing Human Behavior." Rogers chose on this occasion to express some of his own highly personal opinions on the topic of teaching and learning. As he states: "I simply put down what I felt, with assurance that if I had not got it correctly, the discussion would help to set me on the right track."

I wish to present some very brief remarks, in the hope that if they bring forth any reaction from you, I may get some new light on my own ideas.

I find it a very troubling thing to *think*, particularly when I think about my own experiences and try to extract from those experiences the meaning that seems genuinely inherent in them. At first such thinking is very satisfying, because it seems to discover sense and pattern in a whole host of discrete events. But then it very often becomes dismaying, because I realize how ridiculous these thoughts, which have much value to me, would seem to most people. My impression is that if I try to find the meaning of my own experience it leads me, nearly always, in directions regarded as absurd.

So in the next three or four minutes, I will try to digest some of the meanings which have come to me from my classroom experience and the experience I have had in individual and group therapy. They are in no way intended as conclusions for some one else, or a guide to what others should do or be. They are the very tentative meanings, as of April 1952, which my experience has had for me, and some of the bothersome questions which their absurdity raises. I will put each idea or meaning in a separate lettered paragraph, not because they are in any particular logical order, but because each meaning is separately important to me.

a. I may as well start with this one in view of the purposes of this conference. *My experience has been that I cannot teach another person how to teach.* To attempt it is for me, in the long run, futile.

b. *It seems to me that anything that can be taught to another is relatively inconsequential, and has little or no significant influence on behavior.* That sounds so ridiculous I can't help but question it at the same time that I present it.

c. *I realize increasingly that I am only interested in learnings which significantly influence behavior.* Quite possibly this is simply a personal idiosyncrasy.

d. *I have come to feel that the only learning which significantly influences behavior is self-discovered, self-appropriated learning.*

e. *Such self-discovered learning, truth that has been personally appropriated and assimilated in experience, cannot be directly communicated to another.* As soon as an individual tries to communicate such experience directly, often with a quite natural enthusiasm, it becomes teaching, and its results are inconsequential. It was some relief recently to discover that Søren Kierkegaard, the Danish philosopher, had found this too, in his own experience, and stated it very clearly a century ago. It made it seem less absurd.

f. As a consequence of the above, *I realize that I have lost interest in being a teacher.*

g. When I try to teach, as I do sometimes, I am appalled by the results, which seem a little more than inconsequential, because sometimes the teaching appears to succeed. When this happens I find that the results are damaging. It seems to cause the individual to distrust his own experience, and to stifle significant learning. *Hence I have come to feel that the outcomes of teaching are either unimportant or hurtful.*

h. When I look back at the results of my past teaching, the real results seem the same — either damage was done, or nothing significant occurred. This is frankly troubling.

i. As a consequence, *I realize that I am only interested in being a learner, preferably learning things that matter, that have some significant influence on my own behavior.*

j. *I find it very rewarding to learn,* in groups, in relationships with one person as in therapy, or by myself.

k. *I find that one of the best, but most difficult ways for me to learn is to drop my own defensiveness, at least temporarily, and to try to understand the way in which his experience seems and feels to the other person.*

l. *I find that another way of learning for me is to state my own uncertainties, to try to clarify my puzzlements, and thus get closer to the meaning that my experience actually seems to have.*

m. This whole train of experiencing, and the meanings that I have thus far discovered in it, seem to have launched me on a process which is both fascinating and at times a little frightening. *It seems to mean letting my experience carry me on, in a direction which appears to be forward, toward goals that I can but dimly define, as I try to understand at least the current meaning of that experience.* The sensation is that of floating with a complex stream of experience, with the fascinating possibility of trying to comprehend its ever changing complexity.

I am almost afraid I may seem to have gotten away from any discussion of learning, as well as teaching. Let me again introduce a practical note by saying that by themselves these interpretations of my own experience may sound queer and aberrant, but not particularly shocking. It is when I realize the *implications* that I shudder a bit at the distance I have come from the commonsense world that everyone knows is right. I can best illustrate that by saying that if the experiences of others had been the same as mine, and if they had discovered similar meanings in it, many consequences would be implied.

a. Such experience would imply that we would do away with teaching. People would get together if they wished to learn.

b. We would do away with examinations. They measure only the inconsequential type of learning.

c. The implication would be that we would do away with grades and credits for the same reason.

d. We would do away with degrees as a measure of competence partly for the same reason. Another reason is that a degree marks an end or a conclusion of something, and a learner is only interested in the continuing process of learning.

e. It would imply doing away with the exposition of conclusions, for we would realize that no one learns significantly from conclusions.

I think I had better stop there. I do not want to become too fantastic. I want to know primarily whether anything in my inward thinking as I have tried to describe it, speaks to anything in your experience of the classroom as you have lived it, and if so, what the meanings are that exist for you in *your* experience.

SAMUEL TENENBAUM

Educational psychologist and philosopher Samuel Tenenbaum is particularly interested in psychotherapy and in the relationship between education and psychology. He has lectured and served on the faculties of various American colleges and universities and is the author of the book Why Men Hate. *In the area of educational philosophy he has written a study of experimentalist philosopher William Heard Kilpatrick.*

Carl R. Rogers
and Non-Directive Teaching

The first part of this selection was written by Samuel Tenenbaum shortly after he had participated in one of Carl Rogers' "non-directive" seminars conducted at Brandeis University in the summer of 1958. The second part is a very brief account of one of Tenenbaum's own subsequent attempts to apply Rogerian non-directive techniques in one of his own graduate courses in education during the following year.

A DESCRIPTION

As one interested in education, I have participated in a classroom methodology that is so unique and so special that I feel impelled to share the experience. The technique, it seems to me, is so radically different from the customary and the accepted, so undermining of the old, that it should be known more widely. As good a description of the process as any — I suppose the one that Carl R. Rogers, the instructor, himself would be inclined to use — would be "non-directive" teaching.

I had some notion what that term meant, but frankly I was not prepared for anything that proved so overwhelming. It is not that I am convention-bound. My strongest educational influences stem from William Heard Kilpatrick and John Dewey, and anyone who has even the slightest acquaintance with their thinking would know that it does not smack of the narrow or the provincial. But this method which I saw Dr. Rogers carry out in a course which he gave at Brandeis University was so unusual, something I could not believe possible, unless I was part of the experience. I hope I shall manage to describe the method in a way to give you some inkling of the feelings, the emotions, the warmth and the enthusiasms that the method engendered.

The course was altogether unstructured; and it was exactly that. At no moment did anyone know, not even the instructor, what the next moment would bring forth in the classroom, what subject would come up for discussion, what questions would be raised, what personal needs, feelings and emotions aired. This atmosphere of non-structured freedom — as free as human beings could allow each other to be — was set by Dr. Rogers himself. In a friendly, relaxed way, he sat down with the students (about 25 in number) around a large table and said it would be nice if we stated our purpose and introduced ourselves. There ensued a strained silence; no one spoke up. Finally, to break it, one student timidly raised his hand and spoke his piece. Another uncomfortable silence, and then another upraised hand. Thereafter, the hands rose more rapidly. At no time did the instructor urge any student to speak.

Unstructured Approach

Afterwards, he informed the class that he had brought with him quantities of materials — reprints, brochures, articles, books; he handed out a bibliography of recommended reading. At no time did he indicate that he expected students to read or do anything else. As I recall, he made only one request. Would some student volunteer to set up this material in a special room which had been reserved for students of the course? Two students promptly volunteered. He also said he had with him recorded tapes of therapeutic sessions and also reels of motion pictures. This created a flurry of excitement, and students asked whether they could be heard and seen and Dr. Rogers answered yes. The class then decided how it could be done best. Students volunteered to run tape recorders, find a movie projector; for the most part this too was student initiated and arranged.

Thereafter followed four hard, frustrating sessions. During this period, the class didn't seem to get anywhere. Students spoke at random, saying whatever came into their heads. It all seemed chaotic, aimless, a waste of time. A student would bring up some aspect of Rogers' philosophy; and the next student, completely disregarding the first, would take the group away in another direction; and a third, completely disregarding the first two, would start fresh on something else altogether. At times there were some faint efforts at a cohesive discussion, but for the most part the classroom proceedings seemed to lack continuity and direction. The instructor received every contribution with attention and regard. He did not find any student's contribution in order or out of order.

The class was not prepared for such a totally unstructured approach. They did not know how to proceed. In their perplexity and frustration, they demanded that the teacher play the role assigned to him by custom and tradition; that he set forth for us in authoritative language what was right and wrong, what was good and bad. Had they not come from far distances to learn from the oracle himself? Were they not fortunate? Were they not about to be initiated in the right rituals and practices by the great man himself, the founder of the movement that bears his name? The notebooks were poised for the climactic moment when the oracle would give forth, but mostly they remained untouched.

Queerly enough, from the outset, even in their anger, the members of the group felt joined together, and outside the classroom, there was an excitement and a ferment, for even in their frustration, they had communicated as never before in any classroom, and probably never before in quite the way they had. The class was bound together by a common, unique experience. In the Rogers class, they had spoken their minds; the words did not come from a book, nor were they the reflection of the instructor's thinking, nor that of any other authority. The ideas, emotions and feelings came from themselves; and this was the releasing and the exciting process.

In this atmosphere of freedom, something for which they had not bargained and for which they were not prepared, the students spoke up as students seldom do. During this period, the instructor took many blows; and it seemed to me that many times he appeared to be shaken; and although he was the source of our irritation, we had, strange as it may seem, a great affection for him, for it did not seem right to be angry with a man who was so sympathetic, so sensitive to the feelings and ideas of others. We all felt that what was involved was some slight misunderstanding, which once understood and remedied would make everything right again. But our instructor, gentle enough on the surface, had a "whim of steel." He didn't seem to understand; and if he did, he was obstinate and obdurate; he refused to come around. Thus did this tug-of-war continue. We all looked to Rogers and Rogers looked to us. One student, amid general approbation, observed: "We are Rogers-centered, not student-centered. We have come to learn from Rogers."

Encouraging Thinking

Another student had discovered that Rogers had been influenced by Kilpatrick and Dewey, and using this idea as a springboard, he said he thought he perceived what Rogers was trying to get at. He thought Rogers wanted students to think independently, creatively; he wanted students to become deeply involved with their very persons, their very selves, hoping that this might lead to the "reconstruction" of the person—in the Dewey sense of the term—the person's outlook, attitudes, values, behavior. This would be a true reconstruction of experience; it would be learning in a real sense. Certainly, he didn't want the course to end in an examination based on textbooks and lectures, followed by the traditional end-term grade, which generally means completion and forgetting.[1] Rogers had expressed the belief almost from the outset of the course that no one can teach anyone else anything. But thinking, this student insisted, begins at the fork in the road, the famed dilemma set up by Dewey. As we reach the fork in the road, we do not know which road to take if we are to reach our destination; and then we begin to examine the situation. Thinking starts at that point.

Kilpatrick also sought original thinking from his students and also rejected a regurgitant textbook kind of learning, but he presented crucial problems for discussion, and these problems aroused a great deal of interest, and they also created vast changes in the person. Why can't committees of students or individual students get up such problems for discussion?[2] Rogers listened sympathetically and said, "I see you feel strongly about this?" That disposed of that. If I recall correctly, the next student who spoke completely disregarded what had been suggested and started afresh on another topic, quite in conformity with the custom set by the class.

Spasmodically, through the session, students referred favorably to the foregoing suggestion, and they began to demand more insistently that Rogers assume the traditional role of a teacher. At this point, the blows were coming Rogers' way rather frequently and strongly and I thought I saw him bend somewhat before them. (Privately, he denied he was so affected.) During one session, a student made the suggestion that he lecture one hour and that we have a class discussion the next. This one suggestion seemed to fit into his plans. He said he had with him an unpublished paper. He warned us that it was available and we could read it by ourselves. But the student said it would not be the same. The person, the author, would be out of it, the stress, the inflection, the emotion, those nuances which give value and meaning to words. Rogers then asked the students if that was what they wanted. They said yes. He read for over an hour. After the vivid and acrimonious exchanges to which we had become accustomed, this was certainly a letdown, dull and soporific to the extreme. This experi-

1. It should be noted that Dr. Rogers neither agreed nor disagreed. It was not his habit to respond to students' contributions unless a remark was directed specifically to him; and even then he might choose not to answer. His main object, it seemed to me, was to follow students' contributions intelligently and sympathetically.
2. One student compiled such a list, had it mimeographed, distributed it, and for practical purposes that was the end of that.

In this connection, another illustration may be in order. At the first session, Rogers brought to class tape recordings of therapeutic sessions. He explained that he was not comfortable in a teacher's role and he came "loaded," and the recordings served as a sort of security. One student continually insisted that he play the recordings, and after considerable pressure from the class, he did so, but he complied reluctantly; and all told, despite the pressure, he did not play them for more than an hour in all the sessions. Apparently, Rogers preferred the students to make real live recordings rather than listen to those which could only interest them in an academic way.

ence squelched all further demands for lecturing. In one of the moments when he apologized for this episode ("It's better, more excusable, when students demand it."), he said: "You asked me to lecture. It is true I am a resource, but what sense would there be in my lecturing? I have brought a great quantity of material, reprints of any number of lectures, articles, books, tape recordings, movies."

By the fifth session, something definite had happened; there was no mistaking that. Students spoke to one another; they by-passed Rogers. Students asked to be heard and wanted to be heard, and what before was a halting, stammering, self-conscious group became an interacting group, a brand new cohesive unit, carrying on in a unique way; and from them came discussion and thinking such as no other group but this could repeat or duplicate. The instructor also joined in, but his role, more important than any in the group, somehow became merged with the group; the group was important, the center, the base of operation, not the instructor.

What caused it? I can only conjecture as to the reason. I believe that what happened was this: For four sessions students refused to believe that the instructor would refuse to play the traditional role. They still believed that he would set the tasks; that he would be the center of whatever happened and that he would manipulate the group. It took the class four sessions to realize that they were wrong; that he came to them with nothing outside of himself, outside of his own person; that if they really wanted something to happen, it was they who had to provide the content — an uncomfortable, challenging situation indeed. It was they who had to speak up, with all the risks that that entailed. As part of the process, they shared, they took exception, they agreed, they disagreed. At any rate, their persons, their deepest selves were involved; and from this situation, this special, unique group, this new creation was born.

Importance of Acceptance

As you may know, Rogers believes that if a person is accepted, fully accepted, and in this acceptance there is no judgment, only compassion and sympathy, the individual is able to come to grips with himself, to develop the courage to give up his defenses and face his true self. I saw this process work. Amid the early efforts to communicate, to find a *modus vivendi*, there had been in the group tentative exchanges of feelings, emotions and ideas; but after the fourth session, and progressively thereafter, this group, haphazardly thrown together, became close to one another and their true selves appeared. As they interacted, there were moments of insight and revelation and understanding that were almost awesome in nature; they were what, I believe, Rogers would describe as "moments of therapy," those pregnant moments when you see a human soul revealed before you, in all its breathless wonder; and then a silence, almost like reverence, would overtake the class. And each member of the class became enveloped with a warmth and a loveliness that border on the mystic. I for one, and I am quite sure the others also, never had an experience quite like this. It was learning and therapy; and by therapy I do not mean illness, but what might be characterized by a healthy change in the person, an increase in his flexibility, his openness, his willingness to listen. In the process, we all felt elevated, freer, more accepting of ourselves and others, more open to new ideas, trying hard to understand and accept.

This is not a perfect world, and there was evidence of hostility as members differed. Somehow in this setting every blow was softened, as if the sharp edges had been removed; if undeserved, students would go off to something else; and the blow was somehow lost. In my own case, even those students who originally irritated me, with further acquaintance I began to accept and respect, and the thought occurred to me as I tried to understand what was happening: Once you come close to a person, perceive his thoughts, his emotions, his feelings, he becomes not only understandable but good and desirable. Some of the more aggressive ones spoke more than they should, more than their right share, but the group itself, by its own being, not by setting rules, eventually made its authority felt; and unless a person was very sick or insensitive, members more or less, in this respect, conformed to what was expected of them. The problem—the hostile, the dominant, the neurotic—was not too acute; and yet if measured in a formal way, with a stop watch, at no time was a session free of aimless talk and waste of time. But yet as I watched the process, the idea persisted that perhaps this waste of time may be necessary; it may very well be that that is the way man learns best; for certainly, as I look back at the whole experience, I am fairly certain that it would have been impossible to learn as much or as well or as thoroughly in the traditional classroom setting. If we accept Dewey's definition of education as the reconstruction of experience, what better way can a person learn than by becoming involved with his whole self, his very person, his root drives, emotions, attitudes and values? No series of facts or arguments, no matter how logically or brilliantly arranged, can even faintly compare with that sort of thing.

In the course of this process, I saw hard, inflexible, dogmatic persons, in the brief period of several weeks, change in front of my eyes and become sympathetic, understanding and to a marked degree non-judgmental. I saw neurotic, compulsive persons ease up and become more accepting of themselves and others. In one instance, a student who particularly impressed me by his change, told me when I mentioned this: "It is true. I feel less rigid, more open to the world. And I like myself better for it. I don't believe I ever learned so much anywhere." I saw shy persons become less shy and agressive persons more sensitive and moderate.

One might say that this appears to be essentially an emotional process. But that I believe would be altogether inaccurate in describing it. There was a great deal of intellectual content, but the intellectual content was meaningful and crucial to the person, in a sense that it meant a great deal to him as a person. In fact, one student brought up this very question. "Should we be concerned," he asked, "only with the emotions? Has the intellect no play?" It was my turn to ask, "Is there any student who has read as much or thought as much for any other course?"

The answer was obvious. We had spent hours and hours reading; the room reserved for us had occupants until 10 o'clock at night, and then many left only because the university guards wanted to close the building.

Students listened to recordings; they saw motion pictures; but best of all, they talked and talked and talked. In the traditional course, the instructor lectures and indicates what is to be read and learned; students dutifully record all this in their notebooks, take an examination and feel good or bad, depending on the outcome; but in nearly all cases it is a complete experience, with a sense of finality; the laws of forgetting begin to operate rapidly and inexorably. In the Rogers course, students read and thought inside and outside the class; it was they who chose from this reading and thinking what was meaningful to them, not the instructor.

This non-directive kind of teaching, I should point out, was not 100 per cent successful. There were three or four students who found the whole idea distasteful. Even at the end of the course, although nearly all became enthusiastic, one student to my knowledge, was intensely negative in his feelings; another was highly critical. These wanted the instructor to provide them with a rounded-out intellectual piece of merchandise which they could commit to memory and then give back on an examination. They would then have the assurance that they had learned what they should. As one said, "If I had to make a report as to what I learned in this course, what could I say?" Admittedly, it would be much more difficult than in a traditional course, if not impossible.

The Rogers method was free and flowing and open and permissive. A student would start an interesting discussion; it would be taken up by a second; but a third student might take us away in another direction, bringing up a personal matter of no interest to the class; and we would all feel frustrated. But this was like life, flowing on like a river, seemingly futile, with never the same water there, flowing on, with no one knowing what would happen the next moment. But in this there was an expectancy, an alertness, an aliveness; it seemed to me as near a smear of life as one could get in a classroom. For the authoritarian person, who puts his faith in neatly piled up facts, this method I believe can be threatening, for here he gets no reassurance, only an openness, a flowing, no closure.

A New Methodology

I believe that a great deal of the stir and the ferment that characterized the class was due to this lack of closure. In the lunch room, one could recognize Rogers' students by their animated discussions, by their desire to be together; and sometimes, since there was no table large enough, they would sit two and three tiers deep; and they would eat with plates on their laps. As Rogers himself points out, there is no finality in the process. He himself never summarizes (against every conventional law of teaching). The issues are left unresolved; the problems raised in class are always in a state of flux, on-going. In their need to know, to come to some agreement, students gather together, wanting understanding, seeking closure. Even in the matter of grades, there is no closure. A grade means an end; but Dr. Rogers does not give the grade; it is the student who suggests the grade; and since he does so, even this sign of completion is left unresolved, without an end, unclosed. Also, since the course is unstructured, each has staked his person in the course; he has spoken, not with the textbook as the gauge, but with his person, and thus as a self he has communicated with others, and because of this, in contradistinction to the impersonal subject matter that comprises the normal course, there develops this closeness and warmth.

To describe the many gracious acts that occurred might convey some idea of this feeling of closeness. One student invited the class to her home for a cookout. Another student, a priest from Spain, was so taken with the group that he talked of starting a publication to keep track of what was happening to the group members after they disbanded. A group interested in student counseling met on its own. A member arranged for the class to visit a mental hospital for children and adults; also he arranged for us to see the experimental work being done with psychotic patients by Dr. Lindsley. Class members brought in tape recordings and printed matter to add to the library material set aside for our use. In every way the spirit of good-will and friendliness was manifest to an extent that happens only in rare and isolated instances. In the many, many courses I have taken I have not seen the like. In this connection, it should be pointed out that the members comprised a group that had been haphazardly thrown together; they had come from many backgrounds and they included a wide age range.

I believe that what has been described above is truly a creative addition to classroom methodology; it is radically different from the old. That it has the capacity to move people, to make them freer, more open-minded, more flexible, I have no doubt. I myself witnessed the power of this method. I believe that non-directive teaching has profound implications which even those who accept this point of view cannot at present fully fathom. Its importance, I believe, goes beyond the classroom and extends to every area where human beings communicate and try to live with one another.

More specifically, as a classroom methodology, it warrants the widest discussion, inquiry and experimentation. It has the possibility of opening up a whole new dimension of thinking, fresh and original, for in its approach, in its practice, in its philosophy it differs so fundamentally from the old. It seems to me this approach ought to be tried out in every area of learning—elementary, high school, college, wherever human beings gather to learn and improve on the old. At this stage we should not be overly concerned about its limitations and inadequacies, since the method has not been refined and we do not know as much about it as we ought. As a new technique, it starts off with a handicap. We are loath to give up the old. The old is bolstered by tradition, authority and respectability; and we ourselves are its product. If we view education, however, as the reconstruction of experience, does not this presume that the individual must do his own reconstructing? He must do it himself, through the reorganization of his deepest self, his values, his attitudes, his very person. What better method is there to engross the individual; to bring him, his ideas, his feelings into communication with others; to break down the barriers that create isolation in a world where for his own mental safety and health, man has to learn to be part of mankind?

A PERSONAL TEACHING EXPERIENCE
AS REPORTED TO DR. ROGERS

I feel impelled to write to you about my first experience in teaching after being exposed to your thinking and influence. You may or may not know I had a phobia about teaching. Since my work with you, I began to perceive more clearly where the difficulty lay. It was mostly in my concept of the role I had to play as a teacher—the motivator, director and the production chief of a performance. I always feared being "hung up" in the classroom —I believe it's your expression and I have come to like it—the class listless, uninterested, not responding, and my yammering and yammering, until I lost poise, the sentences not forming, coming out artificially, and the time moving slowly, slowly, ever more slowly. This was the horror I imagined. I suppose pieces of this happen to every teacher, but I would put them all together, and I would approach the class with foreboding, not at ease, not truly myself.

And now comes my experience. I was asked to give two summer courses for the Graduate School of Education of Yeshiva University, but I had a perfect alibi. I was going to Europe and I couldn't. Wouldn't I give an interim course, a concentrated course of 14 sessions during the month of June; and this would not interfere with the trip? I had no excuse and I accepted —because I no longer wanted to dodge the situation and more, also, because I was determined once and for all to face it. If I didn't like to teach (I haven't taught for nearly ten years), I would learn something. And if I did, I would also learn something. And if I had to suffer, it was best this way, since the course was concentrated and the time element was short.

You know that I have been strongly influenced in my thinking about education by Kilpatrick and Dewey. But now I had another powerful ingredient—you. When I first met my class, I did something I never did before. I was frank about my feelings. Instead of feeling that a teacher should know and students were there to be taught, I admitted weaknesses, doubts, dilemmas, and NOT KNOWING. Since I sort of dethroned my role as a teacher to the class and myself, my more natural self came out more freely and I found myself talking easily and even creatively. By "creatively" I mean ideas came to me as I spoke, brand new ideas which I felt were good.

Another important difference: It is true that since I was influenced by the Kilpatrick methodology I always welcomed the widest discussion, but I now know, I still wanted and expected my students to know the text and the lecture material set out for them. Even worse, I now know that although I welcomed discussion, I wanted, above all things, that, after all was said and done, the final conclusions of the class to come out according to my way of thinking. Hence none of the discussions were real discussions, in the sense that it was open and free and inquiring; none of the questions were real questions, in the sense that they sought to evoke thinking; all of them were loaded, in the sense that I had pretty definite convictions about what I thought were good answers and at times right answers. Hence, I came to the class with subject matter and my students were really instruments by which situations were manipulated to produce the inclusion of what I regarded as desirable subject matter.

In this last course, I didn't have the courage to discard all subject matter, but this time I really listened to my students; I gave them understanding and sympathy. Although I would spend hours and hours preparing for each session, I found that not once did I refer to a note from the voluminous material with which I entered the room. I allowed students free rein, not holding anyone down to any set course, and I permitted the widest diversion; and I followed wherever the students led.

I remember discussing this with a prominent educator and he said, in what I thought was a disappointed and disapproving tone: "You insist, of course, on good thinking." I quoted William James, who in effect said that man is a speck of reason in an ocean of emotion. I told him that I was more interested in what I would call a "third dimension," the feeling part of the students.

I cannot say I followed you all the way, Dr. Rogers, since I would express opinions and at times, unfortunately, lecture; and that I believe is bad, since students, once authoritative opinions are expressed, tend not to think, but to try to guess what is in the instructor's head and provide him with what he might like, so as to find favor in his eyes. If I had to do it over again, I would have less of that. But I did try and I believe I succeeded in large measure to give to each student a sense of dignity, respect and acceptance; farthest from my mind was to check on them or evaluate and mark them.

And the result—and this is why I am writing you—was for me an unparalleled experience, inexplicable in ordinary terms. I myself cannot fully account for it, except to be grateful that it happened to me. Some of the very qualities which I experienced in your course I found in this which I gave. I found myself liking these particular students as I have never liked any other group of persons, and I found—and they expressed this in their final report—that they themselves began to feel warm and kindly and accepting of one another. Orally and in their papers, they told of how moved they were, how much they learned, how well they felt. For me this was a brand new experience, and I was overwhelmed and humbled by it. I have had students who, I believe, respected and admired me, but I never had a classroom experience from which came such warmth and closeness. Incidentally, following your example, I avoided setting any fixed requirements in terms of reading or classroom preparation.

That the foregoing was not "biased perception" was evidenced from reports I got outside the classroom. The students had said such nice things about me that faculty members wanted to sit in the class. Best of all, the students at the end of the course wrote Dean Benjamin Fine a letter in which they said the nicest things about me. And the Dean in turn wrote me to the same effect.

To say that I am overwhelmed by what happened only faintly reflects my feelings. I have taught for many years but I have never experienced anything remotely resembling what occurred. I, for my part, never have found in the classroom so much of the whole person coming forth, so deeply involved, so deeply stirred. Further, I question if in the traditional setup, with its emphasis on subject matter, examinations, grades, there is, or there can be a place for the "becoming" person, with his deep and manifold needs, as he struggles to fulfill himself. But this is going far afield. I can only report to you what happened and to say that I am grateful and that I am also humbled by the experience. I would like you to know this, for again you have added to and enriched my life and being.[3]

ABRAHAM MASLOW

Abraham Maslow is a professor of psychology at Brandeis University. His major work to date—and the book which best explains his controversial theory of self-actualization—is Motivation and Personality *(1954). He is also the author of numerous other books and articles, including* Toward a Psychology of Being *(1962). He has edited a book dealing with contemporary concepts of value which is entitled* New Knowledge in Human Values *(1959).*

Deficiency Motivation and Growth Motivation

It is important, states Maslow, to recognize that human needs are organized into a "hierarchy of relative prepotency." This hierarchy, beginning with the lowest level, includes five classifications of needs: physiological needs, safety needs, be-*

---

3. That this was not an isolated experience for Dr. Tenenbaum is indicated by a quotation from still another personal communication, many months later. He says: "With another group I taught, following the first one, similar attitudes developed, only they were more accentuated, because, I believe, I was more comfortable with the technique and, I hope, more expert. In this second group there was the same release of the person, the same exhilaration and excitement, the same warmth, the same mystery that attaches to a person as he succeeds in shedding portions of his skin. Students from my group told me that while attending other classes, their eyes would meet, drawn to one another, as if they were unique and apart, as if they were bound together by a special experience. In this second group, also, I found that the students had developed a personal closeness, so that at the end of the semester they talked of having annual reunions. They said that somehow or other they wanted to keep this experience alive and not lose one another. They also spoke of radical and fundamental changes in their person—in outlook, in values, in feelings, in attitudes both toward themselves and toward others."

*Abraham Maslow, *Motivation and Personality* (New York: Harper and Brothers, 1954), p. 83.

longingness and love needs, esteem needs, and the need for self-actualization. Only when the needs at one level have been at least partially satisfied does the individual normally seek to satisfy those at the next level. As Maslow states:

> One main implication of this phrasing is that gratification becomes as important a concept as deprivation in motivation theory, for it releases the organism from the domination of a relatively more physiological need, permitting thereby the emergence of other more social goals. The physiological needs, along with their partial goals, when chronically gratified cease to exist as active determinants or organizers of behavior. They now exist only in a potential fashion in the sense that they may emerge again to dominate the organism if they are thwarted. But a want that is satisfied is no longer a want. The organism is dominated and its behavior organized only by unsatisfied needs. If hunger is satisfied, it becomes unimportant in the current dynamics of the individual.+

In this selection Maslow discusses a provocative new theory of motivation which is closely related both to his concept of a natural hierarchy of needs and to his general theory of self-actualization which is discussed in the following selection.

One major difficulty with [the concept of self-actualization] is its somewhat static character. Self-actualization, since I have found it only in older people, tends to be seen as an ultimate or final state of affairs, a far goal, rather than a dynamic process, active throughout life, Being, rather than Becoming.

If we define growth as the various processes which bring the person toward ultimate self-actualization, then this conforms better with the observed fact that it is going on *all* the time in the life history. It discourages also the stepwise, *all* or none, saltatory conception of motivational progression toward self-actualization in which the basic needs are completely gratified, one by one, before the next higher one emerges into consciousness. Growth is seen then not only as progressive gratification of basic needs to the point where they "disappear," but also in the form of specific growth motivations over and above these basic needs, e.g., talents, capacities, creative tendencies, constitutional potentialities. We are thereby helped also to realize that basic needs and self-actualization do not contradict each other any more than do childhood and maturity. One passes into the other and is a necessary prerequisite for it.

The differentiation between these growth-needs and basic needs . . . is a consequence of the clinical perception of qualitative differences between the motivational lives of self-actualizers and of other people. These differences, listed below, are fairly well though not perfectly described by the names deficiency-needs and growth-needs. For instance, not all physiological needs are deficits, e.g., sex, elimination, sleep and rest.

At a higher level, needs for safety, belongingness, love and respect are

---

+*Ibid.*, p. 84.

all clearly deficits. But the need for self-respect is a doubtful case. While the cognitive needs for curiosity-satisfaction and for a system of explanation can easily be considered deficits to be satisfied, as can also the hypothetical need for beauty, the need to create is another matter, as is also the need to express. Apparently not all basic needs are deficits but the needs whose frustration is pathogenic are deficits. (Clearly also the sensory satisfactions that Murphy has emphasized can not be considered deficits, perhaps not even needs at all.)

In any case, the psychological life of the person, in many of its aspects, is lived out differently when he is deficiency-need-gratification-bent and when he is growth-dominated or "metamotivated" or growth-motivated or self-actualizing. The following differences make this clear.

1. ATTITUDE TOWARD IMPULSE: IMPULSE-REJECTION AND IMPULSE-ACCEPTANCE

Practically all historical and contemporary theories of motivation unite in regarding needs, drives and motivating states in general as annoying, irritating, unpleasant, undesirable, as something to get rid of. Motivated behavior, goal seeking, consummatory responses are all techniques for reducing these discomforts. This attitude is very explicitly assumed in such widely used descriptions of motivation as need reduction, tension reduction, drive reduction, and anxiety reduction.

This approach is understandable in animal psychology and in the behaviorism which is so heavily based upon work with animals. It may be that animals have *only* deficiency needs. Whether or not this turns out to be so, in any case we have treated animals *as if* this were so for the sake of objectivity. A goal object has to be something outside the animal organism so that we can measure the effort put out by the animal in achieving this goal.

It is also understandable that the Freudian psychology should be built upon the same attitude toward motivation that impulses are dangerous and to be fought. After all, this whole psychology is based upon experience with sick people, people who in fact suffer from bad experiences with their needs, and with their gratifications and frustrations. It is no wonder that such people should fear or even loathe their impulses which have made so much trouble for them and which they handle so badly, and that a usual way of handling them is repression.

This derogation of desire and need has, of course, been a constant theme throughout the history of philosophy, theology and psychology. The Stoics, most hedonists, practically all theologians, many political philosophers and most economic theorists have united in affirming the fact that good or happiness or pleasure is essentially the consequence of amelioration of this unpleasant state-of-affairs of wanting, of desiring, of needing.

To put it as succinctly as possible, these people all find desire or impulse to be a nuisance or even a threat and therefore will try generally to get rid of it, to deny it or to avoid it.

This contention is sometimes an accurate report of what is the case.

The physiological needs, the needs for safety, for love, for respect, for information are in fact often nuisances for many people, psychic troublemakers, and problem-creators, especially for those who have had unsuccessful experiences at gratifying them and for those who cannot now count on gratification.

Even with these deficiencies, however, the case is very badly overdrawn: one can accept and enjoy one's needs and welcome them to consciousness if (a) past experience with them has been rewarding, and (b) if present and future gratification can be counted on. For example, if one has in general enjoyed food and if good food is now available, the emergence of appetite into consciousness is welcomed instead of dreaded. ("The trouble with eating is that it kills my appetite.") Something like this is true for thirst, for sleepiness, for sex, for dependency needs and for love needs. However, a far more powerful refutation of the "need-is-a-nuisance" theory is found in the recently merging awareness of, and concern with, growth (self-actualization) motivation.

The multitude of idiosyncratic motives which come under the head of "self-actualization" can hardly be listed since each person has different talents, capacities, potentialities. But some characteristics are general to all of them. And one is that these impulses are desired and welcomed, are enjoyable and pleasant, that the person wants more of them rather than less, and that if they constitute tensions, they are *pleasurable* tensions. The creator ordinarily welcomes his creative impulses, the talented person enjoys using and expanding his talents.

It is simply inaccurate to speak in such instances of tension-reduction, implying thereby the getting rid of an annoying state. For these states are not annoying.

2. DIFFERENTIAL EFFECTS OF GRATIFICATION

Almost always associated with negative attitudes toward the need is the conception that the primary aim of the organism is to get rid of the annoying need and thereby to achieve a cessation of tension, an equilibrium, a homeostasis, a quiescence, a state of rest, a lack of pain.

The drive or need presses toward its own elimination. Its only striving is toward cessation, toward getting rid of itself, toward a state of not wanting. Pushed to its logical extreme, we wind up with Freud's death-instinct.

Angyal, Goldstein, G. Allport, C. Buhler, Schachtel and others have effectively criticized this essentially circular position. If the motivational life consists essentially of a defensive removal of irritating tensions, and if the only end product of tension-reduction is a state of passive waiting for more unwelcome irritations to arise and in their turn, to be dispelled, then how does change, or development or movement or direction come about? Why do people improve? Get wiser? What does zest in living mean?

Charlotte Buhler has pointed out that the theory of homeostasis is different from the theory of rest. The latter theory speaks simply of removing tension which implies that zero tension is best. Homeostasis means coming not to a zero but to an optimum level. This means sometimes reducing tension, sometimes increasing it, e.g., blood pressure may be too low as well as too high.

In either case the lack of constant direction through a lifespan is obvious. In both cases, growth of the personality, increases in wisdom, self-actualization, strengthening of the character, and the planning of one's life are not and cannot be accounted for. Some long-time vector, or directional tendency, must be invoked to make any sense of development through the lifetime.

This theory must be put down as an inadequate description even of deficiency motivation. What is lacking here is awareness of the dynamic principle which ties together and interrelates all these separate motivational episodes. The different basic needs are related to each other in a hierarchical order such that gratification of one need and its consequent removal from the center of the stage brings about not a state of rest or Stoic apathy, but rather the emergence into consciousness of another "higher" need; wanting and desiring continues but at a "higher" level. Thus the coming-to-rest theory isn't adequate even for deficiency motivation.

However, when we examine people who are predominantly growth-motivated, the coming-to-rest conception of motivation becomes completely useless. In such ·people gratification breeds increased rather than decreased motivation, heightened rather than lessened excitement. The appetites become intensified and heightened. They grow upon themselves and instead of wanting less and less, such a person wants more and more of, for instance, education. The person rather than coming to rest becomes more active. The appetite for growth is whetted rather than allayed by gratification. Growth is, *in itself*, a rewarding and exciting process, e.g., the fulfilling of yearnings and ambitions, like that of being a good doctor; the acquisition of admired skills, like playing the violin or being a good carpenter; the steady increase of understanding about people or about the universe, or about oneself; the development of creativeness in whatever field, or, most important, simply the ambition to be a good human being.

Wertheimer long ago stressed another aspect of this same differentiation by claiming, in a seeming paradox, that true goal-seeking activity took up less than 10% of his time. Activity can be enjoyed either intrinsically, for its own sake, or else have worth and value only because it is instrumental in bringing about a desired gratification. In the latter case it loses its value and is no longer pleasurable when it is no longer successful or efficient. More frequently, it is simply *not enjoyed at all*, but only the goal is enjoyed. This is similar to that attitude toward life which values it less for its own sake than because one goes to Heaven at the end of it. The observation upon which this generalization is based is that self-actualizing people enjoy life in general and in practically all its aspects, while most other people enjoy only stray moments of triumph, of achievement or of climax or peak experience.

Partly this intrinsic validity of living comes from the pleasurableness inherent in growing and in being grown. But it also comes from the ability of healthy people to transform means-activity into end-experience, so that even instrumental activity is enjoyed as if it were end activity. Growth motivation may be long-term in character. Most of a lifetime may be involved

in becoming a good psychologist or a good artist. All equilibrium or homeostasis or rest theories deal only with short-term episodes, each of which
has nothing to do with each other. Allport particularly has stressed this
point. Planfulness and looking into the future, he points out, are of the central stuff or healthy human nature. He agrees that "Deficit motives do, in
fact, call for the reduction of tension and restoration of equilibrium.
Growth motives, on the other hand, maintain tension in the interest of distant and often unattainable goals. As such they distinguish human from
animal becoming, and adult from infant becoming."

3. CLINICAL EFFECTS OF GRATIFICATION

Deficit-need gratifications and growth-need gratifications have differential
subjective and objective effects upon the personality. If I may phrase what I
am groping for here in a generalized way, it is this: satisfying deficiencies
avoids illness; growth satisfactions produce positive health. I must grant
that this will be difficult to pin down for research purposes at this time.
And yet there is a real *clinical* difference between fending off threat or attack and positive triumph and achievement, between protecting, defending
and preserving oneself and reaching out for fulfillment, for excitement and
for enlargement. I have tried to express this as a contrast between living
fully and *preparing* to live fully, between growing up and being grown.

4. DIFFERENT KINDS OF PLEASURE

Erich Fromm has made an interesting and important effort to distinguish
higher from lower pleasures, as have so many others before him. This is a
crucial necessity for breaking through subjective ethical relativity and is a
prerequisite for a scientific value theory.

He distinguishes scarcity-pleasure from abundance-pleasure, the
"lower" pleasure of satiation of a need from the "higher" pleasure of production, creation and growth of insight. The glut, the relaxation, and the
loss of tension that follows deficiency-satiation can at best be called "relief"
by contrast with the *Funktions-lust*, the ecstasy, the serenity that one experiences when functioning easily, perfectly and at the peak of one's powers
— in overdrive, so to speak.

"Relief," depending so strongly on something that disappears, is itself
more likely to disappear. It must be less stable, less enduring, less constant
than the pleasure accompanying growth, which can go on forever.

5. ATTAINABLE (EPISODIC)
AND UNATTAINABLE GOAL STATES

Deficiency-need gratification tends to be episodic and climactic. The most
frequent schema here begins with an instigating, motivating state which
sets off motivated behavior designed to achieve a goal-state, which, mount-
ing gradually and steadily in desire and excitement, finally reaches a peak

in a moment of success and consummation. From this peak curve of desire, excitement and pleasure fall rapidly to a plateau of quiet tension-release, and lack of motivation.

This schema, though not universally applicable, in any case contrasts very sharply with the situation in growth-motivation, for here, characteristically, there is no climax or consummation, no orgasmic moment, no end-state, even no goal if this be defined climactically. Growth is instead a continued, more or less steady upward or forward development. The more one gets, the more one wants, so that this kind of wanting is endless and can never be attained or satisfied.

It is for this reason that the usual separation between instigation, goal-seeking behavior, the goal object and the accompanying effect breaks down completely. The behaving is itself the goal, and to differentiate the goal of growth from the instigation to growth is impossible. They too are the same.

6. SPECIES-WIDE GOALS AND IDIOSYNCRATIC GOALS

The deficit-needs are shared by all members of the human species and to some extent by other species as well. Self-actualization is idiosyncratic since every person is different. The deficits, i.e., the species requirements, must ordinarily be fairly well satisfied before real individuality can develop fully.

Just as all trees need sun, water, and foods from the environment, so do all people need safety, love and status from *their* environment. However, in both cases this is just where real development of individuality can begin, for once satiated with these elementary, species-wide necessities, each tree and each person proceeds to develop in his own style, uniquely, using these necessities for his own private purposes. In a very meaningful sense, development then becomes more determined from within rather than from without.

7. DEPENDENCE ON, AND INDEPENDENCE FROM, THE ENVIRONMENT

The needs for safety, belongingness, love relations and for respect can be satisfied only by other people, i.e., only from outside the person. This means considerable dependence on the environment. A person in this dependent position cannot really be said to be governing himself, or in control of his own fate. He *must* be beholden to the sources of supply of needed gratifications. Their wishes, their whims, their rules and laws govern him and must be appeased lest he jeopardize his sources of supply. He *must* be, to an extent, "other-directed," and *must* be sensitive to other people's approval, affection and good will. This is the same as saying that he must adapt and adjust by being flexible and responsive and by changing himself to fit the external situation. *He* is the dependent variable; the environment is the fixed, independent variable.

Because of this, the deficiency-motivated man must be more afraid of the environment, since there is always the possibility that it may fail or disappoint him. We now know that this kind of anxious dependence breeds hostility as well. All of which adds up to a lack of freedom, more or less, depending on the good fortune or bad fortune of the individual.

In contrast, the self-actualizing individual, by definition gratified in his basic needs, is far less dependent, far less beholden, far more autonomous and self-directed. Far from needing other people, growth-motivated people may actually be hampered by them. I have already reported their special liking for privacy, for detachment and for meditativeness.

Such people become far more self-sufficient and self-contained. The determinants which govern them are now primarily inner ones, rather than social or environmental. They are the laws of their own inner nature, their potentialities and capacities, their talents, their latent resources, their creative impulses, their needs to know themselves and to become more and more integrated and unified, more and more aware of what they really are, of what they really want, of what their call or vocation or fate is to be.

Since they depend less on other people, they are less ambivalent about them, less anxious and also less hostile, less needful of their praise and their affection. They are less anxious for honors, prestige and rewards.

Autonomy or relative independence of environment means also relative independence of adverse external circumstances, such as ill fortune, hard knocks, tragedy, stress, deprivation. As Allport has stressed, the notion of the human being as essentially reactive, the S-R man, we might call him, who is set into motion by external stimuli, becomes completely ridiculous and untenable for self-actualizing people. The sources of *their* actions are more internal than reactive. This *relative* independence of the outside world and its wishes and pressures, does not mean of course, lack of intercourse with it or respect for its "demand-character." It means only that in these contacts, the self-actualizer's wishes and plans are the primary determiners, rather than stresses from the environment. This I have called psychological freedom, contrasting it with geographical freedom.

Allport's expressive contrast between "opportunistic" and "propriate" determination of behavior parallels closely our outer-determined, inner-determined opposition. It reminds us also of the uniform agreement among biological theorists in considering increasing autonomy and independence of environmental stimuli as *the* defining characteristics of full individuality, of true freedom, of the whole evolutionary process.

8. INTERESTED AND DISINTERESTED INTERPERSONAL RELATIONS

In essence, the deficit-motivated man is far more dependent upon other people than is the man who is predominantly growth-motivated. He is more "interested," more needful, more attached, more desirous.

This dependency colors and limits interpersonal relations. To see people primarily as need-gratifiers or as sources of supply is an abstractive act. They are seen not as wholes, as complicated, unique individuals, but rather from the point of view of usefulness. What in them is not related to the perceiver's needs is either overlooked altogether, or else bores, irritates, or threatens. This parallels our relations with cows, horses, and sheep, as well as with waiters, taxicab drivers, porters, policemen or others whom we *use*.

Fully disinterested, desireless, objective and holistic perception of another human being becomes possible only when nothing is needed from him, only when *he* is not needed. Idiographic, aesthetic perception of the whole person is far more possible for self-actualizing people (or in moments of self-actualization), and furthermore approval, admiration, and love are based less upon gratitude for usefulness and more upon the objective, intrinsic qualities of the perceived person. He is admired for objectively admirable qualities rather than because he flatters or praises. He is loved because he is love-worthy rather than because he gives out love. This is what will be discussed below as unneeding love, e.g., for Abraham Lincoln.

One characteristic of "interested" and need-gratifying relations to other people is that to a very large extent these need-gratifying persons are interchangeable. Since, for instance, the adolescent girl needs admiration per se, it therefore makes little difference who supplies this admiration; one admiration-supplier is about as good as another. So also for the love-supplier or the safety-supplier.

Disinterested, unrewarded, useless, desireless perception of the other as unique, as independent, as end-in-himself—in other words, as a person rather than as a tool—is the more difficult, the more hungry the perceiver is for deficit satisfaction. A "high-ceiling" interpersonal psychology, i.e., an understanding of the highest possible development of human relationships, cannot base itself on deficit theory of motivation.

9. EGO-CENTERING AND EGO-TRANSCENDENCE

We are confronted with a difficult paradox when we attempt to describe the complex attitude toward the self or ego of the growth-oriented, self-actualized person. It is just this person, in whom ego-strength is at its height, who most easily forgets or transcends the ego, who can be most problem-centered, most self-forgetful, most spontaneous in his activities, most homonomous, to use Angyal's term. In such people, absorption in perceiving, in doing, in enjoying, in creating can be very complete, very integrated and very pure.

This ability to center upon the world rather than to be self-conscious, egocentric and gratification-oriented becomes the more difficult the more need-deficits the person has. The more growth-motivated the person is the more problem-centered can he be, and the more he can leave self-consciousness behind him as he deals with the objective world.

10. INTERPERSONAL PSYCHOTHERAPY
AND INTRAPERSONAL PSYCHOLOGY

A major characteristic of people who seek psychotherapy is a former and/or present deficiency of basic-need gratification. Neurosis can be seen as a

deficiency-disease. Because this is so, a basic necessity for cure is supply-
ing what has been lacking or making it possible for the patient to do this
himself. Since these supplies come from other people, ordinary therapy
must be interpersonal.

But this fact has been badly over-generalized. It is true that people
whose deficiency needs have been gratified and who are primarily growth-
motivated are by no means exempt from conflict, unhappiness, anxiety,
and confusion. In such moments they too are apt to seek help and may very
well turn to interpersonal therapy. And yet it is unwise to forget that frequently the problems and the conflicts of the growth-motivated person are
solved by himself by turning inward in a meditative way, i.e., self-searching,
rather than seeking for help from someone. Even in principle, many of
the tasks of self-actualization are largely intrapersonal, such as the making
of plans, the discovery of self, the selection of potentialities to develop, the
construction of a life-outlook.

In the theory of personality improvement, a place must be reserved for
self-improvement and self-searching, contemplation and meditation. In the
later stages of growth the person is essentially alone and can rely only upon
himself. This improvement of an already well person, Oswald Schwarz has
called psychogogy. If psychotherapy makes sick people not-sick and removes symptoms, then psychogogy takes up where therapy leaves off and
tries to make not-sick people healthy. I was interested to notice in Rogers
that successful therapy raised the patients' average score in The Willoughby
Maturity Scale from the twenty-fifth to the fiftieth percentile. Who shall
then lift him to the seventy-fifth percentile? Or the one hundredth? And
are we not likely to need new principles and techniques to do this with?

11. INSTRUMENTAL LEARNING AND PERSONALITY CHANGE

So-called learning theory in this country has based itself almost entirely on
deficit-motivation with goal objects usually external to the organism, i.e.,
learning the best way to satisfy a need. For this reason, among others, our
psychology of learning is a limited body of knowledge, useful only in small
areas of life and of real interest only to other "learning theorists."

This is of little help in solving the problem of growth and self-
actualization. Here the techniques of repeatedly acquiring from the outside
world satisfactions of motivational deficiencies are much less needed. Associative learning and canalizations give way more to perceptual learning, to the
increase of insight and understanding, to knowledge of self and to the steady
growth of personality, i.e., increased synergy, integration and inner consistency. Change becomes much less an acquisition of habits or associations one by one, and much more a total change of the total person, i.e., a
new person rather than the same person with some habits added like new
external possessions.

This kind of character-change-learning means changing a very complex, highly integrated, holistic organism, which in turn means that many
impacts will make no change at all because more and more such impacts
will be rejected as the person becomes more stable and more autonomous.

The most important learning experiences reported to me by my subjects were very frequently single life experiences such as tragedies, deaths,
traumata, conversions, and sudden insights, which forced change in the
life-outlook of the person and consequently in everything that he did. (Of
course the so-called "working through" of the tragedy or of the insight took
place over a longer period of time but this, too, was not primarily a matter
of associative learning.)

To the extent that growth consists in peeling away inhibitions and
constraints and then permitting the person to "be himself," to emit behavior — "radioactively," as it were — rather than to repeat it, to allow his inner
nature to express itself, to this extent the behavior of self-actualizers is unlearned, created and released rather than acquired, expressive rather than
coping.

12. DEFICIENCY-MOTIVATED
AND GROWTH-MOTIVATED PERCEPTION

What may turn out to be the most important difference of all is the greater
closeness of deficit-satisfied people to the realm of Being. Psychologists
have never yet been able to claim this vague jurisdiction of the philosophers, this area dimly seen but nevertheless having undoubted basis in
reality. But it may now become feasible through the study of self-fulfilling
individuals to have our eyes opened to all sorts of basic insights, old to the
philosophers but new to us.

For instance, I think that our understanding of perception and therefore of the perceived world will be much changed and enlarged if we study
carefully the distinction between need-interested and need-disinterested or
desireless perception. Because the latter is so much more concrete and less
abstracted and selective, it is possible for such a person to see more easily
the intrinsic nature of the percept. Also, he can perceive simultaneously the
opposites, the dichotomies, the polarities, the contradictions and the in-
compatibles. It is as if less developed people lived in an Aristotelian world
in which classes and concepts have sharp boundaries and are mutually exclusive and incompatible, e.g., male-female, selfish-unselfish, adult-child,
kind-cruel, good-bad. A is A and everything else is not-A in the Aristotelian
logic, and never the twain shall meet. But seen by self-actualizing people
is the fact that A and not-A interpenetrate and are one, that any person is
simultaneously good *and* bad, male *and* female, adult *and* child. One cannot
place a whole person on a continuum, only an abstracted aspect of a person.

We may not be aware when *we* perceive in a need-determined way.
But we certainly are aware of it when *we* ourselves are perceived in this
way, e.g., simply as a money-giver, a food-supplier, a safety-giver, someone to depend on, or as a waiter or other anonymous servant or means-
object. When this happens we don't like it at all. We want to be taken for ourselves, as complete and whole individuals. We dislike being perceived as
useful objects or as tools. We dislike being "used."

Because self-actualizing people ordinarily do not have to abstract need-
gratifying qualities nor see the person as a tool, it is much more possible

for them to take a non-valuing, non-judging, non-interfering, non-condemning attitude towards others, a desirelessness, a "choiceless awareness." This permits much clearer and more insightful perception and understanding of what is there. This is the kind of untangled and uninvolved, detached perception that surgeons and therapists are supposed to try for and which self-actualizing people attain *without* trying for.

Especially when the structure of the person or object seen is difficult, subtle, and not obvious is this difference in style of perception most important. Especially then must the perceiver have respect for the nature of the object. Perception must then be gentle, delicate, unintruding, undemanding, able to fit itself passively to the nature of things as water gently soaks into crevices. It must *not* be the need-motivated kind of perception which *shapes* things in a blustering, over-riding, exploiting, purposeful fashion, in the manner of a butcher chopping apart a carcass.

The most efficient way to perceive the intrinsic nature of the world is to be more receptive than active, determined as much as possible by the intrinsic organization of that which is perceived and as little as possible by the nature of the perceiver. This kind of detached, Taoist, passive, non-interfering awareness of all the simultaneously existing aspects of the concrete, has much in common with some descriptions of the aesthetic experience and of the mystic experience. The stress is the same. Do we see the real, concrete world or do we see our own system of rubrics, motives, expectations and abstractions which we have projected onto the real world? Or, to put it very bluntly, do we see or are we blind?

NEEDING LOVE AND UNNEEDING LOVE

The love need as ordinarily studied, for instance by Bowlby, Spitz, and Levy, is a deficit need. It is a hole which has to be filled, an emptiness into which love is poured. If this healing necessity is not available, severe pathology results; if it *is* available at the right time, in the right quantities and with proper style, then pathology is averted. Intermediate states of pathology and health follow upon intermediate states of thwarting or satiation. If the pathology is not too severe and if it is caught early enough, replacement therapy can cure. That is to say the sickness, "love-hunger," can be cured in certain cases by making up the pathological deficiency. Love hunger is a deficiency disease, like salt hunger or the avitaminoses.

The healthy person, not having this deficiency, does not need to receive love except in steady, small, maintenance doses and he may even do without these for periods of time. But if motivation is entirely a matter of satisfying deficits and thus getting rid of needs, then a contradiction appears. Satisfaction of the need should cause it to disappear, which is to say that people who have stood in satisfying love relationships are precisely the people who should be *less* likely to give and to receive love! But clinical study of healthier people, who have been love-need-satiated, shows that although they need less to *receive* love, they are more able to *give* love. In this sense, they are *more* loving people.

This finding in itself exposes the limitation of ordinary (deficiency-need-centered) motivation theory and indicates the necessity for "metamo-tivation theory" (or growth-motivation or self-actualization theory).

I have already described in a preliminary fashion the contrasting dy-namics of B-love (love for the Being of another person, unneeding love, unselfish love) and D-love (deficiency-love, love need, selfish love). At this point, I wish only to use these two contrasting groups of people to exemplify and illustrate some of the generalizations made above.

1. B-love is welcomed into consciousness, and is completely enjoyed. Since it is non-possessive, and is admiring rather than needing, it makes no trouble and is practically always pleasure-giving.

2. It can never be sated; it may be enjoyed without end. It usually grows greater rather than disappearing. It is intrinsically enjoyable. It is end rather than means.

3. The B-love experience is often described as being the same as, and having the same effects as the aesthetic experience or the mystic experience.

4. The therapeutic and psychogogic effects of experiencing B-love are very profound and widespread. Similar are the characterological effects of the relatively pure love of a healthy mother for her baby, or the perfect love of their God that some mystics have described.

5. B-love is, beyond the shadow of a doubt, a richer, "higher," more valuable subjective experience than D-love (which all B-lovers have also previously experienced.) This preference is also reported by my other older, more average subjects, many of whom experience both kinds of love simul-taneously in varying combinations.

6. D-love *can* be gratified. The concept "gratification" hardly applies at all to admiration-love for another person's admiration-worthiness and love-worthiness.

7. In B-love there is a minimum of anxiety-hostility. For all practical human purposes, it may even be considered to be absent. There *can*, of course, be anxiety-for-the-other. In D-love one must always expect some degree of anxiety-hostility.

8. B-lovers are more independent of each other, more autonomous, less jealous or threatened, less needful, more individual, more disinterested, but also simultaneously more eager to help the other toward self-actualization, more proud of his triumphs, more altruistic, generous and fostering.

9. The truest, most penetrating perception of the other is made possi-ble by B-love. It is as much a cognitive as an emotional-conative reaction, as I have already emphasized. So impressive is this, and so often validated by other people's later experience, that, far from accepting the common platitude that love makes people blind, I become more and more inclined to think of the *opposite* as true, namely that non-love makes us blind.

10. Finally, I may say that B-love, in a profound but testable sense, cre-ates the partner. It gives him a self-image, it gives him self-acceptance, a feeling of love-worthiness and respect-worthiness, all of which permit him to grow. It is a real question whether the full development of the human being is possible without it.

Self-Actualizing People:
A Study of Psychological Health

PERSONAL FOREWORD

The study to be reported . . . is unusual in various ways. It was not planned as an ordinary research; it was not a social venture but a private one, motivated by my own curiosity and pointed toward the solution of various personal moral, ethical, and scientific problems. I sought only to convince and to teach myself (as is quite proper in a personal quest) rather than to prove or to demonstrate to others.

Quite unexpectedly, however, these studies have proved to be so enlightening to me, and so laden with exciting implications, that it seems fair that some sort of report should be made to others in spite of its methodological shortcomings.

In addition, I consider the problem of psychological health to be so pressing, that *any* suggestions, *any* bits of data, however moot, are endowed with great heuristic value. This kind of research is in principle so difficult—involving as it does a kind of lifting oneself by one's axiological bootstraps—that if we were to wait for conventionally reliable data, we should have to wait forever. It seems that the only manly thing to do is not to fear mistakes, to plunge in, to do the best that one can, hoping to learn enough from blunders to correct them eventually. At present the only alternative is simply to refuse to work with the problem. Accordingly, for whatever use can be made of it, the following report is presented with due apologies to those who insist on conventional reliability, validity, sampling, etc.

SUBJECTS AND METHODS

The subjects were selected from among personal acquaintances and friends, and from among public and historical figures. In addition, in a first research with young people, three thousand college students were screened, but yielded only one immediately usable subject and a dozen or two possible future subjects.

I had to conclude that self-actualization of the sort I had found in my older subjects was not possible in our society for young, developing people.

Accordingly, in collaboration with Dr. Evelyn Raskin and Dan Freedman, a search was begun for a panel of *relatively* healthy college students. We arbitrarily decided to choose the healthiest 1 percent of the college population. This research, pursued over a two-year period as time permitted, had to be interrupted before completion, but it was, of course, very instructive at the clinical level. It is hoped that the subjects selected may yet be followed up for our further instruction.

It was also hoped that figures created by novelists or dramatists could be used for demonstration purposes, but none were found that were usable in our culture and our time (in itself a thought-provoking finding).

The first clinical definition, on the basis of which subjects were finally chosen or rejected, had a positive as well as a merely negative side. The negative criterion was an absence of neurosis, psychopathic personality, psychosis, or strong tendencies in these directions. Possibly psychosomatic illness called forth closer scrutiny and screening. Wherever possible, Rorschach tests were given, but turned out to be far more useful in revealing concealed psychopathology than in selecting healthy people. The positive criterion for selection was positive evidence of self-actualization (SA), as yet a difficult syndrome to describe accurately. For the purposes of this discussion, it may be loosely described as the full use and exploitation of talents, capacities, potentialities, etc. Such people seem to be fulfilling themselves and to be doing the best that they are capable of doing, reminding us of Nietzsche's exhortation, "Become what thou art!" They are people who have developed or are developing to the full stature of which they are capable. These potentialities may be either idiosyncratic or species-wide, so that the self in self-actualization must not have too individualistic a flavor.

This criterion implies also either gratification, past or present, of the basic emotional needs for safety, belongingness, love, respect, and self-respect, and of the cognitive needs for knowledge and for understanding, or in a few cases, conquest of these needs. This is to say that all subjects felt safe and unanxious, accepted, loved and loving, respect-worthy and respected, and that they had worked out their philosophical, religious, or axiological bearings. It is still an open question as to whether this basic gratification is a sufficient or only a prerequisite condition of self-actualization. It may be that self-actualization means basic gratification plus at least minimum talent, capacity, or richness.

In general, the technique of selection used was that of *iteration*, previously used in studies of the personality syndromes of self-esteem and of security . . . . This consists briefly in starting with the personal or cultural nontechnical state of belief, collating the various extant usages and definitions of the syndrome, and then defining it more carefully, still in terms of actual usage (what might be called the lexicographical stage), with, however, the elimination of the logical and factual inconsistencies customarily found in folk definitions.

On the basis of the corrected folk definition, the first groups of subjects are selected, a group who are high in the quality and a group who are low in it. These people are studied as carefully as possible in the clinical style, and on the basis of this empirical study the original corrected folk definition is further changed and corrected as required by the data now in hand. This gives the first clinical definition. On the basis of this new definition, the original group of subjects is reselected, some being retained, some being dropped, and some new ones being added. This second level group of subjects is then in its turn clinically, and if possible, experimentally and statistically studied, which in turn causes modification, correction, and enrichment of the first clinical definition, with which in turn a new group of subjects is selected and so on. In this way an originally vague and unscientific folk concept can become more and more exact, more and more operational in character, and therefore more scientific.

Of course, external, theoretical, and practical considerations may intrude into this spiral-like process of self-correction. For instance, early in this study, it was found that folk usage was so unrealistically demanding that no living human being could possibly fit the definition. We had to stop excluding a possible subject on the basis of single foibles, mistakes, or foolishness; or to put it in another way, we could not use perfection as a basis for selection, since no subject was perfect.

Another such problem was presented by the fact that in all cases it was impossible to get full and satisfactory information of the kind usually demanded in clinical work. Possible subjects, when informed of the purpose of the research, became self-conscious, froze up, laughed off the whole effort, or broke off the relationship. As a result, since this early experience, all older subjects have been studied indirectly, indeed almost surreptitiously. Only younger people can be studied directly.

Since living people were studied whose names could not be divulged, two desiderata or even requirements of ordinary scientific work became impossible to achieve: namely, repeatability of the investigation and public availability of the data upon which conclusions were made. These difficulties are partly overcome by the inclusion of public and historical figures, and by the supplementary study of young people and children who could conceivably be used publicly.

The subjects have been divided into the following categories:

Cases:	3 fairly sure and 2 highly probable contemporaries
	2 fairly sure historical figures (Lincoln in his last years and Thomas Jefferson)
	6 highly probable public and historical figures (Einstein, Eleanor Roosevelt, Jane Addams, William James, and Spinoza)
Partial Cases:	5 contemporaries who fairly certainly fall short somewhat but who can yet be used for study
	7 historical figures who probably or certainly fall short, but who can yet be used for study (Walt Whitman, Henry Thoreau, Beethoven, F. D. Roosevelt, Freud)
Potential or Possible Cases:	20 younger people who seem to be developing in the direction of self-actualization, and G. W. Carver, Eugene V. Debs, Albert Schweitzer, Thomas Eakins, Fritz Kreisler, Goethe

GATHERING AND PRESENTATION OF THE DATA

Data here consist not so much in the usual gathering of specific and discrete facts as in the slow development of a global or holistic impression of the sort that we form of our friends and acquaintances. It was rarely possible to set up a situation, to ask pointed questions, or to do any testing with my older subjects (although this *was* possible and was done with younger subjects). Contacts were fortuitous and of the ordinary social sort. Friends and relatives were questioned where this was possible.

Because of this and also because of the small number of subjects as well as the incompleteness of the data for many subjects, any quantitative presentation is impossible: only composite impressions can be offered for whatever they may be worth (and of course they are worth much less than controlled objective observation, since the investigator is never *quite* certain about what is description and what is projection).

The holistic analysis of these total impressions yields, as the most important and useful whole characteristics of self-actualizing people for further clinical and experimental study, the following:

MORE EFFICIENT PERCEPTION OF REALITY AND MORE COMFORTABLE RELATIONS WITH IT

The first form in which this capacity was noticed was as an unusual ability to detect the spurious, the fake, and the dishonest in personality, and in general to judge people correctly and efficiently. In an informal experiment with a group of college students, a clear tendency was discerned for the more secure (the more healthy) to judge their professors more accurately than did the less secure students, i.e., high scorers in the S-I test.

As the study progressed, it slowly became apparent that this efficiency extended to many other areas of life — indeed *all* areas that were tested. In art and music, in things of the intellect, in scientific matters, in politics and public affairs, they seemed as a group to be able to see concealed or confused realities more swiftly and more correctly than others. Thus an informal experiment indicated that their predictions of the future from whatever facts were in hand at the time seemed to be more often correct, because less based upon wish, desire, anxiety, fear, or upon generalized, character-determined optimism or pessimism.

At first this was phrased as good taste or good judgment, the implication being relative and not absolute. But for many reasons (some to be detailed below), it has become progressively more clear that this had better be called perception (not taste) of something that was absolutely there (reality, not a set of opinions). It is hoped that this conclusion — or hypothesis — can soon be put to the experimental test.

If this is so, it would be impossible to overstress its importance. Recently Money-Kyrle, an English psychoanalyst, has indicated that he believes it possible to call a neurotic person not only *relatively* but *absolutely* inefficient, simply because he does not perceive the real world so accurately or so efficiently as does the healthy person. The neurotic is not only emotionally sick — he is cognitively *wrong!* If health and neurosis are, respectively, correct and incorrect perceptions of reality, propositions of fact and propositions of value merge in this area, and in principle, value propositions should then be empirically demonstrable rather than merely matters of taste or exhortation. For those who have wrestled with this problem it will be clear that we may have here a partial basis for a true science of values, and consequently of ethics, social relations, politics, religion, etc.

It is definitely possible that maladjustment or even extreme neurosis would disturb perception enough to affect acuity of perception of light or touch or odor. But it is *probable* that this effect can be demonstrated in spheres of perception removed from the merely physiological, e.g., *Einstellung* experiment, etc. It should also follow that the effects of wish, desire, prejudice, upon perception as in many recent experiments should be very much less in healthy people than in sick. A priori considerations encourage the hypothesis that this superiority in the perception of reality eventuates in a superior ability to reason, to perceive the truth, to come to conclusions, to be logical and to be cognitively efficient, in general.

It was found that self-actualizing people distinguished far more easily than most the fresh, concrete, and idiographic from the generic, abstract, and rubricized. The consequence is that they live more in the real world of nature than in the man-made mass of concepts, abstractions, expectations, beliefs, and stereotypes that most people confuse with the world. They are therefore far more apt to perceive what is there rather than their own wishes, hopes, fears, anxieties, their own theories and beliefs, or those of their cultural group. "The innocent eye," Herbert Read has very effectively called it.

The relationship with the unknown seems to be of exceptional promise as another bridge between academic and clinical psychology. Our healthy subjects are uniformly unthreatened and unfrightened by the unknown, being therein quite different from average men. They accept it, are comfortable with it, and, often are even *more* attracted by it than by the known. They not only tolerate the ambiguous and unstructured; they like it. Quite characteristic is Einstein's statement, "The most beautiful thing we can experience is the mysterious. It is the source of all art and science."

These people, it is true, are the intellectuals, the researchers, and the scientists, so that perhaps the major determinant here is intellectual power. And yet we all know how many scientists with high IQ, through timidity, conventionality, anxiety, or other character defects, occupy themselves exclusively with what is known, with polishing it, arranging and rearranging it, classifying it, and otherwise puttering with it instead of discovering, as they are supposed to do.

Since, for healthy people, the unknown is not frightening, they do not have to spend any time laying the ghost, whistling past the cemetery, or otherwise protecting themselves against imagined dangers. They do not neglect the unknown, or deny it, or run away from it, or try to make believe it is really known, nor do they organize, dichotomize, or rubricize it prematurely. They do not cling to the familiar, nor is their quest for the truth a catastrophic need for certainty, safety, definiteness, and order, such as we see in an exaggerated form in Goldstein's brain-injured or in the compulsive-obsessive neurotic. They can be, when the total objective situation calls for it, comfortably disorderly, sloppy, anarchic, chaotic, vague, doubtful, uncertain, indefinite, approximate, inexact, or inaccurate (all, at certain moments in science, art, or life in general, quite desirable).

Thus it comes about that doubt, tentativeness, uncertainty, with the consequent necessity for abeyance of decision, which is for most a torture, can be for some a pleasantly stimulating challenge, a high spot in life rather than a low.

ACCEPTANCE (SELF, OTHERS, NATURE)

A good many personal qualities that can be perceived on the surface and that seem at first to be various and unconnected may be understood as manifestations or derivatives of a more fundamental single attitude, namely, of a relative lack of over-riding guilt, of crippling shame, and of extreme or severe anxiety. This is in direct contrast with the neurotic person who in every instance may be described as crippled by guilt and/or shame and/or anxiety. Even the normal member of our culture feels unnecessarily guilty or ashamed about too many things and has anxiety in too many unnecessary situations. Our healthy individuals find it possible to accept themselves and their own nature without chagrin or complaint or, for that matter, even without thinking about the matter very much.

They can accept their own human nature in the stoic style, with all its shortcomings, with all its discrepancies from the ideal image without feeling real concern. It would convey the wrong impression to say that they are self-satisfied. What we must say rather is that they can take the frailties and sins, weaknesses, and evils of human nature in the same unquestioning spirit with which one accepts the characteristics of nature. One does not complain about water because it is wet, or about rocks because they are hard, or about trees because they are green. As the child looks out upon the world with wide, uncritical, innocent eyes, simply noting and observing what is the case, without either arguing the matter or demanding that it be otherwise, so does the self-actualizing person look upon human nature in himself and in others. This is of course not the same as resignation in the eastern sense, but resignation too can be observed in our subjects, especially in the face of illness and death.

Be it observed that this amounts to saying in another form what we have already described; namely, that the self-actualized person sees reality more clearly: our subjects see human nature as it *is* and not as they would prefer it to be. Their eyes see what is before them without being strained through spectacles of various sorts to distort or shape or color the reality.

The first and most obvious level of acceptance is at the so-called animal level. Those self-actualizing people tend to be good and lusty animals, hearty in their appetites and enjoying themselves mightily without regret or shame or apology. They seem to have a uniformly good appetite for food; they seem to sleep well; they seem to enjoy their sexual lives without unnecessary inhibition and so on for all the relatively physiological impulses. They are able to accept themselves not only on these low levels, but at all levels as well; e.g., love, safety, belongingness, honor, self-respect. All of these are accepted without question as worth while, simply because these people are inclined to accept the work of nature rather than to argue with her for not having constructed things to a different pattern. This shows itself in a relative lack of the disgusts and aversions seen in average people and especially in neurotics, e.g., food annoyances, disgust with body products, body odors, and body functions.

Closely related to self-acceptance and to acceptance of others is (1) their lack of defensiveness, protective coloration, or pose, and (2) their distaste for such artificialities in others. Cant, guile, hypocrisy, front, face, playing a game, trying to impress in conventional ways: these are all absent in themselves to an unusual degree. Since they can live comfortably even with their own shortcomings, these finally come to be perceived, especially in later life, as not shortcomings at all, but simply as neutral personal characteristics.

This is not an absolute lack of guilt, shame, sadness, anxiety defensiveness; it is a lack of unnecessary (because unrealistic) guilt, etc. The animal processes, e.g., sex, urination, pregnancy, menstruation, growing old, etc., are part of reality and so must be accepted. Thus no healthy woman feels guilty or defensive about being female or about any of the female processes.

What healthy people *do* feel guilty about (or ashamed, anxious, sad, or defensive) are (1) improvable shortcomings, e.g., laziness, thoughtlessness, loss of temper, hurting others; (2) stubborn remnants of psychological ill health, e.g., prejudice, jealousy, envy; (3) habits, which, though relatively independent of character structure, may yet be very strong, or (4) shortcomings of the species or of the culture or of the group with which they have identified. The general formula seems to be that healthy people will feel bad about discrepancies between what is and what might very well be or ought to be.

SPONTANEITY

Self-actualizing people can all be described as relatively spontaneous in behavior and far more spontaneous than that in their inner life, thoughts, impulses, etc. Their behavior is marked by simplicity and naturalness, and by lack of artificiality or straining for effect. This does not necessarily mean consistently unconventional behavior. If we were to take an actual count of the number of times that the self-actualizing person behaved in an unconventional manner the tally would not be high. His unconventionality is not superficial but essential or internal. It is his impulses, thought, consciousness that are so unusually unconventional, spontaneous, and natural. Apparently recognizing that the world of people in which he lives could not understand or accept this, and since he has no wish to hurt them or to fight with them over every triviality, he will go through the ceremonies and rituals of convention with a good-humored shrug and with the best possible grace. Thus I have seen a man accept an honor he laughed at and even despised in private, rather than make an issue of it and hurt the people who thought they were pleasing him.

That this conventionality is a cloak that rests very lightly upon his shoulders and is easily cast aside can be seen from the fact that the self-actualizing person practically never allows convention to hamper him or inhibit him from doing anything that he considers very important or basic. It is at such moments that his essential lack of conventionality appears, and not as with the average Bohemian or authority-rebel, who makes great issues of trivial things and who will fight against some unimportant regulation as if it were a world issue.

This same inner attitude can also be seen in those moments when the person becomes keenly absorbed in something that is close to one of his main interests. He can then be seen quite casually to drop off all sorts of rules of behavior to which at other times he conforms; it is as if he has to make a conscious effort to be conventional; as if he were conventional voluntarily and by design.

Finally, this external habit of behavior can be voluntarily dropped when in the company of people who do not demand or expect routine behavior. That this relative control of behavior is felt as something of a burden is seen by our subjects' preference for such company as allows them to be more free, natural, and spontaneous, and that relieves them of what they find sometimes to be effortful conduct.

One consequence or correlate of this characteristic is that these people have codes of ethics that are relatively autonomous and individual rather than conventional. The unthinking observer might sometimes believe them to be unethical, since they can break not only conventions but laws when the situation seems to demand it. But the very opposite is the case. They are the most ethical of people even though their ethics are not necessarily the same as those of the people around them. It is this kind of observation that leads us to understand very assuredly that the ordinary ethical behavior of the average person is largely conventional behavior rather than truly ethical behavior, e.g., behavior based on fundamentally accepted principles.

Because of this alienation from ordinary conventions and from the ordinarily accepted hypocrisies, lies, and inconsistencies of social life, they sometimes feel like spies or aliens in a foreign land and sometimes behave so.

I should not give the impression that they try to hide what they are like. Sometimes they let themselves go deliberately, out of momentary irritation with customary rigidity or with conventional blindness. They may, for instance, be trying to teach someone or they may be trying to protect someone from hurt or injustice or they may sometimes find emotions bubbling up from within them that are so pleasant or even ecstatic that it seems almost sacrilegious to suppress them. In such instances I have observed that they are not anxious or guilty or ashamed of the impression that they make on the onlooker. It is their claim that they usually behave in a conventional fashion simply because no great issues are involved or because they know people will be hurt or embarrassed by any other kind of behavior.

Their ease of penetration to reality, their closer approach to an animal-like or childlike acceptance and spontaneity imply a superior awareness of their own impulses, desires, opinions, and subjective reactions in general. Clinical study of this capacity confirms beyond a doubt the opinion, e.g., of Fromm that the average normal, well-adjusted person often has not the slightest idea of what he is, of what he wants, of what his own opinions are.

It was such findings as these that led ultimately to the discovery of a most profound difference between self-actualizing people and others; namely, that the motivational life of self-actualizing people is not only quantitatively different but also qualitatively different from that of ordinary people. It seems probable that we must construct a profoundly different psychology of motivation for self-actualizing people, e.g., expression motivation or growth motivation, rather than deficiency motivation. Perhaps it will be useful to make a distinction between living and *preparing* to live. Perhaps the concept of motivation should apply *only* to non-self-actualizers. Our subjects no longer strive in the ordinary sense, but rather develop. They attempt to grow to perfection and to develop more and more fully in their own style. The motivation of ordinary men is a striving for the basic need gratifications that they lack. But self-actualizing people in fact lack none of these gratifications; and yet they have impulses. They work, they try, and they are ambitious, even though in an unusual sense. For them motivation is just character growth, character expression, maturation, and development; in a word self-actualization. Could these self-actualizing people be more human, more revealing of the original nature of the species, closer to the species type in the taxonomical sense? Ought a biological species to be judged by its crippled, warped, only partially developed specimens, or by examples that have been overdomesticated, caged, and trained?

PROBLEM CENTERING

Our subjects are in general strongly focused on problems outside themselves. In current terminology they are problem centered rather than ego centered. They generally are not problems for themselves and are not generally much concerned about themselves; e.g., as contrasted with the ordinary introspectiveness that one finds in insecure people. These individuals customarily have some mission in life, some task to fulfill, some problem outside themselves which enlists much of their energies.

This is not necessarily a task that they would prefer or choose for themselves; it may be a task that they feel is their responsibility, duty, or obligation. This is why we use the phrase "a task that they must do" rather than the phrase "a task that they want to do." In general these tasks are nonpersonal or unselfish, concerned rather with the good of mankind in general, or of a nation in general, or of a few individuals in the subject's family.

With a few exceptions we can say that our subjects are ordinarily concerned with basic issues and eternal questions of the type that we have learned to call philosophical or ethical. Such people live customarily in the widest possible frame of reference. They seem never to get so close to the trees that they fail to see the forest. They work within a framework of values that are broad and not petty, universal and not local, and in terms of a century rather than the moment. In a word, these people are all in one sense or another philosophers, however homely.

Of course, such an attitude carries with it dozens of implications for every area of daily living. For instance, one of the main presenting symptoms originally worked with (bigness, lack of smallness, triviality, pettiness) can be subsumed under this more general heading. This impression of being above small things, of having a larger horizon, a wider breadth of vision, of living in the widest frame of reference, *sub specie aeternitatis*, is of the utmost social and interpersonal importance; it seems to impart a certain serenity and lack of worry over immediate concerns that make life easier not only for themselves but for all who are associated with them.

THE QUALITY OF DETACHMENT; THE NEED FOR PRIVACY

For all my subjects it is true that they can be solitary without harm to themselves and without discomfort. Furthermore, it is true for almost all that they positively *like* solitude and privacy to a definitely greater degree than the average person. The dichotomy introvert-extrovert applies hardly at all to these people, and will not be used here. The term that seems to be most useful is detachment.

It is often possible for them to remain above the battle, to remain unruffled, undisturbed by that which produces turmoil in others. They find it easy to be aloof, reserved, and also calm and serene; thus it becomes possible for them to take personal misfortunes without reacting violently as the ordinary person does. They seem to be able to retain their dignity even in undignified surroundings and situations. Perhaps this comes in part from their tendency to stick by their own interpretation of a situation rather than to rely upon what other people feel or think about the matter. This reserve may shade over into austerity and remoteness.

This quality of detachment may have some connection with certain other qualities as well. For one thing it is possible to call my subjects more objective (in *all* senses of that word) than average people. We have seen that they are more problem centered than ego centered. This is true even when the problem concerns themselves, their own wishes, motives, hopes, or aspirations. Consequently, they have the ability to concentrate to a degree not usual for ordinary men. Intense concentration produces as a byproduct such phenomena as absent-mindedness, the ability to forget and to be oblivious of outer surroundings. Examples are the ability to sleep soundly, to have undisturbed appetite, to be able to smile and laugh through a period of problems, worry, and responsibility.

In social relations with most people, detachment creates certain troubles and problems. It is easily interpreted by "normal" people as coldness, snobbishness, lack of affection, unfriendliness, or even hostility. By contrast, the ordinary friendship relationship is more clinging, more demanding, more desirous of reassurance, compliment, support, warmth, and exclusiveness. It is true that self-actualizing people do not need others in the ordinary sense. But since this being needed or being missed is the usual earnest of friendship, it is evident that detachment will not easily be accepted by average people.

AUTONOMY; INDEPENDENCE OF CULTURE AND ENVIRONMENT

One of the characteristics of self-actualizing people, which to a certain extent crosscuts much of what we have already described, is their relative independence of the physical and social environment. Since they are propelled by growth motivation rather than by deficiency motivation, self-actualizing people are not dependent for their main satisfactions on the real world, or other people or culture or means to ends or in general, on extrinsic satisfactions. Rather they are dependent for their own development and continued growth on their own potentialities and latent resources. Just as the tree needs sunshine and water and food, so do most people need love, safety, and the other basic need gratifications that can come only from without. But once these external satisfiers are obtained, once these inner deficiencies are satiated by outside satisfiers, the true problem of individual human development begins, e.g., self-actualization.

This independence of environment means a relative stability in the face of hard knocks, blows, deprivations, frustrations, and the like. These people can maintain a relative serenity and happiness in the midst of circumstances that would drive other people to suicide; they have also been described as "self-contained."

Deficiency-motivated people *must* have other people available, since most of their main need gratifications (love, safety, respect, prestige, belongingness) can come only from other human beings. But growth-motivated people may actually be *hampered* by others. The determinants of satisfaction and of the good life are for them now inner-individual and *not* social. They have become strong enough to be independent of the good opinion of other people, or even of their affection. The honors, the status, the rewards, the prestige, and the love they can bestow must have become less important than self-development and inner growth. We must remember that the best technique we know, even though not the only one, for getting to this point of independence from love and respect, is to have been given plenty of this very same love and respect in the past.

CONTINUED FRESHNESS OF APPRECIATION

Self-actualizing people have the wonderful capacity to appreciate again and again, freshly and naïvely, the basic goods of life, with awe, pleasure, wonder, and even ecstasy, however stale these experiences may have become to others. Thus for such a person, any sunset may be as beautiful as the first one, any flower may be of breath-taking loveliness, even after he has seen a million flowers. The thousandth baby he sees is just as miraculous a product as the first one he saw. He remains as convinced of his luck in marriage thirty years after his marriage and is as surprised by his wife's beauty when she is sixty as he was forty years before. For such people, even the casual workaday, moment-to-moment business of living can be thrilling, exciting, and ecstatic. These intense feelings do not come all the time; they come occasionally rather than usually, but at the most unexpected moments. The person may cross the river on the ferry ten times and at the eleventh crossing have a strong recurrence of the same feelings, reaction of beauty, and excitement as when he rode the ferry for the first time.

There are some differences in choice of beautiful objects. Some subjects go primarily to nature. For others it is primarily children, and for a few subjects it has been primarily great music; but it may certainly be said that they derive ecstasy, inspiration, and strength from the basic experiences of life. No one of them, for instance, will get this same sort of reaction from going to a night club or getting a lot of money or having a good time at a party.

Perhaps one special experience may be added. For several of my subjects the sexual pleasures and particularly the orgasm provided, not passing pleasure alone, but some kind of basic strengthening and revivifying that some people derive from music or nature . . . .

It is probable that this acute richness of subjective experience is an aspect of closeness of relationship to the concrete and fresh, *per se* reality discussed above. Perhaps what we call staleness in experience is a consequence of ticketing off a rich perception into one or another category or rubric as it proves to be no longer advantageous, or useful, or threatening or otherwise ego involved.

THE MYSTIC EXPERIENCE; THE OCEANIC FEELING

Those subjective expressions that have been called the mystic experience and described so well by William James are a fairly common experience for our subjects. The strong emotions described in the previous section sometimes get strong enough, chaotic, and widespread enough to be called mystic experiences. My interest and attention in this subject was first enlisted by several of my subjects who described their sexual orgasms in vaguely familiar terms which later I remembered had been used by various writers to describe what *they* called the mystic experience. There were the same feelings of limitless horizons opening up to the vision, the feeling of being simultaneously more powerful and also more helpless than one ever was before, the feeling of great ecstasy and wonder and awe, the loss of placing in time and space with, finally, the conviction that something extremely important and valuable had happened, so that the subject is to some extent transformed and strengthened even in his daily life by such experiences.

It is quite important to dissociate this experience from any theological or supernatural reference, even though for thousands of years they have been linked. None of our subjects spontaneously made any such tie-up, although in later conversation some semireligious conclusions were drawn by a few, e.g., "life must have a meaning," etc. Because this experience is a natural experience, well within the jurisdiction of science, it is probably better to use Freud's term for it, e.g., the oceanic feeling.

We may also learn from our subjects that such experiences can occur in a lesser degree of intensity. The theological literature has generally assumed an absolute, qualitative difference between the mystic experience and all others. As soon as it is divorced from supernatural reference and studied as a natural phenomenon, it becomes possible to place the mystic experience on a quantitative continuum from intense to mild. We discover then that the *mild* mystic experience occurs in many, perhaps even most individuals, and that in the favored individual it occurs dozens of times a day.

Apparently the acute mystic experience is a tremendous intensification of *any* of the experiences in which there is loss of self or transcendance of it, e.g., problem centering, intense concentration, muga behavior, as described by Benedict, intense sensuous experience, self-forgetful and intense enjoyment of music or art.

GEMEINSCHAFTSGEFÜHL

This word, invented by Alfred Adler, is the only one available that describes well the flavor of the feelings for mankind expressed by self-actualizing subjects. They have for human beings in general a deep feeling of identification, sympathy, and affection in spite of the occasional anger, impatience, or disgust described below. Because of this they have a genuine desire to help the human race. It is as if they were all members of a single family. One's feelings toward his brothers would be on the whole affectionate, even if these brothers were foolish, weak, or even if they were sometimes nasty. They would still be more easily forgiven than strangers.

If one's view is not general enough and if it is not spread over a long period of time, then one may not see this feeling of identification with mankind. The self-actualizing person is after all very different from other people in thought, impulse, behavior, emotion. When it comes down to it, in certain basic ways he is like an alien in a strange land. Very few really understand him, however much they may like him. He is often saddened, exasperated, and even enraged by the shortcomings of the average person, and while they are to him ordinarily no more than a nuisance, they sometimes become bitter tragedy. However far apart he is from them at times, he nevertheless feels a basic underlying kinship with these creatures whom he must regard with, if not condescension, at least the knowledge that he can do many things better than they can, that he can see things that they cannot see, that the truth that is so clear to him is for most people veiled and hidden. This is what Adler called the older-brotherly attitude.

INTERPERSONAL RELATIONS$_{SA}$

Self-actualizing people have deeper and more profound interpersonal relations than any other adults (although not necessarily deeper than those of children). They are capable of more fusion, greater love, more perfect identification, more obliteration of the ego boundaries than other people would consider possible. There are, however, certain special characteristics of these relationships. In the first place, it is my observation that the other members of these relationships are likely to be healthier and closer to self-actualization than the average, often *much* closer. There is high selectiveness here, considering the small proportion of such people in the general population.

One consequence of this phenomenon and of certain others as well is that self-actualizing people have these especially deep ties with rather few individuals. Their circle of friends is rather small. The ones that they love profoundly are few in number. Partly this is for the reason that being very close to someone in this self-actualizing style seems to require a good deal of time. Devotion is not a matter of a moment. One subject expressed it so:

"I haven't got time for many friends. Nobody has, that is, if they are to be *real* friends." The only possible exception in my group was one woman who seemed to be especially equipped socially. It was almost as if her appointed task in life was to have close and warm and beautiful relations with all the members of her family and their families as well as all her friends and theirs. Perhaps this was because she was an uneducated woman who had no formal task or career. This exclusiveness of devotion can and does exist side by side with a widespreading *Gemeinschaftsgefühl*, benevolence, affection, and friendliness (as qualified above). These people *tend* to be kind or at least patient to almost everyone. They have an especially tender love for children and are easily touched by them. In a very real even though special sense, they love or rather have compassion for all mankind.

This love does not imply lack of discrimination. The fact is that they can and do speak realistically and harshly of those who deserve it, and especially of the hypocritical, the pretentious, the pompous, or the self-inflated. But the face-to-face relationships even with these people do not always show signs of realistically low evaluations. One explanatory statement was about as follows: "Most people, after all, do not amount to much but they *could* have. They make all sorts of foolish mistakes and wind up being miserable and not knowing how they got that way when their intentions were good. Those who are not nice are usually paying for it in deep unhappiness. They should be pitied rather than attacked."

Perhaps the briefest possible description is to say that their hostile reactions to others are (1) deserved, (2) for the good of the person attacked or for someone else's good. This is to say, with Fromm, that their hostility is not character based, but is reactive or situational.

All the subjects for whom I have data show in common another characteristic that is appropriate to mention here, namely, that they attract at least some admirers, friends or even disciples or worshippers. The relation between the individual and his train of admirers is apt to be rather one-sided. The admirers are apt to demand more than our individual is willing to give. And furthermore, these devotions are apt to be rather embarrassing, distressing, and even distasteful to the self-actualizing person, since they often go beyond ordinary bounds. The usual picture is of our subject being kind and pleasant when forced into these relationships, but ordinarily trying to avoid them as gracefully as possible.

THE DEMOCRATIC CHARACTER STRUCTURE

All my subjects without exception may be said to be democratic people in the deepest possible sense. I say this on the basis of a previous analysis of authoritarian and democratic character structures that is too elaborate to present here; it is possible only to describe some aspects of this behavior in short space. These people have all the obvious or superficial democratic characteristics. They can be and are friendly with anyone of suitable character regardless of class, education, political belief, race, or color. As a matter of fact it often seems as if they are not even aware of these differences, which are for the average person so obvious and so important.

They have not only this most obvious quality but their democratic feeling goes deeper as well. For instance they find it possible to learn from anybody who has something to teach them—no matter what other characteristics he may have. In such a learning relationship they do not try to maintain any outward dignity or to maintain status or age prestige or the like. It should even be said that my subjects share a quality that could be called humility of a certain type. They are all quite well aware of how little they know in comparison with what *could* be known and what *is* known by others. Because of this it is possible for them without pose to be honestly respectful and even humble before people who can teach them something that they do not know or who have a skill they do not possess. They give this honest respect to a carpenter who is a good carpenter; or for that matter to anybody who is a master of his own tools or his own craft.

The careful distinction must be made between this democratic feeling and a lack of discrimination in taste, of an undiscriminating equalizing of any one human being with any other. These individuals, themselves elite, select for their friends elite, but this is an elite of character, capacity, and talent, rather than of birth, race, blood, name, family, age, youth, fame, or power.

Most profound, but also most vague is the hard-to-get-at tendency to give a certain quantum of respect to *any* human being just because he is a human individual; our subjects seem not to wish to go beyond a certain minimum point, even with scoundrels, of demeaning, of derogating, of robbing of dignity.

DISCRIMINATION BETWEEN MEANS AND ENDS

I have found none of my subjects to be chronically unsure about the difference between right and wrong in his actual living. Whether or not they could verbalize the matter, they rarely showed in their day-to-day living the chaos, the confusion, the inconsistency, or the conflict that are so common in the average person's ethical dealings. This may be phrased also in such terms as: these individuals are strongly ethical, they have definite moral standards, they do right and do not do wrong. Needless to say, their notions of right and wrong are often not the conventional ones.

One way of expressing the quality I am trying to describe was suggested by Dr. David Levy, who pointed out that a few centuries ago these would all have been described as men who walk in the path of God or as godly men. So far as religion is concerned, none of my subjects is orthodoxly religious, but on the other hand I know of only one who describes himself as an atheist (four of the total group studied). The few others for whom I have information hesitate to call themselves atheists. They say that they believe in a God, but describe this God more as a metaphysical concept than as a personal figure. Whether or not they could be called religious people as a group must then depend entirely on the concept or definition of religion that we choose to use. If religion is defined only in social-behavioral terms, then these are all religious people, the atheists included. But if more conservatively we use the term religion so as to include and stress the supernatural element and institutional orthodoxy (certainly the more common usage) then our answer must be quite different, for then almost none of them is religious.

Self-actualizing people most of the time behave as though, for them, means and ends are clearly distinguishable. In general, they are fixed on ends rather than on means, and means are quite definitely subordinated to these ends. This, however, is an oversimple statement. Our subjects make the situation more complex by often regarding as ends in themselves many experiences and activities that are, for other people, only means to ends. Our subjects are somewhat more likely to appreciate for its own sake, and in an absolute way, the doing itself; they can often enjoy for its own sake the getting to some place as well as the arriving. It is occasionally possible for them to make out of the most trivial and routine activity an intrinsically enjoyable game or dance or play. Wertheimer pointed out that most children are so creative that they can transform hackneyed routine, mechanical, and rote experiences, e.g., as in one of his experiments, transporting books from one set of shelves to another, into a structured and amusing game of a sort by doing this according to a certain system or with a certain rhythm.

PHILOSOPHICAL, UNHOSTILE SENSE OF HUMOR

One very early finding that was quite easy to make, because it was common to all my subjects, was that their sense of humor is not of the ordinary type. They do not consider funny what the average man considers to be funny. Thus they do not laugh at hostile humor (making people laugh by hurting someone) or superiority humor (laughing at someone else's inferiority) or authority-rebellion humor (the unfunny, smutty joke). Characteristically what they consider humor is more closely allied to philosophy than to anything else. It may also be called the humor of the real because it consists in large part in poking fun at human beings in general when they are foolish, or forget their place in the universe, or try to be big when they are actually small. This can take the form of poking fun at themselves, but this is not done in any masochistic or clownlike way. Lincoln's humor can serve as a suitable example. Probably Lincoln never made a joke that hurt anybody else; it is also likely that many or even most of his jokes had something to say, had a function beyond just producing a laugh. They often seemed to be education in a more palatable form, akin to parables or fables.

On a simple quantitative basis, our subjects may be said to be humorous less often than the average of the population. Punning, joking, witty remarks, gay repartee, persiflage of the ordinary sort is much less often seen than the rather thoughtful, philosophical humor that elicits a smile more usually than a laugh, that is intrinsic to the situation rather than added to it, that is spontaneous rather than planned, and that very often can never be repeated. It should not be surprising that the average man, accustomed as he is to joke books and belly laughs, considers our subjects to be rather on the sober and serious side.

CREATIVENESS

This is a universal characteristic of all the people studied or observed. There is no exception. Each one shows in one way or another a special kind of creativeness or originality or inventiveness that has certain peculiar characteristics. These special characteristics can be understood more fully in the light of discussion later in this chapter. For one thing, it is different from the special-talent creativeness of the Mozart type. We may as well face the fact that the so-called geniuses display ability that we do not understand. All we can say of them is that they seem to be specially endowed with a drive and a capacity that may have rather little relationship to the rest of the personality and with which, from all evidence, the individuals seem to be born. Such talent we have no concern with here since it does not rest upon psychic health or basic satisfaction. The creativeness of the self-actualized man seems rather to be kin to the naïve and universal creativeness of unspoiled children. It seems to be more a fundamental characteristic of common human nature—a potentiality given to all human beings at birth. Most human beings lose this as they become enculturated, but some few individuals seem either to retain this fresh and naïve, direct way of looking at life, or if they have lost it, as most people do, they later in life recover it.

This creativeness appears in some of our subjects not in the usual forms of writing books, composing music, or producing artistic objects, but rather may be much more humble. It is as if this special type of creativeness, being an expression of healthy personality, is projected out upon the world or touches whatever activity the person is engaged in. In this sense there can be creative shoemakers or carpenters or clerks. Whatever one does can be done with a certain attitude, a certain spirit that arises out of the nature of the character of the person performing the act. One can even *see* creatively as the child does.

This quality is differentiated out here for the sake of discussion, as if it were something separate from the characteristics that precede it and follow it, but this is not actually the case. Perhaps when we speak of creativeness here we are simply describing from another point of view, namely, from the point of view of consequences, what we have described above as a greater freshness, penetration, and efficiency of perception. These people seem to see the true and the real more easily. It is because of this that they seem to other more limited men creative.

Furthermore, as we have seen, these individuals are less inhibited, less constricted, less bound, in a word, less enculturated. In more positive terms, they are more spontaneous, more natural, more human. This too would have as one of its consequences what would seem to other people to be creativeness. If we assume, as we may from our study of children, that all people were once spontaneous, and perhaps in their deepest roots still are, but that these people have in addition to their spontaneity a superficial but powerful set of inhibitions, then this spontaneity must be checked so as not to appear very often. If there were no choking-off forces, we might expect that every human being would show this special type of creativeness.

RESISTANCE TO ENCULTURATION

Self-actualizing people are not well adjusted (in the naïve sense of approval of and identification with the culture). They get along with the culture in various ways, but of all of them it may be said that in a certain profound and meaningful sense they resist enculturation and maintain a certain inner detachment from the culture in which they are immersed. Since in the culture-and-personality literature very little has been said about resistance to molding by the culture, and since, as Riesman has clearly pointed out, the saving remnant is especially important for American society, even our meager data are of some importance.

On the whole the relationship of these healthy people with their much less healthy culture is a complex one; from it can be teased out at least the following components.

1. All these people fall well within the limits of apparent conventionality in choice of clothes, of language, of food, of ways of doing things in our culture. And yet they are not *really* conventional, certainly not fashionable or smart or chic.

The expressed inner attitude is usually that it is ordinarily of no great consequence which folkways are used, that one set of traffic rules is as good as any other set, that while they make life smoother they do not really matter enough to make a fuss about. Here again we see the general tendency of these people to accept most states of affairs that they consider unimportant or unchangeable or not of primary concern to them as individuals. Since choice of shoes, or style of haircut or politeness, or manner of behaving at a party are not of primary concern to any of the individuals studied, they are apt to elicit as a reaction only a shrug of the shoulders.

But since this tolerant acceptance is not warm approval with identification, their yielding to convention is apt to be rather casual and perfunctory, with cutting of corners in favor of directness, honesty, saving of energy, etc. In the pinches, when yielding to conventions is too annoying or too expensive, the apparent conventionality reveals itself for the superficial thing that it is, and is tossed off as easily as a cloak.

2. Hardly any of these people can be called authority rebels in the adolescent or hot sense. They show no active impatience or moment-to-moment, chronic, long-time discontent with the culture or preoccupation with changing it quickly, although they often enough show bursts of indignation with injustice. One of these subjects, who was a hot rebel in his younger days, a union organizer in the days when this was a highly dangerous occupation, has given up in disgust and hopelessness. As he became resigned to the slowness of social change (in this culture and in this era) he turned finally to education of the young. All the others show what might be called a calm, long-time concern with culture improvement that seems to me to imply an acceptance of slowness of change along with the unquestioned desirability and necessity of such change.

This is by no means a lack of fight. When quick change is possible or when resolution and courage are needed, it is available in these people. Although they are not a radical group of people in the ordinary sense, I think they easily *could* be. First of all, this is primarily an intellectual group (it must be remembered who selected them), most of whom already have a mission, and feel that they are doing something really important to improve the world. Second, they are a realistic group and seem to be unwilling to make great but useless sacrifices. In a more drastic situation it seems very likely that they would be willing to drop their work in favor of radical social action, e.g., the anti-Nazi underground in Germany or in France. My impression is that they are not against fighting but only against ineffective fighting.

Another point that came up very commonly in discussion was the desirability of enjoying life and having a good time. This seems to all but one to be incompatible with hot and full-time rebelliousness. Furthermore, it seems to them that this is too great a sacrifice to make for the small returns expected. Most of them have had their episodes of fighting, impatience, and eagerness in youth, and in most cases have learned that their optimism about quick change was unwarranted. What they settled down to as a group was an accepting, calm, good-humored everyday effort to improve the culture, usually from within, rather than to reject it and fight it from without.

3. An inner feeling of detachment from the culture is not necessarily conscious but is displayed by almost all, particularly in discussions of the American culture as a whole, in various comparisons with other cultures, and in the fact that they very frequently seem to be able to stand off from it as if they did not quite belong to it. The mixture of varying proportions of affection or approval and hostility or criticism indicated that they select from American culture what is good in it by their lights and reject what they think bad in it. In a word they weigh it, assay it, taste it, and then make their own decisions.

This is certainly very different from the ordinary sort of passive yielding to cultural shaping displayed for instance by the ethnocentric subjects of the many studies of authoritarian personalities.

Detachment from the culture is probably also reflected in our self-actualizing subjects' detachment from people and their liking for privacy, which has been described above, as also in their lesser than average need for and liking for the familiar and customary.

4. For these and other reasons they may be called autonomous, i.e., ruled by the laws of their own character rather than by the rules of society. It is in this sense that they are not only or merely Americans, but also to a greater degree than others, members at large of the human species. To say that they are above or beyond the American culture would be misleading if interpreted strictly, for after all they speak American, act American, have American characters, etc.

And yet if we compare them with the oversocialized, the robotized, or the ethnocentric, we are irresistibly tempted to hypothesize that this group is not simply another subcultural group, but rather less enculturated, less flattened out, less molded. This implies degree, and placing on a continuum that ranges from relative acceptance of the culture to relative detachment from it.

If this turns out to be a tenable hypothesis, at least one other hypothesis can be deduced from it, that those individuals in different cultures who are more detached from their own culture should not only have less national character but also should be more like each other in certain respects than they are like the less developed members of their own societies. Of course this raises questions about what constitutes the good American.

In summary the perennial question, Is it possible to be a good or healthy man in an imperfect culture? has been answered by the observation that it *is* possible for relatively healthy people to develop in the American culture. They manage to get along by a complex combination of inner autonomy and outer acceptance that of course will be possible only so long as the culture remains tolerant of this kind of detached withholding from complete cultural identification.

Of course this is not ideal health. Our imperfect society clearly forces inhibitions and restraints upon our subjects. To the extent that they have to maintain their little secrecies, to that extent is their spontaneity lessened and to that extent are some of their potentialities not actualized. And since only few people can attain health in our culture, those who do attain it are lonely for their own kind and therefore again less spontaneous and less actualized.

THE IMPERFECTIONS OF SELF-ACTUALIZING PEOPLE

The ordinary mistake that is made by novelists, poets, and essayists about the good human being is to make him so good that he is a caricature, so that nobody would like to be like him. The individual's own wishes for perfection, and his guilt and shame about shortcomings are projected upon various kinds of people from whom the average man demands much more than he himself gives. Thus teachers and ministers are ordinarily conceived to be rather joyless people who have no mundane desires and who have no weaknesses. It is my belief that most of the novelists who have attempted to portray good (healthy) people did this sort of thing, making them into stuffed shirts or marionettes or unreal projections of unreal ideals, rather than into the robust, hearty, lusty individuals they really are. Our subjects show many of the lesser human failings. They too are equipped with silly, wasteful, or thoughtless habits. They can be boring, stubborn, irritating. They are by no means free from a rather superficial vanity, pride, partiality to their own productions, family, friends, and children. Temper outbursts are not rare.

Our subjects are occasionally capable of an extraordinary and unexpected ruthlessness. It must be remembered that they are very strong people. This makes it possible for them to display a surgical coldness when this is called for, beyond the power of the average man. The man who found that a long-trusted acquaintance was dishonest cut himself off from this friendship sharply and abruptly and without any pangs whatsoever. Another woman who was married to someone she did not love, when she decided on divorce, did it with a decisiveness that looked almost like ruthlessness. Some of them recover so quickly from the death of people close to them as to seem heartless.

Not only are these people strong but also they are independent of the opinions of other people. One woman, extremely irritated by the stuffy conventionalism of some individuals she was introduced to at a gathering, went out of her way to shock these people by her language and behavior. One might say it was all right for her to react to irritation in this way, but another result was that these people were completely hostile not only to the woman but to the friends in whose home this meeting took place. While our subject *wanted* to alienate these people, the host and hostess did not.

We may mention one more example that arises primarily from the absorption of our subjects in an impersonal world. In their concentration, in their fascinated interest, in their intense concentration on some phenomenon or question, they may become absent-minded or humorless and forget their ordinary social politeness. In such circumstances, they are apt to show themselves more clearly as essentially not interested in chatting, gay conversation, party-going, or the like, they may use language or behavior that may be very distressing, shocking, insulting, or hurtful to others. Other undesirable (at least from the point of view of others) consequences of detachment have been listed above.

Even their kindness can lead them into mistakes, e.g., marrying out of pity, getting too closely involved with neurotics, bores, unhappy people, and then being sorry for it, allowing scoundrels to impose on them for a while, giving more than they should so that occasionally they encourage parasites and psychopaths, etc.

Finally, it has already been pointed out that these people are *not* free of guilt, anxiety, sadness, self-castigation, internal strife, and conflict. The fact that these arise out of nonneurotic sources is of little consequence to most people today (even to most psychologists) who are therefore apt to think them *un*healthy for this reason.

VALUES AND SELF-ACTUALIZATION

A firm foundation for a value system is automatically furnished to the self-actualizer by his philosophic acceptance of the nature of his self, of human nature, of much of social life, and of nature and physical reality. These acceptance values account for a high percentage of the total of his individual value judgments from day to day. What he approves of, disapproves of, is loyal to, opposes or proposes, what pleases him or displeases him can often be understood as surface derivations of this source trait of acceptance.

Not only is this foundation automatically (and universally) supplied to *all* self-actualizers by their intrinsic dynamics (so that in at least this respect fully developed human nature may be universal and cross-cultural); other determiners are supplied as well by these same dynamics. Among these are (1) his peculiarly comfortable relationships with reality, (2) his *Gemeinschaftsgefühl*, (3) his basically satisfied condition from which flow, as epiphenomena, various consequences of surplus, of wealth, overflowing abundance, (4) his characteristically discriminating relations to means and ends, etc. (see above).

One most important consequence of this attitude toward the world—as well as a validation of it—is the fact that conflict and struggle, ambivalence and uncertainty over choice lessen or disappear in many areas of life. Apparently "morality" is largely an epiphenomenon of nonacceptance or dissatisfaction. Many problems are seen to be gratuitous and fade out of existence in the atmosphere of pagan acceptance. It is not so much that the problem is solved as that it becomes clearly seen that it never was an intrinsic problem in the first place, but only a sick-man-created one, e.g., card-playing, dancing, wearing short dresses, exposing the head (in some churches) or *not* exposing the head (in others), drinking wine, or eating some meats and not others, or eating them on some days but not on others. Not only are such trivialities deflated; the process also goes on at a more important level, e.g., the relations between the sexes, attitudes toward the structure of the body and toward its functioning, and toward death itself.

The pursuit of this finding to more profound levels has suggested to the writer that much else of what passes for morals, ethics, and values may be the gratuitous epiphenomena of the pervasive psychopathology of the average. Many conflicts, frustrations, and threats (which force the kind of choice in which value is expressed), evaporate or resolve for the self-actualizing person in the same way as do, let us say, conflicts over dancing. For him the seemingly irreconcilable battle of the sexes becomes no conflict at all but rather a delightful collaboration. The antagonistic interests of adults and children turn out to be not so antagonistic after all. Just as with sex and age differences, so also is it with natural differences, class and caste differences, political differences, role differences, religious differences, etc. As we know, these are each fertile breeding grounds for anxiety, fear, hostility, aggression, defensiveness, and jealousy. But it begins to appear that they *need not be*, for our subjects' reaction to differences is much less often of this undesirable type.

To take the teacher-student relationship as a specific paradigm, our teacher subjects behaved in a very unneurotic way simply by interpreting the whole situation differently, e.g., as a pleasant collaboration rather than as a clash of wills, of authority, of dignity, etc.; the replacement of artificial dignity — that is easily and inevitably threatened — with the natural simplicity that is *not* easily threatened; the giving up of the attempt to be omniscient and omnipotent; the absence of student-threatening authoritarianism; the refusal to regard the students as competing with each other or with the teacher; the refusal to assume the professor stereotype and the insistence on remaining as realistically human as, say, a plumber or a carpenter; all of these created a classroom atmosphere in which suspicion, wariness, defensiveness, hostility, and anxiety disappeared. So also do similar threat responses tend to disappear in marriages, in families and in other interpersonal situations when threat itself is reduced.

The principles and the values of the desperate man and of the psychologically healthy man must be different in at least some ways. They have profoundly different perceptions (interpretations) of the physical world, the social world and the private psychological world, whose organization and economy is in part the responsibility of the person's value system. For the basically deprived man the world is a dangerous place, a jungle, an enemy territory populated by (1) those whom he can dominate and (2) those who can dominate him. His value system is of necessity, like that of any jungle denizen, dominated and organized by the lower needs, especially the creature needs and the safety needs. The basically satisfied person is in a different case. He can afford out of his abundance to take these needs and their satisfaction for granted and can devote himself to higher gratifications. This is to say that their value systems are different, in fact *must* be different.

The topmost portion of the value system of the self-actualized person is entirely unique and idiosyncratic-character-structure-expressive. This must be true by definition, for self-actualization is actualization of a self, and no two selves are altogether alike. There is only one Renoir, one Brahms, one Spinoza. Our subjects had very much in common, as we have seen, and yet at the same time were more completely individualized, more unmistakably themselves, less easily confounded with others than any average control group could possibly be. That is to say, they are simultaneously very much alike and very much unlike each other. They are more completely individual than any group that has ever been described, and yet are also more completely socialized, more identified with humanity than any other group yet described.

THE RESOLUTION OF DICHOTOMIES IN SELF-ACTUALIZATION

At this point we may finally allow ourselves to generalize and underscore a very important theoretical conclusion derivable from the study of self-actualizing people . . . . It was concluded that what had been considered in the past to be polarities or opposites or dichotomies were so *only in unhealthy people*. In healthy people, these dichotomies were resolved, the polarities disappeared, and many oppositions thought to be intrinsic merged and coalesced with each other to form unities.

For example the age-old opposition between heart and head, reason and instinct, or cognition and conation was seen to disappear in healthy people where they become synergic rather than antagonists, and where conflict between them disappears because they say the same thing and point to the same conclusion. In a word in these people, desires are in excellent accord with reason. St. Augustine's "Love God and do as you will" can easily be translated, "Be healthy and then you may trust your impulses."

The dichotomy between selfishness and unselfishness disappears altogether in healthy people because in principle every act is *both* selfish and unselfish. Our subjects are simultaneously very spiritual and very pagan and sensual. Duty cannot be contrasted with pleasure nor work with play when duty *is* pleasure, when work *is* play, and the person doing his duty and being virtuous is simultaneously seeking his pleasure and being happy. If the most socially identified people are themselves also the most individualistic people, of what use is to retain the polarity? If the most mature are also childlike? And if the most ethical and moral people are also the lustiest and most animal?

Similar findings have been reached for kindness-ruthlessness, concreteness-abstractness, acceptance-rebellion, self-society, adjustment-maladjustment, detachment from others-identification with others, serious-humorous, Dionysian-Apollonian, introverted-extraverted, intense-casual, serious-frivolous, conventional-unconventional, mystic-realistic, active-passive, masculine-feminine, lust-love, and Eros-Agape. In these people, the id, the ego, and the superego are collaborative and synergic; they do not war with each other nor are their interests in basic disagreement as they are in neurotic people. So also do the cognitive, the conative, and the emotional coalesce into an organismic unity and into a non-Aristotelian interpenetration. The higher and the lower are not in opposition but in agreement, and a thousand serious philosophical dilemmas are discovered to have more than two horns, or, paradoxically, no horns at all. If the war between the sexes turns out to be no war at all in matured people, but only a sign of crippling and stunting of growth, who then would wish to choose sides? Who would deliberately and knowingly choose psychopathology? Is it necessary to choose between the good woman and the bad, as if they were mutually exclusive, when we have found that the really healthy woman is both at the same time?

In this, as in other ways, healthy people are so different from average ones, not only in degree but in kind as well, that they generate two very different kinds of psychology. It becomes more and more clear that the study of crippled, stunted, immature, and unhealthy specimens can yield only a cripple psychology and a cripple philosophy. The study of self-actualizing people must be the basis for a more universal science of psychology.

Part 3

"THINKING ABOUT THINKING": CYBERNETICS, COMMUNICATIONS, AND EDUCATION

Introduction

Still another set of revolutionary developments which has had a profound and pervasive impact on American educational thought has occurred in the area of communications theory. In cybernetics — the study of human control functions and of the mechanical and electrical systems designed to replace them — radically new ways of "thinking about thinking" have evolved. Various types of learning — ranging from simple stimulus-response learning to learning by means of generalization and hypothesis-testing — have been built into electrical computers. Researchers have, for example, managed to design a computer which is able to prove many of the theorems in Euclidean geometry, and one researcher has even devised a checker-playing machine which, to quote psychologist Carl I. Hovland,

> *utilizes a type of rote learning which stores all of the checkerboard positions it encounters in play, together with the outcomes following each move. In addition this machine has some capacity to generalize on the basis of past experience and to store the generalizations them-selves. With these learning mechanisms it appears possible for the computer to learn in a short period of time to play a better game of checkers than can be played by the person who wrote the program.*[1]

Perhaps the best-known of the cyberneticists, and the man considered by many to be the founder of the cybernetics movement, was mathematician Norbert Wiener. "We ordinarily think of communication and language," states Wiener, "as being directed from person to person. However, it is quite possible for a person to talk to a machine, a machine to a person, and a machine to a machine."[2] "What distinguishes human communication from the communication of most other animals is (a) the delicacy and complexity of the code used, and (b) the high degree of arbitrariness of this code."[3] "It is my thesis," he states in his book *The Human Use of Human Beings,*

> *that the physical functioning of the living individual and the opera-tion of some of the newer communication machines are precisely parallel in their analogous attempts to control entropy through feed-back. Both of them have sensory receptors as one stage in their cycle of operation: that is, in both of them there exists a special apparatus for collecting information from the outer world at low energy levels, and for making it available in the operation of the individual or of the machine. In both cases these external messages are not taken neat, but through the internal transforming powers of the appara-tus, whether it be alive or dead. The information is then turned into*

1. Carl I. Hovland, "Computer Simulation in the Behavioral Sciences," in *The Behavioral Sciences Today,* ed. Bernard Berelson (New York: Harper & Row, Publishers, 1963), p. 82.
2. Norbert Wiener, *The Human Use Of Human Beings: Cybernetics and Society* (New York: Double-day & Company, Inc., Anchor Books, 1950), p. 76.
3. *Ibid.,* p. 74.

a new form available for the further stages of performance. In both animal and the machine this performance is made to be effective on the outer world. In both of them, their performed action on the outer world, and not merely their intended action, is reported back to the central regulatory apparatus. This complex of behavior is ignored by the average man, and in particular does not play the role that it should in our habitual analysis of society; for just as individual physical responses may be seen from this point of view, so may the organic responses of society itself. I do not mean that the sociologist is unaware of the existence in complex nature of communications in society, but until recently he has tended to overlook the extent to which they are the cement which binds its fabric together . . . .

Cybernetics takes the view that the structure of the machine or of the organism is an index of the performance that may be expected from it. *The fact that the mechanical rigidity of the insect is such as to limit its intelligence while the mechanical fluidity of the human being provides for his almost indefinite intellectual expansion is highly relevant . . . . Theoretically, if we could build a machine whose mechanical structure duplicated human physiology, then we could have a machine whose intellectual capacities would duplicate those of human beings.*[4]

In the selection "The Nature of Mass Communication," Wilbur Schramm, who is a professor of communications and Director of the Institute for Communications Research at Stanford University, discusses the way in which communications operate within society as a whole. Using essentially the same conceptual scheme as Wiener, Schramm discusses, among other things, the factors which determine which presentations by the mass media will be selected by any given individual. "Our society," states Schramm,

like any other communication unit, functions as decoder, interpreter, and encoder. It decodes our environment for us, watches the horizon for danger and promise and entertainment. It then operates to interpret what it has decoded, helps us arrive at a consensus so that we can put policy into effect, helps us keep the ordinary interactions of communal life going . . . .[5]

Still another revolutionary development which has had far-reaching implications for formal education is that typically associated with the name of Marshall McLuhan. McLuhan, who is presently Director of the Center for Communications at Fordham University, advances the thesis that "the medium is the message"—that the mass media have transformed not only

---

4. *Ibid.*, pp. 26–27 and 57. Reprinted by permission.
5. Wilbur Schramm, "The Nature of Mass Communications," in *Mass Media and Education*, ed. Nelson B. Henry, Fifty-Third Yearbook of the National Society for the Study of Education, Part II (Chicago, University of Chicago Press, 1954), p. 132.

our material environment but our basic ways of *perceiving* the world as well. Technology has created a new environment, and this environment is an active process which is vitally implicated in virtually every aspect of daily cognition and not merely a passive feature of the encountered world.

> *"The Medium Is the Message" means, in terms of the electronic age, that a totally new environment has been created. The "content" of this new environment is the old mechanized environment of the industrial age. The new environment reprocesses the old one as radically as TV is reprocessing the film . . . . When machine production was new, it gradually created an environment whose content was the old environment of agrarian life and the arts and crafts. This older environment was elevated to an art form by the new mechanical environment. The machine turned Nature into an art form. For the first time men began to regard Nature as a source of aesthetic and spiritual values. They began to marvel that earlier ages had been so unaware of the world of Nature as Art. Each new technology creates an environment that is itself regarded as corrupt and degrading. Yet the new one turns its predecessor into an art form . . . .*

> *Our conventional response to all media, namely that it is how they are used that counts, is the numb stance of the technological idiot. For the "content" of a medium is like the juicy piece of meat carried by the burglar to distract the watchdog of the mind. The effect of the medium is made strong and intense just because it is given another medium as "content." The content of a movie is a novel or play or opera. The effect of the movie form is not related to its program content. The "content" of writing or print is speech, but the reader is almost entirely unaware either of print or of speech . . . .*

> *The effects of technology do not occur at the level of opinions or concepts, but alter sense ratios or patterns of perception steadily and without any resistance. The serious artist is the only person able to encounter technology with impunity, just because he is an expert aware of the changes in sense perception.[6]*

> *The young student today grows up in an electrically configured world. It is a world not of wheels but circuits, not of fragments but of integral patterns. The student today lives mythically and in depth. At school, however, he encounters a situation organized by means of classified information. The subjects are unrelated. They are visually conceived in terms of a blueprint. The student can find no possible means of involvement for himself, nor can he discover how the educational scene relates to the "mythic" world of electronically processed data and experience that he takes for granted . . . .*

---

6. Marshall McLuhan, *Understanding Media: The Extensions of Man* (New York: McGraw-Hill Book Company, 1964), pp. vii–viii and 18. Reprinted by permission.

Before printing, much of the time in school and college classrooms was spent in making . . . texts. The classroom tended to be a scriptorium with a commentary. The student was an editor-publisher. . . . The book was the first teaching machine and also the first mass-produced commodity. . . . Print provided a vast new memory for past writings that made a personal memory inadequate[7]

[Today] the culturally disadvantaged child is the TV child. For TV has established a new environment of low visual orientation and high involvement that makes accommodation to our older educational establishment quite difficult.[8]

In the selection entitled "The Medium Is the Message," which is adapted from his book *Understanding Media*, McLuhan expands on his central concept and discusses some of its major implications for modern society. In the selection "Classroom Without Walls," McLuhan discusses some of the ways in which the new communication media are likely to affect traditional classroom procedures.

Father John M. Culkin, also of the Center for Communications at Fordham, attempts to identify the central concepts in McLuhan's radical theory of communications in his article "A Schoolman's Guide to Marshall McLuhan." He then traces their overall relevance for present-day educational practices.

In his selection entitled "The New Languages," anthropologist Edmund Carpenter, a long-time associate of McLuhan and also a colleague at the Fordham Center for Communications, further discusses the ways in which the new communications media actually function as new "languages," as recodifications of reality which appreciably alter the manner in which we select and organize our impressions of the surrounding world. "Teachers," comments Carpenter, "have had captive audiences for so long that few are equipped to compete for attention via the new media."[9]

When we read, another person thinks for us: we merely repeat his mental process. The greater part of the work of thought is done for us. This is why it relieves us to take up a book after being occupied by our own thoughts. In reading, the mind is only the playground for another's ideas. People who spend most of their lives in reading often lose the capacity for thinking, just as those who always ride forget how to walk . . . .

Face-to-face discourse is not as selective, abstract, nor explicit as any mechanical medium; it probably comes closer to communicating

---

7. *Ibid.*, pp. vii and 173–174.
8. *Ibid.*, p. ix.
9. Edmund Carpenter, "The New Languages," in *Explorations in Communication*, ed. Edmund Carpenter and Marshall McLuhan (Boston: Beacon Press, 1960), p. 177.

an unabridged situation than any of them, and, insofar as it exploits the give-take of dynamic relationship, it's clearly the most indispensably human one.[10]

Essayist-critic Susan Sontag, while in substantial agreement with the positions presented by McLuhan and Carpenter, is very much concerned with the even more basic topic of how *style*, or mode of expression, relates to *content*, or the information expressed. What is required, she comments in her book *Against Interpretation*, is more attention to form. "What is needed is a vocabulary—a descriptive, rather than prescriptive, vocabulary—for forms."[11]

Miss Sontag's remarks about art can largely be extended to the art of teaching and, indeed, to the entire area of nonaesthetic (or cognitive) communication as well. As she notes,

> *every style embodies an epistemological decision, an interpretation of how and what we perceive . . . . The circular repetitive style of Gertrude Stein's* Melanctha *expresses her interest in the dilution of immediate awareness by memory and anticipation, what she calls "association," which is obscured in language by the system of the tenses. Stein's insistence on the presentness of experience is identical with her decision to keep to the present tense, to choose commonplace short words and repeat groups of them incessantly, to use an extremely loose syntax and abjure most punctuation. Every style is a means of insisting on something.*[12]

According to Sontag, a "new sensibility" is emerging and, along with it, a new culture.

> *Having one's sensorium challenged or stretched hurts . . . . The commonest complaint about the films of Antonioni or the narratives of Beckett or Burroughs is that they are hard to look at or to read, that they are "boring" . . . . Boredom is only another name for a certain species of frustration. And the new languages which the interesting art of our time speaks are frustrating to the sensibilities of most educated people.*[13]

> *The primary feature of the new sensibility is that its model product is not the literary work, above all, the novel. A new non-literary culture exists today, of whose very existence, not to mention significance, most literary intellectuals are entirely unaware. This new establishment includes certain painters, sculptors, architects, social*

---

10. *Ibid.*, pp. 172–173.
11. Susan Sontag, *Against Interpretation* (New York: Farrar, Straus & Giroux, Inc., 1961), p. 299.
12. *Ibid.*, p. 35. Reprinted by permission.
13. *Ibid.*, p. 303.

planners, film-makers, TV technicians, neurologists, musicians, electronics engineers, dancers, philosophers, and sociologists.

Simply ignorant of the vital and enthralling (so called "avant-garde") developments in the other arts, and blinded by their personal investment in the perpetuation of the older notion of culture, they continue to cling to literature as the model for creative statement.[14]

In the concluding selection of this part, educational philosopher Philip H. Phenix discusses the relationship between the mass media and education. Increasingly, states Phenix, mass communications have become central to the processes of public education. "We have entered an era in which the mass media may be the *real* public schools — the institutions in which the public is not only formed and instructed but also brought into being as a public with common standards and assumptions."[15]

In the age of the mass media the teacher's functions shift to emphasis on selection, evaluation, interpretation, application, and individual guidance. To put it another way, the center of attention in education is moving from teaching to learning, because published materials offer at least the possibility of such rich resources of well-organized, authoritative, and expertly presented instructional materials that students need only the time and the incentives to learn.[16]

14. *Ibid.*, p. 298.
15. Philip H. Phenix, "Education and Mass Communications," *Phi Delta Kappan*, October 1961, p. 15.
16. *Ibid.*

NORBERT WIENER

Norbert Wiener was a professor of mathematics at Massachusetts Institute of Technology. He was one of the founders—many would say the originator—of the cybernetics movement and is best known for his work Cybernetics *(1948) and for the later popularization and extension of his ideas in* The Human Use of Human Beings: Cybernetics and Society *(1950).*

Rigidity and Learning:
Two Patterns of Communicative Behavior

Certain kinds of machines and some living organisms—particularly the higher living organisms—can, as we have seen, modify their patterns of behavior on the basis of past experience so as to achieve specific anti-entropic ends. In these higher forms of communicative organisms the environment, considered as the past experience of the individual, can modify the pattern of behavior into one which in some sense or other will deal more effectively with the future environment. In other words, the organism is not like the clockwork monad of Leibnitz with its pre-established harmony with the universe, but actually seeks a new equilibrium with the universe and its future contingencies. Its present is unlike its past and its future unlike its present. In the living organism as in the universe itself, exact repetition is absolutely impossible.

The work of Dr. W. Ross Ashby is probably the greatest modern contribution to this subject insofar as it concerns the analogies between living organisms and machines. Learning, like more primitive forms of feedback, is a process which reads differently forward and backward in time. The whole conception of the apparently purposive organism, whether it is mechanical, biological, or social, is that of an arrow with a particular direction in the stream of time rather than that of a line segment facing both ways which we may regard as going in either direction. The creature that learns is not the mythical amphisbaena of the ancients, with a head at each end and no concern with where it is going. It moves ahead from a known past into an unknown future and this future is not interchangeable with that past.

From *The Human Use of Human Beings: Cybernetics and Society* by Norbert Wiener. Reprinted by permission of Houghton Mifflin Company.

Let me give still another example of feedback which will clarify its function with respect to learning. When the great control rooms at the locks of the Panama Canal are in use, they are two-way message centers. Not only do messages go out controlling the motion of the tow locomotives, the opening and closing of the sluices, and the opening and closing of the gates; but the control room is full of telltales which indicate not merely that the locomotives, the sluices, and the gates have received their orders, but that they have in fact effectively carried out these orders. If this were not the case, the lock master might very easily assume that a towing locomotive had stopped and might rush the huge mass of a battleship into the gates, or might cause any one of a number of similar catastrophes to take place.

This principle in control applies not merely to the Panama locks, but to states, armies, and individual human beings. When in the American Revolution, orders already drawn up had failed, through carelessness, to go from England commanding a British army to march down from Canada to meet another British army marching up from New York at Saratoga, Burgoyne's forces met a catastrophic defeat which a well conceived program of two-way communications would have avoided. It follows that administrative officials, whether of a government or a university or a corporation, should take part in a two-way stream of communication, and not merely in one descending from the top. Otherwise, the top officials may find that they have based their policy on a complete misconception of the facts that their underlings possess. Again, there is no task harder for a lecturer than to speak to a dead-pan audience. The purpose of applause in the theater—and it is essential—is to establish in the performer's mind some modicum of two-way communication.

This matter of social feedback is of very great sociological and anthropological interest. The patterns of communication in human societies vary widely. There are communities like the Eskimos, among whom there seems to be no chieftainship and very little subordination, so that the basis of the social community is simply the common desire to survive against enormous odds of climate and food supply. There are socially stratified communities such as are found in India, in which the means of communication between two individuals are closely restricted and modified by their ancestry and position. There are communities ruled by despots, in which every relation between two subjects becomes secondary to the relation between the subject and his king. There are the hierarchical feudal communities of lord and vassal, and the very special techniques of social communication which they involve.

Most of us in the United States prefer to live in a moderately loose social community, in which the blocks to communication among individuals and classes are not too great. I will not say that this ideal of communication is attained in the United States. Until white supremacy ceases to belong to the creed of a large part of the country it will be an ideal from which we fall short. Yet even this modified formless democracy is too anarchic for many of those who make efficiency their first ideal. These worshipers of efficiency would like to have each man move in a social orbit meted out to him from his childhood, and perform a function to which he is bound as the serf was bound to the clod. Within the American social picture, it is shameful to have these yearnings, and this denial of opportunities implied by an uncertain future. Accordingly, many of those who are most attached to this orderly state of permanently allotted functions would be confounded if they were forced to admit this publicly. They are only in a position to display their clear preferences through their actions. Yet these actions stand out distinctly enough. The businessman who separates himself from his employees by a shield of yes-men, or the head of a big laboratory who assigns each subordinate a particular problem, and begrudges him the privilege of thinking for himself so that he can move beyond his immediate problem and perceive its general relevance, show that the democracy to which they pay their respects is not really the order in which they would prefer to live. The regularly ordered state of pre-assigned functions toward which they gravitate is suggestive of the Leibnitzian automata and does not suggest the irreversible movement into a contingent future which is the true condition of human life.

In the ant community, each worker performs its proper functions. There may be a separate caste of soldiers. Certain highly specialized individuals perform the functions of king and queen. If man were to adopt this community as a pattern, he would live in a fascist state, in which ideally each individual is conditioned from birth for his proper occupation: in which rulers are perpetually rulers, soldiers perpetually soldiers, the peasant is never more than a peasant, and the worker is doomed to be a worker.

. . . this aspiration of the fascist for a human state based on the model of the ant results from a profound misapprehension both of the nature of the ant and of the nature of man. I wish to point out that the very physical development of the insect conditions it to be an essentially stupid and unlearning individual, cast in a mold which cannot be modified to any great extent. I also wish to show how these physiological conditions make it into a cheap mass-produced article, of no more individual value than a paper pie plate to be thrown away after it is once used. On the other hand, I wish to show that the human individual, capable of vast learning and study, which may occupy almost half of his life, is physically equipped, as the ant is not, for this capacity. Variety and possibility are inherent in the human sensorium — and are indeed the key to man's most noble flights — because variety and possibility belong to the very structure of the human organism.

While it is possible to throw away this enormous advantage that we have over the ants, and to organize the fascist ant-state with human material, I certainly believe that this is a degradation of man's very nature, and economically a waste of the great human values which man possesses.

I am afraid that I am convinced that a community of human beings is a far more useful thing than a community of ants; and that if the human being is condemned and restricted to perform the same functions over and over again, he will not even be a good ant, not to mention a good human being. Those who would organize us according to permanent individual functions and permanent individual restrictions condemn the human race to move at much less than half-steam. They throw away nearly all our human possibilities and by limiting the modes in which we may adapt ourselves to future contingencies, they reduce our chances for a reasonably long existence on this earth.

Let us now turn to a discussion of the restrictions on the make-up of
the ant which have turned the ant community into the very special thing it
is. These restrictions have a deep-seated origin in the anatomy and the
physiology of the individual insect. Both the insect and the man are air-
breathing forms, and represent the end of a long transition from the easy-
going life of the water-borne animal to the much more exacting demands
of the land-bound. This transition from water to land, wherever it has occurred, has involved radical improvements in breathing, in the circulation
generally, in the mechanical support of the organism, and in the sense
organs.

The mechanical reinforcement of the bodies of land animals has taken
place along several independent lines. In the case of most of the mollusks,
as well as in the case of certain other groups which, though unrelated, have
taken on a generally mollusk-like form, part of the outer surface secretes a
non-living mass of calcareous tissue, the shell. This grows by accretion
from an early stage in the animal until the end of its life. The spiral and hel-
ical forms of those groups need only this process of accretion to account for
them.

If the shell is to remain an adequate protection for the animal, and the
animal grows to any considerable size in its later stages, the shell must be a
very appreciable burden, suitable only for land animals of the slowly moving and inactive life of the snail. In other shell-bearing animals, the shell is
lighter and less of a load, but at the same time much less of a protection.
The shell structure, with its heavy mechanical burden, has had only a limited
success among land animals.

Man himself represents another direction of development—a direction
found throughout the vertebrates, and at least indicated in invertebrates as
highly developed as the limulus and the octopus. In all these forms, certain
internal parts of the connective tissue assume a consistency which is no
longer fibrous, but rather that of a very hard, stiff jelly. These parts of the
body are called *cartilage*, and they serve to attach the powerful muscles
which animals need for an active life. In the higher vertebrates, this primary
cartilaginous skeleton serves as a temporary scaffolding for a skeleton of
much harder material: namely, bone, which is even more satisfactory for
the attachment of powerful muscles. These skeletons, of bone or cartilage,
contain a great deal of tissue which is not in any strict sense alive, but
throughout this mass of intercellular tissue there is a living structure of
cells, cellular membranes, and nutritive blood vessels.

The vertebrates have developed not only internal skeletons, but other
features as well which suit them for active life. Their respiratory system,
whether it takes the form of gills or lungs, is beautifully adapted to the active interchange of oxygen between the external medium and a blood, and
the latter is made much more efficient than the average invertebrate blood
by having its oxygen-carrying respiratory pigment concentrated in corpuscles. This blood is pumped through a closed system of vessels, rather than
through an open system of irregular sinuses, by a heart of relatively high
efficiency.

The insects and crustaceans, and in fact all the arthropods, are built for
quite another kind of growth. The outer wall of the body is surrounded by

a layer of chitin secreted by the cells of the epidermis. This chitin is a stiff substance rather closely related to cellulose. In the joints the layer of chitin is thin and moderately flexible, but over the rest of the animal it becomes that hard external skeleton which we see on the lobster and the cockroach. An internal skeleton such as man's can grow with the animal. An external skeleton (unless, like the shell of the snail, it grows by accretion) cannot. It is dead tissue, and possesses no intrinsic capability of growth. It serves to give a firm protection to the body and an attachment for the muscles, but it amounts to a strait jacket.

Internal growth among the arthropods can be converted into external growth only by discarding the old strait jacket, and by developing under it a new one, which is initially soft and pliable and can take a slightly new and larger form, but which very soon acquires the rigidity of its predecessor. In other words, the stages of growth are marked by definite moults, relatively frequent in the crustacean, and much less so in the insect. There are several such stages possible during the larval period. The pupal period represents a transition moult, in which the wings, that have not been functional in the larva, develop internally toward a functional condition. This becomes realized when the pre-final pupal stage, and the moult which terminates it gives rise to a perfect adult. The adult never moults again. It is in its sexual stage and although in most cases it remains capable of taking nourishment, there are insects in which the adult mouth-parts and the digestive tube are aborted, so that the *imago*, as it is called, can only mate, lay eggs, and die.

The nervous system takes part in this process of tearing down and building up. While there is a certain amount of evidence that some memory persists from the larva through to the imago, this memory cannot be very extensive. *The physiological condition for memory and hence for learning seems to be a certain continuity of organization, which allows the alterations produced by outer sense impressions to be retained as more or less permanent changes of structure or function.* Metamorphosis is too radical to leave much lasting record of these changes. It is indeed hard to conceive of a memory of any precision which can survive this process of radical internal reconstruction.

There is another limitation on the insect, which is due to its method of respiration and circulation. The heart of the insect is a very poor and weak tubular structure, which opens, not into well-defined blood vessels, but into vague cavities or sinuses conveying the blood to the tissues. This blood is without pigmented corpuscles, and carries the blood-pigments in solution. This mode of transferring oxygen seems to be definitely inferior to the corpuscular method.

In addition, the insect method of oxygenation of the tissues makes at most only local use of the blood. The body of the animal contains a system of branched tubules, carrying air directly from the outside into the tissues to be oxygenated. These tubules are stiffened against collapse by spiral fibers of chitin, and are thus passively open, but there is nowhere evidence of an active and effective system of air pumping. Respiration occurs by diffusion alone.

Notice that the same tubules carry by diffusion the good air in and the spent air, polluted with carbon dioxide, out to the surface. In a diffusion mechanism, the time of diffusion varies not as the length of the tube, but as the square of the length. Thus, in general, the efficiency of this system tends to fall off very rapidly with the size of the animal, and falls below the point of survival for an animal of any considerable size. So not only is the insect structurally incapable of a first-rate memory, he is also structurally incapable of an effective size.

To know the significance of this limitation in size, let us compare two artificial structures — the cottage and the skyscraper. The ventilation of a cottage is quite adequately taken care of by the leak of air around the window frames, not to mention the draft of the chimney. No special ventilation system is necessary. On the other hand, in a skyscraper with rooms within rooms, a shutdown of the system of forced ventilation would be followed in a very few minutes by an intolerable foulness of the air in the work spaces. Diffusion and even convection are no longer enough to ventilate such a structure.

The absolute maximum size of an insect is smaller than that attainable by a vertebrate. On the other hand, the ultimate elements of which the insect is composed are not always smaller than they are in man, or even in a whale. The nervous system partakes of this small size, and yet consists of neurons not much smaller than those in the human brain, though there are many fewer of them, and their structure is far less complex. In the matter of intelligence, we should expect that it is not only the relative size of the nervous system that counts, but in a large measure its absolute size. There is simply no room in the reduced structure of an insect for a nervous system of great complexity, nor for a large stored memory.

In view of the impossibility of a large stored memory, as well as of the fact that the youth of an insect such as an ant is spent in a form which is insulated from the adult phase by the intermediate catastrophe of metamorphosis, there is no opportunity for the ant to learn much. Add to this, that its behavior in the adult stage must be substantially perfect from the beginning, and it then becomes clear that the instructions received by the insect nervous system must be pretty much a result of the way it is built, and not of any personal experience. Thus the insect is rather like the kind of computing machine whose instructions are all set forth in advance on the "tapes," and which has next to no feedback mechanism to see it through the uncertain future. The behavior of an ant is much more a matter of instinct than of intelligence. *The physical strait jacket in which an insect grows up is directly responsible for the mental strait jacket which regulates its pattern of behavior.*

Here the reader may say: "Well, we already know that the ant as an individual is not very intelligent, so why all this fuss about explaining why it cannot be intelligent?" The answer is that *Cybernetics takes the view that the structure of the machine or of the organism is an index of the performance that may be expected from it.* The fact that the mechanical rigidity of the insect is such as to limit its intelligence while the mechanical fluidity of the human being provides for his almost indefinite intellectual expansion is highly relevant to the point of view of this book. Theoretically, if we could build a machine whose mechanical structure duplicated human physiology, then we could have a machine whose intellectual capacities would duplicate those of human beings.

In the matter of rigidity of behavior, the greatest contrast to the ant is not merely the mammal in general, but man in particular. It has frequently been observed that man is a neoteinic form: that is, that if we compare man with the great apes, his closest relatives, we find that mature man in hair, head, shape, body proportions, bony structure, muscles, and so on, is more like the newborn ape than the adult ape. Among the animals, man is a Peter Pan who never grows up.

This immaturity of anatomical structure corresponds to man's prolonged childhood. Physiologically, man does not reach puberty until he has already completed a fifth of his normal span of life. Let us compare this with the ratio in the case of a mouse, which lives three years and starts breeding at the end of three months. This is a ratio of twelve to one. The mouse's ratio is much more nearly typical of the large majority of mammals than is the human ratio.

Puberty for most mammals either represents the end of their epoch of tutelage, or is well beyond it. In our community, man is recognized as immature until the age of twenty-one, and the modern period of education for the higher walks of life continues until about thirty, actually beyond the time of greatest physical strength. Man thus spends what may amount to forty per cent of his normal life as a learner, again for reasons that have to do with his physical structure. It is as completely natural for a human society to be based on learning as for an ant society to be based on an inherited pattern.

Man like all other organisms lives in a contingent universe, but man's advantage over the rest of nature is that he has the physiological and hence the intellectual equipment to adapt himself to radical changes in his environment. The human species is strong only insofar as it takes advantage of the innate adaptive, learning faculties that its physiological structure makes possible.

We have already indicated that effective behavior must be informed by some sort of feedback process, telling it whether it has equalled its goal or fallen short. The simplest feedbacks deal with gross successes or failures of performance, such as whether we have actually succeeded in grasping an object that we have tried to pick up, or whether the advance guard of an army is at the appointed place at the appointed time. However, there are many other forms of feedback of a more subtle nature.

It is often necessary for us to know whether a whole policy of conduct, a strategy so to say, has proved successful or not. The animal we teach to traverse a maze in order to find food or to avoid electric shocks, must be able to record whether the general plan of running through the maze has been on the whole successful or not, and it must be able to change this plan in order to run the maze efficiently. This form of learning is most certainly a feedback, but it is a feedback on a higher level, a feedback of policies and not of simple actions. It differs from more elementary feedbacks in what Bertrand Russell would call its "logical type."

This pattern of behavior may also be found in machines. A recent innovation in the technique of telephonic switching provides an interesting mechanical analogy to man's adaptive faculty. Throughout the telephone industry, automatic switching is rapidly completing its victory over manual switching, and it may seem to us that the existing forms of automatic switching constitute a nearly perfect process. Nevertheless, a little thought will show that the present process is very wasteful of equipment. The number of people with whom I actually wish to talk over the telephone is limited, and in large measure is the same limited group day after day and week after week. I use most of the telephone equipment available to me to communicate with members of this group. Now, as the present technique of switching generally goes, the process of reaching one of the people whom we call up four or five times a day is in no way different from the process of reaching those people with whom we may never have a conversation. From the standpoint of balanced service, we are using either too little equipment to handle the frequent calls or too much to handle the infrequent calls, a situation which reminds me of Oliver Wendell Holmes' poem on the "one-hoss shay." This hoary vehicle, as you recollect, after one hundred years of service, showed itself to be so carefully designed that neither wheel, nor top, nor shafts, nor seat contained any part which manifested an uneconomical excess of wearing power over any other part. Actually, the "one-hoss shay" represents the pinnacle of engineering, and is not merely a humorous fantasy. If the tires had lasted a moment longer than the spokes or the dashboard than the shafts, these parts would have carried into disuse certain economic values. These values could either have been reduced without hurting the durability of the vehicle as a whole, or they could have been transferred equally throughout the entire vehicle to make the whole thing last longer. Indeed, any structure not of the nature of the "one-hoss shay" is wastefully designed.

This means that for the greatest economy of service it is not desirable that the process of my connection with Mr. A., whom I call up three times a day, and with Mr. B., who is for me only an unnoticed item in the telephone directory, should be of the same order. If I were allotted a slightly more direct means of connection with Mr. A., then the time wasted in having to wait twice as long for Mr. B. would be more than compensated for. If then, it is possible without excessive cost to devise an apparatus which will record my past conversations, and reapportion to me a degree of service corresponding to the frequency of my past use of the telephone channels, I should obtain a better service, or a less expensive one, or both. The Philips Lamp Company in Holland has succeeded in doing this. The quality of its service has been improved by means of a feedback of Russell's so-called "higher logical type." It is capable of greater variety, more adaptability, and deals more effectively than conventional equipment with the entropic tendency for the more probable to overwhelm the less probable.

I repeat, feedback is a method of controlling a system by reinserting into it the results of its past performance. If these results are merely used as numerical data for the criticism of the system and its regulation, we have the simple feedback of the control engineers. If, however, the information which proceeds backward from the performance is able to change the general method and pattern of performance, we have a process which may well be called learning.

Another example of the learning process appears in connection with the problem of the design of prediction machines. At the beginning of World War II, the comparative inefficiency of anti-aircraft fire made it necessary to introduce apparatus which would follow the position of an airplane, compute its distance, determine the length of time before a shell could reach it, and figure out where it would be at the end of that time. If the plane were able to take a perfectly arbitrary evasive action, no amount of skill would permit us to fill in the as yet unknown motion of the plane between the time when the gun was fired and the time when the shell should arrive approximately at its goal. However, under many circumstances the aviator either does not, or cannot, take arbitrary evasive action. He is limited by the fact that if he makes a rapid turn, centrifugal force will render him unconscious; and by the other fact that the control mechanism of his plane and the course of instructions which he has received practically force on him certain regular habits of control which show themselves even in his evasive action. These regularities are not absolute but are rather statistical preferences which appear most of the time. They may be different for different aviators, and they will certainly be for different planes. Let us remember that in the pursuit of a target as rapid as an airplane, there is not time for the computer to take out his instruments and figure where the plane is going to be. All the figuring must be built into the gun control itself. This figuring must include data which depend on our past statistical experience of airplanes of a given type under varying flight conditions. The present stage of anti-aircraft fire consists in an apparatus which uses either fixed data of this sort, or a selection among a limited number of such fixed data. The proper choice among these may be switched in by means of the voluntary action of the gunner.

However, there is another stage of the control problem which may also be dealt with mechanically. The problem of determining the flight statistics of a plane from the actual observation of its flight, and then of transforming these into rules for controlling the gun, is itself a definite and mathematical one. Compared with the actual pursuit of the plane, in accordance with given rules, it is a relatively slow action, and involves a considerable observation of the past flight of the airplane. It is nevertheless not impossible to mechanize this long-time action as well as the short-time action. We thus may construct an anti-aircraft gun which observes by itself the statistics concerning the motion of the target plane, which then works these into a system of control, and which finally adopts this system of control as a quick way for adjusting its position to the observed position and motion of the plane.

To my knowledge this has not yet been done, but it is a problem which lies along lines we are considering, and expect to use in other problems of prediction. The adjustment of the general plan of pointing and firing the gun according to the particular system of motions which the target has made is essentially an act of learning. It is a change in the *taping* of the gun's computing mechanism, which alters not so much the numerical data, as the process by which they are interpreted. It is, in fact, a very general sort of feedback, affecting the whole method of behavior of the instrument.

The advanced process of learning which we have here discussed is still limited by the mechanical conditions of the system in which it occurs, and clearly does not correspond to the normal process of learning in man. But from this process we can infer quite different ways in which learning of a complex sort can be mechanized. These indications are given respectively by the Lockean theory of association, and by Pavlov's theory of the conditioned reflex. Before I take these up, however, I wish to make some general remarks to cover in advance certain criticisms of the suggestion that I shall present.

Let me recount the basis on which it is possible to develop a theory of learning. By far the greater part of the work of the nerve physiologist has been on the conduction of impulses by nerve fibers or neurons, and this process is given as an all-or-none phenomenon. That is, if a stimulus reaches the point or threshold where it will travel along a nerve fiber at all, and not die out in a relatively short distance, the effect which it produces at a comparatively remote point on the nerve fiber is substantially independent of its initial strength.

These nerve impulses travel from fiber to fiber across connections known as *synapses*, in which one ingoing fiber may come in contact with many outgoing fibers, and one outgoing fiber in contact with many ingoing fibers. In these synapses, the impulse given by a single incoming nerve fiber is often not enough to produce an effective outgoing impulse. In general, if the impulses arriving at a given outgoing fiber by incoming synaptic connections are too few, the outgoing fiber will not respond. When I say too few, I do not necessarily mean that all incoming fibers act alike, nor even that with any set of incoming active synaptic connections the question of whether the outgoing fiber will respond may be settled once for all. I also do not intend to ignore the fact that some incoming fibers, instead of tending to produce a stimulus in the outgoing fibers with which they connect, may tend to prevent these fibers from accepting new stimuli.

Be that as it may, while the problem of the conduction of impulses along a fiber may be described in a rather simple way as an all-or-none phenomenon, the problem of the transmission of an impulse across a layer of synaptic connections depends on a complicated pattern of responses, in which certain combinations of incoming fibers, firing within a certain limited time, will cause the message to go further, while certain other combinations will not. These combinations are not a thing fixed once for all, nor do they even depend solely on the past history of messages received into that synaptic layer. They are known to change with temperature, and may well change with many other things.

This view of the nervous system corresponds to the theory of those machines that consist in a sequence of switching devices in which the opening of a later switch depends on the action of precise combinations of earlier switches leading into it, which open at the same time. This all-or-none machine is called a *digital* machine. It has great advantages for the most varied problems of communication and control. In particular, the sharpness of the decision between "yes" and "no" permits it to accumulate information in such a way as to allow us to discriminate very small differences in very large numbers.

Besides these machines which work on a yes-and-no scale, there are other computing and control machines which measure rather than count. These are known as *analogy* machines, because they operate on the basis of analogous connections between the measured quantities and the numerical quantities supposed to represent them. An example of an analogy machine is a slide rule, in contrast with a desk computing machine which operates digitally. Those who have used a slide rule know that the scale on which the marks have to be printed and the accuracy of our eyes give sharp limits to the precision with which the rule can be read. These limits are not as easily extended as one might think, by making the slide rule larger. A ten-foot slide rule will give only one decimal place more accuracy than a one-foot slide rule, and in order to do this, not only must each foot of the larger slide rule be constructed with the same precision as the smaller one, but the orientation of these successive feet must conform to the degree of accuracy to be expected for each one-foot slide rule. Furthermore, the problems of keeping the larger rule rigid are much greater than those which we find in the case of the smaller rule, and serve to limit the increase in accuracy which we get by increasing the size. In other words, for practical purposes, machines that measure, as opposed to machines that count, are very greatly limited in their precision. Add this to the prejudices of the physiologist in favor of all-or-none action, and we see why the greater part of the work which has been done on the mechanical simulacra of the brain has been on machines which are more or less on a digital basis.

However, if we insist too strongly on the brain as a glorified digital machine, we shall be subject to some very just criticism, coming in part from the physiologists and in part from the somewhat opposite camp of those psychologists who prefer not to make use of the machine comparison. I have said that in a digital machine there is a *taping,* which determines the sequence of operations to be performed, and that a change in this taping on the basis of past experience corresponds to a learning process. In the brain, the clearest analogy to taping is the determination of the synaptic thresholds, of the precise combinations of the incoming neurons which will fire an outgoing neuron with which they are connected. We have already seen that these thresholds are variable with temperature, and we have no reason to believe that they may not be variable with the chemistry of the blood and with many other phenomena which are not themselves originally of an all-or-none nature. It is therefore necessary that in considering the problem of learning, we should be most wary of assuming an all-or-none theory of the nervous system, without having made an intellectual criticism of the notion, and without specific experimental evidence to back our assumption.

It will often be said that there is no theory of learning whatever that will be reasonable for the machine. It will also be said that in the present stage of our knowledge, any theory of learning which I may offer will be premature, and will probably not correspond to the actual functioning of the nervous system. I wish to walk a middle path between these two criticisms. On the one hand, I wish to give a method of constructing learning machines, a method which will not only enable me to build certain special machines of this type, but will give me a general engineering technique for constructing a very large class of such machines. Only if I reach this degree of generality will I have defended myself in some measure from the criticism that the mechanical process which I claim is similar to learning, is, in fact, something of an essentially different nature from learning.

On the other hand, I wish to describe such machines in terms which are not too foreign to the actual observables of the nervous system, and of human and animal conduct. I am quite aware that I cannot expect to be right in detail in presenting the actual human mechanism, and that I may even be wrong in principle. Nevertheless, if I give a device which can be verbally formulated in terms of the concepts belonging to the human mind and the human brain, I shall give a point of departure for criticism, and a standard with which to compare the performance to be expected on the basis of other theories.

Locke, at the end of the seventeenth century, considered that the content of the mind was made up of what he calls *ideas*. The mind for him is entirely passive, a clean blackboard, *tabula rasa*, on which the experiences of the individual write their own impressions. If these impressions appear often, either under circumstances of simultaneity, or in a certain sequence, or in situations which we ordinarily attribute to cause and effect, then according to Locke, these impressions or ideas will form complex ideas, with a certain positive tendency for the component elements to stick together. The mechanism by which the ideas stick together lies in the ideas themselves; but there is throughout Locke's writing a singular unwillingness to describe such a mechanism. His theory can bear only the sort of relation to reality that a picture of a locomotive bears to a working locomotive. It is a diagram without any working parts. This is not remarkable when we consider the date of Locke's theory. It was in astronomy, and not in engineering or in psychology, that the dynamic point of view, the point of view of working parts, first reached its importance; and this was at the hands of Newton, who was not a predecessor of Locke, but a contemporary.

For several centuries, science, dominated by the Aristotelian impulse to classify, neglected the modern impulse to search for ways in which phenomena function. Indeed, with the plants and animals yet to be explored, it is hard to see how biological science could have entered a properly dynamic period except through the continual gathering of more descriptive natural history. The great botanist Linnaeus will serve us as an example. For Linnaeus, species and genera were fixed Aristotelian forms, rather than signposts for a process of evolution; but it was only on the basis of a thoroughly Linnaean description that any cogent case could ever be made for evolution. The early natural historians were the practical frontiersmen of the intellect; too much under the compulsion to seize and occupy new territory to be very precise in treating the problem of explaining the new forms that they had observed. After the frontiersman comes the operative farmer, and after the naturalist comes the modern scientist.

In the last quarter of the last century and the first quarter of the present one, another great scholar, Pavlov, covered in his own way essentially the same ground that Locke had covered earlier. His study of the conditioned reflexes, however, progressed experimentally, not theoretically as Locke's had. Moreover, he treated it as it appears among the lower animals rather than as it appears in man. The lower animals cannot speak in man's language, but in the language of behavior. Much of their more conspicuous behavior is emotional in its motivation and much of their emotion is concerned with food. It was with food that Pavlov began, and with the physical symptom of salivation. It is easy to insert a canula into the salivary duct of a dog and to observe the secretion that is stimulated by the presence of food.

Ordinarily many things unconnected with food, as objects seen, sounds heard, etc., produce no effect on salivation, but Pavlov observed that if a certain pattern or a certain sound had been systematically introduced to a dog at feeding time, then the display of the pattern or sound alone was sufficient to excite salivation. That is, the reflex of salivation was conditioned by a past association.

Here we have on the level of the animal reflex, something analogous to Locke's association of ideas, an association which occurs in reflex responses whose emotional content is presumably very strong. Let us notice the rather complicated nature of the antecedents which are needed to produce a conditioned reflex of the Pavlov type. To begin with, they generally center about something important to the life of the animal: in this case, food, even though in the reflex's final form the food element may be entirely elided. We may, however, illustrate the importance of the initial stimulus of a Pavlovian conditioned reflex by the example of electric fences enclosing a cattle farm.

On cattle farms, the construction of wire fences strong enough to turn a steer is not easy. It is thus economical to replace a heavy fence of this type by one where one or two relatively thin strands of wire carry a sufficiently high electric voltage to impress upon an animal a quite appreciable shock when the animal short-circuits it by contact with its body. Such a fence may have to resist the pressure of the steer once or twice; but after that, the fence acts, not because it can hold up mechanically under pressure, but because the steer has developed a conditioned reflex which tends to prevent it from coming into contact with the fence at all. Here the original trigger to the reflex is pain; and the withdrawal from pain is vital for the continued life of any animal. The transferred trigger is the sight of the fence. There are other triggers which lead to conditioned reflexes besides hunger and pain. It will be using anthropomorphic language to call these emotional situations, but there is no such anthropomorphism needed to describe them as situations which generally carry an emphasis and importance not belonging to many other animal experiences. Such experiences, whether we may call them emotional or not, produce strong reflexes. In the formation of conditioned reflexes in general the reflex response is transferred to one of these trigger situations. This trigger situation is one which frequently occurs concurrently with the original trigger. The change in the stimulus for which a given response takes place must have some such nervous correlate as the opening of a synaptic pathway leading to the response which would otherwise have been closed, or the closing of one which would otherwise have been open; and thus constitutes what Cybernetics calls a *change in taping*.

Such a change in taping is preceded by the continued association of the old, strong, natural stimulus for a particular reaction and the new concomitant one. It is as if the old stimulus had the power to change the permeability of those pathways which were carrying a message at the same time as it was active. The interesting thing is that the new, active stimulus need have almost nothing predetermined about it except the fact of repeated concomitance with the original stimulus. Thus the original stimulus seems to produce a long-time effect in all those pathways which were carrying a message at the time of its occurrence or at least in a large number of them. The insignificance of the substitute stimulus indicates that the modifying effect of the original stimulus is widespread, and is not confined to a few special pathways. Thus we assume that there may be some kind of general message released by the original stimulus, but that it is active only in those channels which were carrying a message at about the time of the original stimulus. The effect of this action may perhaps not be permanent, but is at least fairly long-lived. The most logical site at which to suppose this secondary action to take place is in the synapses, where it most probably affects their thresholds.

The concept of an undirected message spreading out until it finds a receiver, which is then stimulated by it, is not an unfamiliar one. Messages of this sort are used very frequently as alarms. The fire siren is a call to all the citizens of the town, and in particular to members of the fire department, wherever they may be. In a mine, when we wish to clear out all remote passages because of the presence of fire damp, we break a tube of ethyl mercaptan in the air-intake. There is no reason to suppose that such messages may not occur in the nervous system. If I were to construct a learning machine of a general type, I would be very much disposed to employ this method of the conjunction of general spreading "To-whom-it-may-concern" messages with localized channeled messages. It ought not to be too difficult to devise electrical methods of performing this task. This is very different, of course, from saying that learning in the animal actually occurs by such a conjunction of spreading and of channeled messages. Frankly, I think it is quite possible that it does, but our evidence is as yet not enough to make this more than a conjecture.

As to the nature of these "To-whom-it-may-concern" messages, supposing them to exist, I am on still more speculative ground. They might indeed be nervous, but I am rather inclined to attribute them to the nondigital, analogy side of the mechanism responsible for reflexes and thought. It is a truism to attribute synaptic action to chemical phenomena. Actually, in the action of a nerve, it is impossible to separate chemical potentials and electrical potentials, and the statement that a certain particular action is chemical is almost devoid of meaning. Nevertheless, it does no violence to current thought to suppose that at least one of the causes or concomitants of synaptic change is a chemical change which manifests itself locally, no matter what its origin may be. The presence of such a change may very well be locally dependent on release signals which are transmitted nervously. It is at least equally conceivable that changes of the sort may be due in part to chemical changes transmitted generally through the blood, and not by the nerves. It is conceivable that "To-whom-it-may-concern" messages are transmitted nervously, and make themselves locally apparent in the form of that sort of chemical action which accompanies synaptic changes. To me, as an engineer, the transmission of "To-whom-it-may-concern" messages would appear to be more economically performed through the blood than through the nerves. However, I have no evidence.

Let us remember that these "To-whom-it-may-concern" influences bear a certain similarity to the sort of changes in the anti-aircraft control apparatus which carry all new statistics to the instrument, rather than to those which directly carry only specific numerical data. In both cases, we have an action which has probably been piling up for a long time, and which will produce effects due to continue for a long time.

The rapidity with which the conditioned reflex responds to its stimulus is not necessarily an index that the conditioning of the reflex is a process of comparable speed. Thus it seems to me appropriate for a message causing such a conditioning to be carried by the slow but pervasive influence of the blood stream.

It is already a considerable narrowing of what my point of view requires, to suppose that the fixing influence of hunger or pain or whatever stimulus may determine a conditioned reflex passes through the blood. It would be a still greater restriction if I should try to specify the nature of this unknown blood-borne influence, if any such exists. That the blood carries in it substances which may alter nervous action directly or indirectly seems to me very likely, and to be suggested by the actions of some at least of the hormones or internal secretions. This, however, is not the same as saying that the influence on thresholds which determines learning is the product of specific hormones. Again, it is tempting to find the common denominator of hunger and the pain caused by the electrified fence in something that we may call an emotion, but it is certainly going too far to attach emotion to all conditioners of reflexes, without any further discussion of their particular nature.

Nevertheless, it is interesting to know that the sort of phenomenon which is recorded subjectively as emotion may not be merely a useless epiphenomenon of nervous action, but may control some essential stage in learning, and in other similar processes. I definitely do not say that it does, but I do say that those psychologists who draw sharp and uncrossable distinctions between man's emotions and those of other living organisms and the responses of the modern type of automatic mechanisms, should be just as careful in their denials as I should be in my assertions.

WILBUR SCHRAMM

Wilbur Schramm is a professor of communications and Director of the Institute for Communication Research at Stanford University. He is the author of the books The Process and Effects of Mass Communications Television in the Lives of Our Children, *(1954) and* The Impact of Educational Television *(1960).*

The Nature of Mass Communication

The chief *sender*, in mass communication, is a communication organization or an institutionalized person. By a communication organization we mean a newspaper, a broadcasting network or station, a film studio, a book- or magazine-publishing house. By an institutionalized person we mean such a person as the editor of a newspaper, who speaks in his editorial columns through the facilities of the institution and with more voice and prestige than he would have if he were speaking without the institution.

The organization works exactly as the individual communicator does. It operates as decoder, interpreter, and encoder. On a newspaper, for example, the input to be decoded flows in through the news wires and the reporters. It is evaluated, checked, amplified where necessary, written into a story, assigned headline and position, printed, distributed. This is the same process as goes on within an individual communicator, but it is carried out by a group of persons rather than by one individual. The quality of organization required to get a group of reporters, editors, and printers working together as a smooth communication unit, decoding, interpreting, and encoding so that the whole operation and product has an individual quality, is a quite remarkable thing. We have become so accustomed to this performance that we have forgotten how remarkable it is.

Another difference between the communication institution and the individual communicator is that the institution has a very high ratio of output to input. Individuals vary, of course, in their output-input ratios. Persons who are in the business of communicating (preachers or teachers, for example) ordinarily have higher ratios than others, and so do naturally talkative persons who are not professional communicators. Very quiet persons have relatively higher input. But the communication organization is so designed as to be able to encode thousands—sometimes millions—of identical messages at the same time. To carry these, intricate and efficient channels must be provided. There have to be provisions for printing and delivering thousands of newspapers, magazines, or books, for making prints of a film and showing them in hundreds or thousands of theaters, for translating sound waves into electricity and distributing it through wires and through the air to millions of receiving sets.

The *receivers* of mass communication are individuals at the ends of these channels — individuals reading the evening paper, looking through the new magazine, reading the new book, sitting in the motion-picture theater, turning the dial on the radio set. This receiving situation is much different from that which pertains in face-to-face communication, for one thing, because there is very little direct *feedback* from the receivers to the sender. The receiver who, in a face-to-face situation, will nod his head and smile or frown while the sender is speaking, and then encode a reply himself, will very seldom talk back to the radio network or write a letter to the editor.

The kind of feedback that comes to a mass communication organization is a kind of inferential expression — receivers stop buying the publication, or no longer listen to the program, or cease to buy the product advertised. Only in rare instances do these organizations have an opportunity to see, more directly than that, how their messages are going over. That is one reason why mass communication conducts so much audience research, to find out what programs are being listened to, what stories are being read, what advertisements are attended to. It is one of their few substitutes for the feedback which makes interpersonal communication so relatively easy to plan and control.

. . . These audiences cluster not only around the newspaper, the magazine, or the television station but also around certain stories in the paper, certain parts of the magazine, certain television or radio programs. For example, Station A will not have the same audience at eight o'clock as it had at seven o'clock, because some of these listeners will have moved to Stations B and C, and some of the listeners from B and C will have moved to A. Newspaper D will not have the same audience on its sports pages as on its society pages, although there will be some overlap. What determines which offering of mass communication will be selected by any given individual? Perhaps the easiest way to put it is to say that choice is determined by the "fraction of selection":

$$\frac{\text{Expectation of Reward}}{\text{Effort Required}}$$

You can increase the value of that fraction either by increasing the numerator or decreasing the denominator, which is to say that an individual is more likely to select a certain communication if it promises him more reward or requires less effort than comparable communications. You can see how this works in your own experience. You are much more likely to read the newspaper or magazine at hand than to walk six blocks to the newsstand to buy a preferred newspaper or magazine. You are more likely to listen to a station which has a loud, clear signal than to one which is faint and fading and requires constant effort from you to hear the program. But if the big game of the week is on that faint station, or if your favorite author is in the magazine at the newsstand, then there is more likelihood that you will make the additional effort.

If you were a member of the underground in occupied France during World War II, you probably risked your life to hear news from the forbidden Allied radio. You aren't likely to stay up until 2:00 A.M. simply to hear a radio program, but if by staying up that long you can find out how the Normandy invasion is progressing or who has won the presidential election — then you will probably make the extra effort just as most of the rest of us did. It is hardly necessary to point out that no two listeners may have exactly the same fraction of selection. One of them may expect more reward from Milton Berle than will the other. One of them may consider it less effort to walk six blocks to the newsstand than does the other. The significant fact is that the audience of mass communication in any given situation is determined by the way this fraction of selection looks to the interested individuals.

Unlike lecture audiences and small groups, mass communication audiences (with the exception of the people in a motion-picture theater at the same time) have very little contact with each other. People in one house listening to Jack Benny don't know whether anybody in the next house is listening to him or not. A person reading an editorial in the *New York Times* has little group feeling for the other people in this country who read editorials in the *New York Times*. These audiences are individuals, rather than groups. But each individual is connected with a group or groups — his family, his close friends, his occupational or school group — and this is a very important thing to remember about mass communication.

The more we study it, the more we are coming to think that the great effects of mass communication are gained by feeding ideas and information into small groups through individual receivers. In some groups, as you well know, it is a sign of status to be familiar with some part of mass communication (for example, in the teenage group to hear the currently screamable crooner, or in some business groups to read the *Wall Street Journal*). In many a group, it is a news story from the radio, or an editorial from the *Times*, or an article from the *Tribune*, or an article from one of the big magazines, that furnishes the subject of conversation on a given day. The story, or article, or editorial is then reinterpreted by the group, and the result is encoded in group opinion and perhaps in group action. Thus, it may well be that the chief influence of mass communication on individuals is really a kind of secondary influence, reflected to the group and back again.

We are ready now to draw a diagram of mass communication and to talk about the kind of messages this sort of system requires and what we know about predicting their effects. The way mass communication seems to work is illustrated [on page 284].

It is easy to see that there will be certain restrictions on the kinds of program which can be carried over these identical circuits to these little-known and changing audiences. The communication organization knows it is dealing with individuals, yet it does not know them as individuals. Its audience-research classifies rather than individualizes the audience. That is, audience-research says that so many people are listening at a given time, that so many men and so many women are likely to read a given kind of

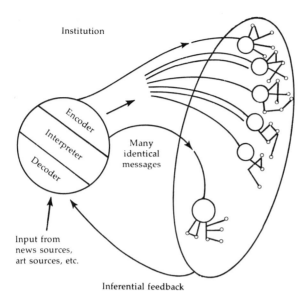

Institution

Encoder

Interpreter

Decoder

Many
identical
messages

Input from
news sources,
art sources, etc.

Inferential feedback

The "mass audience":
many receivers, each de-
coding, interpreting, en-
coding — each connected
with a group, where mes-
sage is reinterpreted and
often acted upon.

article, or that the readers of a given magazine are in the upper economic
bracket and have had, on the average, twelve years of schooling. Whereas
the individual communicator is dealing with individuals and is able to
watch the way his message is received and may modify it, if necessary, the
organization is dealing only with averages and classes. It must pitch its
reading level somewhere below the estimated average of its audience, in
order not to cut off too many of the lower half of the audience. It must
choose its content according to the best estimate it can make of what the
broadest classes of receivers want and need. Whereas the individual communicator is free to experiment because he can instantly correct any mistake, the organization is loathe to experiment. When it finds an apparently
successful formula, it keeps on that way; or it changes the details but not
the essentials. If one institution makes a great success with a given kind of
message, others tend to copy it — not because of any lack of originality but
because this is one of the few kinds of feedback available from the mass
audience. That is why we have so much sameness on the radio, why one
successful comic strip tends to be followed by others of the same kind, one
successful news or digest magazine by others, one kind of comedy program
by others of the same kind, and so forth.

What can we say about the effects of these mass-communication messages? For one thing, mass communication has pervasive effect because in
many respects it has taken over the function of *society communicating*. Our
society, like any other communication unit, functions as decoder, interpreter,
and encoder. It decodes our environment for us, watches the horizon for
danger and promise and entertainment. It then operates to interpret what it
has decoded, helps us arrive at a consensus so that we can put policy into
effect, helps us keep the ordinary interactions of communal life going, as
illustrated by the accompanying diagram [on page 285].

Our society helps us enjoy life. It also encodes — messages to maintain our relations with other societies in the world, and messages to transmit our culture to its new members. Mass communication, which has the power to extend our eyes and ears almost indefinite distances and to multiply our voices and written words as far as we can find listeners or readers, has taken over a large share of the responsibility for this social communication. Newspapers, radio, and television watch the horizon for us. By telling us what our leaders and experts think, by conducting a discussion of public issues, these media, and magazines and films as well, help us interpret what is seen on the horizon and help us decide what to do about it. The textbook and educational film have led all the other media in encoding our culture so that the young persons coming into our society may learn as quickly and easily as possible the history, standards, roles, and skills they must know in order to be good members of society.

This is not to say that all the media do not contribute in some degree to all these functions. For example, a book like Orwell's *1984* may be as much a report of the horizon as the most current news story. On the other hand, it is certainly true that a great deal of our culture is transmitted currently through television, radio, newspapers, and magazines. But the faster media are better equipped to be watchmen and are more often so used. The slower, longer-lasting media are better equipped to be teaching aids and are so used. The important thing for the teacher to realize is that *all* the mass media have important uses in providing the network of understandings without which the modern large community could not exist.

So much for the basic effect, which we see every day in the customs around us, the people and problems talked about, and the language we speak. This is the slow, imperceptible effect. This is like building the stalagmite. But how about the specific effect of a given message transmitted by mass communication? How can we predict what the effect will be on the mass audience?

We can't predict the effect on the mass audience. We can only predict the effect on individuals. Communication organizations have developed group encoding, but there is only individual decoding. Therefore, we can predict the effect of mass communication only in the way we try to predict the effect of other communication — that is, in terms of the interaction of message, situation, personality, and group. Inasmuch as there are many

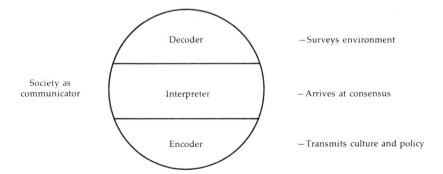

different combinations of personality, situation, and group in any mass audience, there are likely to be many different kinds of effects. It is equally obvious that, since mass communication doesn't know much about the individuals in its audience, predicting effects is going to be extremely difficult.

Nevertheless, there are certain things to be said. The problem of attention constantly faces mass communication. The average American probably gives four or five hours a day to mass communication. If he lives in a big city, he gets a paper that would itself take half that time to read. He is offered the equivalent of two weeks of radio and television every day, from which he can choose. He is offered a bewildering array of magazines and books and films. From these, also, he must choose. Other attractive ways to spend leisure compete with communication. He sometimes combines them—listening to music while he reads, playing cards or eating while he hears a newscast, playing with the baby while he watches television.

We can, therefore, predict at least that any individual will have a fairly small chance of selecting any given item in mass communication and that, if he does select it, his level of attention may be rather low. This is responsible for many cases of "mishearing" radio. We know also that readership of the average newspaper story falls off sharply after the first few paragraphs, so that a member of the mass audience is likely not to see at all the latter part of a long newspaper story.

There are, of course, many cases in which markedly high attention is aroused by mass communication and plentiful instances of listeners identifying themselves closely with radio characters and adopting the mannerisms and language of movie heroes. It has been said that the mass media have brought Hollywood, Broadway, and Washington nearer than the next town, and there is a great deal of truth in this. There are, also, some cases in which very spectacular overt results have been accomplished by mass communication.

Let us recall one of them. Can you remember when CBS broadcast Orson Welles' performance of H. G. Wells' *War of the Worlds*? The script featured the invasion of the United States by armies from outer space. Perhaps you were one of the people who ran screaming for the hills, or armed yourself to wait for the invaders, or tried to call your loved ones long distance for a farewell talk. Or perhaps you were not. Perhaps you were one of those who heard the CBS announcers explain carefully that it was a play made from a book of fiction. Those who didn't hear those announcements were engaged in proving what we have just said about the low level of attention to some parts of mass communication.

But that doesn't entirely explain why people became hysterical and did things they were rather ashamed of the next day. And, in truth, this is one of the really spectacular examples of mass-communication effect. This happened without any specific reference to groups; it happened spontaneously in thousands of homes near the supposed scene of invasion. Why did it happen? Research men have studied the incident and think they have put together the puzzle. For one thing, it was a tense time. People were full of anxiety, which could have been triggered off in many ways. In the second place, people trusted—still trust—radio news; the play was in the form of newscasts and commentaries. Therefore, the communication, as it was interpreted, really represented a spectacular change in the situation: The Martians were invading! Apparently the group element played no large part in this event, but the other three did. The message was accepted (minus the important identification as fiction). The receivers had a good deal of anxiety ready to be used. The message convinced them that the situation had indeed changed for the worse. Each, according to his own personality and situation, then took action.

As we have said, this was, fortunately, one of the few really spectacular examples of mass behavior. Another was the gold rush that resulted when the newspapers, in the 1890's, brought word of gold in Alaska. Some people might say that what the Communists have been able to accomplish is a spectacular advertisement for the power of mass communication, and this interpretation is worth considering because it shows us not only some of the differences between the way we use the mass media and the way dictators use them but also some of the principles of communication effect.

One of the first acts of the Communists, when they take over a country, is to seize the mass-communication system. (That was also one of Hitler's first acts.) They also seize the police power and the control of productive resources, and they organize an intricate system of party groups and meetings. I don't know of any case in which the Communists have put the whole burden of convincing people and gaining members on mass communications alone. They always provide a group structure, where a convert can get reinforcement, and meetings, to which a potential convert can be drawn. They use mass media of communication almost as an adjunct to these groups. In Korea and China, the mass media actually become texts for the groups. And the Communists do one thing more. If at all possible, they secure a monopoly on the mass-communication facilities which reach the people whom they are taking over. When they took Seoul, Korea, in 1950, they confiscated radio receivers wherever they found receivers, despite the fact that they had captured intact Radio Seoul, the most powerful transmitter in that part of Asia. They were willing to give up the use of Radio Seoul, if by so doing they could keep their subjects from listening to foreign radio programs.

A state monopoly on communication, as well as control of resources and organization of a police state, is obviously a long way from our American system. As long as our mass media are permitted free criticism and reporting, and as long as they represent more than one political point of view, we have little to worry about in a political way from them. But even though we may look with revulsion at the Communist way of using mass communication, still we can study it. Let us refer back to the four elements which we said were instrumental in bringing about communication effects — message, situation, personality, and group. The Communists control the messages. By their police power, control of resources (and, hence, of food and pay), they can structure the situation as they see fit. Their group organization is most careful and offers a place — in fact compels a place — for every person. Thus, they control three of the four elements and can use those three to work on the fourth — the personalities of their receivers.

The Communists, who have now had thirty-five years' practice in the intensive use of mass communication for accomplishing specified effects, are apparently unwilling to predict the results of their communication unless they can control three of the four chief elements which enter into the effect.

Let us take one final example. There is a great deal of violence in mass-communication content today. Violence is interesting to children. Yet only a few children actually engage in acts of criminal violence. Most children do no such things. They sample the violent material and decide they would rather play football. Or they attend faithfully to the violent material, use it to clear out vicariously some of the aggressions they have been building up, and emerge none the worse for the experience. Or they adopt some of the patterns in a mild and inoffensive way when they play cops and robbers. Only a few children learn, from the mass media, techniques of crime and violence which they and their pals actually try out. Now what is it that determines which of those children will be affected harmfully by those messages of violence and which will not?

We can answer this question fairly well from cases we have studied. And the answer is simply that the other three elements — personality, situation, and group influence — will probably determine the use made of the message. If the child is busy with athletics, Scouts, church, or other wholesome activities, he is not likely to feel the need of violent and antisocial actions. On the other hand, if he is bored and frustrated, he may experiment with dangerous excitement. If he has a healthy personality, if he has learned a desirable set of values from his family group, he is less likely to give in to motivation toward violence. On the other hand, if his value standards are less certain, if he has lost some of his sense of belonging and being loved (possibly because of a broken home), he may entertain more hospitably the invitation to violence. If the group he admires has a wholesome set of standards, he is not likely to try an undesirable response, because the group will not reinforce it. On the other hand, if he belongs to a "gang," there is every reason to expect that he will try some of the violence, because in so doing he will win admiration and status in the group. Therefore, what he does will depend on the delicate balancing of these influences at a given time. Certainly no one could predict from merely seeing such a message exactly what the response to it would be. Moreover, it is entirely probable in the case we have mentioned that the community, the home, and the school — because they influence so greatly the other three elements — would have much more to do with the young person's response than would the message itself.

The all-pervasive effect of mass communication, the groundswell of learning that derives from mass communication acting as *society communicating* — this we can be sure of, and over a long period we can identify its results in our lives and beliefs. The more specific effects, however, we must predict only with caution and never from the message alone without knowing a great deal about the situation, the personality, and the group relationship where the message is to be acted upon.

MARSHALL McLUHAN

Marshall McLuhan is currently Director of the Center for Communications at Fordham University. In addition to his widely discussed Understanding Media: The Extensions of Man, *he is also the author of such controversial studies as* The Mechanical Bride *(1951) and* The Gutenberg Galaxy *(1962) and co-author with Quentin Fiore of* The Medium Is the Massage *(1967) and* War and Peace in the Global Village *(1968). With his colleague, anthropologist Edmund Carpenter, he co-edited the volume* Explorations in Communication.

The Medium Is the Message

In a culture like ours, long accustomed to splitting and dividing all things as a means of control, it is sometimes a bit of a shock to be reminded that, in operational and practical fact, the medium is the message. This is merely to say that the personal and social consequences of any medium — that is, of any extension of ourselves — result from the new scale that is introduced into our affairs by each extension of ourselves, or by any new technology. Thus, with automation, for example, the new patterns of human association tend to eliminate jobs, it is true. That is the negative result. Positively, automation creates roles for people, which is to say depth of involvement in their work and human association that our preceding mechanical technology had destroyed.

Many people would be disposed to say that it was not the machine, but what one did with the machine, that was its meaning or message. But in terms of the ways in which the machine altered our relations to one another and to ourselves, it mattered not in the least whether it turned out cornflakes or Cadillacs. The restructuring of human work and association was shaped by the technique of fragmentation that is the essence of machine technology. The essence of automation technology is the opposite. It is integral and decentralist in depth, just as the machine was fragmentary, centralist, and superficial in its patterning of human relationships.

The instance of the electric light may prove illuminating in this connection. The electric light is pure information. It is a medium without a message, as it were, unless it is used to spell out some verbal ad or name.

Adapted by the author from *Understanding Media: The Extensions of Man* by Marshall McLuhan. Copyright © 1964 by Marshall McLuhan. Reprinted with permission of McGraw Hill Book Company and Routledge & Kegan Paul Ltd.

This fact, characteristic of all media, means that the "content" of any medium is always another medium. The content of writing is speech, just as the written word is the content of print, and print is the content of the telegraph. If it is asked, "What is the content of speech?" it is necessary to say, "It is an actual process of thought, which is in itself nonverbal."

An abstract painting represents direct manifestation of creative thought processes as they might appear in computer designs. What we are considering here, however, are the psychic and social consequences of the designs or patterns as they amplify or accelerate existing processes. For the "message" of any medium or technology is the change of scale or pace or pattern that it introduces into human affairs. The railway did not introduce movement or transportation or wheel or road into human society, but it accelerated and enlarged the scale of previous human functions, no matter what freight it carried.

Let us return to the electric light. Whether the light is being used for brain surgery or night baseball makes no difference to human society. It could be argued that these activities are in some way the "content" of the electric light, since they could not exist without the electric light. This argument merely underlines the point that the medium is the message because it is the medium that shapes and controls the scale and form of human association and action. The content or uses of media are as diverse as they are ineffectual in shaping the form of human association.

Indeed, it is typical that the "content" of any medium blinds us to the character of the medium. Only today have industries become aware of the various kinds of business in which they are engaged. When IBM discovered that it was not in the business of making office equipment or business machines, but that it was in the business of processing information, then it began to navigate with clear vision. The General Electric Company makes a considerable portion of its profits from electric light bulbs and lighting systems. It has not yet discovered that, quite as much as AT&T, it is in the business of moving information.

The electric light escapes attention as a communication medium just because it has no "content." And this makes it an invaluable instance of how people fail to study media at all. For it is not till the electric light is used to spell out some brand name that it is noticed as a medium. Then it is not the light but the "content" (or what is really another medium) that is noticed. The message of the electric light is like the message of electric power in industry, totally radical, pervasive, and decentralized. For electric light and power are separate from their uses, yet they eliminate time and space factors in human association exactly as do radio, telegraph, telephone, and TV, creating involvement in depth.

In accepting an honorary degree from a university a few years ago, the chairman of the board of one of the television networks made this statement: "We are too prone to make technological instruments the scapegoats for the sins of those who wield them. The products of modern science are not in themselves good or bad; it is the way they are used that determines their value." That is the voice of the current somnambulism. Suppose we were to say, "Apple pie is in itself neither good nor bad; it is the way it is used that determines its value." Or, "The smallpox virus is in itself neither good nor bad: it is the way it is used that determines its value." Again, "Firearms are in themselves neither good nor bad; it is the way they are used that determines their value."

I am not being perverse. There is simply nothing in the speaker's statement that will bear scrutiny, for it ignores the nature of the medium, of any and all media, in the true Narcissus style of one hypnotized by the amputation and extension of his own being in a new technical form.

The paradox of mechanization is that although it is itself the cause of maximal growth and change, the principle of mechanization excludes the very possibility of growth or the understanding of change. For mechanization is achieved by fragmentation of any process and by putting the fragmented parts in a series. Yet, as David Hume showed in the eighteenth century, there is no principle of causality in a mere sequence. That one thing follows another accounts for nothing.

The greatest of all reversals occurred with electricity, which ended sequence by making things instant. With instant speed, the causes of things began to emerge to awareness again as they had not done with things in sequence. Instead of asking which came first, the chicken or the egg, it suddenly seemed that a chicken was an egg's idea for getting more eggs.

Mechanization was never so vividly fragmented or sequential as in the birth of the movies, the moment that translated us beyond mechanism into the world of growth and organic interrelation. The movie, by sheer speeding up of the mechanical, carried us from the world of sequence connections into the world of creative configuration and structure. The message of the movie medium is that of transition from lineal connections to configurations.

To a highly literate and mechanized culture, the movie appeared as a world of triumphant illusions and dreams that money could buy. It was at this moment of the movie that cubism occurred. Cubism has been described by E. H. Gombrich (*Art and Illusion*) as "the most radical attempt to stamp out ambiguity and to enforce one reading of the picture—that of a man-made construction, a colored canvas." For cubism substitutes all facets of an object simultaneously for the "point of view" or facet of perspective illusion. Instead of the specialized illusion of the third dimension on canvas, cubism sets up an interplay of planes and contradiction or dramatic conflict of patterns, lights, textures that "drives home the message" by involvement.

In other words, cubism, by giving the inside and outside, the top, bottom, back, and front and the rest, in two dimensions, drops the illusion of perspective in favor of instant sensory awareness of the whole. Cubism, by seizing on instant total awareness, suddenly announced that the medium is the message. Is it not evident that the moment that sequence yields to the simultaneous, one is in the world of the structure and of configuration? Is that not what has happened in physics as in painting, poetry, and in communication? Specialized segments of attention have shifted to total field, and we can now say quite naturally, "The medium is the message."

Before electric speed and total field, it was not obvious that the medium is the message. The message, it seemed, was the "content," as people used to ask what a painting was *about*. Yet they never thought to ask what a melody was about, nor what a house or a dress was about. In such matters, people retained some sense of the whole pattern, of form and function as a unity. But in the electric age this integral idea of structure and configuration has become so prevalent that educational theory has taken up the matter. Instead of working with specialized "problems" in arithmetic, the structural approach now follows the lines of force in the field of number and has small children meditating about number theory and "sets."

Detribalization by literacy and its traumatic effects on tribal man is the theme of a book by the psychiatrist, J. C. Carothers, *The African Mind in Health and Disease* (World Health Organization, Geneva, 1953). Much of his material reappeared in an article in *Psychiatry* magazine, November 1959, entitled "The Culture, Psychiatry, and the Written Word." Again, it is electric speed that has revealed the lines of force operating from Western technology in the remotest areas of bush, savannah, and desert. One example is the Bedouin with his battery radio on board the camel. Submerging natives with floods of concepts for which nothing has prepared them is the normal action of all of our technology. But with electric media Western man himself experiences exactly the same inundation as the remote native. We are no more prepared to encounter radio and TV in our literate milieu than the native of Ghana is able to cope with the literacy that takes him out of his collective tribal world and beaches him in individual isolation. We are as numb in our new electric world as the native involved in our literate and mechanical culture.

Electric speed mingles the cultures of prehistory with the dregs of industrial marketeers, the nonliterate with the semiliterate and the postliterate. Mental breakdown of varying degrees is the very common result of uprooting and of inundation with new information and endless new patterns of information. In our own world as we become more aware of the effects of technology on psychic formation and manifestation, we are losing all confidence in our right to assign guilt. Ancient prehistoric societies regarded violent crime as pathetic. The killer was regarded as we do a cancer victim. "How terrible it must be to feel like that," they said.

Literate man is quite inclined to see others who cannot conform as somewhat pathetic. Especially the child, the cripple, the woman, and the colored person appear in a world of visual and typographic technology as victims of injustice. On the other hand, in a culture that assigns roles instead of jobs to people—the dwarf, the eccentric, the child create their own spaces. They are not expected to fit into some uniform and repeatable niche that is not their size anyway.

Consider the phrase, "It's a man's world." As a quantitative observation endlessly repeated from within a homogenized culture, this phrase refers to the men in such a culture who have to be homogenized Dagwoods in order to belong at all. In our IQ testing we have produced the greatest flood of misbegotten standards. Unaware of our typographic cultural bias, our testers assume that uniform and continuous habits are a sign of intelligence, thus eliminating the ear man and the tactile man.

The American stake in literacy as a technology or uniformity applied to every level of education, government, industry, and social life is totally threatened by the electric technology. The electric technology is within the gates, and we are numb, deaf, blind, and mute about its encounter with the

Gutenberg technology, on and through which the American way of life was formed. It is, however, no time to suggest strategies when the threat has not even been acknowledged to exist. I am in the position of Louis Pasteur telling doctors that their greatest enemy was quite invisible, and quite unrecognized by them.

Our conventional response to all media, namely that it is how they are used that counts, is the numb stance of the technological idiot. For the "content" of a medium is like the juicy piece of meat carried by the burglar to distract the watchdog of the mind. The effect of the medium is made strong and intense just because it is given another medium as "content." The content of a movie is a novel or a play or an opera. The effect of the movie form is not related to its program content. The "content" of writing or print is speech, but the reader is almost entirely unaware either of print or of speech.

Arnold Toynbee apparently has not turned his attention to how media have shaped history. He seriously suggests that adult education is a useful counterforce to the popular press. He considers that, although all of the oriental societies have in our time accepted the industrial technology and its political consequences: "On the cultural plane . . . there is no uniform corresponding tendency." This is like the voice of the literate man, floundering in a milieu of ads, who boasts, "Personally, I pay no attention to ads."

The spiritual and cultural reservations that the oriental peoples may have about our technology will avail them not at all. The effects of technology do not occur at the level of opinions or concepts, but alter sense ratios or patterns of perception steadily and without any resistance. The serious artist is the only person able to encounter technology with impunity, just because he is an expert aware of the changes in sense perception.

The operation of the money medium in seventeenth-century Japan had effects not unlike the operation of typography in the West. The penetration of the money economy, wrote G. B. Sansom, "caused a slow but irresistible revolution, culminating in the breakdown of feudal government and the resumption of intercourse with foreign countries after more than two hundred years of seclusion." Money has reorganized the sense life of peoples just because it is an *extension* of our sense lives. This change does not depend upon approval or disapproval of those living in the society.

Arnold Toynbee made one approach to the transforming power of media in his concept of "etherialization," which he holds to be the principle of progressive simplification and efficiency in any organization or technology. Typically, he is ignoring the *effect* of the challenge of these forms upon the response of our senses. He imagines that it is the response of our opinions that is relevant to the effect of media and technology in society, a "point of view" that is plainly the result of the typographic spell. For the man in a literate and homogenized society ceases to be sensitive to the diverse and discontinuous life or forms. He acquires the illusion of the third dimension and the "private point of view" as part of his Narcissus fixation, and is quite shut off from the old truism that we become what we behold.

If the formative energies in the media are the media themselves, that raises an important consideration that can only be mentioned here, although it deserves volumes: Namely, that technological media are staples or natural resources, exactly as are coal and cotton and oil. Anybody will concede that a society whose economy is dependent upon one or two major staples like cotton or grain or lumber or fish or cattle is going to have some obvious social patterns of organization as a result.

Stress on a few major staples creates extreme instability in the economy but great endurance in the population. For a society configured by reliance on a few commodities accepts them as a social bond quite as much as the metropolis does the press. Cotton and oil, like radio and TV, become "fixed charges" on the entire psychic life of the community. And this pervasive fact creates the unique cultural flavor of any society. It pays through the nose and all its other senses for each staple that shapes its life.

That our human senses, of which all media are extensions, are also fixed charges on our personal energies and that they also configure the awareness and experience of each one of us may be perceived in another connection mentioned by the psychologist C. G. Jung:

"Every Roman was surrounded by slaves. The slave and his psychology flooded ancient Italy, and every Roman became inwardly, and of course unwittingly, a slave. Because living constantly in the atmosphere of slaves, he became infected through the unconscious with their psychology. No one can shield himself from such an influence."

Classroom Without Walls

It's natural today to speak of "audio-visual aids" to teaching, for we still think of the book as norm, of other media as incidental. We also think of the new media (press, radio, TV) as *mass media* and think of the book as an individualistic form — individualistic because it isolated the reader in silence and helped create the Western "I." Yet it was the first product of mass production.

With it everybody could have the same books. It was impossible in medieval times for different students, different institutions, to have copies of the same book. Manuscripts, commentaries, were dictated. Students memorized. Instruction was almost entirely oral, done in groups. Solitary study was reserved for the advanced scholar. The first printed books were "visual aids" to oral instruction.

Before the printing press, the young learned by listening, watching,

---

"Classroom Without Walls" by Marshall McLuhan is reprinted by permission of the Beacon Press from *Explorations in Communication*, edited by Edmund Carpenter and Marshall McLuhan. Copyright © 1960 by the Beacon Press.

doing. So, until recently, our own rural children learned the language and skills of their elders. Learning took place outside the classroom. Only those aiming at professional careers went to school at all. Today in our cities, most learning occurs outside the classroom. The sheer quantity of information conveyed by press-magazines-film-TV-radio far exceeds the quantity of information conveyed by school instruction and texts. This challenge has destroyed the monopoly of the book as a teaching aid and cracked the very walls of the classroom so suddenly that we're confused, baffled.

In this violently upsetting social situation, many teachers naturally view the offerings of the new media as entertainment, rather than education. But this carries no conviction to the student. Find a classic that wasn't first regarded as light entertainment. Nearly all vernacular works were so regarded until the 19th century.

Many movies are obviously handled with a degree of insight and maturity at least equal to the level permitted in today's textbooks. Olivier's *Henry V* and *Richard III* assemble a wealth of scholarly and artistic skill, which reveals Shakespeare at a very high level, yet in a way easy for the young to enjoy.

The movie is to dramatic representation what the book was to the manuscript. It makes available to many and at many times and places what otherwise would be restricted to a few at few times and places. The movie, like the book, is a ditto device. TV shows to 50,000,000 simultaneously. Some feel that the value of experiencing a book is diminished by being extended to many minds. This notion is always implicit in the phrases "mass media," "mass entertainment" — useless phrases obscuring the fact that English itself is a mass medium.

Today we're beginning to realize that the new media aren't just mechanical gimmicks for creating worlds of illusion, but new languages with new and unique powers of expression. Historically, the resources of English have been shaped and expressed in constantly new and changing ways. The printing press changed not only the quantity of writing but also the character of language and the relations between author and public. Radio, film, TV pushed written English toward the spontaneous shifts and freedom of the spoken idiom. They aided us in the recovery of intense awareness of facial language and bodily gesture. If these "mass media" should serve only to weaken or corrupt previously achieved levels of verbal and pictorial culture, it won't be because there's anything inherently wrong with them. It will be because we've failed to master them as new languages in time to assimilate them to our total cultural heritage.

These new developments, under quiet analytic survey, point to a basic strategy of culture for the classroom. When the printed book first appeared, it threatened the oral procedures of teaching and created the classroom as we now know it. Instead of making his own text, his own dictionary, his own grammar, the student started out with these tools. He could study not one but several languages. Today these new media threaten, instead of merely reinforce, the procedures of this traditional classroom. It's customary to answer this threat with denunciations of the unfortunate character and effect of movies and TV, just as the comic book was feared and scorned and rejected from the classroom. Its good and bad features in form and content, when carefully set beside other kinds of art and narrative, could have become a major asset to the teacher.

Where student interest is already focused is the natural point at which to be in the elucidation of other problems and interests. The educational task is not only to provide basic tools of perception but also to develop judgment and discrimination with ordinary social experience.

Few students ever acquire skill in analysis of newspapers. Fewer have any ability to discuss a movie intelligently. To be articulate and discriminating about ordinary affairs and information is the mark of an educated man. It's misleading to suppose there's any basic difference between education and entertainment. This distinction merely relieves people of the responsibility of looking into the matter. It's like setting up a distinction between didactic and lyric poetry on the ground that one teaches, the other pleases. However, it's always been true that whatever pleases teaches more effectively.

JOHN M. CULKIN, S.J.

Father John M. Culkin is a member of the Center for Communications at Fordham University.

A Schoolman's Guide to Marshall McLuhan

Education, a seven-year-old assures me, is "how kids learn stuff." Few definitions are as satisfying. It includes all that is essential—a who, a what, and a process. It excludes all the people, places, and things which are only sometimes involved in learning. The economy and accuracy of the definition, however, are more useful in locating the problem than in solving it.

From *Saturday Review*, L, March 18, 1967. Copyright Saturday Review, Inc., 1967. Reprinted by permission of the author and publisher.

We know little enough about *kids*, less about *learning*, and considerably more than we would like to know about *stuff*.

In addition, the whole process of formal schooling is now wrapped inside an environment of speeded-up technological change which is constantly influencing kids and learning and stuff. The jet-speed of this technological revolution, especially in the area of communications, has left us with more reactions to it than reflections about it. Meanwhile back at the school, the student, whose psyche is being programed for tempo, information, and relevance by his electronic environment, is still being processed in classrooms operating on the postulates of another day. The cold war existing between these two worlds is upsetting for both the student and the schools. One thing is certain: It is hardly a time for educators to plan with nostalgia, timidity, or old formulas. Enter Marshall McLuhan.

He enters from the North, from the University of Toronto where he teaches English and is director of the Center for Culture and Technology. He enters with the reputation as "the oracle of the electric age" and as "the most provocative and controversial writer of this generation." More importantly for the schools, he enters as a man with fresh eyes, with new ways of looking at old problems. He is a man who gets his ideas first and judges them later. Most of these ideas are summed up in his book, *Understanding Media*. His critics tried him for not delivering these insights in their most lucid and practical form. It isn't always cricket, however, to ask the same man to crush the grapes and serve the wine. Not all of McLu is nu or tru, but then again neither is *all* of anybody else. This article is an attempt to select and order those elements of McLuhanism which are most relevant to the schools and to provide the schoolman with some new ways of thinking about the schools.

McLuhan's promise is modest enough: "All I have to offer is an enterprise of investigation into a world that's quite unusual and quite unlike any previous world and for which no models of perception will serve." This unexplored world happens to be the present. McLuhan feels that very few men look at the present with a present eye, that they tend to miss the present by translating it into the past, seeing it through a rearview mirror. The unnoticed fact of our present is the electronic environment created by the new communications media. It is as pervasive as the air we breathe (and some would add that it is just as polluted), yet its full import eludes the judgments of commonsense or content-oriented perception. The environments set up by different media are not just containers for people; they are processes which shape people. Such influence is deterministic only if ignored. There is no inevitability as long as there is a willingness to contemplate what is happening.

Theorists can keep reality at arm's length for long periods of time. Teachers and administrators can't. They are closeted with reality all day long. In many instances they are co-prisoners with electronic-age students in the old pencil box cell. And it is the best teachers and the best students who are in the most trouble because they are challenging the system constantly. It is the system which has to come under scrutiny. Teachers and students can say, in the words of the Late Late Show, "Baby, this thing is bigger than both of us." It won't be ameliorated by a few dashes of good will or a little more hard work. It is a question of understanding these new kids and these new media and of getting the schools to deal with the new electronic environment. It's not easy. And the defenders of the old may prove to be the ones least able to defend and preserve the values of the old. For some people, analysis of these newer technologies automatically implies approbation of them. Their world is so full of *shoulds* that it is hard to squeeze in an *is*. McLuhan suggests a more positive line of exploration:

> At the moment, it is important that we understand cause and process. The aim is to develop an awareness about print and the newer technologies of communication so that we can orchestrate them, minimize their mutual frustrations and clashes, and get the best out of each in the educational process. The present conflict leads to elimination of the motive to learn and to diminution of interest in all previous achievement: It leads to loss of the sense of relevance. Without an understanding of media grammars, we cannot hope to achieve a contemporary awareness of the world in which we live.

We have been told that it is the property of true genius to disturb all settled ideas. McLuhan is disturbing in both his medium and his message. His ideas challenge the normal way in which people perceive reality. They can create a very deep and personal threat since they touch on everything in a person's experience. They are just as threatening to the establishment whose way of life is predicated on the postulates he is questioning. The establishment has no history of organizing parades to greet its disturbers.

His medium is perhaps more disturbing than his message. From his earliest work he has described his enterprise as "explorations in communication." The word he uses most frequently today is "probe." His books demand a high degree of involvement from the reader. They are poetic and intuitive rather than logical and analytic. Structurally, his unit is the sentence. Most of them are topic sentences—which are left undeveloped. The style is oral and breathless and frequently obscure. It's a different kind of medium.

"The medium is the message," announced McLuhan a dozen years ago in a cryptic and uncompromising aphorism whose meaning is still being explored. The title of his latest book, an illustrated popular paperback treatment of his theories, playfully proclaims that *The Medium Is the Massage*—a title calculated to drive typesetters and critics to hashish and beyond. The original dictum can be looked at in four ways, the third of which includes a massage of importance.

The first meaning would be better communicated orally—"The *medium* is the message." The *medium* is the thing to study. The *medium* is the thing you're missing. Everybody's hooked on content; pay attention to form, structure, framework, *medium*. The play's the thing. The medium's the thing. McLuhan makes the truth stand on its head to attract attention. Why the medium is worthy of attention derives from its other three meanings.

Meaning number two stresses the relation of the medium to the content. The form of communication not only alters the content, but each form also has preferences for certain kinds of messages. Content always exists in some form and is, therefore, to some degree governed by the dynamics of that form. If you don't know the medium, you don't know the message. The insight is neatly summed up by Dr. Edmund Carpenter: "English is a mass medium. All languages are mass media. The new mass media—film, radio, TV—are new languages, their grammars as yet unknown. Each codifies reality differently; each conceals a unique metaphysics. Linguists tell us it's possible to say anything in any language if you use enough words or images, but there's rarely time; the natural course is for a culture to exploit its media biases . . . ."

It is always content-in-form which is mediated. In this sense, the medium is co-message. The third meaning for the M-M formula emphasizes the relation of the medium to the individual psyche. The medium alters the perceptual habits of its users. Independent of the content, the medium itself gets through. Pre-literate, literate, and post-literate cultures see the world through different-colored glasses. In the process of delivering content the medium also works over the sensorium of the consumer. To get this subtle insight across, McLuhan punned on message and came up with massage. The switch is intended to draw attention to the fact that a medium is not something neutral—it does something to people. It takes hold of them, it jostles them, it bumps them around, it massages them. It opens and closes windows in their sensorium. Proof? Look out the window at the TV generation. They are rediscovering texture, movement, color, and sound as they retribalize the race. TV is a real grabber; it really massages those lazy, unused senses.

The fourth meaning underscores the relation of the medium to society. Whitehead said, "The major advances in civilization are processes that all but wreck the societies in which they occur." The media massage the society as well as the individual. The results pass unnoticed for long periods of time because people tend to view the new as just a little bit more of the old. Whitehead again: "The greatest invention of the nineteenth century was the invention of the method of invention. A new method entered into life. In order to understand our epoch, we can neglect all details of change, such as railways, telegraphs, radios, spinning machines, synthetic dyes. We must concentrate on the method in itself: That is the real novelty which has broken up the foundations of the old civilization." Understanding the medium or process involved is the key to control.

The media shape both content and consumer and do so practically undetected. We recall the story of the Russian worker whose wheelbarrow was searched every day as he left the factory grounds. He was, of course, stealing wheelbarrows. When your medium is your message and they're only investigating content, you can get away with a lot of things—like wheelbarrows, for instance. It's not the picture but the frame. Not the contents but the box. The blank page is not neutral; nor is the classroom.

McLuhan's writings abound with aphorisms, insights, for-instances, and irrelevancies which float loosely around recurring themes. They provide the raw materials of a do-it-yourself kit for tidier types who prefer to do their exploring with clearer charts. What follows is one man's McLuhan served up in barbarously brief form. Five postulates, spanning nearly 4,000 years, will serve as the fingers in this endeavor to grasp McLuhan:

1) 1967 B.C. — *All the senses get into the act.* A conveniently symmetrical year for a thesis which is partially cyclic. It gets us back to man before the Phoenician alphabet. We know from our contemporary ancestors in the jungles of New Guinea and the wastes of the Arctic that preliterate man lives in an all-at-once sense world. The reality which bombards him from all directions is picked up with the omni-directional antennae of sight, hearing, touch, smell, and taste. Films such as *The Hunters* and *Nanook of the North* depict primitive men tracking game with an across-the-board sensitivity which mystifies Western, literate man. We mystify them too. And it is this cross-mystification which makes inter-cultural abrasions so worthwhile.

Most people presume that their way of perceiving the world is *the* way of perceiving the world. If they hang around with people like themselves, their mode of perception may never be challenged. It is at the poles (literally and figuratively) that the violent contrasts illumine our own unarticulated perceptual prejudices. Toward the North Pole, for example, live Eskimos. A typical Eskimo family consists of a father, a mother, two children, and an anthropologist. When the anthropologist goes into the igloo to study Eskimos, he learns a lot about himself. Eskimos see pictures and maps equally well from all angles. They can draw equally well on top of a table or underneath it. They have phenomenal memories. They travel without visual bearings in their white-on-white world and can sketch cartographically accurate maps of shifting shorelines. They have forty or fifty words for what we call "snow." They live in a world without linearity, a world of acoustic space. They are Eskimos. Their natural way of perceiving the world is different from our natural way of perceiving the world.

Each culture develops its own balance of the senses in response to the demands of its environment. The most generalized formulation of the theory would maintain that the individual's modes of cognition and perception are influenced by the culture he is in, the language he speaks, and the media to which he is exposed. Each culture, as it were, provides its constituents with a custom-made set of goggles. The differences in perception are a question of degree. Some cultures are close enough to each other in perceptual patterns so that the differences pass unnoticed. Other cultural groups, such as the Eskimo and the American teen-ager, are far enough away from us to provide esthetic distance.

2) *Art imitates life.* In *The Silent Language* Edward T. Hall offers the thesis that all art and technology is an extension of some physical or psychic element of man. Today man has developed extensions for practically everything he used to do with his body: stone axe for hand, wheel for foot, glasses for eyes, radio for voice and ears. Money is a way of storing energy. This externalizing of individual, specialized functions is now, by definition, at its most advanced stage. Through the electronic media of telegraph, telephone, radio, and television, man has now equipped his world with a nervous system similar to the one within his own body. President Kennedy is shot and the world instantaneously reels from the impact of the bullets. Space and time dissolve under electronic conditions. Current concern for the United Nations, the Common Market, ecumenism, reflects this organic

thrust toward the new convergence and unity which is "blowing in the wind." Now in the electric age, our extended faculties and senses constitute a single instantaneous and coexistent field of experience. It's all-at-once. It's shared-by-all. McLuhan calls the world "a global village."

3) *Life imitates art.* We shape our tools and thereafter they shape us. These extensions of our senses begin to interact with our senses. These media become a massage. The new change in the environment creates a new balance among the senses. No sense operates in isolation. The full sensorium seeks fulfillment in almost every sense experience. And since there is a limited quantum of energy available for any sensory experience, the sense-ratio will differ for different media.

The nature of the sensory effect will be determined by the medium used. McLuhan divides the media according to the quality or definition of their physical signal. The content is not relevant in this kind of analysis. The same picture from the same camera can appear as a glossy photograph or as a newspaper wirephoto. The photograph is well-defined, of excellent pictorial quality, hi-fi within its own medium. McLuhan calls this kind of medium "hot." The newspaper photo is grainy, made up of little dots, low definition. McLuhan calls this kind of medium "cool." Film is hot; television is cool. Radio is hot; telephone is cool. The cool medium or person invites participation and involvement. It leaves room for the response of the consumer. A lecture is hot; all the work is done. A seminar is cool; it gets everyone into the game. Whether all the connections are causal may be debated, but it's interesting that the kids of the cool TV generation want to be so involved and so much a part of what's happening.

4) *We shaped the alphabet and it shaped us.* In keeping with the McLuhan postulate that "the medium is the message," a literate culture should be more than mildly eager to know what books do to people. Everyone is familiar enough with all the enrichment to living mediated through fine books to allow us to pass on to the subtler effects which might be attributed to the print medium independent of the content involved. Whether one uses the medium to say that *God is dead* or that *God is love* (--- -- ----), the structure of the medium itself remains unchanged. Nine little black marks with no intrinsic meaning of their own are strung along a line with spaces left after the third and fifth marks. It is this stripping away of meaning which allows us to X-ray the form itself.

As an example, while lecturing to a large audience in a modern hotel in Chicago, a distinguished professor is bitten in the leg by a cobra. The whole experience takes three seconds. He is affected through the touch of the reptile, the gasp of the crowd, the swimming sights before his eyes. His memory, imagination, and emotions come into emergency action. A lot of things happen in three seconds. Two weeks later he is fully recovered and wants to write up the experience in a letter to a colleague. To communicate this experience through print means that it must first be broken down into parts and then mediated, eyedropper fashion, one thing at a time, in an abstract, linear, fragmented, sequential way. That is the essential structure of print. And once a culture uses such a medium for a few centuries, it begins to perceive the world in a one-thing-at-a-time, abstract, linear, fragmented, sequential way. And it shapes its organizations and schools according to the same premises. The form of print has become the form of thought. The medium has become the message.

For centuries now, according to McLuhan, the straight line has been the hidden metaphor of literate man. It was unconsciously but inexorably used as the measure of things. It went unnoticed, unquestioned. It was presumed as natural and universal. It is neither. Like everything else it is good for the things it is good for. To say that it is not everything is not to say that it is nothing. The electronic media have broken the monopoly of print; they have altered our sensory profiles by heightening our awareness of aural, tactile, and kinetic values.

5) 1967 A.D. — *All the senses want to get into the act*. Print repressed most sense-life in favor of the visual. The end of print's monopoly also marks the end of a visual monopoly. As the early warning system of art and popular culture indicates, all the senses want to get into the act. Some of the excesses in the current excursions into aural, oral, tactile, and kinetic experience may in fact be directly responsive to the sensory deprivation of the print culture. Nature abhors a vacuum. No one glories in the sight of kids totally out of control in reaction to the Beatles. Some say, "What are the Beatles doing to these kids?" others say, "What have we done to these kids?" All the data isn't in on what it means to be a balanced human being.

Kids are what the game is all about. Given an honest game with enough equipment to go around, it is the mental, emotional, and volitional capacity of the student which most determines the outcome. The whole complicated system of formal education is in business to get through to kids, to motivate kids, to help kids learn stuff. Schools are not in business to label kids, to grade them for the job market or to babysit. They are there to communicate with them.

Communication is a funny business. There isn't as much of it going on as most people think. Many feel that it consists in saying things in the presence of others. Not so. It consists not in saying things but in having things heard. Beautiful English speeches delivered to monolingual Arabs are not beautiful speeches. You have to speak the language of the audience — of the *whom* in the "who-says-what-to-whom" communications diagram. Sometimes the language is lexical (Chinese, Japanese, Portuguese), sometimes it is regional or personal (125th Street-ese, Holden Caulfield-ese, anybody-ese). It has little to do with words and much to do with understanding the audience. The word for good communication is "Whom-ese" — the language of the audience, of the "whom."

All good communicators use Whom-ese. The best writers, film-makers, advertising men, lovers, preachers, and teachers all have the knack for thinking about the hopes, fears, and capacity of the other person and of being able to translate their communication into terms which are *relevant* for that person. Whitehead called "inert ideas" the bane of education. Relevance, however, is one of those subjective words. It doesn't pertain to the object in itself but to the object as perceived by someone. The school may decide that history is *important for* the student, but the role of the teacher is to make history *relevant to* the student.

If *what* has to be tailored to the *whom*, the teacher has to be constantly engaged in audience research. It's not a question of keeping up with the latest slang or of selling out to the current mores of the kids. Neither of these tactics helps either learning or kids. But it is a question of knowing what values are strong in their world, of understanding the obstacles to communication, of sensing their style of life. Communication doesn't have to end there, but it can start nowhere else. If they are tuned in to FM and you are broadcasting on AM, there's no communication. Communication forces you to pay a lot of attention to other people.

McLuhan has been paying a great deal of attention to modern kids. Of necessity they live in the present since they have no theories to diffract or reflect what is happening. They are also the first generation to be born into a world in which there was always television. McLuhan finds them a great deal different from their counterparts at the turn of the century when the electric age was just getting up steam.

A lot of things have happened since 1900 and most of them plug into walls. Today's six-year-old has already learned a lot of stuff by the time he shows up for the first day of school. Soon after his umbilical cord was cut he was planted in front of a TV set "to keep him quiet." He liked it enough there to stay for some 3,000 to 4,000 hours before he started the first grade. By the time he graduates from high school he has clocked 15,000 hours of TV time and 10,800 hours of school time. He lives in a world which bombards him from all sides with information from radios, films, telephones, magazines, recordings, and people. He learns more things from the windows of cars, trains, and even planes. Through travel and communications he has experienced the war in Vietnam, the wide world of sports, the civil rights movement, the death of a President, thousands of commercials, a walk in space, a thousand innocuous shows, and, one may hope, plenty of Captain Kangaroo.

This is all merely descriptive, an effort to lay out what *is*, not what should be. Today's student can hardly be described by any of the old educational analogies comparing him to an empty bucket or a blank page. He comes to the information machine called school and he is already brimming over with information. As he grows his standards for relevance are determined more by what he receives outside the school than what he receives inside. A recent Canadian film tells the story of a bright, articulate middle class teen-ager who leaves school because there's "no reason to stay." He daydreams about Vietnam while his teacher drones on about the four reasons for the spread of Christianity and the five points such information is worth on the exam. Only the need for a diploma was holding him in school; learning wasn't, and he left. He decided the union ticket wasn't worth the gaff. He left. Some call him a dropout. Some call him a pushout.

The kids have one foot on the dock and one foot on the ferryboat. Living in two centuries makes for that kind of tension. The gap between the classroom and the outside world and the gap between the generations is wider than it has ever been. Those tedious people who quote Socrates on the conduct of the young are trying vainly to reassure themselves that this is just the perennial problem of communication between generations. 'Tain't so. "Today's child is growing up absurd, because he lives in two worlds, and neither of them inclines him to grow up," says McLuhan in

The Medium Is the Massage. "Growing up—that is our new work, and it is *total.* Mere instruction will not suffice."

Learning is something that people do for themselves. People, places, and things can facilitate or impede learning; they can't make it happen without some cooperation from the learner. The learner these days comes to school with a vast reservoir of vicarious experiences and loosely related facts; he wants to use all his senses in his learning as an active agent in the process of discovery; he knows that all the answers aren't in. The new learner is the result of the new media, says McLuhan. And a new learner calls for a new kind of learning.

Leo Irrera said, "If God had anticipated the eventual structure of the school system, surely he would have shaped man differently." Kids are being tailored to fit the Procrustean forms of schedules, classrooms, memorizing, testing, etc., which are frequently relics from an obsolete approach to learning. It is the total environment which contains the philosophy of education, not the title page in the school catalogue. And it is the total environment which is invincible because it is invisible to most people. They tend to move things around within the old boxes or to build new and cleaner boxes. They should be asking whether or not there should be a box in the first place.

The new learner, who is the product of the all-at-once electronic environment, often feels out of it in a linear, one-thing-at-a-time school environment. The total environment is now the great teacher; the student has competence models against which to measure the effectiveness of his teachers. Nuclear students in linear schools make for some tense times in education. Students with well developed interests in science, the arts and humanities, or current events need assistance to suit their pace, not that of the state syllabus. The straight line theory of development and the uniformity of performance which it so frequently encourages just don't fit many needs of the new learner. Interestingly, the one thing which most of the current educational innovations share is their break with linear or print-oriented patterns: team teaching, nongraded schools, audio-lingual language training, multi-media learning situations, seminars, student research at all levels of education, individualized learning, and the whole shift of responsibility for learning from the teacher to the student. Needless to say, these are not as widespread as they should be, nor were they brought about through any conscious attention to the premises put forward by McLuhan. Like the print-oriented and linear mentality they now modify, these premises were plagiarized from the atmosphere. McLuhan's value is in the power he gives us to predict and control these changes.

There is too much stuff to learn today. McLuhan calls it an age of "information overload." And the information levels outside the classroom are now higher than those in the classroom. Schools used to have a virtual monopoly on information; now they are part-time competitors in the electronic informational surround. And all human knowledge is expanding at computer speed.

Every choice involves a rejection. If we can't do everything, what priorities will govern our educational policies? "The medium is the message" may not be bad for openers. We can no longer teach kids all about a subject; we can teach them what a subject is all about. We have to introduce them to the form, structure, gestalt, grammar, and process of the knowledge involved. What does a math man do when a math man does do math? This approach to the formal element of a discipline can provide a channel of communication between specialists. Its focus is not on content or detail but on the postulates, ground rules, frames of reference, and premises of each discipline. It stresses the modes of cognition and perception proper to each field. Most failures in communication are based on disagreement about items which are only corollaries of a larger thesis. It happens between disciplines, individuals, media, and cultures.

The arts play a new role in education because they are explorations in perception. Formerly conceived as a curricular luxury item, they now become a dynamic way of tuning up the sensorium and of providing fresh ways of looking at familiar things. When exploration and discovery become the themes, the old lines between art and science begin to fade. We have to guide students to becoming their own data processors to operate through pattern recognition. The media themselves serve as both aids to learning and as proper objects of study in this search for an all-media literacy. Current interest in film criticism will expand to include all art and communication forms.

And since the knowledge explosion has blown out the walls between subjects, there will be a continued move toward interdisciplinary swapping and understanding. Many of the categorical walls between things are artifacts left over from the packaging days of print. The specialist's life will be even lonelier as we move further from the Gutenberg era. The trends are all toward wholeness and convergence.

These things aren't true just because Marshall McLuhan says they are. They work. They explain problems in education that nobody else is laying a glove on. When presented clearly and with all the necessary examples and footnotes added, they have proven to be a liberating force for hundreds of teachers who were living through the tension of this cultural fission without realizing that the causes for the tension lay outside themselves. McLuhan's relevance for education demands the work of teams of simultaneous translators and researchers who can both shape and substantiate the insights which are scattered through his work. McLuhan didn't invent electricity or put kids in front of TV sets; he is merely trying to describe what's happening out there so that it can be dealt with intelligently. When someone warns you of an oncoming truck, it's frightfully impolite to accuse him of driving the thing. McLuhan can help kids to learn stuff better.

EDMUND CARPENTER

Anthropologist Edmund Carpenter is presently associated with communications theorist Marshall McLuhan at the Center for Communications at Fordham University. For a period of time he was co-editor, with McLuhan, of the journal Explorations, *which dealt with advanced thinking in the area of communications. He and McLuhan also co-edited the book* Explorations in Communication *which contains a selection of articles from that journal.*

The New Languages

English is a mass medium. All languages are mass media. The new mass media—film, radio, TV—are new languages, their grammars as yet unknown. Each codifies reality differently; each conceals a unique metaphysics. Linguists tell us it's possible to say anything in any language if you use enough words or images, but there's rarely time; the natural course is for a culture to exploit its media biases.

Writing, for example, didn't record oral language; it was a new language, which the spoken word came to imitate. Writing encouraged an analytical mode of thinking with emphasis upon lineality. Oral languages tended to be polysynthetic, composed of great, tight conglomerates, like twisted knots, within which images were juxtaposed, inseparably fused; written communications consisted of little words chronologically ordered. Subject became distinct from verb, adjective from noun, thus separating actor from action, essence from form. Where preliterate man imposed form diffidently, temporarily—for such transitory forms lived but temporarily on the tip of his tongue, in the living situation—the printed word was inflexible, permanent, in touch with eternity: it embalmed truth for posterity.

This embalming process froze language, eliminated the art of ambiguity, made puns "the lowest form of wit," destroyed word linkages. The word became a static symbol, applicable to and separate from that which it symbolized. It now belonged to the objective world; it could be seen. Now came the distinction between being and meaning, the dispute as to whether the Eucharist *was* or only *signified* the body of the Sacrifice. The word became a neutral symbol, no longer an inextricable part of a creative process.

Gutenberg completed the process. The manuscript page with pictures, colors, correlation between symbol and space, gave way to uniform type, the black-and-white page, read silently, alone. The format of the book favored lineal expression, for the argument ran like a thread from cover to cover: subject to verb to object, sentence to sentence, paragraph to paragraph, chapter to chapter, carefully structured from beginning to end, with value embedded in the climax. This was not true of great poetry and drama, which retained multi-perspective, but it was true of most books, particularly texts, histories, autobiographies, novels. Events were arranged chronologically and hence, it was assumed, causally; relationship, not being, was valued. The author became an *authority*; his data were serious, that is, *serially* organized. Such data, if sequentially ordered and printed, conveyed value and truth; arranged any other way, they were suspect.

The newspaper format brought an end to book culture. It offers short, discrete articles that give important facts first and then taper off to incidental details, which may be, and often are, eliminated by the make-up man. The fact that reporters cannot control the length of their articles means that, in writing them, emphasis can't be placed on structure, at least in the traditional linear sense, with climax or conclusion at the end. Everything has to be captured in the headline; from there it goes down the pyramid to incidentals. In fact there is often more in the headline than in the article; occasionally, no article at all accompanies the banner headline.

The position and size of articles on the front page are determined by interest and importance, not content. Unrelated reports from Moscow, Sarawak, London, and Ittipik are juxtaposed; time and space, as separate concepts, are destroyed and the *here* and *now* presented as a single Gestalt. Subway readers consume everything on the front page, then turn to page 2 to read, in incidental order, continuations. A Toronto banner headline ran: TOWNSEND TO MARRY PRINCESS; directly beneath this was a second headline: *Fabian Says This May Not Be Sex Crime*. This went unnoticed by eyes and minds conditioned to consider each newspaper item in isolation.

Such a format lends itself to simultaneity, not chronology or lineality. Items abstracted from a total situation aren't arranged in causal sequence, but presented holistically, as raw experience. The front page is a cosmic *Finnegans Wake*.

The disorder of the newspaper throws the reader into a producer role. The reader has to process the news himself; he has to co-create, to cooperate in the creation of the work. The newspaper format calls for the direct participation of the consumer.

In magazines, where a writer more frequently controls the length of his article, he can, if he wishes, organize it in traditional style, but the majority don't. An increasingly popular presentation is the printed symposium, which is little more than collected opinions, pro and con. The magazine format as a whole opposes lineality; its pictures lack tenses. In *Life*, extremes are juxtaposed: space ships and prehistoric monsters, Flemish monasteries and dope addicts. It creates a sense of urgency and uncertainty: the next page is unpredictable. One encounters rapidly a riot in Teheran, a Hollywood marriage, the wonders of the Eisenhower administration, a two-headed calf, a party on Jones beach, all sandwiched between ads. The eye takes in the page as a whole (readers may pretend this isn't so, but the success of advertising suggests it is), and the page—indeed, the whole magazine—becomes a single Gestalt where association, though not causal, is often lifelike.

The same is true of the other new languages. Both radio and TV offer short, unrelated programs, interrupted between and within by commercials. I say "interrupted," being myself an anachronism of book culture, but my children don't regard them as interruptions, as breaking continuity. Rather, they regard them as part of a whole, and their reaction is neither one of annoyance nor one of indifference. The ideal news broadcast has half a dozen speakers from as many parts of the world on as many subjects. The London correspondent doesn't comment on what the Washington correspondent has just said; he hasn't even heard him.

The child is right in not regarding commercials as interruptions. For the only time anyone smiles on TV is in commercials. The rest of life, in news broadcasts and soap operas, is presented as so horrible that the only way to get through life is to buy this product: then you'll smile. Aesop never wrote a clearer fable. It's heaven and hell brought up to date: Hell in the headline, Heaven in the ad. Without the other, neither has meaning.

There's pattern in these new media—not line, but knot; not lineality or causality or chronology, nothing that leads to a desired climax; but a Gordian knot without antecedents or results, containing within itself carefully selected elements, juxtaposed, inseparably fused; a knot that can't be untied to give the long, thin cord of lineality.

This is especially true of ads that never present an ordered, sequential, rational argument but simply present the product associated with desirable things or attitudes. Thus Coca-Cola is shown held by a beautiful blonde, who sits in a Cadillac, surrounded by bronze, muscular admirers, with the sun shining overhead. By repetition these elements become associated, in our minds, into a pattern of sufficient cohesion so that one element can magically evoke the others. If we think of ads as designed solely to sell products, we miss their main effect: to increase pleasure in the consumption of the product. Coca-Cola is far more than a cooling drink; the consumer participates, vicariously, in a much larger experience. In Africa, in Melanesia, to drink a Coke is to participate in the American way of life.

Of the new languages, TV comes closest to drama and ritual. It combines music and art, language and gesture, rhetoric and color. It favors simultaneity of visual and auditory images. Cameras focus not on speakers but on persons spoken to or about; the audience *hears* the accuser but *watches* the accused. In a single impression it hears the prosecutor, watches the trembling hands of the big-town crook, and sees the look of moral indignation on Senator Tobey's face. This is real drama, in process, with the outcome uncertain. Print can't do this; it has a different bias.

Books and movies only pretend uncertainty, but live TV retains this vital aspect of life. Seen on TV, the fire in the 1952 Democratic Convention threatened briefly to become a conflagration; seen on newsreel, it was history, without potentiality.

The absence of uncertainty is no handicap to other media, if they are properly used, for their biases are different. Thus it's clear from the beginning that Hamlet is a doomed man, but, far from detracting in interest, this heightens the sense of tragedy.

Now, one of the results of the time-space duality that developed in Western culture, principally from the Renaissance on, was a separation within the arts. Music, which created symbols in time, and graphic art, which created symbols in space, became separate pursuits, and men gifted in one rarely pursued the other. Dance and ritual, which inherently combined them, fell in popularity. Only in drama did they remain united.

It is significant that of the four new media, the three most recent are dramatic media, particularly TV, which combines language, music, art, dance. They don't, however, exercise the same freedom with time that the stage dares practice. An intricate plot, employing flash backs, multiple time perspectives and overlays, intelligible on the stage, would mystify on the screen. The audience has no time to think back, to establish relations between early hints and subsequent discoveries. The picture passes before the eyes too quickly; there are no intervals in which to take stock of what has happened and make conjectures of what is going to happen. The observer is in a more passive state, less interested in subtleties. Both TV and film are nearer to narrative and depend much more upon the episodic. An intricate time construction can be done in film, but in fact rarely is. The soliloquies of *Richard III* belong on the stage; the film audience was unprepared for them. On stage Ophelia's death was described by three separate groups: one hears the announcement and watches the reactions simultaneously. On film the camera flatly shows her drowned where "a willow lies aslant a brook."

Media differences such as these mean that it's not simply a question of communicating a single idea in different ways but that a given idea or insight belongs primarily, though not exclusively, to one medium, and can be gained or communicated best through that medium.

Thus the book was ideally suited for discussing evolution and progress. Both belonged, almost exclusively, to book culture. Like a book, the idea of progress was an abstracting, organizing principle for the interpretation and comprehension of the incredibly complicated record of human experience. The sequence of events was believed to have a direction, to follow a given course along an axis of time; it was held that civilization, like the reader's eye (in J. B. Bury's words), "has moved, is moving, and will move in a desirable direction. Knowledge will advance, and with that advance, reason and decency must increasingly prevail among men." Here we see the three main elements of book lineality: the line, the point moving along that line, and its movement toward a desirable goal.

The Western conception of a definite moment in the present, of the present as a definite moment or a definite point, so important in book-dominated languages, is absent, to my knowledge, in oral languages. Absent as well, in oral societies, are such animating and controlling ideas as Western individualism and three-dimensional perspective, both related to this conception of the definite moment, and both nourished, probably bred, by book culture.

Each medium selects its ideas. TV is a tiny box into which people are crowded and must live; film gives us the wide world. With its huge screen, film is perfectly suited for social drama, Civil War panoramas, the sea, land erosion, Cecil B. DeMille spectaculars. In contrast, the TV screen has room for two, at the most three, faces, comfortably. TV is closer to stage, yet different. Paddy Chayefsky writes:

> The theatre audience is far away from the actual action of the drama. They cannot see the silent reactions of the players. They must be told in a loud voice what is going on. The plot movement from one scene to another must be marked, rather than gently shaded as is required in television. In television, however, you can dig into the most humble, ordinary relationships; the relationship of bourgeois children to their mother, of middle-class husband to his wife, of white-collar father to his secretary—in short, the relationships of the people. We relate to each other in an incredibly complicated manner. There is far more exciting drama in the reasons why a man gets married than in why he murders someone. The man who is unhappy in his job, the wife who thinks of a lover, the girl who wants to get into television, your father, your mother, sister, brothers, cousins, friends—all these are better subjects for drama than Iago. What makes a man ambitious? Why does a girl always try to steal her kid sister's boy friends? Why does your uncle attend his annual class reunion faithfully every year? Why do you always find it depressing to visit your father? These are the substances of good television drama; and the deeper you probe into and examine the twisted, semi-formed complexes of emotional entanglements, the more exciting your writing becomes.[1]

This is the primary reason, I believe, why Greek drama is more readily adapted to TV than to film. The boxed-in quality of live TV lends itself to static literary tragedy with greater ease than does the elastic, energetic, expandable movie. Guthrie's recent movie of *Oedipus* favored the panoramic shot rather than the selective eye. It consisted of a succession of tableaux, a series of elaborate, unnatural poses. The effect was of congested groups of people moving in tight formation as though they had trained for it by living for days together in a self-service elevator. With the lines, "I grieve for the City, and for myself and you . . . and walk through endless ways of thought," the inexorable tragedy moved to its horrible "come to realize" climax as though everyone were stepping on everyone else's feet.

The tight, necessary conventions of live TV were more sympathetic to Sophocles in the Aluminium Hour's *Antigone*. Restrictions of space are imposed on TV as on the Greek stage by the size and inflexibility of the studio. Squeezed by physical limitations, the producer was forced to expand the viewer's imagination with ingenious devices.

When T. S. Eliot adapted *Murder in the Cathedral* for film, he noted a difference in realism between cinema and stage:

---

1. *Television Plays* (New York: Simon and Schuster, Inc., 1955), pp. 176–178. Reprinted by permission of the publisher.

> *Cinema, even where fantasy is introduced, is much more realistic than the stage. Especially in an historical picture, the setting, the costume, and the way of life represented have to be accurate. Even a minor anachronism is intolerable. On the stage much more can be overlooked or forgiven; and indeed, an excessive care for accuracy of historical detail can become burdensome and distracting. In watching a stage performance, the member of the audience is in direct contact with the actor playing a part. In looking at a film, we are much more passive; as audience, we contribute less. We are seized with the illusion that we are observing an actual event, or at least a series of photographs of the actual event; and nothing must be allowed to break this illusion. Hence the precise attention to detail.*[2]

If two men are on a stage in a theatre, the dramatist is obliged to motivate their presence; he has to account for their existing on the stage at all. Whereas if a camera is following a figure down a street or is turned to any object whatever, there is no need for a reason to be provided. Its grammar contains that power of statement of motivation, no matter what it looks at.

In the theatre, the spectator sees the enacted scene as a whole in space, always seeing the whole of the space. The stage may present only one corner of a large hall, but that corner is always totally visible all through the scene. And the spectator always sees that scene from a fixed, unchanging distance and from an angle of vision that doesn't change. Perspective may change from scene to scene, but within one scene it remains constant. Distance never varies.

But in film and TV, distance and angle constantly shift. The same scene is shown in multiple perspective and focus. The viewer sees it from here, there, then over here; finally he is drawn inexorably into it, becomes part of it. He ceases to be a spectator. Balázs writes:

> *Athough we sit in our seats, we do not see Romeo and Juliet from there. We look up into Juliet's balcony with Romeo's eyes and look down on Romeo with Juliet's. Our eye and with it our consciousness is identified with the characters in the film, we look at the world out of their eyes and have no angle of vision of our own. We walk amid crowds, ride, fly or fall with the hero and if one character looks into the other's eyes, he looks into our eyes from the screen, for, our eyes are in the camera and become identical with the gaze of the characters. They see with our eyes. Herein lies the psychological act of identification. Nothing like this "identification" has ever occurred as the effect of any other system of art and it is here that the film manifests its absolute artistic novelty.*
> *. . . Not only can we see, in the isolated "shots" of a scene, the very atoms of life and their innermost secrets revealed at close*

---

2. George Hoellering and T. S. Eliot, *Film of Murder in the Cathedral* (New York: Harcourt, Brace and Company, 1952), p. vi (London: Faber & Faber, Ltd., 1952). Reprinted by permission of the publisher.

> quarters, but we can do so without any of the intimate secrecy being
> lost, as always happens in the exposure of a stage performance or of
> a painting. The new theme which the new means of expression of
> film art revealed was not a hurricane at sea or the eruption of a vol-
> cano: it was perhaps a solitary tear slowly welling up in the corner
> of a human eye.
>   . . . Not to speak does not mean that one has nothing to say.
> Those who do not speak may be brimming over with emotions which
> can be expressed only in forms and pictures, in gesture and play of
> feature. The man of visual culture uses these not as substitutes for
> words, as a deaf-mute uses his fingers.[3]

The gestures of visual man are not intended to convey concepts that
can be expressed in words, but inner experiences, nonrational emotions,
which would still remain unexpressed when everything that can be told
has been told. Such emotions lie in the deepest levels. They cannot be approached by words that are mere reflections of concepts, any more than
musical experiences can be expressed in rational concepts. Facial expression is a human experience rendered immediately visible without the inter-
mediary of word. It is Turgenev's "living truth of the human face."

Printing rendered illegible the faces of men. So much could be read
from paper that the method of conveying meaning by facial expression fell
into desuetude. The press grew to be the main bridge over which the more
remote interhuman spiritual exchanges took place; the immediate, the personal, the inner, died. There was no longer need for the subtler means of
expression provided by the body. The face became immobile; the inner life,
still. Wells that dry up are wells from which no water is dipped.

Just as radio helped bring back inflection in speech, so film and TV are
aiding us in the recovery of gesture and facial awareness—a rich, colorful
language, conveying moods and emotions, happenings and characters,
even thoughts, none of which could be properly packaged in words. If film
had remained silent for another decade, how much faster this change might
have been!

Feeding the product of one medium through another medium creates a
new product. When Hollywood buys a novel, it buys a title and the publicity
associated with it: nothing more. Nor should it.

Each of the four versions of the *Caine Mutiny*—book, play, movie, TV
—had a different hero: Willie Keith, the lawyer Greenwald, the United States
Navy, and Captain Queeg, respectively. Media and audience biases were
clear. Thus the book told, in lengthy detail, of the growth and making of
Ensign William Keith, American man, while the movie camera with its colorful shots of ships and sea, unconsciously favored the Navy as hero, a bias
supported by the fact the Navy cooperated with the movie makers. Because
of stage limitations, the play was confined, except for the last scene, to the
courtroom, and favored the defense counsel as hero. The TV show, aimed at
a mass audience, emphasized patriotism, authority, allegiance. More im-

---

3. Béla Balázs, *Theory of Film* (New York, Roy Publishers, Inc., 1953), pp. 48, 31, and 40; (London: Denis Dobson, 1952). Reprinted by permission of the publishers.

portant, the cast was reduced to the principals and the plot to its principles; the real moral problem — the refusal of subordinates to assist an incompetent, unpopular superior — was clear, whereas in the book it was lost under detail, in the film under scenery. Finally, the New York play, with its audience slanted toward Expense Account patronage — Mr. Sampson, Western Sales Manager for the Cavity Drill Company — became a morality play with Willie Keith, innocent American youth, torn between two influences: Keefer, clever author but moral cripple, and Greenwald, equally brilliant but reliable, a businessman's intellectual. Greenwald saves Willie's soul.

The film *Moby Dick* was in many ways an improvement on the book, primarily because of its explicitness. For *Moby Dick* is one of those admittedly great classics, like *Robinson Crusoe* or Kafka's *Trial*, whose plot and situation, as distilled apart from the book by time and familiarity, are actually much more imposing than the written book itself. It's the drama of Ahab's defiance rather than Melville's uncharted leviathan meanderings that is the greatness of *Moby Dick*. On film, instead of laborious tacks through leagues of discursive interruptions, the most vivid descriptions of whales and whaling become part of the action. On film, the viewer was constantly aboard ship: each scene an instantaneous shot of whaling life, an effect achieved in the book only by illusion, by constant, detailed reference. From start to finish, all the action of the film served to develop what was most central to the theme — a man's magnificent and blasphemous pride in attempting to destroy the brutal, unreasoning force that maims him and turns man-made order into chaos. Unlike the book, the film gave a spare, hard, compelling dramatization, free of self-conscious symbolism.

Current confusion over the respective roles of the new media comes largely from a misconception of their function. They are art-forms, not substitutes for human contact. Insofar as they attempt to usurp speech and personal, living relations, they harm. This, of course, has long been one of the problems of book culture, at least during the time of its monopoly of Western middle-class thought. But this was never a legitimate function of books, nor of any other medium. Whenever a medium goes claim jumping, trying to work areas where it is ill-suited, conflicts occur with other media, or, more accurately, between the vested interests controlling each. But, when media simply exploit their own formats, they become complementary and cross-fertile.

Some people who have no one around talk to cats, and you can hear their voices in the next room, and they sound silly, because the cat won't answer, but that suffices to maintain the illusion that their world is made up of living people, while it is not. Mechanized mass media reverse this: now mechanical cats talk to humans. There's no genuine feedback.

This charge is often leveled by academicians at the new media, but it holds equally for print. The open-mouthed, glaze-eyed TV spectator is merely the successor of the passive, silent, lonely reader whose head moved back and forth like a shuttlecock.

When we read, another person thinks for us: we merely repeat his mental process. The greater part of the work of thought is done for us. This is why it relieves us to take up a book after being occupied by our own thoughts. In reading, the mind is only the playground for another's ideas.

People who spend most of their lives in reading often lose the capacity for thinking, just as those who always ride forget how to walk. Some people read themselves stupid. Chaplin did a wonderful take-off of this in *City Lights*, when he stood up on a chair to eat the endless confetti that he mistook for spaghetti.

Eliot remarks: "It is often those writers whom we are lucky enough to know whose books we can ignore; and the better we know them personally, the less need we may feel to read what they write."

Frank O'Connor highlights a basic distinction between oral and written traditions: " 'By the hokies, there was a man in this place one time by name of Ned Sullivan, and he had a queer thing happen to him late one night and he coming up the Valley Road from Durlas.' This is how a folk story begins, or should begin . . . . Yet that is how no printed short story should begin, because such a story seems tame when you remove it from its warm nest by the cottage fire, from the sense of an audience with its interjections, and the feeling of terror at what may lurk in the darkness outside."

Face-to-face discourse is not as selective, abstract, nor explicit as any mechanical medium; it probably comes closer to communicating an unabridged situation than any of them, and, insofar as it exploits the give-take of dynamic relationship, it's clearly the most indispensably human one.

Of course, there can be personal involvement in the other media. When Richardson's *Pamela* was serialized in 1741, it aroused such interest that in one English town, upon receipt of the last installment, the church bell announced that virtue had been rewarded. Radio stations have reported receiving quantities of baby clothes and bassinets when, in a soap opera, a heroine had a baby. One of the commonest phrases used by devoted listeners to daytime serials is that they "visited with" Aunt Jenny or Big Sister. BBC and *News Chronicle* report cases of women viewers who kneel before TV sets to kiss male announcers good night.

Each medium, if its bias is properly exploited, reveals and communicates a unique aspect of reality, of truth. Each offers a different perspective, a way of seeing an otherwise hidden dimension of reality. It's not a question of one reality being true, the others distortions. One allows us to see from here, another from there, a third from still another perspective; taken together they give us a more complete whole, a greater truth. New essentials are brought to the fore, including those made invisible by the "blinders" of old languages.

This is why the preservation of book culture is as important as the development of TV. This is why new languages, instead of destroying old ones, serve as a stimulant to them. Only monopoly is destroyed. When actor-collector Edward G. Robinson was battling actor-collector Vincent Price on art on TV's *$64,000 Challenge*, he was asked how the quiz had affected his life; he answered petulantly, "Instead of looking at the pictures in my art books, I now have to read them." Print, along with all old languages, including speech, has profited enormously from the development of the new media. "The more the arts develop," writes E. M. Forster, "the more they depend on each other for definition. We will borrow from painting first and call it pattern. Later we will borrow from music and call it rhythm."

The appearance of a new medium often frees older media for creative effort. They no longer have to serve the interests of power and profit. Elia Kazan, discussing the American theatre, says:

> Take 1900 - 1920. The theatre flourished all over the country. It had no competition. The box office boomed. The top original fare it had to offer was The Girl of the Golden West. Its bow to culture was fusty productions of Shakespeare . . . . Came the moving pictures. The theatre had to be better or go under. It got better. It got so spectacularly better so fast that in 1920–1930 you wouldn't have recognized it. Perhaps it was an accident that Eugene O'Neill appeared at that moment—but it was no accident that in that moment of strange competition, the theatre had room for him. Because it was disrupted and hard pressed, it made room for his experiments, his unheard-of subjects, his passion, his power. There was room for him to grow to his full stature. And there was freedom for the talents that came after his.[4]

Yet a new language is rarely welcomed by the old. The oral tradition distrusted writing, manuscript culture was contemptuous of printing, book culture hated the press, that "slag-heap of hellish passions," as one 19th century scholar called it. A father, protesting to a Boston newspaper about crime and scandal, said he would rather see his children "in their graves while pure in innocence, than dwelling with pleasure upon these reports, which have grown so bold."

What really disturbed book-oriented people wasn't the sensationalism of the newspaper, but its nonlineal format, its nonlineal codifications of experience. The motto of conservative academicians became: *Hold that line!*

A new language lets us see with the fresh, sharp eyes of the child; it offers the pure joy of discovery. I was recently told a story about a Polish couple who, though long resident in Toronto, retained many of the customs of their homeland. Their son despaired of ever getting his father to buy a suit cut in style or getting his mother to take an interest in Canadian life. Then he bought them a TV set, and in a matter of months a major change took place. One evening the mother remarked that "Edith Piaf is the latest thing on Broadway," and the father appeared in "the kind of suit executives wear on TV." For years the father had passed this same suit in store windows and seen it both in advertisements and on living men, but not until he saw it on TV did it become meaningful. This same statement goes for all media: each offers a unique presentation of reality, which when new has a freshness and clarity that is extraordinarily powerful.

This is especially true of TV. We say, "We have a radio" but "We have television"—as if something had happened to us. It's no longer "The skin

4. "Writers and Motion Pictures," The Atlantic Monthly, No. 199, (1957), p. 69. Copyright © 1957 by Newtown Productions, Inc. Reprinted by permission of the author.

you love to touch" but "The Nylon that loves to touch you." We don't watch TV; it watches us: it guides us. Magazines and newspapers no longer convey "information" but offer ways of seeing things. They have abandoned realism as too easy: they substitute themselves for realism. *Life* is totally advertisements: its articles package and sell emotions and ideas just as its paid ads sell commodities.

Several years ago, a group of us at the University of Toronto undertook the following experiment: 136 students were divided, on the basis of their over-all academic standing of the previous year, into four equal groups who either (1) heard and saw a lecture delivered in a TV studio, (2) heard and saw this same lecture on a TV screen, (3) heard it over the radio, or (4) read it in manuscript. Thus there were, in the CBC studios, four controlled groups who simultaneously received a single lecture and then immediately wrote an identical examination to test both understanding and retention of content. Later the experiment was repeated, using three similar groups; this time the same lecture was (1) delivered in a classroom, (2) presented as a film (using the kinescope) in a small theatre, and (3) again read in print. The actual mechanics of the experiment were relatively simple, but the problem of writing the script for the lecture led to a consideration of the resources and limitations of the dramatic forms involved.

It immediately became apparent that no matter how the script was written and the show produced, it would be slanted in various ways for and against each of the media involved; no show could be produced that did not contain these biases, and the only real common denominator was the simultaneity of presentation. For each communication channel codifies reality differently and thus influences, to a surprising degree, the content of the message communicated. A medium is not simply an envelope that carries any letter; it is itself a major part of that message. We therefore decided not to exploit the full resources of any one medium, but to try to chart a middle-of-the-road course between all of them.

The lecture that was finally produced dealt with linguistic codifications of reality and metaphysical concepts underlying grammatical systems. It was chosen because it concerned a field in which few students could be expected to have prior knowledge; moreover, it offered opportunities for the use of gesture. The cameras moved throughout the lecture, and took close-ups where relevant. No other visual aids were used, nor were shots taken of the audience while the lecture was in progress. Instead, the cameras simply focused on the speaker for 27 minutes.

The first difference we found between a classroom and a TV lecture was the brevity of the latter. The classroom lecture, if not ideally, at least in practice, sets a slower pace. It's verbose, repetitive. It allows for greater elaboration and permits the lecturer to take up several *related* points. TV, however, is stripped right down; there's less time for qualifications or alternative interpretations and only time enough for *one* point. (Into 27 minutes we put the meat of a two-hour classroom lecture.) The ideal TV speaker states his point and then brings out different facets of it by a variety of illustrations. But the classroom lecturer is less subtle and, to the agony of the better students, repeats and repeats his identical points in the hope, perhaps, that ultimately no student will miss them, or perhaps simply because he is dull. Teachers have had captive audiences for so long that few are equipped to compete for attention via the new media.

The next major difference noted was the abstracting role of each medium, beginning with print. Edmund M. Morgan, Harvard Law Professor, writes:

> One who forms his opinion from the reading of any record alone is prone to err, because the printed page fails to produce the impression or convey the idea which the spoken word produced or conveyed. The writer has read charges to the jury which he had previously heard delivered, and has been amazed to see an oral deliverance which indicated a strong bias appear on the printed page as an ideally impartial exposition. He has seen an appellate court solemnly declare the testimony of a witness to be especially clear and convincing which the trial judge had orally characterized as the most abject perjury.[5]

Selectivity of print and radio are perhaps obvious enough, but we are less conscious of it in TV, partly because we have already been conditioned to it by the shorthand of film. Balázs writes:

> A man hurries to a railway station to take leave of his beloved. We see him on the platform. We cannot see the train, but the questing eyes of the man show us that his beloved is already seated in the train. We see only a close-up of the man's face, we see it twitch as if startled and then strips of light and shadow, light and shadow flit across it in quickening rhythm. Then tears gather in the eyes and that ends the scene. We are expected to know what happened and today we do know, but when I first saw this film in Berlin, I did not at once understand the end of this scene. Soon, however, everyone knew what had happened: the train had started and it was the lamps in its compartments which had thrown their light on the man's face as they glided past ever faster and faster.[6]

As in a movie theatre, only the screen is illuminated, and, on it, only points of immediate relevance are portrayed; everything else is eliminated. This explicitness makes TV not only personal but forceful. That's why stage hands in a TV studio watch the show over floor monitors, rather than watch the actual performance before their eyes.

The script of the lecture, timed for radio, proved too long for TV. Visual aids and gestures on TV not only allow the elimination of certain words, but require a unique script. The ideal radio delivery stresses pitch and intonation to make up for the absence of the visual. That flat, broken speech in "sidewalk interviews" is the speech of a person untrained in radio delivery.

The results of the examination showed that TV had won, followed by

5. G. Louis Joughin and Edmund M. Morgan, *The Legacy of Sacco and Vanzetti* (New York: Harcourt, Brace and Company, 1948), p. 34. Reprinted by permission of G. Louis Joughin.
6. Béla Balázs, *op. cit.*, pp. 35–36.

lecture, film, radio, and finally print. Eight months later the test was read-ministered to the bulk of the students who had taken it the first time. Again it was found that there were significant differences between the groups exposed to different media, and these differences were the same as those on the first test, save for the studio group, an uncertain group because of the chaos of the lecture conditions, which had moved from last to second place. Finally, two years later, the experiment was repeated, with major modifications, using students at Ryerson Institute. Marshall McLuhan reports:

> In this repeat performance, pains were taken to allow each medium full play of its possibilities with reference to the subject, just as in the earlier experiment each medium was neutralized as much as possible. Only the mimeograph form remained the same in each experiment. Here we added a printed form in which an imaginative typographical layout was followed. The lecturer used the blackboard and permitted discussion. Radio and TV employed dramatization, sound effects and graphics. In the examination, radio easily topped TV. Yet, as in the first experiment, both radio and TV manifested a decisive advantage over the lecture and written forms. As a conveyor both of ideas and information, TV was, in this second experiment, apparently enfeebled by the deployment of its dramatic resources, whereas radio benefited from such lavishness. "Technology is explicitness," writes Lyman Bryson. Are both radio and TV more explicit than writing or lecture? Would a greater explicitness, if inherent in these media, account for the ease with which they top other modes of performance?[7]

Announcement of the results of the first experiment evoked considerable interest. Advertising agencies circulated the results with the comment that here, at last, was scientific proof of the superiority of TV. This was unfortunate and missed the main point, for the results didn't indicate the superiority of one medium over others. They merely directed attention toward differences between them, differences so great as to be of kind rather than degree. Some CBC officials were furious, not because TV won, but because print lost.

The problem has been falsely seen as democracy *vs.* the mass media. But the mass media *are* democracy. The book itself was the first mechanical mass medium. What is really being asked, of course, is: can books' monopoly of knowledge survive the challenge of the new languages? The answer is: no. What should be asked is: what can print do better than any other medium and is that worth doing?

---

7. From a personal communication to the author.

SUSAN SONTAG

Susan Sontag's essays have appeared in a variety of magazines and journals. While she is best known for her essays and criticism, she is also a novelist. Her most recent works include a novel, The Death Kit *(1967), and a collection of essays,* Styles of Radical Will *(1969).*

One Culture and the New Sensibility

This selection by writer-critic Susan Sontag is primarily concerned with litera-ture and the arts and is only indirectly addressed to the problems confronting public education. She does, however, discuss two topics which are basic to a great number of educational problems, the problem of style as opposed to content (which, in educational terms, is generally expressed as a distinction between "methods" and "content") and the problem of the "new sensibility," as well as a variety of closely related problems that are ordinarily subsumed under such topics as "the media revolution," "the new morality," and "the crisis in communications."

In the last few years there has been a good deal of discussion of a purported chasm which opened up some two centuries ago, with the advent of the Industrial Revolution, between "two cultures," the literary-artistic and the scientific. According to this diagnosis, any intelligent and articulate mod-ern person is likely to inhabit one culture to the exclusion of the other. He will be concerned with different documents, different techniques, different problems; he will speak a different language. Most important, the type of effort required for the mastery of these two cultures will differ vastly. For the literary-artistic culture is understood as a general culture. It is ad-dressed to man insofar as he is man; it is culture or, rather, it promotes cul-ture, in the sense of culture defined by Ortega y Gasset: that which a man has in his possession when he has forgotten everything that he has read. The scientific culture, in contrast, is a culture for specialists; it is founded on remembering and is set down in ways that require complete dedication of the effort to comprehend. While the literary-artistic culture aims at internalization, ingestion—in other words, cultivation—the scientific culture aims at accumulation and externalization in complex instruments for problem-solving and specific techniques for mastery.

Though T. S. Eliot derived the chasm between the two cultures from a period more remote in modern history, speaking in a famous essay of a "dissociation of sensibility" which opened up in the 17th century, the connection of the problem with the Industrial Revolution seems well taken. There is a historic antipathy on the part of many literary intellectuals and artists to those changes which characterize modern society—above all, industrialization and those of its effects which everyone has experienced, such as the proliferation of huge impersonal cities and the predominance of the anonymous style of urban life. It has mattered little whether industrialization, the creature of modern "science" is seen on the 19th and early 20th century model, as noisy smoky artificial processes which defile nature and standardize culture, or on the newer model, the clean automated technology that is coming into being in the second half of the 20th century. The judgment has been mostly the same. Literary men, feeling that the status of humanity itself was being challenged by the new science and the new technology, abhorred and deplored the change. But the literary men, whether one thinks of Emerson and Thoreau and Ruskin in the 19th century, or of 20th century intellectuals who talk of modern society as being in some new way incomprehensible, "alienated," are inevitably on the defensive. They know that the scientific culture, the coming of the machine, cannot be stopped.

The standard response to the problem of "the two cultures"—and the issue long antedates by many decades the crude and philistine statement of the problem by C. P. Snow in a famous lecture some years ago—has been a facile defense of the function of the arts (in terms of an ever vaguer ideology of "humanism") or a premature surrender of the function of the arts to science. By the second response, I am not referring to the philistinim of scientists (and those of their party among artists and philosophers) who dismiss the arts as imprecise, untrue, at best mere toys. I am speaking of serious doubts which have arisen among those who are passionately engaged in the arts. The role of the individual artist, in the business of making unique objects for the purpose of giving pleasure and educating conscience and sensibility, has repeatedly been called into question. Some literary intellectuals and artists have gone so far as to prophesy the ultimate demise of the art-making activity of man. Art, in an automated scientific society, would be unfunctional, useless.

But this conclusion, I should argue, is plainly unwarranted. Indeed, the whole issue seems to me crudely put. For the question of "the two cultures" assumes that science and technology are changing, in motion, while the arts are static, fulfilling some perennial generic human function (consolation? edification? diversion?). Only on the basis of this false assumption would anyone reason that the arts might be in danger of becoming obsolete.

Art does not progress, in the sense that science and technology do. But the arts do develop and change. For instance, in our own time, art is becoming increasingly the terrain of specialists. The most interesting and creative art of our time is not open to the generally educated; it demands special effort; it speaks a specialized language. The music of Milton Babbitt and Morton Feldman, the painting of Mark Rothko and Frank Stella, the dance of Merce Cunningham and James Waring demand an education of sensibility whose difficulties and length of apprenticeship are at least comparable to the difficulties of mastering physics or engineering. (Only the novel, among the arts, at least in America, fails to provide similar examples.) The parallel between the abstruseness of contemporary art and that of modern science is too obvious to be missed. Another likeness to the scientific culture is the history-mindedness of contemporary art. The most interesting works of contemporary art are full of references to the history of the medium; so far as they comment on past art, they demand a knowledge of at least the recent past. As Harold Rosenberg has pointed out, contemporary paintings are themselves acts of criticism as much as of creation. The point could be made as well of much recent work in the films, music, the dance, poetry, and (in Europe) literature. Again, a similarity with the style of science—this time, with the accumulative aspect of science—can be discerned.

The conflict between "the two cultures" is in fact an illusion, a temporary phenomenon born of a period of profound and bewildering historical change. What we are witnessing is not so much a conflict of cultures as the creation of a new (potentially unitary) kind of sensibility. This new sensibility is rooted, as it must be, in *our* experience, experiences which are new in the history of humanity—in extreme social and physical mobility; in the crowdedness of the human scene (both people and material commodities multiplying at a dizzying rate); in the availability of new sensations such as speed (physical speed, as in airplane travel; speed of images, as in the cinema); and in the pan-cultural perspective on the arts that is possible through the mass reproduction of art objects.

What we are getting is not the demise of art, but a transformation of the function of art. Art, which arose in human society as a magical-religious operation, and passed over into a technique for depicting and commenting on secular reality, has in our own time arrogated to itself a new function—neither religious, nor serving a secularized religious function, nor merely secular or profane (a notion which breaks down when its opposite, the "religious" or "sacred," becomes obsolescent). Art today is a new kind of instrument, an instrument for modifying consciousness and organizing new modes of sensibility. And the means for practicing art have been radically extended. Indeed, in response to this new function (more felt than clearly articulated), artists have had to become self-conscious aestheticians: continually challenging their means, their materials and methods. Often, the conquest and exploitation of new materials and methods drawn from the world of "non-art"—for example, from industrial technology, from commercial processes and imagery, from purely private and subjective fantasies and dreams—seems to be the principal effort of many artists. Painters no longer feel themselves confined to canvas and paint, but employ hair, photographs, wax, sand, bicycle tires, their own toothbrushes and socks. Musicians have reached beyond the sounds of the traditional instruments to use tampered instruments and (usually on tape) synthetic sounds and industrial noises.

All kinds of conventionally accepted boundaries have thereby been challenged: not just the one between the "scientific" and the "literary-artistic" cultures, or the one between "art" and "non-art"; but also many established distinctions within the world of culture itself — that between form and content, the frivolous and the serious, and (a favorite of literary intellectuals) "high" and "low" culture.

The distinction between "high" and "low" (or "mass" or "popular") culture is based partly on an evaluation of the difference between unique and mass-produced objects. In an era of mass technological reproduction, the work of the serious artist had a special value simply because it was unique, because it bore his personal, individual signature. The works of popular culture (and even films were for a long time included in this category) were seen as having little value because they were manufactured objects, bearing no individual stamp — group concoctions made for an undifferentiated audience. But in the light of contemporary practice in the arts, this distinction appears extremely shallow. Many of the serious works of art of recent decades have a decidedly impersonal character. The work of art is reasserting its existence as "object" (even as manufactured or mass-produced object, drawing on the popular arts) rather than as "individual personal expression."

The exploration of the impersonal (and trans-personal) in contemporary art is the new classicism; at least, a reaction against what is understood as the romantic spirit dominates most of the interesting art of today. Today's art, with its insistence on coolness, its refusal of what it considers to be sentimentality, its spirit of exactness, its sense of "research" and "problems," is closer to the spirit of science than of art in the old-fashioned sense. Often, the artist's work is only his idea, his concept. This is a familiar practice in architecture, of course. And one remembers that painters in the Renaissance often left parts of their canvases to be worked out by students, and that in the flourishing period of the concerto the cadenza at the end of the first movement was left to the inventiveness and discretion of the performing soloist. But similar practices have a different, more polemical meaning today, in the present post-romantic era of the arts. When painters such as Joseph Albers, Ellsworth Kelly, and Andy Warhol assign portions of the work, say, the painting in of the colors themselves, to a friend or the local gardener; when musicians such as Stockhausen, John Cage, and Luigi Nono invite collaboration from performers by leaving opportunities for random effects, switching around the order of the score, and improvisations — they are changing the ground rules which most of us employ to recognize a work of art. They are saying what art need not be. At least, not necessarily.

The primary feature of the new sensibility is that its model product is not the literary work, above all, the novel. A new non-literary culture exists today, of whose very existence, not to mention significance, most literary intellectuals are entirely unaware. This new establishment includes certain painters, sculptors, architects, social planners, film-makers, TV technicians, neurologists, musicians, electronics engineers, dancers, philosophers, and sociologists. (A few poets and prose writers can be included.) Some of the basic texts for this new cultural alignment are to be found in the writings of

Nietzsche, Wittgenstein, Antonin Artaud, C. S. Sherrington, Buckminster Fuller, Marshall McLuhan, John Cage, André Breton, Roland Barthes, Claude Lévi-Strauss, Siegfried Gidieon, Norman O. Brown, and Gyorgy Kepes.

Those who worry about the gap between "the two cultures," and this means virtually all literary intellectuals in England and America, take for granted a notion of culture which decidedly needs reexamining. It is the notion perhaps best expressed by Matthew Arnold (in which the central cultural act is the making of literature, which is itself understood as the criticism of culture). Simply ignorant of the vital and enthralling (so called "avant-garde") developments in the other arts, and blinded by their personal investment in the perpetuation of the older notion of culture, they continue to cling to literature as the model for creative statement.

What gives literature its preeminence is its heavy burden of "content," both reportage and moral judgment. (This makes it possible for most English and American literary critics to use literary works mainly as texts, or even pretexts, for social and cultural diagnosis—rather than concentrating on the properties of, say, a given novel or a play, as an art work.) But the model arts of our time are actually those with much less content, and a much cooler mode of moral judgment—like music, films, dance, architecture, painting, sculpture. The practice of these arts—all of which draw profusely, naturally, and without embarrassment, upon science and technology—are the locus of the new sensibility.

The problem of "the two cultures," in short, rests upon an uneducated, uncontemporary grasp of our present cultural situation. It arises from the ignorance of literary intellectuals (and of scientists with a shallow knowledge of the arts, like the scientist-novelist C. P. Snow himself) of a new culture, and its emerging sensibility. In fact, there can be no divorce between science and technology, on the one hand, and art, on the other, any more than there can be a divorce between art and the forms of social life. Works of art, psychological forms, and social forms all reflect each other, and change with each other. But, of course, most people are slow to come to terms with such changes—especially today, when the changes are occurring with an unprecedented rapidity. Marshall McLuhan has described human history as a succession of acts of technological extension of human capacity, each of which works a radical change upon our environment and our ways of thinking, feeling, and valuing. The tendency, he remarks, is to upgrade the old environment into art form (thus Nature became a vessel of aesthetic and spiritual values in the new industrial environment) "while the new conditions are regarded as corrupt and degrading." Typically, it is only certain artists in any given era who "have the resources and temerity to live in immediate contact with the environment of their age . . . . That is why they may seem to be 'ahead of their time' . . . . More timid people prefer to accept the . . . previous environment's values as the continuing reality of their time. Our natural bias is to accept the new gimmick (automation, say) as a thing that can be accommodated in the old ethical order." Only in the terms of what McLuhan calls the old ethical order does the problem of "the two cultures" appear to be a genuine problem. It is not a problem for most of the creative artists of our time (among whom one could include very few novelists) because most of these artists have broken, whether they know it or not, with the Matthew Arnold notion of culture, finding it historically and humanly obsolescent.

The Matthew Arnold notion of culture defines art as the criticism of life—this being understood as the propounding of moral, social, and political ideas. The new sensibility understands art as the extension of life—this being understood as the representation of (new) modes of vivacity. There is no necessary denial of the role of moral evaluation here. Only the scale has changed; it has become less gross, and what it sacrifices in discursive explicitness it gains in accuracy and subliminal power. For we are what we are able to see (hear, taste, smell, feel) even more powerfully and profoundly than we are what furniture of ideas we have stocked in our heads. Of course, the proponents of "the two cultures" crisis continue to observe a desperate contrast between unintelligible, morally neutral science and technology, on the one hand, and morally committed, human-scale art on the other. But matters are not that simple, and never were. A great work of art is never simply (or even mainly) a vehicle of ideas or of moral sentiments. It is, first of all, an object modifying our consciousness and sensibility, changing the composition, however slightly, of the humus that nourishes all specific ideas and sentiments. Outraged humanists, please note. There is no need for alarm. A work of art does not cease being a moment in the conscience of mankind, when moral conscience is understood as only one of the functions of consciousness.

Sensations, feelings, the abstract forms and styles of sensibility count. It is to these that contemporary art addresses itself. The basic unit for contemporary art is not the idea, but the analysis of and extension of sensations. (Or if it is an "idea," it is about the form of sensibility.) Rilke described the artist as someone who works "toward an extension of the regions of the individual senses"; McLuhan calls artists "experts in sensory awareness." And the most interesting works of contemporary art (one can begin at least as far back as French symbolist poetry) are adventures in sensation, new "sensory mixes." Such art is, in principle, experimental—not out of an elitist disdain for what is accessible to the majority, but precisely in the sense that science is experimental. Such an art is also notably apolitical and undidactic, or, rather, infra-didactic.

When Ortega y Gasset wrote his famous essay *The Dehumanization of Art* in the early 1920's, he ascribed the qualities of modern art (such as impersonality, the ban on pathos, hostility to the past, playfulness, willful stylization, absence of ethical and political commitment) to the spirit of youth which he thought dominated our age.[1] In retrospect, it seems this "dehumanization" did not signify the recovery of childlike innocence, but was rather a very adult, knowing response. What other response than anguish, followed by anesthesia and then by wit and the elevating of intelligence over sentiment, is possible as a response to the social disorder and mass atrocities of our time, and—equally important for our sensibilities, but less often remarked on—to the unprecedented change in what rules our

---

1. Ortega remarks, in this essay: "Were art to redeem man, it could do so only by saving him from the seriousness of life and restoring him to an unexpected boyishness."

environment from the intelligible and visible to that which is only with difficulty intelligible, and is invisible? Art, which I have characterized as an instrument for modifying and educating sensibility and consciousness, now operates in an environment which cannot be grasped by the senses.

Buckminster Fuller has written:

> *In World War I industry suddenly went from the visible to the invisible base, from the track to the trackless, from the wire to the wireless, from visible structuring to invisible structuring in alloys. The big thing about World War I is that* man went off the sensorial spectrum forever *as the prime criterion of accrediting innovations . . . . All major advances since World War I have been in the* infra *and the* ultra*sensorial frequencies of the electromagnetic spectrum. All the important technical affairs of men today are invisible . . . . The old masters, who were sensorialists, have unleashed a Pandora's box of non-sensorially controllable phenomena, which they had avoided accrediting up to that time . . . . Suddenly they lost their true mastery, because from then on they didn't personally understand what was going on. If you don't understand you cannot master . . . . Since World War I, the old masters have been extinct . . . .*

But, of course, art remains permanently tied to the senses. Just as one cannot float colors in space (a painter needs some sort of surface, like a canvas, however neutral and textureless), one cannot have a work of art that does not impinge upon the human sensorium. But it is important to realize that human sensory awareness has not merely a biology but a specific history, each culture placing a premium on certain senses and inhibiting others. (The same is true for the range of primary human emotions.) Here is where art (among other things) enters, and why the interesting art of our time has such a feeling of anguish and crisis about it, however playful and abstract and ostensibly neutral morally it may appear. Western man may be said to have been undergoing a massive sensory anesthesia (a concomitant of the process that Max Weber calls "bureaucratic rationalization") at least since the Industrial Revolution, with modern art functioning as a kind of shock therapy for both confounding and unclosing our senses.

One important consequence of the new sensibility (with its abandonment of the Matthew Arnold idea of culture) has already been alluded to —namely, that the distinction between "high" and "low" culture seems less and less meaningful. For such a distinction—inseparable from the Matthew Arnold apparatus—simply does not make sense for a creative community of artists and scientists engaged in programming sensations, uninterested in art as a species of moral journalism. Art has always been more than that, anyway.

Another way of characterizing the present cultural situation, in its most creative aspects, would be to speak of a new attitude toward pleasure. In one sense, the new art and the new sensibility take a rather dim view of pleasure. (The great contemporary French composer, Pierre Boulez, entitled an important essay of his twelve years ago, "Against Hedonism in Music.") The seriousness of modern art precludes pleasure in the familiar sense—the pleasure of a melody that one can hum after leaving the concert hall, of characters in a novel or play whom one can recognize, identify with, and dissect in terms of realistic psychological motives, of a beautiful landscape or a dramatic moment represented on a canvas. If hedonism means sustaining the old ways in which we have found pleasure in art (the old sensory and psychic modalities), then the new art is anti-hedonistic. Having one's sensorium challenged or stretched hurts. The new serious music hurts one's ears, the new painting does not graciously reward one's sight, the new films and the few interesting new prose works do not go down easily. The commonest complaint about the films of Antonioni or the narratives of Beckett or Burroughs is that they are hard to look at or to read, that they are "boring." But the charge of boredom is really hypocritical. There is, in a sense, no such thing as boredom. Boredom is only another name for a certain species of frustration. And the new languages which the interesting art of our time speaks are frustrating to the sensibilities of most educated people.

But the purpose of art is always, ultimately, to give pleasure — though our sensibilities may take time to catch up with the forms of pleasure that art in a given time may offer. And, one can also say that, balancing the ostensible anti-hedonism of serious contemporary art, the modern sensibility is more involved with pleasure in the familiar sense than ever. Because the new sensibility demands less "content" in art, and is more open to the pleasures of "form" and style, it is also less snobbish, less moralistic — in that it does not demand that pleasure in art necessarily be associated with edification. If art is understood as a form of discipline of the feelings and a programming of sensations, then the feeling (or sensation) given off by a Rauschenberg painting might be like that of a song by the Supremes. The brio and elegance of Budd Boetticher's *The Rise and Fall of Legs Diamond* or the singing style of Dionne Warwick can be appreciated as a complex and pleasurable event. They are experienced without condescension.

This last point seems to me worth underscoring. For it is important to understand that the affection which many younger artists and intellectuals feel for the popular arts is not a new philistinism (as has so often been charged) or a species of anti-intellectualism or some kind of abdication from culture. The fact that many of the most serious American painters, for example, are also fans of "the new sound" in popular music is *not* the result of the search for mere diversion or relaxation; it is not, say, like Schoenberg also playing tennis. It reflects a new, more open way of looking at the world and at things in the world, our world. It does not mean the renunciation of all standards: there is plenty of stupid popular music, as well as inferior and pretentious "avant-garde" paintings, films, and music. The point is that there *are* new standards, new standards of beauty and style and taste. The new sensibility is defiantly pluralistic; it is dedicated both to an excruciating seriousness and to fun and wit and nostalgia. It is also extremely history-conscious; and the voracity of its enthusiasms (and of the supercession of these enthusiasms) is very high-speed and hectic. From the vantage point of this new sensibility, the beauty of a machine or of the solution to a mathematical problem, of a painting by Jasper Johns, of a film by Jean-Luc Godard, and of the personalities and the music of the Beatles is equally accessible.

PHILIP H. PHENIX

Philip H. Phenix is a professor of education at Teachers College, Columbia University. A distinguished philosopher of education, his books include Education and the Common Good, *(1961) and* Realms of Meaning, *(1964).*

Education
and Mass Communications

One of the most insistent ethical concerns in American civilization is the development of high standards for the mass media of communication. The quality and purposes of these media are of profound educational significance, because today they are among the most powerful and pervasive of all educational influences.

Young people—and older people too—are caught in a continual and almost inescapable barrage of sights and sounds from the various organs of publicity. Until recent years the average person had to seek out sources of information and entertainment. Now he has to find refuge from their omnipresent importunity. Whether or not he wills it, everybody is, as it were, bathed in a flood of symbols pouring in from the mass media—music, news, sports, weather, market information. Thus, the perennial stimuli of the natural and social environments have been complemented by the more insistent stimuli of this new symbolic environment.

Since these influences inevitably have a marked effect on the development of personality, broadcasters, writers, and publishers in our day play the role of powerful educators. It is they—perhaps more than schoolteachers and parents—who set the intellectual and moral tone of our society and suggest the values which govern the conduct of life. We have entered an era in which the mass media may be the *real* public schools—the institutions in which the public is not only formed and instructed but also brought into being as a public with common standards and assumptions.

But even within our existing framework of educational institutions, the channels of public communication are educationally important, because of the wealth of teaching materials and models which they provide for teachers and parents. The teacher is no longer a person whose main function is to impart information or even to demonstrate skills, since so many re-

From *Phi Delta Kappan*, XLIII, October 1961. Reprinted by permission of the publisher.

sources are available and conveniently organized in a variety of published forms. In the age of the mass media the teacher's functions shift to emphasis on *selection, evaluation, interpretation, application,* and *individual guidance.* To put it another way, the center of attention in education is moving from teaching to learning, because published materials offer at least the possibility of such rich resources of well-organized, authoritative, and expertly presented instructional materials that students need only the time and the incentives to learn.

This is to say that the most influential and important teachers, to some extent today and even more so tomorrow, will be those who speak and write for the mass media. Under these conditions, a continuing and increasingly necessary task of parents and regular classroom teachers will be to help young people develop the trained perception and critical judgment which will enable them to use published materials profitably and responsibly.

Since authors, broadcasters, advertisers, and others who speak through the public channels are themselves nurtured in homes and schools, these traditional institutions of education may have considerable power in determining the character and purposes of what is done through the newer agencies. In a healthy society the influences of home and school should complement and sustain those of the mass media, replacing the chaotic and frequently antagonistic relationships that now so largely prevail. This mutuality presupposes common standards of values for judging mass communications. The chief aim of the present article is to attempt the statement of such standards.

For our American civilization one general idea is surely that the mass media should be democratic. In one sense they are automatically democratic, because they create a common world in which everybody has an equal place: newspapers, magazines, radio, and television are no respecters of persons; what is for one is for all.

On the other hand, the economics of production introduce antidemocratic tendencies. Since considerable equipment is required to produce, distribute, and market mass materials, publication is a privilege of those who command the requisite resources of wealth and power. The ability of a relatively few already powerful people and organizations to exert still further pervasive influence introduces the possibility of tyranny and misuse of power in some respects even more devastating than that caused by physical compulsion.

THE HOW OF PUBLIC CONTROL

The problem, then, is how to organize our society so as to realize the democratic potentialities in the mass media and at the same time to guard against their undemocratic misuse by egoistic interests. The clue to such a society is the recognition that values are more than individual or group preferences; rather, they are ideals to which our common loyalty and allegiance are due and by which our wants and interests are judged worthy or not. The fulfillment of democracy in respect to the mass media calls for public control of them by reference to objective standards of worth, in such manner as to prevent their arbitrary employment for the advantage of private interests, either through deliberate manipulation or through profitable catering to popular demand without regard for quality.

I shall suggest four principles as democratic standards for the mass media. These principles are offered as a basis for evaluating social policy respecting the mass media, in the light of their profound educational significance and in view of the special responsibility of school people in this aspect of public affairs.

THE PRINCIPLE OF FREE SPEECH

The first principle is that of *free speech*. If truth is to be known and right is to be done, there must be opportunity for exploration and for search, hence for diversity of beliefs and for the public expression of this diversity. The basic assumption of the free and open society is that no one can say with full and final authority what is true and right. There must be no official public view to which all are obliged to hold and from which no variance is permitted.

It follows that the mass media should be organized so as to permit and encourage the creation of many "publics." A single system of production and distribution, resulting in the making of a single public, would destroy the contrast and variation which are the source of cultural enrichment and social progress. Ideal democracy is pluralistic. A monolithic society, consisting of only one public, is a threat to truth and justice. Freedom of publication is a prerequisite for this necessary pluralism.

Freedom of speech is not, however, an absolute and unconditional ideal. It has conditions, the most basic of which is the presumed good faith of those who publish. It is one thing to defend plurality on the ground that no one can rightly claim complete knowledge of the good and the true. It is quite something else to uphold it on the basis of the demand for individual autonomy. To stand for freedom in the name of a truth which is beyond the reach of finite mortals is wholly different from defending it for the sake of personal license. Good faith is faith in the good. It is action predicated on loyalty to the good. Bad faith is conduct based on the principle of autonomy and of deliberate self-interest. It follows that free speech is appropriate in a democracy whose citizens are committed to objective ideals, but not where values are defined as what yields satisfaction, for human desires are no sure indication of what is right.

THE NEED TO APPROXIMATE TRUTH

The second principle for the mass media stems from recognition of the need to approximate truth through the finite and fallible forms of human existence. This is the principle of *regulation*, which sets bounds to the permissible freedom. While plurality of published influences is desirable in order to allow for criticism and improvement, not any and every influence may be permitted. Any society needs some minimal standards which prescribe in broad terms the range of allowable public communications. Such limits are necessary because even people who are committed to the good are never completely devoid of egoism, and because there are many others who deliberately pursue their own interests without regard for any common good.

Every society censors communications which would immediately endanger the security of the commonwealth. For example, the use of mass media to incite to rebellion against the established government, or the publication of military or diplomatic secrets, are obviously inadmissible on the grounds of corporate self-preservation. Other matters which would be repugnant to most people, such as gross misrepresentation of facts important to health and safety, or public displays of vicious and immoral conduct, would also normally be prohibited.

Who should do the regulating? Ultimately, the responsibility lies with the agencies of government. Courts may adjudicate claims brought against publishers or broadcasters. Legislatures, too, may prescribe limits, and various regulatory bodies may be set up by the executive branch of government.

Producers of the mass media may regulate themselves through their own associations both on an advisory basis and by invoking sanctions on delinquents. Individual producers too can restrict themselves in the light of standards of excellence to which they have pledged their loyalty. Such self-limitation is not actually regulation at all, but simply the responsible exercise of freedom. In fact, to be fully free means not unrestrained license but regulation of one's own conduct in accordance with what is good.

Another important means of control are the distributors of the materials of mass communication. Subscription agents and booksellers to some extent can choose what they will and will not sell and to whom. Motion picture theaters can sometimes determine the films to be shown, and to a degree they can restrict the viewing to appropriate persons. Since television and radio programs, on the other hand, are open to everybody without limitation, it is necessary to maintain a broader standard of public propriety than applies to the other forms of mass communication.

Finally, voluntary regulation may be exercised by the receiving public as individuals and as groups. Associations such as churches and clubs may adopt their own standards of quality, and may employ their own corporate disciplines to enforce the observance of these standards. Of special importance in this respect are families, in which books, magazines, newspapers, movies, and broadcasts may be chosen with reference to standards of worth higher than those generally prevailing. The quality of family life is regularly subject to erosion from the inflow of debased materials from the mass media—as in the brutality and immorality of many so-called "comic books," the triviality, sensationalism, and distortion of most journalism, and the preoccupation with crime and violence in many television programs. It is the duty of parents to maintain at least minimal standards in the home by appropriate regulation of the reading, listening, and viewing activities of their children.

Similarly, libraries may regulate the quality of the materials acquired and the manner of their use by the public. Schools, too, play an important part in the screening of published materials, both in choosing what is used in regular instruction and in influencing students' habits of viewing and listening.

The ultimate goal of control of the mass media is to educate the public in self-regulation — to develop in all people, whether producers or recipients, a reliable sense of what is worthy and what is not worthy of being made public. In this manner the principle of regulation may serve as support and confirmation for the principle of free speech.

SOCIAL SUPPORT FOR EXCELLENCE

A third principle for the mass media in a democracy dedicated to worth is that of *social support for excellence*. When mass communications are supported on a commercial basis, as largely prevails in this country today, excellence when it is achieved at all is largely a chance by-product. Newspaper publishers for the most part find it more profitable not to print the whole truth nor interpret the news in a searching and balanced fashion. Movie, radio, and television producers cannot normally afford to offer a steady flow of high level programs. Under the commercial system, there is no commitment to excellence as such, but only as it may happen to be a useful tool of sales promotion.

By contrast, in a democracy committed first to standards of excellence, the agencies of mass communication are given direct social support for the publication of valuable materials. This can be accomplished in various ways. The most obvious is for the government to operate its own general press, radio, and television services for the public good. While various levels of government in this country, for reasons of law and tradition, have not undertaken such activities to any large extent, in many other countries government-controlled mass media are the rule. Sometimes, as in the case of the B.B.C., notable contributions to public well-being have been made. In other cases the dangers to liberty in official government press and radio have been demonstrated. This peril is most ominous when the government has a monopoly of the mass media. Since democratic freedom depends on a plurality of public-making agencies, non-government mass media should exist, and safeguards should be provided through government to insure high professional and ethical standards in such independent agencies.

Social support for excellence in the mass media may be provided through private, non-profit organizations devoted directly and exclusively to the production of high quality materials. Non-commercial educational radio and television stations and certain non-profit publishers and film producers exemplify this approach. Some commercial publishing enterprises are also specifically committed to excellence and are supported by direct consumer purchase of the product by a discriminating and loyal clientele. The plan of subscription television follows this principle of establishing a direct relation between program and viewer, thus creating a means of responding to a demand for high quality productions.

Ideally, the mass media should be recognized for what they are — as prime agencies of public education — and their work should be made an integral part of the work of the institutions of education and supported as such. The acknowledgement of this relationship would shift the purpose of mass communications from special advantage and private profit to the advancement of truth and excellence, which are traditional objectives of schools. A growing recognition of the educative role of the mass media may result in substantial changes both in the schools and in the agencies of publication and broadcasting. Teachers of exceptional ability in writing and speaking may increasingly be employed to make their talents available by press, radio, and television to the public at large. At the same time, teachers in school classrooms may concentrate much more on guidance, testing, and individual application than on the presentation of materials for learning. The primary function of most teachers should eventually be to stimulate and channel the students' dedication to make use of the abundant resources available through modern publishing techniques.

The universities should also become centers of public education in a new sense. They should not merely cherish their own intellectual life, serving only those who come to them for instruction. They should become major centers of mass communication, carrying on a continuous work of adult education of the public in the letters, sciences, and arts, by the printed word, by films, and by radio and television. For this work they should receive the substantial material support which would be required to do the job at a high level of competence.

THE DEMOCRATIC PRINCIPLE OF CRITICISM

A fourth and final principle of democracy in mass communication is that of *criticism*, that is to say, of evaluative response by the receiving public. Only by criticism can the one-way nature of mass communication be overcome. In a democracy devoted to objective values the critical response ought to be based not on the consumer's personal wants and preferences, but on standards of excellence.

Criticism may be accomplished in several ways. One way is by direct communication with the author, publisher, or producer. A relatively small number of thoughtful letters or conversations may have a significant influence on the quality of what is published. A second mode of criticism is by the publication of reviews by expert critics. Evaluations by such reviewers have considerable effect upon the professional standing of authors and producers and upon the judgment of the public. They are particularly important in a society devoted to standards of excellence, to keep before the public a clear vision of ideal ends to be served and to show explicitly in what respects materials offered for public reception are or are not valuable. Third, indirect and inarticulate but nonetheless effective criticism may be exercised by giving or withholding support for the agencies of mass communication. This can be done in the case of commercial agencies through consumer reaction in the market and in the case of publicly supported agencies by political pressure.

It is with respect to the critical function that the pertinence of the institutions of education to the mass media is perhaps most evident. Criticism is integral to the educative process. It is an activity essential to good practice in all schools, colleges, and universities. When mass communication occurs under the auspices of non-school agencies, criticism in the schools is important for forming standards of personal choice and of responsible consumer reaction. If the mass media should increasingly become an arm of the schools, the critical function would become a natural extension of the self-appraising, reflective activity which is an essential feature of all good teaching and learning. It is this commitment to practical self-examination in the interest of what is right and true that makes the institutions of education uniquely appropriate as centers for mass communication in a democracy serving the common good.

Part 4

PROGNOSIS
AND PRESCRIPTION

Introduction

What, then, is to be done? What—in view of the foregoing ideas and theories—is the proper course for contemporary public education to pursue? In this concluding part, four noted authorities—educational theorists Theodore Brameld and William Van Til, psychologist Jerome Bruner, and anthropologist Margaret Mead—offer their ideas about the probable course of future developments in public education.

In his article "Is Progressive Education Obsolete?" William Van Til takes the position that, contrary to public opinion, "progressive education has never been tried on any significant scale."

> *If their work is to have meaning, rather than to be innovation for unclear purposes, the sponsors and users of the new technology, organization, and approaches to discipline must come to terms with the questions that engaged the intellectual leadership of the progressive movement in education. Questions of "why" and "what" have necessary precedence over questions of "how" and "when."*[1]

Jerome S. Bruner, in his selection "After John Dewey, What?" finds himself in partial disagreement with Van Til. Many of Dewey's ideas, states Bruner, have been vulgarized and sentimentalized.

> *One writes against the background of one's day. Dewey was writing with an eye to the sterility and rigidity of school instruction in the 1890s—particularly its failure to appreciate the nature of the child. His emphasis upon the importance of direct experience and social action was an implied critique of the empty formalism that did little to relate learning to the child's world of experience. Dewey did mighty service in inspiring a correction. But an excess of virtue is vice. We, in our day, are reconsidering education against the background of such an excess.*[2]

What is needed today, states Bruner, is "the nurturing of images of excellence."[3] A thorough analysis of the nature of knowledge eventuates in two convictions.

> *The first is that the structure of knowledge—its connectedness and the derivations that make one idea follow from another—is the proper emphasis in education. For it is structure, the great conceptual inventions that bring order to the congeries of disconnected ob-*

---

1. William Van Til, "Is Progressive Education Obsolete?" *Saturday Review*, February 17, 1962, p. 83.
2. Jerome S. Bruner, "After John Dewey, What?" *On Knowing: Essays for the Left Hand* (New York: Atheneum, 1965), p. 115.
3. *Ibid.*, p. 119.

servations, that gives meaning to what we may learn and makes possible the opening up of new realms of experience. The second conviction is that the unity of knowledge is to be found within knowledge itself, if the knowledge is worth mastering.[4]

For educational philosopher Theodore Brameld, the need for a reconstructed philosophy of education entails far more than a consideration of purely academic matters. It involves a thoroughgoing review of existing social attitudes and practices as well. The world is in a profound state of crisis, states Brameld, brought about largely by the consequences of radical and accelerating social and technological changes. From the educational point of view, perhaps the most significant revolution has occurred in the area of the behavioral sciences. These changes not only necessitate a radical revision of traditional philosophical assumptions about the nature of knowledge and of value; they demand an overhaul of the traditional educational theories which have been founded upon obsolete—i.e., pre-scientific and pre-psychological—foundations. Values are now scientifically ascertainable and testable, and they therefore translate into truly objective educational goals. The proper role of the school is to confront the contemporary crisis, to analyze it objectively, and to work for consensus on the basis of verifiable scientific solutions.

In the final selection anthropologist Margaret Mead offers her proposal for adapting the schools to the needs of the future. The traditional concept of what constitutes teaching and learning, she states, "has exploded in our faces."[5] Our entire educational system is faced with the overriding problem of obsolescence. We must confront "the most vivid truth of the new age: *no one will live all his life in the world into which he was born, and no one will die in the world in which he worked in his maturity.*"[6]

Change has become so rapid that adjustment cannot be left to the next generation; adults must—not once, but continually—take in, adjust to, use, and make innovations in a steady stream of discovery and new conditions . . . . An educational system that was designed to teach what was known to little children and to a selected few young men (after which they could be regarded as "educated") may not fit a world in which the most important factors in everyone's life are those things that are not yet, but soon will be, known.[7]

"What is needed and what we are already moving toward," states Mead, "is the inclusion of another whole dimension of learning: the *lateral* transmission, to every sentient member of society, of what has just been discovered, invented, created, manufactured, or marketed."[8]

---

4. *Ibid.*, pp. 120–121.
5. Margaret Mead, "Thinking Ahead," *Harvard Business Review*, XXXVI (November–December 1958), p. 23.
6. *Ibid.*, p. 34.
7. *Ibid.*, p. 26.
8. *Ibid.*, p. 23.

WILLIAM VAN TIL

William Van Til is currently a professor of education and chairman of the depart-
ment of secondary education at New York University. He has written various
articles on educational topics and is the author of several books, including The
Making of a Modern Educator.

Is Progressive Education Obsolete?

Is progressive education outmoded? One's first impulse is to say "yes."
Who today, among the voices being heard on education, is talking about
the concerns which characterized many leaders of education during the
first half of the twentieth century? Specifically, who today is talking about
the ideas which occupied John Dewey, George Counts, Boyd H. Bode, and
William Heard Kilpatrick, those symbols of the intellectual leadership of
the "new education," symbols of the varied versions of the progressive
movement in education? Practically nobody, at least nobody who is being
heard widely.

Instead, American education in the early 1960s is engrossed with the
application of technology to education, with competing new proposals for
organization of the school program, and with stress on reconstruction of
academic disciplines. The mass media foster the interest in technology,
organization, and disciplines. If an educator tries to be heard on more fundamental aspects, he often encounters the silent treatment.

The Industrial Revolution has finally reached education. As a result,
matters of technology have virtually become table talk in education today.
In professional discussions and in the mass media reporting we hear constantly about educational television, language laboratories, courses on film,
and programmed learning through teaching machines.

A second stress in today's education emphasizes organization of the
school program. Proposals are varied and often conflicting. They include
such organizational proposals as team teaching, the dual progress plan, the
nongraded school, and increasing the course requirements within the existing Carnegie unit structure.

Currently, a third stress is the new interest in the academic disciplines.
In part, the emphasis is upon updating knowledge through efforts by spe-

cialists in the disciplines. The work of such groups as the Physical Science Study Committee and the varied mathematics programs at Yale, Maryland, and Illinois are watched intently. Science, mathematics, and foreign languages ride high as the favored fields of the national government, which has become a significant curriculum maker on the elementary and high school levels. The fields of English and physical education make frantic and failing attempts to latch onto the benefits of the National Defense Education Act; leadership in reconstruction of the curriculum in these fields has been assumed by the College Entrance Examination Board and by a football coach, respectively. There are indications that Commissioner McMurrin intends to attempt to do for the arts as well as for English what post-Sputnik apprehension did for the sciences. Rumors, alarms, and confusions surround the status of the social studies. The phrase "structures of the disciplines" is being bandied about, with none too clear a definition emerging as yet.

Technology, organization, and the disciplines seem a far cry from the philosophical, social, and psychological ideas that engaged the leaders of the progressive movement in education in the first half of the twentieth century. There appears to have been a change in "fashions in ideas," to use the chilling and accurate phrase Irwin Edman coined for a phenomenon of our times. Consequently, progressive education seems outmoded. Lawrence A. Cremin even consigned it to history in his "The Transformation of the School: Progressivism in American Education, 1876–1957." He began his preface as follows: "The death of the Progressive Education Association in 1955 and the passing of its journal, *Progressive Education*, two years later marked the end of an era in American pedagogy. Yet one would scarcely have known it from the pitifully small group of mourners at both funerals." Martin Mayer recapitulated the Cremin position in his widely read book, "The Schools."

One might readily conclude that progressive education is outmoded save for a stubborn fact. The fact is that the questions raised by the progressive movement in education are not obsolete. They will not die. They cannot be killed. They cannot be exorcised by any voodooism yet known to technology, organization, or the reconstruction of disciplines which remains aloof from these questions.

The basic questions which men like John Dewey, William Heard Kilpatrick, George Counts, and Boyd H. Bode raised are inescapable questions: What are the aims of education? Upon what foundations should the school program be built? Given such aims and foundations, what should the schools teach? To these probing and fundamental questions, matters of organization and technique, while important, are necessarily subordinate.

The progressive education movement of the first half of the twentieth century, symbolized by Dewey, Kilpatrick, Counts, and Bode, was essentially a quest for workable answers for our times to questions such as these. No one claims that the Holy Grail was found; no one claims that the questioners came up with final, definitive, eternal answers. The "new educators" did not completely agree among themselves on workable answers for our times. But at least the "new educators" asked the right questions.

One wing of the progressive movement sought the answers primarily in the potential of the individual learner. A pioneer in this respect was the man whose ninetieth birthday was celebrated on November 20, 1961 — William Heard Kilpatrick. Many of today's schoolmen will remember Kilpatrick's classes in the Horace Mann Auditorium of Teachers College, Columbia University. Hundreds attended each session, yet the quiet man with the mane of white hair used committees and reports so skillfully that each student found opportunities to speak out and battle over ideas.

The heart of Kilpatrick's first major contribution to education, "The Project Method," was founded on his faith in the potential of the individual learner. In back of the recurrent Kilpatrickian phrases which valued "purposeful activity," "intrinsic motivation," "planning," in back of his opposition to "extrinsic subject matter" which disregarded individuals, in back of his opposition to meaningless rote learning, lay Kilpatrick's belief that clues to significant content can be found within the learner and can be developed fully in collaboration with a mature adult who fosters self-direction and independent thought. The later Kilpatrick increased his stress on the importance of social orientation and the urgency of meeting social problems. But the mark Kilpatrick lastingly left on the progressive movement still derives largely from his faith in the potentiality of the learner when that potentiality is cultivated by skillful and sensitive teachers. To many educators, probably to most, insight into the relationship between the individual and his education was the major contribution of the progressive education which Kilpatrick espoused, though he was concerned for philosophical and social, as well as psychological, foundations. And — mistake it not — the insight derived from Kilpatrick made a massive contribution to education in an era that had lost sight of the importance of the learner and his purposes and potential.

A second wing of the progressive movement set forth answers to the perennial questions of aims, foundations, and content largely in terms of the society which surrounded the schools. George Counts, a battler for socially oriented schools in a democracy, serves as a symbol of this emphasis. To George Counts, for instance, the times cried out for an education realistically geared to the new social order which was emerging. He threw his eloquent challenge to the Progressive Education Association assembled in convention in 1932. He amplified his ideas in the pamphlet "Dare the Schools Build a New Social Order?" and for years educators found themselves forced to face the issues Counts raised. Whether one condemned aspects of his viewpoint as indoctrination and a potential abuse of the method of intelligence, thus classifying it as a new liberal's version of authoritarianism, or whether one hailed it as a realistic recognition of the overpowering importance of social problems, as an indication that the social sciences had come of age, an educator who heard Counts had to take into account stress on society. The role of education with respect to social change and to reform was an imperative and recurrent theme with Counts and his fellow social reconstructionists. The pivotal place of social realities in education could not be forgotten after Counts was heard, even though indoctrination might be repudiated.

George Counts lived his faith. He helped turn back Communist infiltration of teachers' unions. He was a tower of strength in the Liberal Party;

he was a candidate for public office and in the vanguard of social movements of his time. He is still active in his retirement.

To others equally immersed in the progressive movement, democratic values were central to all considerations. For instance, to Boyd H. Bode, the Lincoln-like man from Illinois who made his major contribution through Ohio State University, the crucial need was for the clarification of differences between the democratic way of life and the way of its authoritarian competitors. As he saw it, the road out of value confusion led through a remorseless and unremitting use of the method of intelligence in human affairs. To Bode, progressive education was at the crossroads and a child-centered view would never suffice. Nor was indoctrination the road to a better world. He conducted his classes in philosophy of education through the Socratic method and he fostered thought with every heckling, humorous, or trenchant exchange of ideas into day-by-day learning experiences.

I venture for your consideration the bold hypothesis that each of these men touched on part of the whole, that each perceived and particularly stressed an aspect of education which we neglect at our peril, that each succeeded nobly, and, where he failed, failed gallantly in building the "new education." Each asked the right questions; each responded with relevant contributions toward workable answers for our times.

The thinker who came closest to the reconciliation of the individual, society, and philosophical foundations — was the extraordinary John Dewey, whose centennial was celebrated by the John Dewey Society three years ago through meetings in scores of universities across the nation. The word "extraordinary" is used advisedly. During his long lifetime, this incredible man lived a full life as a person, participated in social and civic action, conducted the most famous laboratory school in history, became the father figure of the progressive education movement (and, to shift the analogy, sometimes served as mother hen by reconciling conflicts and even smoothing ruffled feathers in the flock), became a towering figure in philosophy, and, in the process, managed to leave for posterity a legacy of 5,000 pages of articles and 18,000 pages in book form.

Yet even Dewey, prodigious though his endeavors were, never achieved extensive translation of his ideas into a new curriculum. Underbrush in philosophy needed to be cleared. After his Laboratory School experimentation, and after setting forth his pedagogical creed in such books as "The School and Society" and "Democracy and Education," Dewey gave himself to this Herculean labor as he built his philosophy of experimentalism. He constantly reacted to trends and tendencies in progressive education, as he did in his critique "Experience and Education." He made only occasional critical forays into program building. He would be the first to admit, were he alive, that much remained to be done to implement his ideas on what he preferred to term simply "education," rather than "progressive education."

So we turn back to the thinking of representative intellectual leaders of the progressive movement in education, not in any spirit of ancestor worship, but for the inescapable questions they raised and for the insights they contributed toward workable solutions for our times. Cremin says it well in his final paragraphs: "There remained a timelessness about many of the

problems the progressives raised and the solutions they proposed . . . .
And for all the talk about pedagogical breakthroughs and crash programs,
the authentic progressive vision remained strangely pertinent to the problems of mid-century America. Perhaps it only awaited the reformulation
and resuscitation that would ultimately derive from a larger research and
reform in American life and thought." With these words Cremin partially
redeems the strange inconsistency of pointing out brilliantly in early chapters that social currents created progressive education well before the official establishment of a Progressive Education Association, yet conveying
the impression in his final chapter that the demise of an organization and a
magazine meant the death of progressive education. The fact that ideas live
beyond organizations apparently escaped the overanxious gravediggers
who gleefully greeted Cremin's book as the definitive obituary for progressive education as a force in American ideas.

The questions raised and many of the tentative answers ventured by
the early leaders of progressive education are not dead nor will they die. In
time, the sponsors of new educational technology, the advocates of varied
forms of educational organization, the proponents of study of the structure
of separate disciplines, must face the inescapable questions and consider
the possible solutions proposed.

The problem for sponsors and users of programmed learning through
teaching machines does not lie in the capacity of the machine to produce
positive reinforcement, whether it takes the form of a kind word, a pat on
the head, or, indeed, a bottle of Coca-Cola. Given technical ingenuity, a
reinforcing reward will be forthcoming. The harder problem for sponsors
and users of the teaching machine is whether positive reinforcement will
be used to bring nearer George Orwell's "1984" and Aldous Huxley's
"Brave New World," or whether programmed learning, using positive reinforcement selectively and with discrimination, will reduce the skill-drudgery
of education and free teachers and students for more humane aspects of
learning and human development, such as creativity, the use of reflective
thought, and experiences in freedom. Consider, for instance, this quotation
from "Walden Two," a Utopia envisioned by the pioneer of teaching machines, B. F. Skinner of Harvard, a Utopia which appears to some of us an
authoritarian nightmare world of behavioristic conditioning. T. E. Frazier,
spokesman for "Walden Two," says approvingly, "Now that we *know* how
positive reinforcement works and why negative doesn't . . . we can be
more deliberate, and hence more successful, in our cultural design. We can
achieve a sort of control under which the controlled, even though they are
following a code much more scrupulously than was ever the case under the
old system, nevertheless *feel free*. They are doing what they want to do, not
what they are forced to do. That's the source of the tremendous power of
positive reinforcement — there's no restraint and no revolt. By a careful cultural design, we control not the final behavior, but the *inclination* to behave — the motives, the desires, the wishes.

"The curious thing is that in that case *the question of freedom never
arises.*"

In the light of this quotation we can understand why Aldous Huxley
recently reminded us in "Brave New World Revisited" that it may be later

than we think. He wrote as his conclusion, "The older dictators fell because they never could supply their subjects with enough bread, enough circuses, enough miracles and mysteries. Nor did they possess a really effective system of mind-manipulation . . . . Under a scientific dictator, education will really work — with the result that most men and women will grow up to love their servitude and will never dream of revolution. There seems to be no good reason why a thoroughly scientific dictatorship should ever be overthrown."

The problem before the sponsors of educational television is not how wide a circle over six states, or indeed a nation, can be reached by a plane flying for Midwest Airborne Television. Nor is it bouncing beams off satellites for global television. Technology will solve those problems. The real problem is whether the device will realize the gloomy prophecy of an old Vanderbilt University professor who once said at a meeting of the American Association of University Professors, "Gentlemen, the time is coming when one Harvard University professor will determine through his history course on television what history is taught in the United States — and even if it's Arthur Schlesinger, Jr., I say the hell with it!" — or whether imaginative educational TV will provide learners with a magic carpet to a wider world of experience made at once more expansive and more closely detailed.

The problem before the sponsors and users of team teaching is not precisely how many students to instruct at any given time in any given space. It is not whether a new magical number combination, proposed for better staff utilization, or some flexible magic of numbers out of Lexington, Massachusetts, will take the place of the former magic number — 25 or 30 in each classroom. Experience and, we hope, genuine controlled experimentation, will supply the answer here. The real problem is whether team teaching actually will improve learning, whether it will evolve toward emphasis on the *interrelationships* of subject matter, whether it can provide sufficient personalized contacts with teachers and sufficient firsthand experiences by students to enable young people to deal with significant problems.

The problem before the sponsors and users of the dual progress plan is not the technical difficulty of introducing specialized science, mathematics, and arts teachers into elementary school organization through the demonstrations at Ossining and Long Beach in New York. The real problem for the sponsors and users of the dual progress plan is recognized by the originator of the plan as whether the dual progress plan will or will not better answer some of Dewey's persistent queries; George Stoddard poses the issue in his new book, "The Dual Progress Plan," which should be read along with the Association for Supervision and Curriculum Development pamphlet, "The Self-Contained Classroom," for differing organizational approaches to possibly compatible goals.

The problem before the liberal arts professors currently reconstructing and updating knowledge in such disciplines as physics, biology, and mathematics is not whether they can cram all of man's new knowledge into separate watertight compartments, which will then be siphoned off during the elementary and high school years. They can't. Even if they could, they would endlessly face true obsolescence, for knowledge swiftly dates and, like fish, won't keep. The real problem, of which some of the reconstructors of disciplines are aware and of which others appear quite unaware, is whether the scholars can identify concepts in their new knowledge which can be made meaningful to children and youth, appropriate to both the general and specialized education needed for living in today's society, crucial in the process of critical thinking and problem solving—or whether their reconstructed and amplified knowledge, however new, will prove to be inert subject matter in Alfred North Whitehead's sense.

The problem for those who are studying the structures of the disciplines may be first to make clear what they mean. Granted that they can and do, the question will face them as to whether their studies of structures of disciplines are to be achieved as culminations built upon the experience of learners, as Dewey recommended. Or will their studies of structures of disciplines be evasions of problems central to general education, formal orientations to content which bear little relationship to how young people live and learn?

One can derive little encouragement for the future of study of the structure of the disciplines from the views of Charles R. Keller, director of the John Hay Fellows Program, who believes "too many social studies teachers have emphasized the creation of good citizens rather than the content and discipline of their subjects." He says, "Attitudes cannot be taught in formal classroom situations. We weaken education—and schools—when we try to do so. What students should do in school is to study subjects and become acquainted with facts and ideas. Subjects as such have disciplines that will help to develop students' minds." Is this the conception of educational aims and psychology of learning which is to characterize the new advocacy of studying the structure of disciplines? Surely this was not the conception of Arthur W. Foshay when, in his presidential address to the Association for Supervision and Curriculum Development in 1961, he advised "that we educators take directly into account the nature of the organized bodies of knowledge, in addition to the nature of the growing child and the nature of our society, as we try to make curriculum decisions."

If their work is to have meaning, rather than to be innovation for unclear purposes, the sponsors and users of the new technology, organization, and approaches to disciplines must come to terms with the questions that engaged the intellectual leadership of the progressive movement in education. Questions of "why" and "what" have necessary precedence over questions of "how" and "when." The inescapable questions relate to the aims of education, the foundations of the program, and what the schools should teach as appropriate content based on such aims and foundations.

Is, then, the progressive movement in education obsolete? I think not. The questions raised by the "new education" are remorseless, inevitable, demanding. The answers provided by the intellectual leaders of the progressive movement were promising beginnings, useful leads, valid foreshadowings.

When considerations of "why" are dodged, we get prescriptions which simply cannot be appraised. One cannot truly evaluate the proposals made in widely read books which are characterized by indifference to aims and purposes in the early chapters and which then constantly smuggle in unanalyzed value assumptions through the remainder of the pages. Two knights entered in the educational jousting show this tendency: both the great and good James B. Conant and the provocative and prancing Martin Mayer.

Conant, for instance, does not set forth aims for education in "The American High School Today." Yet he steadily makes assumptions as to what knowledge is of most worth.

In "Slums and Suburbs," Conant says, "It is after visits to schools like these that I grow impatient with both critics and defenders of public education who ignore the realities of school situations to engage in fruitless debate about educational philosophy, purposes, and the like. These situations call for action, not hair-splitting arguments." Yet "Slums and Suburbs" is permeated with proposals for action which must be based on philosophic assumptions.

In "The Schools," Martin Mayer colorfully rejects all possible formulations of aims. He says, "It is well to rid oneself immediately of this business of the 'aims of education.' Discussions on this subject are among the dullest and most fruitless of human pursuits. Whatever the ideal general aims of education' may be, they certainly cannot be accomplished in schools." He then proceeds to lace through his book individualistic approbations and denunciations based on his acceptance of undefined aims.

One of the myths of our times is that the several tendencies which characterized what is broadly termed progressive education prevailed, were fully achieved, and are now being repudiated. This sedulously cultivated myth is incomprehensible. The reality is that progressive education has never been tried on any significant scale.

As the inescapable queries reassert themselves and the tentative proposals of the varied interpretations of progressive education are reconsidered, educators will find it necessary to utilize the insights of Dewey, Bode, Counts, and Kilpatrick. An education which takes into account the individual, his society, and his values—an education which builds upon the soundest possible scholarship derivative from psychological, social, and philosophical foundations—is imperative in developing a curriculum appropriate for twentieth-century man.

The central questions posed and the relevant contributions toward workable answers for our times made by such interpreters of the progressive movement in education are not obsolete. They must and will persist. In time, they will be embodied in the form of new proposals for modern education, new syntheses which build upon our predecessors, as is common in the world of ideas. The overanxious gravediggers, and those who currently give them comfort, will discover as this twentieth century moves along that what they have mistaken for a corpse is indeed very much alive.

JEROME S. BRUNER

Psychologist Jerome S. Bruner is presently a professor of psychology in the Center for Cognitive Studies at Harvard University. A recognized authority in the study of cognitive processes (and particularly in the areas of perception, memory, and thinking), Bruner's ideas have had a great impact on education through such books as The Process of Education *(1960),* On Knowing *(1962), and* Toward a Theory of Instruction *(1966).*

After John Dewey, What?

In 1897, at the age of thirty-eight, John Dewey published a stirring and prophetic work entitled *My Pedagogic Creed.* Much of his later writing on education is foreshadowed in this brief document. Five articles of faith are set forth. The first defines the educational process: "All education proceeds by the participation of the individual in the social consciousness of the race. This process begins unconsciously almost at birth, and is continually shaping the individual's powers, saturating his consciousness, forming his habits, training his ideas, and arousing his feelings and emotions."

The second article of faith embodies Dewey's concept of the school: "Education being a social process, the school is simply that form of community life in which all those agencies are concentrated that will be most effective in bringing the child to share in the inherited resources of the race, and to use his own powers for social ends. Education, therefore, is a process of living and not a preparation for future living." In the third thesis Dewey speaks to the subject matter of education: "The social life of the child is the basis of concentration or correlation in all his training or growth. The social life gives the unconscious unity and the background of all his efforts and all his attainments . . . . The true center . . . is not science, nor literature, nor history, nor geography, but the child's own social activities." A view of educational method gives form to Dewey's fourth article: "The law for presenting and treating material is the law implicit in the child's own nature." For Dewey, the law was that of action: "the active side precedes the passive in the development of the child-nature. I believe that consciousness is essentially motor or impulsive; that conscious states tend to project themselves in action." And, finally, Dewey's fifth thesis: "Education is the fundamental method of social progress and reform."

One reads the document today with mixed feelings. Its optimism is classically American in its rejection of the tragic view of life. It defines truth in the pragmatic spirit: truth is the fruit of inquiry into the consequences of action. It expresses a firm faith not only in the individual's capacity to grow but in society's capacity to shape man in its own best image. The final lines of the creed are these: "Every teacher should realize the dignity of his calling; that he is a social servant set apart for the maintenance of proper social order and the securing of the right social growth. In this way the teacher always is the prophet of the true God and the usherer in of the true kingdom of heaven."

Yet the very wholesomeness — the optimism, the pragmatism, the acceptance of man's harmonious continuity with society — leaves one uneasy. For in the two thirds of a century between 1897 and today, there has been a profound change not only in our conception of nature but also of society and the world of social institutions. Perhaps more important, we have lived through a revolution in our understanding of the nature of man, his intelligence, his capabilities, his passions, and the forms of his growth.

Dewey's thinking reflected the changes, though he was limited by the premises of his philosophical position. But between Dewey's first premises and our day, there bristles a series of revolutionary doctrines and cataclysmic events that change the very character of the inquiry. Two world wars, the dark episode of Hitler and genocide, the Russian revolution, the relativistic revolution in physics and psychology, the Age of Energy with its new technology, the sardonic reign of skeptical philosophy — all of these have forced a reappraisal of the underlying terms by which we construct a philosophy of education.

Let us then re-examine the terms, guided by what we know today of the world and of human nature. There is matter here, however, that is liable to some misinterpretation and we do well to clear it up at the outset. One writes against the background of one's day. Dewey was writing with an eye to the sterility and rigidity of school instruction in the 1890's — particularly its failure to appreciate the nature of the child. His emphasis upon the importance of direct experience and social action was an implied critique of the empty formalism that did little to relate learning to the child's world of experience. Dewey did mighty service in inspiring a correction. But an excess of virtue is vice. We, in our day, are reconsidering education against the background of such an excess.

Then, too, misunderstanding often converted Dewey's ideas into the sentimental practices he so deplored: "Next to deadness and dullness, formalism and routine," he wrote in his creed, "our education is threatened by no greater evil than sentimentalism." The sentimental cult of "the class project," of "life adjustment" courses, the reluctance to expose the child to the startling sweep of man and nature for fear it might violate the comfortable domain of his direct experience, the cloying concept of "readiness" — these are conceptions about children, often with no experimental support, that are justified in the name of Dewey. His was a noble yet tender view in his time. But what of our times? In what form shall we speak our beliefs?

WHAT EDUCATION IS

Education seeks to develop the power and sensibility of mind. On the one hand, the educational process transmits to the individual some part of the accumulation of knowledge, style, and values that constitutes the culture of a people. In doing so, it shapes the impulses, the consciousness, and the way of life of the individual. But education must also seek to develop the processes of intelligence so that the individual is capable of going beyond the cultural ways of his social world, able to innovate in however modest a way so that he can create an interior culture of his own. For whatever the art, the science, the literature, the history, and the geography of a culture, each man must be his own artist, his own scientist, his own historian, his own navigator. No person is master of the whole culture; indeed, this is almost a defining characteristic of that form of social memory that we speak of as culture. Each man lives a fragment of it. To be whole, he must create his own version of the world, using that part of his cultural heritage he has made his own through education.

In our time, the requirements of technology constrain the freedom of the individual to create images of the world that are satisfying in the deepest sense. Our era has also witnessed the rise of ideologies that subordinate the individual to the defined aims of a society, a form of subordination that is without compassion for idiosyncrasy and respects only the instrumental contribution of a man to the progress of the society. At the same time, and in spite of ideologies, man's understanding of himself and of his world — both the natural and social world — has deepened to a degree that warrants calling our age an intellectually golden one. The need is now to employ our deeper understanding not only for the enrichment of society but also for the enrichment of the individual.

It is true, as Dewey said, that all education proceeds by the participation of the individual in the social consciousness of the race, but it is a truth with a double edge. For all education, good and bad alike, is of this order. We know now to what degree this is so. To take but one example, the very language one speaks conditions the style and structure of thought and experience. Indeed, as we have seen, there is reason to believe that thought processes themselves are internalizations of social intercourse, an inner colloquy patterned by early external dialogues. It is this that makes education possible. But education, by giving shape and expression to our experience, can also be the principal instrument for setting limits on the enterprise of mind. The guarantee against limits is the sense of alternatives. Education must, then, be not only a process that transmits culture but also one that provides alternative views of the world and strengthens the will to explore them.

After a half century of startling progress in the psychological sciences, we know that mental health is only a minimum condition for the growth of mind. The tragedy of mental illness is that it so preoccupies the person with the need to fend off realities with which he cannot cope that it leaves him without either the nerve or the zest to learn. But mental health is only a state from which to start: the powers of mind grow with their exercise. Adjustment is too modest an ideal, if it is an ideal at all. Competence in the use of one's powers for the development of individually defined and socially relevant excellence is much more to the point. After a half century of Freud, we know that the freeing of instinct and inclination is not an end in itself but a way station along the road to competence. What is most prophetic for us about Freud in this second half of the century is not his battle against the fetters of rigid moralism, but his formula: "Where there was id, let there be ego."

Education must begin, as Dewey concluded his first article of belief, "with a psychological insight into the child's capacities, interests, habits," but a point of departure is not an itinerary. It is just as mistaken to sacrifice the adult to the child as to sacrifice the child to the adult. It is sentimentalism to assume that the teaching of life can be fitted always to the child's interests just as it is empty formalism to force the child to parrot the formulas of adult society. Interests can be created and stimulated. In this sphere it is not far from the truth to say that supply creates demand, that the provocation of what is available creates response. One seeks to equip the child with deeper, more gripping, and subtler ways of knowing the world and himself.

WHAT THE SCHOOL IS

The school is an entry into the life of the mind. It is, to be sure, life itself and not merely a preparation for living. But it is a special form of living, one carefully devised for making the most of those plastic years that characterize the development of *homo sapiens* and distinguish our species from all others. School should provide more than a continuity with the broader community or with everyday experience. It is primarily the special community where one experiences discovery by the use of intelligence, where one leaps into new and unimagined realms of experience, experience that is discontinuous with what went before. A child recognizes this when he first understands what a poem is, or what beauty and simplicity inhere in the idea of the conservation theorems, or that measure is universally applicable. If there is one continuity to be singled out, it is the slow converting of the child's artistic sense of the omnipotence of thought into the realistic confidence in the use of thought that characterizes the effective man.

In insisting upon the continuity of the school with the community on the one side and the family on the other, John Dewey overlooked the special function of education as an opener of new perspectives. If the school were merely a transition zone from the intimacy of the family to the life of the community, it would be a way of life easily enough arranged. In the educational systems of primitive societies, there almost always comes a point, usually at puberty, where there is a sharp change in the life of a boy, marked by a *rite de passage* that establishes a boundary between childhood ways and the ways of the adolescent.

It would be romantic nonsense to pattern our practices upon those found in preliterate societies. I would only ask that we attend to one parallel: education must not confuse the child with the adult and must recognize that the transition to adulthood involves an introduction to new realms of experience, the discovery and exploration of new mysteries, the gaining of new powers.

In the *shtetl* of Eastern Europe, the traditional Jewish ghetto, the scholar was a particularly important figure—the *talmid khokhem*. In his mien, his mode of conversation so rich in allusion, his form of poise, the wise man was the image not of a competent but, rather, of a beautiful person. Traditional Chinese society also had its image of the beautiful person, one who blended knowledge and sentiment and action in a beautiful way of life. The ideal of the gentleman served much the same function in the Europe of the seventeenth and eighteenth centuries. It is perhaps in this spirit that Alfred North Whitehead declared that education must involve an exposure to greatness if it is to leave its mark. For me the yeast of education is the idea of excellence, and that comprises as many forms as there are individuals to develop a personal image of excellence. The school must have as one of its principal functions the nurturing of images of excellence.

A detached conception of idealized excellence is not enough. A doctrine of excellence, to be effective, must be translatable into the individual lives of those who come in contact with it. What is compelling about the *talmid khokhem*, the Chinese scholar-administrator, and the eighteenth-century gentleman is that they embody ways of life to which any man can aspire in his own way and from which he can draw in his own style. I believe, then, that the school must also contain men and women who, in their own way, seek and embody excellence. This does not mean that we shall have to staff our schools with men and women of great genius but that the teacher must embody in his own approach to learning a pursuit of excellence. And, indeed, with the technical resources opened by television and its adjuncts, one can present the student and also his teacher with the working version of excellence in its highest sense. In the years ahead, we shall find that the great scholar, scientist, or artist can speak as easily and honestly to the beginner as to the graduate student.

THE SUBJECT MATTER OF EDUCATION

The issue of subject matter in education can be resolved only by reference to one's view of the nature of knowledge. Knowledge is a model we construct to give meaning and structure to regularities in experience. The organizing ideas of any body of knowledge are inventions for rendering experience economical and connected. We invent concepts such as force in physics, the bond in chemistry, motives in psychology, style in literature as means to the end of comprehension.

The history of culture is the history of the development of great organizing ideas, ideas that inevitably stem from deeper values and points of view about man and nature. The power of great organizing concepts is in large part that they permit us to understand and sometimes to predict or change the world in which we live. But their power lies also in the fact that ideas provide instruments for experience. Having grown up in a culture dominated by the ideas of Newton, and so with a conception of time flowing equably, we experience time moving inexorably and steadily, marked by a one-way arrow. Indeed, we know now, after a quarter of a century of research on perception, that experience is not to be had directly and neatly, but filtered through the programmed readiness of our senses. The program is constructed with our expectations and these are derived from our models or ideas about what exists and what follows what.

From this, two convictions follow. The first is that the structure of knowledge — its connectedness and the derivations that make one idea follow from another — is the proper emphasis in education. For it is structure, the great conceptual inventions that bring order to the congeries of disconnected observations, that gives meaning to what we may learn and makes possible the opening up of new realms of experience. The second conviction is that the unity of knowledge is to be found within knowledge itself, if the knowledge is worth mastering.

To attempt a justification of subject matter, as Dewey did, in terms of its relation to the child's social activities is to misunderstand what knowledge is and how it may be mastered. The significance of the concept of commutativity in mathematics does not derive from the social insight that two houses with fourteen people in each is not the same as fourteen houses with two people in each. Rather, it inheres in the power of the idea to create a way of thinking about number that is lithe and beautiful and immensely generative — an idea at least as powerful as, say, the future conditional tense in formal grammar. Without the idea of commutativity, algebra would be impossible. If set theory — now often the introductory section in newer curriculums in mathematics — had to be justified in terms of its relation to immediate experience and social life, it would not be worth teaching. Yet set theory lays a foundation for the understanding of order and number that could never be achieved with the social arithmetic of interest rates and bales of hay at so much per bale. Mathematics, like any other subject, must begin with experience, but progress toward abstraction and understanding requires precisely that there be a weaning away from the obviousness of superficial experience.

There is one consideration of cognitive economy, discussed in an earlier chapter, that is paramount. One cannot "cover" any subject in full, not even in a lifetime, if coverage means visiting all the facts and events and morsels. Subject matter presented so as to emphasize its structure will perforce be of that generative kind that permits reconstruction of the details or, at very least, prepares a place into which the details, when encountered, can be put.

What then of subject matter in the conventional sense? The answer to the question, "What shall be taught?" turns out to be the answer to the question, "What is nontrivial?" If one can first answer the question, "What is worth knowing about?" then it is not difficult to distinguish between the aspects of it that are worth teaching and learning and those that are not. Surely, knowledge of the natural world, knowledge of the human condition, knowledge of the nature and dynamics of society, knowledge of the past so that it may be used in experiencing the present and aspiring to the future — all of these, it would seem reasonable to suppose, are essential to an educated man. To these must be added another: knowledge of the products of our artistic heritage that mark the history of our aesthetic wonder and delight.

A problem immediately arises concerning the symbolism in terms of which knowledge is understood and talked about. There is language in its natural sense and language in its mathematical sense. I cannot imagine an educated man a century from now who will not be largely bilingual in this special sense—concise and adept in both a natural language and mathematics. For these two are the tools essential to the unlocking of new experience and the gaining of new powers. As such, they must have a central place in any curriculum.

Finally, it is as true today as it was when Dewey wrote that one cannot foresee the world in which the child we educate will live. Informed powers of mind and a sense of potency in action are the only instruments we can give the child that will be invariable across the transformations of time and circumstance. The succession of studies that we give the child in the ideal school need be fixed in only one way: whatever is introduced, let it be pursued continuously enough to give the student a sense of the power of mind that comes from a deepening of understanding. It is this, rather than any form of extensive coverage, that matters most.

THE NATURE OF METHOD

The process and the goal of education are one and the same thing. The goal of education is disciplined understanding; that is the process as well.

Let us recognize that the opposite of understanding is not ignorance or simply "not knowing." To understand something is, first, to give up some other way of conceiving of it. Confusion all too often lies between one way of conceiving and another, better way. It is one of our biological inheritances that confusion produces emergency anxiety, and with anxiety there come the defensive measures—flight, fright, or freezing—that are antithetical to the free and zestful use of the mind. The binding fact of mental life in child and adult alike is that there is a limited capacity for processing information—our span, as it is called, can comprise six or seven unrelated items simultaneously. Go beyond that and there is overload, confusion, forgetting. As George Miller has put it, the principle of economy is to fill our seven mental-input slots with gold rather than dross. The degree to which material to be learned is put into structures by the learner will determine whether he is working with gold or dross.

For this reason, as well as for reasons already stated, it is essential that, before being exposed to a wide range of material on a topic, the child first have a general idea of how and where things fit. It is often the case that the development of the general idea comes from a first round of experience with concrete embodiments of ideas that are close to a child's life. The cycle of learning begins, then, with particulars and immediately moves toward abstraction. It comes to a temporary goal when the abstraction can then be used in grasping new particulars in the deeper way that abstraction permits.

Insofar as possible, a method of instruction should have the objective of leading the child to discover for himself. Telling children and then test-ing them on what they have been told inevitably has the effect of produc-ing bench-bound learners whose motivation for learning is likely to be ex-trinsic to the task—pleasing the teacher, getting into college, artificially maintaining self-esteem. The virtues of encouraging discovery are of two kinds. In the first place, the child will make what he learns his own, will fit his discovery into the interior world of culture that he creates for himself. Equally important, discovery and the sense of confidence it provides is the proper reward for learning. It is a reward that, moreover, strengthens the very process that is at the heart of education—disciplined inquiry.

The child must be encouraged to get the full benefit from what he learns. This is not to say that he should be required to put it to immediate use in his daily life, though so much the better if he has the happy oppor-tunity to do so. Rather, it is a way of honoring the connectedness of knowl-edge. Two facts and a relation joining them is and should be an invitation to generalize, to extrapolate, to make a tentative intuitive leap, even to build a tentative theory. The leap from mere learning to using what one has learned in thinking is an essential step in the use of the mind. Indeed, plausible guessing, the use of the heuristic hunch, the best employment of necessarily insufficient evidence—these are activities in which the child needs practice and guidance. They are among the great antidotes to passivity.

Most important of all, the educational process must be free of intellec-tual dishonesty and those forms of cheating that explain without providing understanding. I have expressed the conviction elsewhere that any subject can be taught to anybody at any age in some form that is honest. It is not honest to present a fifth-grade social-studies class with an image of town government as if it were a den of cub scouts presided over by a parent fig-ure interpreting the charter—even if the image set forth does happen to mesh with the child's immediate social experience. A lie is still a lie—even if it sounds like familiar truth. Nor is it honest to present a sixth-grade sci-ence class with a garbled but concrete picture of the atom that is, in its way, as sweeteningly false as the suburban image of town government given them the year before. A dishonest image can only discourage the self-generating intellectual inquiry out of which real understanding grows.

THE SCHOOL AND SOCIAL PROGRESS

I believe that education is the fundamental method of social change. Revo-lutions themselves are no better and are often less good than the ideas they embody and the means invented for their application. Change is swifter in our times than ever before in human history and news of it is almost in-stantaneous. If we are to be serious in the belief that school must be life it-self and not merely preparation for life, then school must reflect the changes through which we are living.

The first implication of this belief is that means must be found to feed back into our schools the ever deepening insights that are developed on the frontiers of knowledge. This is an obvious point in science and mathemat-ics, and continuing efforts are now being instituted to assure that new, more powerful, and often simpler ways of understanding find their way back into the classrooms of our primary and secondary schools. But it is equally important to have this constant refreshment from fields other than the sciences — where the frontiers of knowledge are not always the universities and research laboratories but political and social life, the arts, literary endeavor, and the rapidly changing business and industrial community. Everywhere there is change, and with change we are learning.

I see the need for a new type of institution, a new conception in curriculum. What we have not had and what we are beginning to recognize as needed is something that is perhaps best called an "institute for curriculum studies" — not one of them, but many. Let it be the place where scholars, scientists, men of affairs, and artists come together with talented teachers continually to revise and refresh our curriculums. It is an activity that transcends the limits of any of our particular university faculties — be they faculties of education, arts and science, medicine, or engineering. We have been negligent in coming to a sense of the quickening change of life in our time and its implications for the educational process. We have not shared with our teachers the benefits of new discovery, new insight, new artistic triumph. Not only have we operated with the notion of the self-contained classroom but also with the idea of the self-contained school — and even the self-contained educational system.

The Nobel poet or the ambassador to the United Nations, the brilliant cellist or the perceptive playwright, the historian making use of the past or the sociologist seeking a pattern in the present — these men, like the student, are seeking understanding and mastery over new problems. They represent excellence at the frontiers of endeavor. If a sense of progress and change toward greater excellence is to illuminate our schools, there must be a constant return of their wisdom and effort to enliven and inform teacher and student alike. There is no difference in kind between the man at the frontier and the young student at his own frontier, each attempting to understand. Let the educational process be life itself as fully as we can make it.

THEODORE BRAMELD

Theodore Brameld is one of the most prominent educational philosophers in America today. Currently a professor of educational philosophy at Boston University, he has also served as president of the Philosophy of Education Society. He is an extremely prolific writer, and his books include Toward a Reconstructed Philosophy of Education *(1956),* Education as Power *(1965), and* The Use of Explosive Ideas in Education *(1965).*

Imperatives for a Reconstructed Philosophy of Education

Recently an invitation came to me, as it did to others, that was unusual not only in itself but because of its signers. I was asked to comment for the impending 10th Anniversary Conference of the New Lincoln School on this kind of question: "What should American education become in the next ten years?" The signers were: William H. Kilpatrick, Jerrold Zacharias, Arthur Bestor, and Robert M. Hutchins. Almost anyone would be intrigued by such an invitation: could it mean that leaders representing such extremely diverse educational views as Kilpatrick and Hutchins were actually going to listen carefully to one another? My reply provides the framework for this article.

Addressing myself to Dr. Kilpatrick, I wrote as follows:

> *Your desire to include the views of people of very different educational outlooks is most commendable and surely much needed in a time of extraordinary concern . . . . As you know, my own philosophic position in education is quite unorthodox and differs at rather crucial points not only from your own but particularly from that of Dr. Bestor and Dr. Hutchins whose names accompany your own . . . . I assume that, since you have written me, you wish to have my viewpoint heard along with others.*
>
> *. . . The challenge of the sputnik has not only aroused the*

From *School and Society*, LXXXVII, January 17, 1959. Reprinted by permission of the Society for the Advancement of Education, Inc.

American people from their educational lethargy as few if any events have done, but it has since demonstrated the appalling confusion among us as to the functions and purposes of education in our democracy. Even more appalling, if that is possible, is the evidence that exceedingly powerful voices in America—exemplified by Life *and* Time—*oversimplify and prejudge the issues. The editorial in the March 31st [1958] issue of* Life, *reprinted in* Time, The New York Times, *and elsewhere, so outrageously falsified these issues that the Philosophy of Education Society in its annual meeting, Indianapolis, April 2, 1958, unanimously went on record in condemnation of such "irresponsible" journalism. The President of the Society, incidentally, was Father R. J. Henle, S. J., and many members are in disagreement with the philosophy of John Dewey, which was especially under attack in the editorial.*

And yet, in one respect, the thesis of the Life *editorial represents the attitudes of millions of so-called, self-appointed "authorities" on American education. This thesis is, of course, that education must ultimately choose between two points of view—the one, represented by the progressivism of Dewey and his disciples; the other, represented by the kind of neo-conservatism which* Life *itself espouses and which, typified by the writings of such earnest persons as Professor Bestor, has the support of all those forces in the culture that identify education with traditional forms of learning and classical subject matters.*

. . . This kind of either-or choice is quite as false as is the kind of pseudo-syntheses and patchwork proposals exemplified in the equally earnest writings of Professor Paul Woodring. There is, I submit, a radically different approach to the problem which we shall have to give consideration if we are not to be deluded indefinitely by oversimplifications and fuzzy or nostalgic thinking. This approach is based upon at least two fundamental premises.

The first premise is that we live today in one of the greatest periods of crisis in human history. Granting that all history consists of recurrent crises, this one is unprecedented in several ways, the most monstrous of which is the fact that man has achieved the capacity to destroy civilization over night. America, living as it does in an aura of deceptive prosperity and complacency, refuses thus far to admit this fact with any real conviction. In many other parts of the world, however, the masses of people are very deeply concerned—so deeply that, as anyone knows who follows world events, our own country is looked upon with more and more skepticism, less and less as the great democratic vanguard which it once was.

The second premise is that, just as the physical sciences have recently passed through a revolution which was, indeed, partly responsible for the crisis itself, so today the behavioral sciences . . . are rapidly entering upon a revolution of their own. This revolution is already awakening those familiar with it to the realization that mankind is now approaching the opportunity to achieve a world civilization of abundance, health, and humane ca-

pacity that is as life-affirming and promising as the crisis symbolized by sputniks and hydrogen bombs is life-denying and dreadful.

The kind of education needed in America must, I submit, be reconstructed upon these two premises. It can become an education that inspires young people to adventure and creation and yet is at diametrically opposite poles from its one real opponent—the totalitarian education of the communist orbit. Instead of being based upon outmoded conceptions of learning and discipline, such as are at bottom endorsed by the neo-conservative forces, it can utilize the richest resources of the behavioral sciences and a theory of unified man which those resources elucidate. The superficial arguments of the pro-science versus the pro-humanities groups are overarched in the same way as are those between the so-called educationists and academicians.

Teacher training, for example, would of course be reorganized once such a conception took hold. Of course it is cluttered with busy work, with over-emphasis upon method, and with all sorts of absurdities. But so, too, would the liberal-arts program of the typical high school and college require reorganization—characterized as it often is with a chaos of unrelated courses, bad teaching, and unmotivated learning. Neither teacher training nor liberal arts can be called satisfactory because neither is governed by a philosophy of education and culture suitable to a world in crisis. And neither is satisfactory because neither is aware (except vaguely at most) that a revolution in the behavioral sciences, which is breaking down old classifications and opening new vistas of human potentiality, is already well under way.

I cannot now indicate in any detail what this conception would mean for the curriculum, for standards of scholarship, for school administration, or for the profession of teaching; I can only suggest that it does mean a completely new look at all of them. The question of how to move from the high level of generalization to the concrete level of practice is, however, answerable in one way here. There is pressing need for new forms of educational experimentation—new designs in the form of testable hypotheses . . . . The time has come to initiate audacious, imaginative pilot projects based upon the conception I have tried to indicate. Teachers and students alike would enter into them with an excitement that could be contagious, and that could affect education not only throughout America but throughout other countries that are attuned to the crisis of our time and await our leadership again.

The remaining paragraphs spell out a little further the implications of the above statement.

The first premise—that we live in an age of crisis—is supportable in a great many ways besides the one selected for mention. Granting that destruction by nuclear war is the most horrifying fear of our time, only a little less horrifying are the insidious disintegrations threatened by radioactive fallouts. Add to these the record of two bloody intercontinental wars within a quarter-century, the rise of a mighty totalitarian system that already jeopardizes America's position as the foremost industrial power, and now the looming conquest of space with its portents of evil as well as good. For any educational system not to give these events priority, for it not to provide every possible opportunity to diagnose their causes and to consider how the growing generation may cope with them while time remains, is for that system to shirk its most urgent responsibility.

Although certain other viewpoints besides the one I support would agree on the fact of major crisis, no other derives from it similar educational imperatives. The most crucial of these rest upon the second major premise — the revolution occurring in the behavioral sciences. This revolution requires education to re-examine its whole conventional structure and to consider new ways of (1) ordering its subject matters, (2) engaging in the processes by which they are taught and learned, and (3) formulating the purposes of school and society.

None of these imperatives would have been practicably realizable before the emergence of such young sciences as cultural anthropology and psychiatry, or the interrelating of these with such older ones as economics, sociology, and history. None of them depends upon metaphysical or otherwise speculative doctrines of the classical philosophies. All of them, while open to a great deal of further clarification and verification, are potentially demonstrable and defensible in the same way that all science is demonstrable and defensible.

Let me try now to illustrate each of the three imperatives in educational terms.

1. Up to this time, the structure of the typical school and college curriculum has been largely a jumble of discrete subject matters that, for the average student, have little or no meaningful relations to one another — languages, mathematics, social science, natural science, and others — each of which is often again subdivided into further discrete units. The behavioral sciences are now demonstrating that, as far at least as all the areas having to do with biopsychological experience are concerned, these divisions and subdivisions are less and less tenable. Concepts such as organism, connoting relationships between parts as much as the parts related, are replacing the older atomistic concepts. Human life, individually and culturally, is increasingly seen in terms of patterns and configurations.

Programs of general or integrated education, recognizing that something must be done to give meaningful unity to the curriculum structure, have sometimes been tangentially affected by this interdisciplinary view of human behavior. Unfortunately, however, they also have been plagued by the same confusions in theory and practice that are chronic to other educational programs. Some general educationists, for example, take their cue from the physical sciences; others, from neo-scholasticism or like doctrines. Few as yet regard the tasks and goals of human beings as the first and most important concern of vital education in an age such as ours, or, for that matter, in any age.

This is not to say that the physical sciences, any more than the humanities, should be neglected by the needed new framework. It does mean that they are encompassed by it. A theory of unified man, both derived from and contributing to our experimental knowledge of human behavior in its multiple perspectives, not only should integrate all other fields of knowledge; it should provide them with a fresh and potent significance.

2. The required rebuilding of teaching and learning processes is heralded by a great body of recent behavioral research, only a fraction of which has begun to permeate educational practice. Perhaps the one point where permeation has occurred at all fruitfully thus far is in the methodology of "group dynamics." Yet, even here, as so commonly happens in educational circles, it has acquired more often the earmarks of a superficial fad than of a profound process dependent upon a widening range of discoveries about the "fields of forces" that constitute the interactions of human beings in their multiple roles.

Even more promising is the "culture-and-personality" frontier. Here anthropologists and psychologists are joining hands. And they are demonstrating that learning, for example, involves polaristic dimensions of inner and outer experience, some of it quite unconscious, that have been almost totally neglected by the orthodox formulations still underlying classroom routines.

Again, the problem of how to enlist education in the processes of institutional change so that it functions, not merely to transmit but to modify and reconstruct outmoded arrangements, can now be attacked with the aid of substantial knowledge. The concept of crisis itself exemplifies this opportunity. Citing outstanding authorities in the behavioral sciences, I have pointed out elsewhere that

> there is no good reason, except timidity or irresponsibility, that prevents high schools and colleges from encouraging young people to analyze both the meaning of crisis theoretically and its manifestations overtly. Leaders ought accordingly to clarify their orientation here: they ought to face the issue of whether education is to be regarded as capable of sharing importantly in the control and resolution of crises, or as a pawn of overpowering material or spiritual forces beyond control and resolution.[1]

3. The shaping of new purposes for education and culture is also becoming feasible in a way that could hardly have been conceived even three or four decades ago. In other words, the behavioral sciences are beginning to prove, really for the first time in history, that it is possible to formulate human goals not for sentimental, romantic, mystical, or similarly arbitrary reasons, but on the basis of what we are learning about cross-cultural and even universal values. Though studies in this difficult field have moved only a little way, they have moved far enough so that it is already becoming plausible both to describe these values objectively and to demonstrate that most human beings prefer them to alternative values.

Freedom is an example. By analyzing drives and motivations, by determining what human beings in many different cultures most deeply need

---

1. *Cultural Foundations of Education — An Interdisciplinary Exploration* (New York: Harper and Brothers, 1957), p. 153.

and want, freedom both as fact and norm undergoes something of a metamorphosis of meaning. Yet it preserves the rich kernel of significance intuited by Jefferson and other geniuses of a pre-scientific age.

This way of constructing educational purposes rests, too, upon an expanding inventory of research evidence. Human resources for a happy life on earth are infinitely greater than we have ever dreamed possible — resources that we have hardly begun to tap because we are so often blinded by conflict, ignorance, and fear. A truly goal-centered education could contribute more than any other agency to displacing these destructive forces by scientifically ascertainable and testable hopes for the future of mankind.

To what extent is educational theory presently concerned with the kind of imperatives that I have indicated? I regret to say: very little, indeed. The only recent books that, in my judgment, help (each in a different way) are three: *The Ideal and the Community — A Philosophy of Education,* by I. B. Berkson;[2] *Philosophy of Education for Our Time,* by Frederick Mayer;[3] and *Philosophy and Education,* edited by Israel Scheffler.[4]

It is difficult, however, to feel that the dominant neo-conservative mood of the moment is anything more than passing. The single most encouraging fact about the behavioral sciences as they are now swiftly developing (I have been able, of course, to reveal only a few glimpses) is that they offer so little comfort to those of such a timid if not defeatist mood and so much support to those who continue deeply to believe in the need of a philosophy and program appropriate to our revolutionary age.

MARGARET MEAD

Margaret Mead is a prominent anthropologist who is currently an associate curator of ethnology at the American Museum of Natural History in New York City and an adjunct professor of anthropology at Columbia University. Perhaps best known for her studies of the native peoples of the Pacific area, she has also turned her attention to such topics as cultural change, the problems of family life and child rearing, and the relationship between education and culture. Among

2. New York: Harper and Brothers, 1958.
3. New York: The Odyssey Press, Inc., 1958.
4. Boston: Allyn & Bacon, Inc., 1958.

her best-known books are Coming of Age in Samoa *(1928)*, Growing Up in New Guinea *(1935)*, Sex and Temperament in Three Primitive Societies *(1935), and* Male and Female *(1949). She has also authored several books which are of particular interest to educators:* The School in American Culture *(1951) and* Growth and Culture: A Photographic Study of Balinese Childhood *(1951). With Martha Wolfenstein she has edited the volume* Childhood in Contemporary Cultures *(1955).*

Thinking Ahead

When we look realistically at the world in which we are living today and become aware of what the actual problems of learning are, our conception of education changes radically. Although the educational system remains basically unchanged, we are no longer dealing primarily with the *vertical* transmission of the tried and true by the old, mature, and experienced teacher to the young, immature, and inexperienced pupil. This was the system of education developed in a stable, slowly changing culture. In a world of rapid change, vertical transmission of knowledge alone no longer serves the purposes of education.

What is needed and what we are already moving toward is the inclusion of another whole dimension of learning: the *lateral* transmission, to every sentient member of society, of what has just been discovered, invented, created, manufactured, or marketed. This need for lateral transmission exists no less in the physics or genetics laboratory than it does on the assembly line with its working force of experienced and raw workmen. The man who teaches another individual the new mathematics or the use of a newly invented tool is not sharing knowledge he acquired years ago. He learned what was new yesterday, and his pupil must learn it today.

The whole teaching-and-learning continuum, which once was tied in an orderly and productive way to the passing of generations and the growth of the child into a man—this whole process has exploded in our faces. Yet even as we try to catch hold of and patch up the pieces, we fail to recognize what has happened.

Why should the businessman be concerned with this apparently academic issue? In our rapidly changing world, industry has taken the lead in practical consideration of problems of obsolescence and in many ways is capable of taking a position of leadership in the task of reorienting the training of people to live in this new world.

In order to understand the issues, let us begin by looking at some of the features and underlying assumptions of our American educational system as it is today. Even a brief examination of the picture we carry in our minds of "education" and of "students" will indicate the state of confusion at which we have arrived and the immediate need for creative leadership in working out a more realistic system of education.

We have moved into a period in which the break with the past provides an opportunity for creating a new framework for activity in almost every field—but in each field the fact that there has been a break must be rediscovered. In education there has been up to now no real recognition of the extent to which our present system is outmoded. Meanwhile, as the turmoil over our educational system grows, the various responsible groups in the United States are jockeying for position. But some of them, particularly those representing industry, have as yet hardly entered the field.

Historians point sagely to the last two educational crises—the first of which ended with the establishment of the universal elementary school and the second with the establishment of the universal high school—and with remarkable logic and lack of imagination they predict that the present crisis will follow the same pattern. (And what is history for if not to tell us exactly how to make the same mistakes as in the past!) According to such present predictions, the crisis will last until 1970, when it will end with the establishment of universal college education, accessible in principle to all young Americans.

Implicit in this prediction is a series of other ideas, such as:

—The assumption that our educational system has fallen behind in something (though it is not now clear what the "something" is—the work training of German apprentices, or the technical training of young Soviets, or the linguistic mastery of Netherlands students), and that it should therefore arrange to catch up.

—The explanation that our difficulties are due to the "bulge"—the host of babies that tricked the statisticians peacefully extrapolating their population curves and bedeviled a people who had decided that orphan asylums could slowly be turned into homes for the aged and elementary schools into high schools as a population with a falling birth rate aged into maturity. (Only a few people followed out the simile to senility!)

—The thinking of the people who are sure that the pendulum is swinging back to sense—to discipline and dunce caps, switches and multiplication tables, and the highly satisfactory forms of torture which somebody (they themselves or at least their grandfathers) once suffered in the cause of learning.

But in the midst of the incessant discussion and the search for scapegoats to take the blame for what everyone admits is a parlous state, extraordinarily little attention is paid to any basic issues. Everyone simply wants more of what we already have: more children in more schools for more hours studying more of something. The scientists want more students to be taught more mathematics, while the liberal arts advocates want more of their subject matter included in the curriculum. The planners want more school buildings built, and the educators want more teachers trained who have studied more hours and who will get more pay. Meanwhile, the child labor committees want more inspection and more attention to migratory children, and the youth boards want more social workers and more special schools and more clinics provided.

Likewise, extraordinarily little attention is paid to the fact that two great new educational agencies—the armed services and industry—have entered the field, and there is little awareness of the ways in which operations in these institutions are altering traditional education. Recruitment programs of the armed services now include explicit statements of their role as educational institutions. For instance:

> The United States Armed Forces Institute . . . has enabled thousands upon thousands of young men to finish their high school education and begin college-level studies. A second Army program enables young men to attend courses at many civilian schools and colleges in off-duty hours . . . . [A third program teaches soldiers—on their bases] such subjects as typing, stenography, foreign languages, literature, and many more.[1]

But most important, the pattern itself is hardly questioned. For we *think* we know what education is and what a good education ought to be; and however deficient we may be as a people, as taxpayers, or as educators, we may be actualizing our ideals. An occasional iconoclast can ask wistfully: "Wouldn't it be fine if we could scrap our whole school system and start anew?" But he gets no hearing because everyone knows that what he is saying is nonsense. Wishful dreams about starting all anew are obviously impractical but this does not mean that someone should not ask these crucial questions:

—Is our present historic idea of education suitable for people in the mid-twentieth century, who have a life expectancy of 70 years, and who live in a world of automation and global communication, ready to begin space exploration and aware of the possibility that we can bring about the suicide of the entire human species?

—As all these present and pressing concerns of the human race are new, is it not possible that a system of education may be out of date which was designed for small societies that were connected by horse-drawn coaches and sailing ships, and where any war could threaten only small sections of the human species at any one time?

—Is it not possible that the problem of the educational system's obsolescence goes beyond such issues as methods of teaching reading or physics, or the most desirable age for leaving school, or the payment of teachers, or the length of summer holidays, or the number of years best devoted to college, or even the comparative advantages of working while going to high school or college?

—Is not the break between past and present—and so the whole problem of outdating in our educational system—related to a change in the rate of change? For change has become so rapid that adjustment cannot be left

---

1. U.S. Army Recruitment Service, "Pathway to Maturity: A U.S. Army Booklet for Parents."

to the next generation; adults must—not once, but continually—take in, adjust to, use, and make innovations in a steady stream of discovery and new conditions.

—Our educational system, besides being the oldest system of universal free primary education in the world, bears the marks of its long history. But is it not possible to think that an educational system that was designed to teach what was known to little children and to a selected few young men (after which they could be regarded as "educated") may not fit a world in which the most important factors in everyone's life are those things that are not yet, but soon will be, known?

—Is it not equally possible that our present definition of a pupil or a student is out of date when we define the learner as a child (or at best an immature person) who is entitled to those things to which a child is entitled—moral protection and a meager subsistence in a dependency position —and who is denied those things which are denied to a child—moral autonomy, sex and parenthood, alcoholic beverages, and exposure to hazards?

In the picture which we have of the student, we have muddled together *both* a conception of the young child who is unable to fend for himself or to protect himself against moral and physical hazards, and who is entitled to be fed and sheltered *and* our own historical conception of the scholar's role as one in which some few men could claim lifelong support provided they themselves accepted an economic dependency that was demeaning to other men and a type of life in which they were subject to supervision (and, until recently in Christian history, gave up sex and parenthood).

This composite picture is one into which we can fit the scholarly monk, the Cambridge don who was not permitted to marry, and the student who lives in college and whose degree depends on his sleeping there (a touchingly infantile method of attaining a degree). All of these match our conception of the learner as a dependent who is subject to the supervision appropriate to a child and who must pay for his learning by abnegating some of the rewards of maturity.

Yet the combined ideas of the child and the monk do not complete our picture of the student; we have added still other things to it. With the industrial revolution there came new possibilities of exploiting human labor. Work, which through long ages had often been disliked by members of the upper classes and had been delegated to women, slaves, or serfs, became something different—more hazardous, more menacing. In this situation children were the most easily identifiable victims, and their fate was dramatized as a conflict between their right to an education and their subjection to dangerous and ruthless exploitation in the mines, in the factories, in dives, and in the street trades. The common school, born at a period in the United States when we were particularly concerned with extending the rights of the common man, was sponsored and fought for by labor groups. In this way the common school became doubly identified as the means of making all children literate and as the official enemy of child labor. A vote to raise the school-leaving age was a vote against child labor, and, like sin or cancer, child labor became something no one could be in favor of, officially.

So, as inevitably happens when different institutions in a culture become intertwined, raising the school-leaving age came to stand for several things: it was, on the one hand, a way of increasing the privileges of every child born in the United States and, on the other hand, a way of protecting children against the hazards of work to their health and morals.

That our picture of harmful labor is itself very complex can be seen even from a cursory examination of federal and state child labor laws. Looking at these we find that work outdoors is better than work indoors, that work in small cities is better than work in large cities, that work in summer and during vacations is less harmful than work in winter or during school terms, that work done for parents does not count as work, and that there is one form of work in which all the rules can be broken about age, hours, places, hazards from the weather, weight of objects dealt with, being on the streets, going to strange places, and so forth, — which, characteristically and in the best spirit of Horatio Alger, is delivering newspapers.

This one exception to our children's right to protection highlights the whole picture. In the American myth, men rise to success and greatness by working hard as children, and as we have progressively forbidden them this traditional preparation for greatness, we have left them the one symbolic activity of delivering newspapers. (Nowadays, however, it may be the father — bank president or chief justice — who actually delivers the papers because the son is in bed with a cold under the care of an expensive pediatrician.)

Slowly, as a society, we have codified both the rights and the disabilities of minors and also the conditions under which a minor may take on the privileges appropriate to adults because they require maturity. These are problems which are dealt with in the most primitive societies, though the way in which they are thought of may contrast with ours. What has happened in our contemporary society is that the codified rules, each intended to serve some specific need, fail to fit the contemporary situation — and the result is confusion.

The state of confusion that characterizes our attitudes toward maturity in students shows up in a variety of ways. For instance:

—School regulations may forbid a married student to attend high school even though he or she may be below the age and the grade when it is legal to leave high school.

—Even more quaintly, in one large city the schoolgirl who has an illegitimate child may go back to school after the child has been born but the married girl who becomes a mother may not return.

—In some school systems, not only expectant mothers but also expectant *fathers* are barred from the daytime high school.

The complexity of the total picture and the confusion about the relationship of being a child, a minor, a student, and a morally incapable individual are further increased when we include, as nowadays we must, the armed services. For in different degrees, the armed services permit a boy to enlist who is too young to marry, to leave school, to buy cigarettes or to drink beer, to vote, to make a legal contract, to bequeath property, to change his citizenship, to work in a hazardous occupation or in other occupations between the hours of seven and seven, or to have contact with dangerous machinery. Yet by enlisting he is enabled to operate the complex instruments of death and to die for his country.

So, when we think about education and try to identify the student, we have in our minds—whether or not we are aware of it—an exceedingly complex picture, the elements of which are compounded and confused in their historic connections. Yet we must identify what they are if we are to remodel our educational system so that it is devoted to the kind of teaching and learning that is appropriate to the United States today. For this purpose a look at education in other societies will be helpful:

—Education which is limited to small children is appropriate in a very primitive society like that of the Eskimo. The nine-year-old Eskimo child has learned, from father or from mother, the basic skills of a spoken language, the handling of tools and equipment, knowledge of the weather, relevant personal relations, and religious taboos. He must wait until he is physically mature before he can marry; as he grows older he will gain proficiency in hunting, in religious practices, in his knowledge of time, the seasons, and the landscape; and he may come to exercise leadership. But his education, in the sense of learning whatever adults could teach him directly, was over long before.[2]

—In other societies that are more complex, education may not be completed before adolescence, when some young people may elect, or may be chosen, to learn more complicated skills and may memorize the classics, master complex weaving skills, or become skilled craftsmen or leaders of ritual activities.

After the invention of writing and the development of mathematics and medicine, these did not become part of the whole tradition which had to be imparted to everyone. Like techniques of gold working or a knowledge of magical charms, they were taught by a few to a few in a long continuum of teaching-and-learning, in which the teacher responded as much to the pupil as the pupil did to the demands of the teacher, and both attempted not so much to add to the sum total of knowledge as to increase the skill of its manipulation.[3] Under these circumstances, new knowledge was added so gradually that the slow web of transmission of ancient skills was not torn.

Parallel to these developments was the special education given by specially chosen tutors and teachers to the children of the aristocracy; such an education was designed to ground the pupils well in many arts and graces and in a scholarship which they would not practice but would wear as an adornment or use for wise government.[4]

—In a country governed by a conqueror or in a country to which large

2. Franz Boas, "The Central Eskimo," *Sixth Annual Report of the Bureau of American Ethnology* (Washington, 1888), p. 399.

3. Margaret Mead, "Our Educational Emphases in Primitive Perspective," in *Education and the Cultural Process*, ed. Charles S. Johnson (Nashville: Fisk University Press, 1943), pp. 5–12.

4. Thomas Woody, *Life and Education in Early Societies* (New York: The Macmillan Company, 1949).

numbers of immigrants come, there are special problems of education as the government becomes responsible for people who speak a different language and have different customs. For, in these situations, the function—or at least one function—of the educational system is not the transmission to the next generation of something that all adults or that specialized groups of adults know, but rather the transmission of something the parents' generation does *not* know to children whom the authorities wish to have educated.[5]

So, looking at our educational system today, we can see that in various ways it combines these different functions:

—The protection of the child against exploitation and the protection of society against precocity and inexperience.
—The maintenance of learners in a state of moral and economic dependency.
—Giving to all children the special, wider education once reserved for the children of privileged groups, in an attempt to form the citizen of a democracy as once the son of a noble house was formed.
—The teaching of complex and specialized skills which, under our complex system of division of labor, is too difficult and time-consuming for each set of parents to master or to hand on to their own children.
—The transmission of something which the parents' generation does *not* know (in the case of immigrants with varied cultural and linguistic backgrounds) to children whom the authorities or the parents wish to have educated.

To these multiple functions of an educational system, which, in a slowly changing society, were variously performed, we have added slowly and reluctantly a quite new function: *education for rapid and self-conscious adaptation to a changing world.* Yet we hardly recognize how new this function of our educational system is. It is implicit in the demands of educators that schools develop flexibility, open-mindedness, and creativity; but such demands might equally well have been made 200 years ago, well before the rhythm of change had radically altered.

That we have as yet failed to recognize the new character of change is apparent in a thousand ways. Despite the fact that a subject taught to college freshmen may have altered basically by the time the same students are seniors, it is still said that colleges are able to give students "a good education"—finished, wrapped up, and scaled with a degree.

A student who is still in college can "go on" to a higher degree because he has not as yet "completed" his education, i.e., the lump of the known which he has decided to bite off. But a student who has once let a year go by after he is "out of school" does not "*go on*," but rather "goes *back*" to school. And as we treat education as the right of a minor who has not yet completed high school (for the position of a boy who has completed high

5. Margaret Mead, *The School in American Culture* (Cambridge, Mass.: Harvard University Press, 1951).

school at the age of 14 is a different and anomalous one, in which he is exempt from most of the forms of protection accorded minors because a high school diploma is equated with physiological maturity, the capacity for parenthood, and the ability to resist the seductions of hostel and bowling-alley life), just so we equate marriage and parenthood with getting a diploma; both indicate that one's education is "finished."

Consistent with these ideas and with our conception of what a student is, our educational institutions are places where we keep "children" for a shorter or longer period. The length of time depends in part on their intelligence and motivation and in part on their parents' incomes and the immediately recognized national needs for particular skills or types of training—and as long as they are there, we treat them as minors.

Once they have left, we regard them as in some sense finished, neither capable of nor in need of further "education," for we still believe that education should come all in one piece, or rather, in a series of connected pieces, each presented as a whole at the elementary school, the high school, and the college level. All other behaviors are aberrant. So we speak of "interrupted" education—that is, education which has been broken into by sickness, delinquency, or military service—and we attempt to find means of repairing this interruption. Indeed, the whole GI bill, which in a magnificent way gave millions of young men a chance for a different kind of education than they would otherwise have got, was conceived of primarily as a means of compensating young men for an unsought but unavoidable interruption.

Thus we avoid facing the most vivid truth of the new age: *no one will live all his life in the world into which he was born, and no one will die in the world in which he worked in his maturity.*

For those who work on the growing edge of science, technology, or the arts, contemporary life changes at even shorter intervals. Often, only a few months may elapse before something which previously was easily taken for granted must be unlearned or transformed to fit the new state of knowledge or practice.

In this world, no one can "complete an education." The students we need are not just children who are learning to walk and talk and to read and write plus older students, conceived of as minors, who are either "going on" with or "going back" to specialized education. Rather, we need children *and* adolescents *and* young *and* mature *and* "senior" adults, each of whom is learning at the appropriate pace and with all the special advantages and disadvantages of experience peculiar to his own age.

If we are to incorporate fully each new advance, we need simultaneously:

—The wide-eyed freshness of the inquiring child.

—The puzzlement of the near-dunce who, if the system is to work, must still be part of it.

—The developing capacities of the adolescent for abstract thinking.

—The interest of the young adult whose motives have been forged in the responsibilities of parenthood and first contacts with a job.

—The special awareness of the mature man who has tempered experience, skepticism, and the power to implement whatever changes he regards as valuable.

— The balance of the older man who has lived through cycles of change and can use the wisdom to place what is new.

Each and every one of these is a learner, not of something old and tried — the alphabet or multiplication tables or Latin declensions or French irregular verbs or the rules of rhetoric or the binomial theorem, all the paraphernalia of learning which children with different levels of aspiration must acquire — but of new, hardly tried theories and methods: pattern analysis, general system theory, space lattices, cybernetics, and so on.

Learning of this kind must go on not only at special times and in special places, but all through production and consumption — from the technician who must handle a new machine to the factory supervisor who must introduce its use, the union representative who must interpret it to the men, the foreman who must keep the men working, the salesmen who must service a new device or find markets for it, the housewife who must understand how to care for a new material, the mother who must answer the questions of an observant four-year-old.

In this world the age of the teacher is no longer necessarily relevant. For instance, children teach grandparents how to manage TV, young expediters come into the factory along with the new equipment, and young men invent automatic programing for computers over which their seniors struggle because they, too, need it for their research.

This, then, is what we call the *lateral transmission* of knowledge. It is not an outpouring of knowledge from the "wise old teacher" into the minds of young pupils, as in vertical transmission. Rather, it is a sharing of knowledge by the informed with the uninformed, whatever their ages. The primary prerequisite is the desire to know.

Given this situation, which of the institutions that are concerned with the revision of our educational system is to take the initiative: the educational world, the government, the armed services, citizens' voluntary organizations, churches, or industry? Each has a stake in the outcome; each has power to influence what happens; each has its own peculiar strengths and weaknesses.

Industry, however, has the peculiar advantage of understanding the major evil from which our whole educational system is suffering — *obsolescence*. Modern ideas of obsolescence have come out of studies of industrial processes, and industrialists have made these ideas so much a part of their thinking that making allowance for the costs of obsolescence and supporting continuing research on problems of obsolescence are a normal part of their professional behavior. In any major effort to modernize our educational system, of course, it would be appropriate for all the institutions to have a voice. It would be well, for example:

— For educators to watch out so that all they know would not be lost in the shuffle.

— For government to guard the needs of the nation.

— For church and synagogue to protect the religious values of the past.

—For the armed services to concentrate on our defense needs.

—For citizens to organize means of protecting the health, safety, and welfare (present and future) of their own and the community's children.

In these circumstances, would it not be most appropriate for industry to take the lead in highlighting the obsolescence of our present educational system? In the United States, in 1958, approximately 67% of the civilian labor force are engaged in some kind of work in industry. Of the advances which account for obsolescence, a very large proportion have come out of industry. But, at the same time, much of the thinking that is holding up a real revision of our school system is based on an outmoded public image of industry as a monstrous and wicked institution which, if not restrained, would permit little boys to be sent down into coal mines or to work in conditions in which their lungs would be filled with powdered silicon.

In fact, industry has already taken the lead—within its own walls—in developing a new type of education that includes all levels of competence and training and that freely faces the need for education at the senior levels of management. In their recent survey, Clark and Sloan have presented a masterful picture of the very real contribution that education within industry is making to educational change.[6] The thinking that has gone into this contribution, however, has not yet become an articulate, leading part of our rethinking of the educational system as a whole. But if industry, as represented by individual leaders from management and labor in many parts of the country, would come forward with plans which dramatized our dilemma, such plans would be heard.

What might these plans be? First, in regard to work performed by young people, industry could say to all those who believe that children should be kept in school primarily so that they will not be on the streets or at work under bad conditions: "We will agree that young people need more supervision than older workers—that someone should know where they are each day, that their health should be protected and checked, and that they should be protected from organized attempts to deprave them. We will undertake to train and supervise the young people who *at this time* cannot gain anything by remaining in school."

But this would not be enough. This offer would need to be accompanied by a second one: "As soon as *any* worker—of any age, at any level—in our plant, office, or laboratory is ready to study again, we will facilitate his, or her, doing so."

This is, admittedly, a large order. But we cannot have one without the other. For as long as we continue to think that free and, when necessary, subsidized education is appropriate *only* when it is *preliminary* to work (though, exceptionally, it may be continued after some inevitable "interruption"), just so long the guardians of character, of political literacy, and of our store of talent that comes from all classes and in many cases shows itself only very slowly will argue for—and will get—longer and longer years of compulsory education and longer and longer years of free education.

6. Harold F. Clark and Harold S. Sloan, *Classrooms in the Factories: An Account of Educational Activities Conducted by American Industries* (Rutherford, N.J.: Institute of Research, Fairleigh-Dickinson College, 1958).

Under these circumstances, the meaning of education and the purpose of schools — especially for young people between the ages of 14 and 20 — will only become more confused. On the one hand, the education that is absolutely necessary for those who, at an early age, are ready to go on to become scientists, statesmen, philosophers, and poets will be hamstrung by the presence of those others who, at the same age, do not want schooling; and on the other hand, the lives and characters of the temporary nonlearners will be ruined, and they will be incapacitated as potential later learners.

What we need to do, instead, is to separate primary and secondary education — in an entirely new way:

By *primary education* we would mean the stage of education in which all children are taught what they need to know in order to be fully human in the world in which they are growing up — including the basic skills of reading and writing and a basic knowledge of numbers, money, geography, transportation and communication, the law, and the nations of the world.

By *secondary education* we would mean an education that is based on primary education and that can be obtained *in any amount* and *at any period* during the individual's whole lifetime.

By so doing, we could begin to deal effectively with the vast new demands that are being made on us. The high schools would be relieved of the nonlearners, among whom are found a large number of delinquents. But, more important, men and women, instead of preparing for a single career to which — for lack of any alternative — they must stick during their entire active lives, would realize that they might learn something else. The very knowledge that this was so would relieve much of the rigidity that now bedevils management. Women, after their children became older, could be educated for particular new tasks — instead of facing the rejection that today is related to fears about new learning that is acquired in middle age.

Whatever their age, those who were obtaining a secondary education at any level (high school, college, or even beyond) would be in school because they *wanted* to learn and *wanted* to be there — *then*. A comparison of GI and non-GI students has shown how great have been the achievements of students who have chosen to go to school.[7] Furthermore, the student — of whatever age — who was obtaining a secondary education would no longer be defined as someone without adult rights who must accept dependency and meager stipends and have a dedicated delight in poverty.

In an educational system of this kind we could give primary education and protection to actual children as well as protection and sensitive supervision to adolescents. We could back up to the hilt the potentiality of every human being — of whatever age — to learn at each level. And we could do this proudly.

The kind and amount of leadership that industry can best take in making individual plans for sending workers — *on pay* — to get more education, and the kind and amount of leadership that can best come from tax-

---

7. Norman Frederiksen and W. B. Schrader, "The Academic Achievement of Veteran and Nonveteran Students," *Psychological Monographs*, LXVI, No. 15.

supported activities is a problem that will have to be threshed out. In the United States, we usually depend upon private initiative to make the first experiments before tax-supported agencies pick up the check. So, too, we shall have to work out the problem of providing special work situations for adolescents and on this basis make our decisions as to whether tax-supported institutions—rather than individual industries—should become chiefly responsible for the employment of adolescents.

But we also need to recognize articulately that there are other routes to competence than the one route provided by the conventional school. Experimental cooperative-work plans in the public schools need to be supplemented by experiments in industry. Such a plan is the one being conceptualized by Pylon, in which the sons of successful parents, who are financially able to continue their studies but find nothing rewarding in school work, are given a chance to learn under meaningful, money-making conditions.[8]

The right to obtain a secondary education when and where the individual could use it would include not only the right of access to existing conventional types of schools but also the right of access to types of work training not yet or only now being developed—new kinds of apprenticeship and also new kinds of work teams . . . .

In thinking about an effective educational system we should recognize that the adolescent's need and right to work is as great as (perhaps greater than) his immediate need and right to study. And we must recognize that the adult's need and right to study more is as great as (perhaps greater than) his need and right to hold the same job until he is 65 years old. Recent publications of the Department of Labor show that we are already beginning to recognize the importance of work for youth.

Among the nations whose industrial capacities make them our competitors, the United States has a comparatively small total population. The more completely we are able to educate each individual man and woman, the greater will be our productive capacity. But we cannot accomplish the essential educational task merely by keeping children and young adults —whom we treat like children—in school longer. We can do it by creating an educational system in which all individuals will be assured of the secondary and higher education they want and can use any time throughout their lives.

---

8. Don A. Luscombe, *Pylon: A New Concept and a New Institution (a nonprofit organization chartered under the Laws of Pennsylvania)*, (Gwynedd, Pennsylvania, no date).